1989

Data Base

Data Base: Structured Techniques for Design, Performance, and Management

Second Edition

Shaku Atre

Atre International Consultants, Inc.
Rye, New York

WILEY

JOHN WILEY & SONS

New York · Chichester · Brisbane · Toronto · Singapore

Library of Congress Cataloging-in-Publication Data:

Atre, S., 1940-
    Data base : structured techniques for design, performance, and
management / Shaku Atre. -- 2nd ed.

        p.   cm.
    Includes index.
    ISBN 0-471-85251-1
    1. Data base management. 2. Data base management--Case
studies. 3. Electronic data processing--Structured techniques.
I. Title.
QA76.9.D3A9 1988
005.74--dc19

Printed in the United States of America

10 9 8 7 6 5 4 3 2

Preface

We are reaching the stage where the problems that we must solve are going to become insoluble without computers. I do not fear computers. I fear the lack of them.

Isaac Asimov

The computer revolution promises to simplify, ease, and otherwise enhance life in ways undreamed of even by the Utopians. In organizations of all kinds, the computer stores and retrieves vast amounts of information. The volume of data processed in all types of industries, medical services, financial institutions, and governmental agencies is expanding geometrically, and it is very difficult to imagine how these organizations would function without computers. Organizations of various natures are called "enterprises."

The repository of information, called a "data base," is the foundation of the entire computer system for an enterprise. Thus the design and the performance of the data base are perhaps two of the most important areas in information processing.

Although several articles and books have been published that give scholarly treatment to this area, or give survey information regarding existing data base management systems and data models, few offer specific answers to these questions:

1. What are the responsibilities of the people involved?
2. How can a data base that will satisfy performance criteria be designed?
3. What problems may arise in different phases?

This book is intended to fill the need for this and related information. It demonstrates the principles for designing a data base that will achieve the functions and performance needed to satisfy the requirements of the information processing environment. It addresses the roles of the data base administrators, systems programmers, systems analysts, application programmers, information processing managers, data processing managers, and data base users. The material is simple without becoming simplistic and shows a step-by-step approach to data base design. The chapters are organized so that data base designers can follow their sequence during the process of designing a data base. The methodology is independent of any software package; it does not concentrate on any one manufacturer's data base management system.

This book can be used effectively by practitioners in business as well as in government, and also as a single-semester course in a business or technical school where students are interested in the "how to" as well as the "why" of information processing approaches.

A case study approach has been adopted. A case study for designing a data base for a banking environment is carried through from the very beginning to the end in Appendix A. In Appendix B a case study of a university environment is presented in its entirety. The step-by-step approach to designing a data base and the application of this approach to the two case studies are major features of the book.

The material presented was developed in the courses that I have taught for a number of years at IBM's Systems Research Institute. A version of the manuscript was used as a text in a course with the same title, "Data Base: Structured Techniques for Design, Performance, and Management." Portions were presented at various professional seminars, including local chapter meetings of the Association for Computing Machinery (ACM) and the Data Processing Management Association (DPMA). Questions and suggestions from students and colleagues helped to make the material more timely and digestible, while the overall enthusiastic response at these lectures led to the decision to present the material as a book.

The book is divided into three parts, each consisting of a number of chapters. Part 1, "Data Base Administration," deals with installing and maintaining a data base. The first chapter sets the stage by discussing the issues that will be treated later. Chapter 2 describes the function of the data base administrator (DBA) and the roles that the DBA and his or her staff play in the information processing system. The third chapter, titled "Data Dictionary," discusses a valuable tool for collecting information about the data base environment.

Part 2, "Data Base Design (Conceptual Model and Logical Model)," demonstrates the conceptual and logical data base design process. The fourth chapter creates the basis of any data base management system—the data models. A brief treatment is given of three popular approaches—the relational, hierarchical, and network data models. Chapter 5 describes the design process for developing a conceptual model. Chapter 6 gives the design process for a logical model. Both chapters demonstrate the techniques in detail, with specific examples.

Part 3, "Data Base Performance," describes the equally important aspects of the performance of information processing with the data base. The main emphasis is on how to design for good performance, that is, how to optimize the design. Chapter 7 reviews data access techniques, which are key issues of performance. The eighth chapter presents some implementations of these access methods. Chapter 9 discusses the data base design of a physical model with the estimation of space and time. Chapter 10 treats specific performance problems in the design phase, implementation phase, and operations phase.

Appendix A demonstrates a case study of a banking environment. Appendix B contains a case study of a university environment. Finally, Appendix C gives the basic concepts of probability theory and mathematical statistics used in Chapter 9.

And now only the pleasant task of acknowledging my students, friends, and colleagues remains. I am grateful to the numerous students who patiently read the manuscript and made many constructive comments. I also want to thank Charles Bontempo, Robert Bower, Gary D. Bowers, Robert G. Brown, George T. Fadok, Joan Foster, Ron Gale, George Hubbard, Judy King, Barry Kingsbury, Frank Post, Jay Schmoll, Cora Tangney, and everyone else who helped along the way.

S. ATRE

New York, New York
July 1980

Preface to the Second Edition

The urgent need for a coordinated and complete data base design methodology, surfacing in all sectors of the data processing community, has resulted in the continuing success of this book. Moreover, seminars emphasizing the practical step-by-step nature of the methodology have been enthusiastically received and applied in commercial and academic as well as many government installations throughout the world. The book, in fact, has been translated into several foreign languages. These events have prompted revision to include new developments and insights gained, while preserving all the strengths of the first edition.

Part 1, "Data Administration," has undergone minor alterations. The introductory Chapter 1 remains unchanged. Chapter 2 has been revised to reflect the evolution of the previous DBA function into two functions: Data Administration (DA), responsible for planning and setting policies; and Data Base Administration (DBA), responsible for day-to-day technical implementation of policies. Chapter 3, "Data Dictionary," has been slightly revised to sharpen distinctions between active and passive and between integrated and freestanding data dictionaries.

Part 2, "Data Base Design (Conceptual Model and Logical Model)," has been expanded to include the inverted file data model. Several prominent and widely used data base management systems are based predominantly upon file inversion. The needs of data base designers for these systems have to be addressed in a methodology that claims to be comprehensive. Accordingly, Chapter 4 now includes the inverted file data model as a separate and distinct data model. Chapter 5, "Data Base Design (Conceptual Model)," which is independent of the DBMS used, remains unchanged. Chapter 6 treats mapping the conceptual model to a logical model based on file inversion, in addition to the other popular logical models.

The biggest changes in the new edition are in Part 3, "Data Base Performance," although Chapter 7, "Data Storage and Access Methods," remains the same. Chapter 8 previously discussed Implementation of the Access Methods for several data base management systems. Chapter 9 did the same for Designing and Evaluating the Physical Model. The new Chapters 8, 9, and 10 treat IMS/VS, IDMS/R, and ADABAS, respectively.

Each has three sections: (1) Implementations of the Access Methods; (2) Design a Physical Model of a Data Base; (3) Evaluate the Physical Model of a Data Base. Chapter 8 unifies material previously found in the old Chapters 8 and 9. The new Chapters 9 and 10 contain completely new material and are much more detailed and specific than anything in the first edition. Recasting the treatments of the three DBMSs—IMS, IDMS/R, and ADABAS—in a unified and balanced form will make them more readily accessible to a reader interested in just one of them. Contrasting and comparing the three systems is also facilitated. Finally, the new Chapter 11, "Performance Issues," is the old Chapter 10 unchanged.

The even and comprehensive handling of three different data base management systems has also been carried over into Appendices A and B, the Banking and University Case Studies. These have been improved for the conceptual and IMS models. In addition, logical and physical models have been created and evaluated for IDMS/R and for ADABAS.

Finally, to enhance the instructional value of the book and to respond to requests from teachers in numerous colleges and universities, sets of questions have been included for all chapters.

And now I would like to thank two individuals, in particular, who made this second edition possible: Franz Schneider, Principal Consultant, and Nancy Carafa, Office Manager, who have worked with me at Atre International Consultants, Inc. for the past several years.

SHAKU ATRE

Rye, New York
November 1987

Works by the Author

PAPERS & ARTICLES BY SHAKU ATRE

"End-User Designed/Driven Data Bases," S. Atre, *Computerworld/Extra*, September 1, 1982.

"Spreading the Wealth of DBMS," S. Atre, *Computerworld Buyer's Guide: Software*, December 14, 1983.

"Information Center & Data Base: Synergy for Success!" S. Atre, *Technology Transfer Institute Newsletter*, Vol. 2, No. 1, 1983.

"Nothing Succeeds Like Access," S. Atre, *Data Training*, January 1984.

"Information Center Implementation," interview with S. Atre, *Data Base Newsletter*, January/February 1984.

"Info Centers and P. C.s: Should They Be Synonymous?" S. Atre, *P. C. Week*, July 3, 1984.

"Information Center Software," S. Atre, *Computerworld: Office Automation*, August 15, 1984.

"Create That Opportunity," interview with S. Atre, *InfoSystems*, December 1984.

"Will The Real Fourth-Generation Languages Please Stand Up?" S. Atre, *Softline, Computerworld*, June 17, 1985.

"Technology, Intelligent Software Guide Market Growth," S. Atre, *Computerworld Special Report*, June 24, 1985.

"The Information Center and Productivity Tools: Working in Harmony," S. Atre, *Computerworld Focus*, September 18, 1985.

"Information Center Strategy," interview with S. Atre, by Elisabeth Horwitt, *Business Computer Systems*, September 1985.

"Mini and Mainframe DBMS, The Seven-Step Solution," S. Atre, Product Spotlight, *Computerworld*, March 31, 1986.

"IC Directors' Problems: Management, Understaffing," interview with Shaku Atre, by Bob Rhein, *MIS Week*, August 4, 1986.

"Integrating tools speeds and simplifies application building process," Shaku Atre, Product Spotlight/Application Generators, *Computerworld*, Vol. XX, No. 31, August 4, 1986.

"The Information Center Holds," S. Atre, *PC World*, August 1986.

"Storing Data About Data," S. Atre, *Information Center*, Weingarten Publications, Inc., July 1986.

BOOKS BY SHAKU ATRE

Data Base: Structured Techniques for Design, Performance, and Management, S. Atre, New York: John Wiley, 1980.

Data Base Management Systems for the Eighties, S. Atre, Wellesley, Massachusetts: Q.E.D. Information Sciences, 1984.

Information Center: Strategies and Case Studies, S. Atre, Rye, New York: Atre International Consultants, Inc., 1986.

CONSULTING EDITOR, SHAKU ATRE

The Macmillan Database/Data Communications Series:

AVAILABLE

Cave-Maymon   *Software Lifecycle Management*
Fadok   *Effective Design of CODASYL Data Base*
Potter   *Local Area Networks: Applications and Design*
Ranade/Ranade   *VSAM: Multiprogramming with Virtual Storage*
St. Amand   *A Guide to Packet-Switched Value-Added Networks*
Towner   *The ADS/On-Line Cookbook*

Contents

CONTENTS

CHAPTER 1

Data

One of the foundations of an enterprise is the information needed for its survival and prosperity. This chapter indicates where this information comes from and how data processing requirements for using the information caused data base systems to evolve. One of the desirable characteristics of a successful data base is flexibility. Flexibility makes a data base less sensitive to changes in information processing requirements. This chapter discusses the issues regarding flexibility and gives a preview of the steps involved in designing a data base to provide adequate performance.

1.1 SOURCES OF DATA

The processing of information has been one of the basic tasks in any civilization. Because of economic and population growth, there are ever increasing needs to administer large quantities of interrelated data for commercial and administrative purposes. The interrelated data taken together is called a "system." Any system that will create important simplifications in human affairs is likely to need a very complex model of the real world, in addition to other conventional forms of knowledge.

The heart of any information system is its stored data. For an enterprise, the data usually crosses the boundaries of different divisions. For example, management decisions often need information from across the enterprise. For decisions on manufacturing processes, it is necessary to have inventory information, as well as orders received, sales strategy, and so forth. This means that the data spanning the enterprise should be stored in an easily and readily accessible form.

In the early days of electronic data processing, data was stored on paper tapes and punched cards. Hardware equipment could read the tapes and cards. Application programs were written to process the data and transform it into reports. Compilers were used to translate the application programs from source language into machine instructions. To coordinate the electronic data processing, operating systems evolved. As the years passed, the operating systems, compilers, equipment, and procedures used to operate the electronic data processing system became increasingly sophisticated.

The basic goals, however, remained the same. Today the data processing system may be an old fashioned one with a clerk entering the data manually in a binder, or it may be a modern one with the fastest computers and the most sophisticated hardware and software available. The basic goal is always to provide the correct information at the right time, to the right person, at the right place, and at the right cost. The enterprise may be a bank, a manufacturing plant, a utility company, a university, a hospital, a supermarket, a department store, or an agricultural farm, to name just a few.

To understand electronic data processing, it is necessary to know some of the terms used to describe data and its representation.

1.1.1 Enterprise

An "enterprise" is any kind of organization such as a bank, a university, a manufacturing plant, or a hospital.

A problem arises here in distinguishing between a total enterprise (e.g., a big corporation such as an automobile manufacturer, computer manufacturer, chemical concern, or steel manufacturer) and an organizational unit of a big corporation. The organizational unit may represent an enterprise in its own right (e.g., a body manufacturing division of a big automobile manufacturer, or a data processing division of a computer manufacturer). In a situation like this, the divisions themselves may be called enterprises and regarded as such.

A number of enterprises may require information about one or more of the following functions: personnel, payroll, inventories, purchase orders, accounts receivable, sales reports, laboratory tests, course enrollments, financial transactions, medical history reports. The information concerning these items is about a person, place, thing, event, or concept.

1.1.2 Entity

An "entity" is a person, place, thing, event, or concept about which information is recorded.

In a banking environment examples of entities are CUSTOMERS, BANK ACCOUNTS, and MORTGAGE LOANS. In a warehouse the entities are SUPPLIERS, PARTS, SHIPMENTS, and the like.

1.1.3 Attributes (or Data Elements)

Every entity has some basic "attributes" that characterize it. A house can be described by its size, color, age, and surroundings. A customer of a bank may be described by such attributes as name, address, and possibly a customer identification number. A bank account can be represented by an account type, an account number, and an account balance. Customer identification number, customer name, and customer address are three attributes describing the entity CUSTOMER of a bank (see Figure 1.1). An attribute is often called a data element, a data field, a field, a data item, or an elementary item.

1.1.4 Data Value

A "data value" is the actual data or information contained in each data element. The data element "customer name" can take values like "Prof. Higgins" and "Mark Twain." The values taken by the data elements can be quantitative, qualitative, or descriptive, depending on how the data elements describe an entity. Figure 1.1 shows the difference between entities, data elements, and values taken by the data elements.

The information about an enterprise can be represented with the help of a number of entities, and an individual entity can be represented by a number of data elements. The values taken by the data elements are referred to as data. One set of values taken by the data elements of an entity is called an entity occurrence. The entities are interconnected by

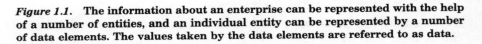

Entity	Attributes (or Data Elements)	Values (Data)
CUSTOMER	Customer identification number ———➤	123456789
	Customer name ———➤	Prof. Higgins
	Customer address ———➤	55 Snow Street New York, N.Y.
ACCOUNT	Account type ———➤	Checking
	Account number ———➤	634250
	Account balance ———➤	20.53
SUPPLIER	Supplier name ———➤	William Shakespeare
	Supplier number ———➤	S1
	Supplier address ———➤	100 Book Street New York, N.Y.

Figure 1.1. **The information about an enterprise can be represented with the help of a number of entities, and an individual entity can be represented by a number of data elements. The values taken by the data elements are referred to as data.**

certain relationships. An inherent model of the entities with the data elements representing them, together with the relationships interconnecting the entities, is called a "conceptual model." The conceptual model gives an overall view of the structure of the data in the enterprise.

The discussion of data is frequently confused by a failure to distinguish between the entity, the data element, and the value taken by the data element. In referring to a customer, there is an entity CUSTOMER; there are some data elements that represent the customer (e.g., the customer identification number, the customer name, and the customer address); and there are values taken by the data elements, such as "123456789," "Prof. Higgins," and "55 Snow Street, New York, N.Y." It is important to distinguish between the *entity*, the *data element*, and the *value* taken by the data element.

1.1.5 Key Data Element

Some data elements have the property that, knowing the value taken by a particular data element of an entity, we can identify the values taken by other data elements of the same entity. By knowing the customer identification number "123456789," we can determine that the person in question is "Prof. Higgins" and that Professor Higgins has a checking account at the bank. These data elements, from which we can infer other data elements, are called "key data elements." Key data elements can also be called entity identifiers.

It is possible that there are two or more data elements that can uniquely identify an entity. In that case we call those data elements "candidates" for becoming key data elements. Someone (the user or designer) decides which one of the candidates is to be used to access the entity. The designation of key data elements should be done very carefully because the right selection may help one to design the conceptual model correctly.

1.1.6   Data Record

A "data record" is a collection of values taken by related data elements. In Figure 1.2, the data elements are customer name, customer identification number, account type, . . . , remarks. One of the data records is "Prof. Higgins 123456789 Checking . . . Notify Customer Tel. 555-1234." The values taken by the data elements are for the entities CUSTOMER, AC-COUNT, and TRANSACTION. These values form the data records. The data records are stored on some medium. The medium can be a human brain, a piece of paper, a memory of a computer, or an auxiliary storage device of a computer such as a tape, disk, or drum, to name just a few examples.

1.1.7   Data File

The data records form a "data file": A data file is thus a collection of data records. In Figure 1.2, "Branch Manager's Report (Exception)" is an example of a data file in printed form. It contains data records that are identical, that is, are of the same type. A data file of this type, where all the records are alike (i.e., are made up of the same number of data elements), is called a "flat" file. A data file may also consist of heterogeneous types of data records; that is, it may contain records of different types. A data file is also called a file or a data set.

1.2   DATA FILE ENVIRONMENT

Sources of data are the basic necessities of information processing in an enterprise. Some examples of enterprises and their sources of data are listed below.

Entity CUSTOMER		Entity ACCOUNT			Entity TRANSACTION					

Branch Number: 1234
Branch Name: Downtown Branch
Branch Address: 1 First Street, New York, N.Y. 10001

Manager's Name: ABC
Report for: January 10, 1988

Date: January 11, 1988

Customer Name	Customer Identification Number	Account Type	Account Number	Amount Involved	Date of Transaction	Time of Transaction	Transaction Code	Reason Code	Action Code	Remarks
Prof. Higgins	123456789	Checking	653210	268.50	1/10/88	10:15:20	Check withdraw	Checking over-drawn	Auto-matic loan	Notify customer Tel. 555-1234
Zalaf, Amir	345678901	Savings	12345-1	10,000.00	1/10/88	15:02:10	Check deposit	Savings exceeds 100,000 limit	No deposit	Send back check and inform customer

A Data Element

A "Value" of the Data Element

A Data Record

A Data File

- Values taken by the data elements form a data record.
- Data records form a data file.

Figure 1.2. Report 1. Popular Bank—Branch Manager's Report (Exception).

Enterprise	Sources of Data
Brokerage firms	Stock activities, historical trends of the stock market
Manufacturing companies	Inventories
Airlines	Flights, crews, passengers, reservations, maintenance, inventory
Police precincts	Criminal patterns, types of crime
Hospitals	Patient medical records, bed utilization, billing, inventory of supplies
Insurance companies	Policyholder vitae, claims, premiums
Universities	Student records, courses offered, degree requirements, course schedulings
Banks	Checking accounts, savings accounts, installment loans, mortgage loans

The conventional data processing approach is to develop a program or a number of programs for each different application, for example, banking applications such as checking and savings accounts, installment loans, and mortgage loans. This results, most probably, in one or more data files for every application. This type of development is reflected in Figure 1.3.

Each application of the enterprise, such as checking, savings, installment loan, and mortgage loan, has its own view of data. In the early days of data processing, every application programmer had to write the data file handling routines to add, delete, replace, and retrieve data from the data files associated with the programs. A big improvement was the advent of generalized routines.

1.2.1 Advantages of Generalized Routines

The generalized routines provided predefined access methods. These methods freed the application programmer from having to code, test, and debug methods specific to a particular application. The common access methods are thus generalized routines that add, delete, replace, and retrieve data from the auxiliary storage such as tape, disk, and drum. These access methods then become integral parts of the operating systems.

Figure 1.4 shows that a checking application can be written to create or access a checking account data file using generalized access methods. However, most generalized access methods do not allow other applications with different views of the common data to share and access that data. All users are constrained to a single view of the data. Different views may be provided using various sorting techniques.

The access methods, or the generalized access routines, provide varying degrees of physical data storage independence, since some changes in

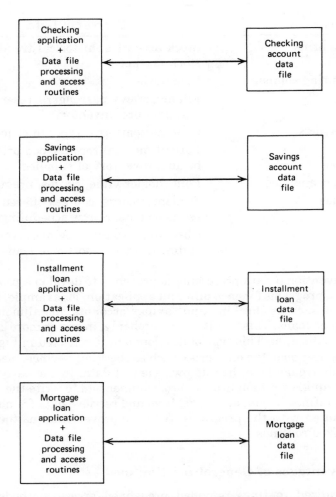

Figure 1.3. **Popular Bank. One-to-one correspondence between an application, its data file processing, its access routines, and a data file. In the early days of data processing, every application programmer had to write the data file handling routines to add, delete, replace, and retrieve data from the data files associated with the programs.**

physical storage can be reflected in the access methods without having to rewrite the application programs. In a later section we will see how the application programs can be detached further from the physical characteristics of data storage devices. First, however, we shall examine some drawbacks of the conventional data file environment.

1.2.2 Drawbacks of the Conventional Data File Environment

Consider the banking environment illustrated in Figure 1.5. Information processing has to deal with the following problems when working in an environment with a number of data files, such as the one illustrated.

Data Redundancy. It is unavoidable that some data elements such as name, address, and customer identification number are used in a number of applications. Since data is required by multiple applications, it often is recorded in multiple data files. In most cases, the data is stored repeatedly. This situation, called "data redundancy," leads to many problems concerning the integrity of data. Data redundancy requires multiple input, updating, and reporting procedures.

Data Integrity Problems. One reason for inadequate data integrity is data redundancy. It is inevitable that some inconsistency will result from storing the same information in more than one place. Figure 1.5 shows that the address of the same customer is stored in four different data sets: checking account data file, savings account data file, installment loan data file, and mortgage loan data file. If the customer moves, the

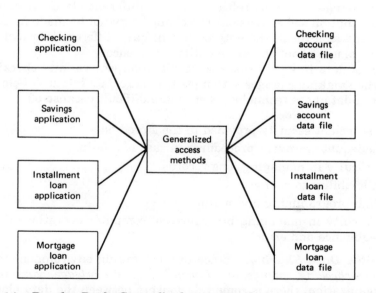

Figure 1.4. **Popular Bank. Generalized access methods can be used in place of individual data file handling routines. Every application programmer did not have to write the data file handling routines. But most generalized access methods do not allow other applications with different views of the common data to share and access that data. All users are constrained to a single view of the data.**

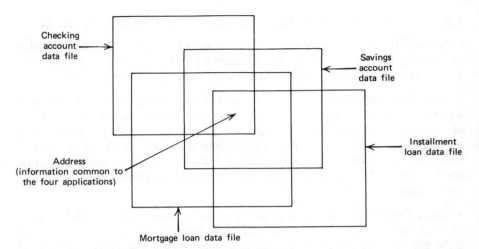

Figure 1.5. Redundant data stored in a number of data files. Savings account data file has redundant data stored with checking account data file, mortgage loan data file, and installment loan data file. All data files in this example contain redundant data. Address is common to all the four data files.

address change has to be reflected in four different places. It is highly probable that on some occasions the change may not be made in all four places, and as a result the enterprise will have different information in different places about the same entity occurrence.

Lack of data integrity can also result from poor validity checking of data when making changes. Attempts to ensure data integrity before the advent of data base technology were more difficult because of:

- Insufficient security provided to the stored data
- Inadequate recovery procedures in case of a failure
- Difficulty in managing long records
- Inflexibility to changes
- High programming and maintenance costs
- Difficulty in managing procedures of computer operations (human negligence and error)

Limited Data Sharing. Since in our banking environment the applications *checking, savings, installment loan,* and *mortgage loan* represent one organization, there is some relationship between the data elements of different data files. When the data files are implemented as separate units, however, it is difficult if not impossible to relate the data elements across the applications. For an enterprise to function as one unit of organization, it is desirable to share data among different data files.

Data Availability Constraints. In today's fast moving environments, data must be available at the right time to an authorized person. When data is scattered in a number of data files, the availability of the combined data from these files is somewhat constrained.

Difficulty in Management Control. As a result of data redundancy in the data files, it is difficult to implement new guidelines across the whole enterprise. For example, as a result of the Privacy Act of 1974, the social security number may not be used as an identification number in governmental agencies. Where the social security number has been used, it will be time-consuming to implement the change through all the data files.

To solve these kinds of problems, data base systems were developed.

1.3 DATA BASE ENVIRONMENT

1.3.1 What Is a Data Base?

A "data base" is a collection of related data about an enterprise with multiple uses. In a data base the data definitions and the relations between the data are separated from the procedural statements of a program. The question to be asked here is, "What is the major distinction between a data base and a data file?" A data base may have more than one use, and the multiple uses may satisfy multiple views of the data stored. A data file may have more than one use, but only one view of the stored data can be satisfied. Multiple views of a data file can be satisfied only after the data has been sorted. In a data base environment, multiple uses may be the result of multiple users; for example, in a banking environment the information about customers may have several users, such as checking, savings, installment loan, and mortgage loan. Thus data sharing is a major objective of an enterprise data base system.

Figure 1.4 shows that generalized access methods were developed to create and access the data files separately from the application programs. Some extension of the common access methods is needed to handle the data base separately from the application programs. This extension is called a data base management system.

1.3.2 Data Base Management System (DBMS)

A system is needed that will integrate the data files into a data base and that can provide different views to different users. The software, the hardware, the firmware, and the procedures that manage the data base comprise a "data base management system" (DBMS). A data base management system makes it possible to access integrated data that crosses

operational, functional, or organizational boundaries within an enterprise.
See Figure 1.6.

1.3.3 Drawbacks of Data Integration

Integration of data about an enterprise into a central place may pose
some disadvantages. Because the data from individual data files is integrated in a central place in a data base, the sense of ownership and, as
a result, the responsibility for data are easily lost. As a result, inaccurate
data may not be detected. This can cause serious problems unless extensive
data integrity and data validity measures are implemented. The data
base can also become a target of security breaches unless stringent security
disciplines are maintained. Moreover, a data base can increase political
and organizational struggles within the organization because it serves
the needs of multiple users, some of whom may have legitimate conflicts
of interest and may have different requirements. An integrated data base
may also threaten privacy. Traditionally, privacy has been defined as the
right of an individual to be left alone. In an integrated data base environment, it becomes easier to collect information about people and organizations and then expose the information to some unauthorized person

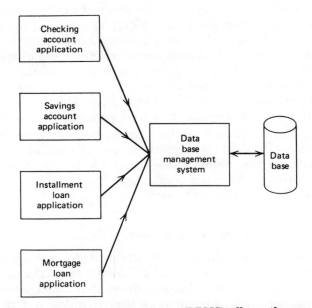

Figure 1.6. **Data base management system (DBMS) allows the use of data that
crosses operational, functional, or organizational boundaries. DBMS enables the
data base users to satisfy multiple views of the data stored.**

or organization. Therefore, if the data base management system does not ensure adequate integrity, security, and privacy and if the data base is not designed properly, the data base environment may result in new problems.

To avoid these potential drawbacks we may say that a data base management system (DBMS) should satisfy the following objectives:

- Different functions of an enterprise can be served effectively by the same DBMS.
- The amount of redundancy in stored data can be minimized.
- Consistent information can be supplied for the decision-making process.
- Security controls can be applied.
- Application programs can be developed, maintained, and enhanced faster and more economically, with fewer skilled personnel.
- Physical reorganization of the stored data is easy.
- Centralized control of the data base is possible.
- Easier procedures for computer operations can be established.

How should the collected information about the entities of the enterprise be organized, and what relationships should be provided to interconnect the information about the various entities? How can the enterprise's data base be made less sensitive to the expansion and reorganization of the business? How should the security, integrity, and validity measures be implemented and controlled? How should the recovery and backup procedures be provided, that is, how should the data base be designed, implemented, and maintained efficiently?

To answer these questions, an in-depth knowledge of the enterprise's environment, as well as technical expertise, is required. It is necessary to establish a central function that can provide an efficient data structure of the entities and their relationships to a community of users. This data structure is efficient for the community of users rather than for any one particular user. The central function is called a data administration function.

1.4 DATA ADMINISTRATOR

In a data base environment, multiple users are involved. A function that can review different requirements and resolve conflicts of interest is absolutely necessary. To coordinate and carry out all the steps in designing, implementing, and maintaining an integrated data base, an ongoing administrative function must be established.

Thus data administration is a function made up of people responsible for protecting a valuable resource—data. In the conventional data processing environment, an application programmer possesses a data file.

Users lock their data, keeping others from using it and forcing them to collect the same data. The data base era has removed the sense of individual property. The person in charge of the data administration function is called a "data administrator" (DA). The data administrator is not the *possessor* of data but the *protector* of it. For a sophisticated enterprise, the information generation and decision processes become complicated as the spectrum of the functions expands. Since direct data control is taken away from the application programmer, he or she loses the feeling of personal contact and responsibility for it. This loss of personal contact forces the enterprise to develop procedures to assure that data integrity is not compromised. This goal should be coordinated through the data administration function.

Data administration is a function providing services to users of the data base. An analogy could be drawn between the DA and the comptroller of the enterprise. The comptroller protects the resource of the enterprise called *money*, and the DA protects the resource called *data*. In many organizations, the DA function is considered merely that of a highly technical person. This categorization defeats the purpose of a DA. The DA function should be high enough in the hierarchy of the organization to have authority over, as well as responsibility for, the data structures and their access. The person in charge of the DA function also must have an understanding of how the enterprise works and how it uses data. Although it is desirable for the DA to be technically competent, an understanding of the enterprise and the ability and responsibility to interact with people and to submit alternatives to standard procedures are more important. Otherwise, the DA function is not as effective.

Although it is beneficial to have an authoritative DA function, the placement of the data administrator may vary from organization to organization. The first major factor in determining this placement is the importance of the data base for survival of the organization. The second factor is the sophistication of the organization both in data processing and in the nature of its business. In today's data base environment, the DA function most often remains in the DP department, and usually within an application area of this department.

The DA has to coordinate the tasks of collecting information about data and designing, implementing, and maintaining the data base and its security. The DA's mission does not terminate at the implementation of the data base. Integration of new functions into the data base makes the DA more necessary than ever. One of the major functions of the DA is to pay attention to the future as well as to the present information requirements of the enterprise. To fulfill this function, the data base design should be as flexible or data independent as possible.

The DA function is clearly important in multiuser data base system operations. We should not, however, rule out the possibility that some of these operations will some day be automated. Also, we should not forget the future importance of personal data bases over which the user has total control. Even with a single user, it is possible to take different views of the data or to make nonprocedural requests. But in the data base environment of today and of the near future, the DA will play a major role.

The data administration function, together with the function of attending to day-to-day data base operations called "data base administration" (DBA), is discussed in more detail in Chapter 2.

1.5 DATA INDEPENDENCE

1.5.1 What Is Data Independence?

In the conventional data set environment, the application programmer has to know answers to the following questions before manipulating the data:

What is its format?
Where is it located?
How is it accessed?

Changes in any of these three items may affect the application program and result in other changes, since the details of these three points may be locked into the application code. Let us assume that the details about data regarding *where*, *how*, and *what* are coded in the application program. In that case any changes to *where*, *how*, and *what* in the data have to be reflected in the application code, and the application programs must be recompiled and maintained. It is highly probable that as the needs of the enterprise change, the format of the data may change. The data set has to be expanded by the addition of new data elements representing new entities.

With enhancements in computer architecture and improved efficiency in software and hardware, the methods of accessing and the means of storing the data are likely to change. The access methods and the storage means are built into the application logic. As a result, programmers must spend an increasing percentage of their time in program maintenance and updating. This is both a source of error and a division of resources. The users (application programmers and terminal users) of the data base should be oriented toward the information content of the data and should not be concerned with details of representation and location. The ability to use the data base without knowing the representation details is called "data independence."

Data independence is crucial from the economic viewpoint. An enterprise may spend thousands of dollars for implementing very simple changes, such as increasing a field length or adding a new field. An ideal data base design should provide, to some degree, for changes of this nature without affecting the application programs. But one thing not to be forgotten is that the extent of data independence provided depends on the data base design, as well as on the data base management system (DBMS).

Data independence provides, at a central location, a solution to the problems mentioned above. The individual application programmer no longer must change the application programs to accommodate changes in access method or location or format of the data. Unfortunately, DBMS packages available today do not appear to achieve full data independence. Since a data base design depends on the DBMS package, it seems difficult to achieve total data independence, even with the best data base design.

The central location for reflecting changes in the method of storing, the ways of accessing, the format of the data elements, and the relationships between the data elements representing the entities of the enterprise should be anchored in the DBMS. The issue here is when, where, why, and who should specify the changes to the DBMS. And who should control these changes? These responsibilities should be given to the data base administrator.

In summary, the reasons for data independence are as follows:*

"1. To allow the DBA to make changes in the content, location, representation and organization of a data base without causing reprogramming of application programs which use the data base.

2. To allow the supplier of data processing equipment and software to introduce new technologies without causing reprogramming of the customer's application.

3. To facilitate data sharing by allowing the same data to appear to be organized differently for different application programs.

4. To simplify application program development and, in particular, to facilitate the development of programs for interactive data base processing.

5. To provide the centralization of control needed by the data base administrator to insure the security and integrity of the data base."

1.5.2 Two Stages of Data Independence

The data base design process starts with the conceptual requirements of a number of users. (See Figure 1.7.) The conceptual requirements can also be specified for some applications that will not be implemented in the near future. These requirements of individual users are integrated into a single community view, called a "conceptual model." The conceptual model represents the entities and their relationships. It gives us the ability to view all the data entities and their relationships to each other

---

* From R. W. Engels, "A Tutorial on Data Base Organization" (see complete reference at the end of this chapter).

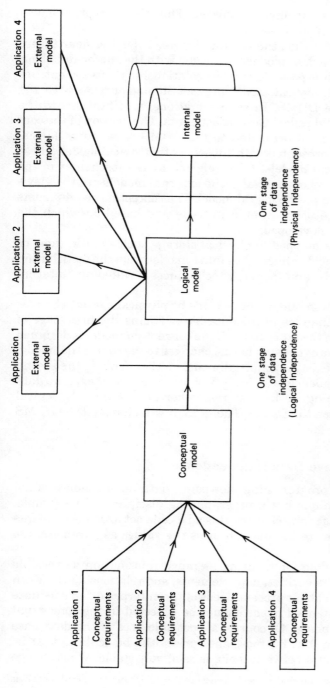

Figure 1.7. Two stages of data independence:

1. Logical independence.
2. Physical independence.

- *Conceptual Model.* The conceptual requirements of individual users are integrated into a single community view, called a "conceptual" model.
- *Logical Model.* The version of the conceptual model that can be presented to the data base management system is called a "logical" model.
- *Internal Model.* The physical model that takes into consideration the distribution of data, access methods, and indexing techniques is called an "internal" model.

17

with no concern about their physical storage. Thus the conceptual model is the inherent model of the enterprise.

The conceptual model that the community needs for the near future is then translated into a data model compatible with the chosen data base management system. It is possible that the relationships between entities as reflected in the conceptual model are not implementable with the chosen package of the DBMS. In such situations, modifications to the conceptual model should reflect these constraints. The version of the conceptual model that can be presented to the DBMS is called a "logical model." The users are presented with subsets of this logical model. These subsets, called "external models" (also referred to as subschemas in the literature), are the views of the users. The external models are the views that the users get based on the logical model. The conceptual requirements are the views that the users wanted initially and based on which the conceptual model was developed.

The logical model is mapped to physical storage such as disk, tape, or drum. The physical model, which takes into consideration the distribution of data, access methods, and indexing techniques, is called an "internal model."*

The external models should not be affected by physical storage changes or by access method changes to the data base. This is the first stage of data independence. On the other hand, if the conceptual model is designed so that it reflects future expansion needs, changes to the conceptual model should not affect the existing external models either. This is the second stage of data independence. Figure 1.7 shows the two stages of data independence. One thing we have to remember here is that the logical model is forced to match the DBMS. Therefore it will change if the DBMS changes.

1.5.3   How to Achieve Data Independence

From an application programming viewpoint, data independence is not a programming technique but a programming discipline. For example, to avoid recompilation for any changes, it is advisable not to define constants in a program. A better technique is to pass the values as parameters to the program.

The DA is responsible for tracking as much information as possible about the enterprise, its entities, data elements, and relationships between them. All information about present needs of the enterprise and adequate information about intended needs should be reflected in the conceptual model in the design phase. Of course, all possible uses of the data base cannot be anticipated, but for most enterprises the basic data, that is, entities and relationships between them, is relatively stable. What change

---

* The terminology such as "internal model," "conceptual model," and "external model" is from American National Standards Institute (ANSI/X3/Sparc) Data Base Management System's Study Group.

are information needs, that is, ways in which data is used to produce information. Another aspect of data independence is that the internal representation of the data may differ from the form in which the application program wishes to use it. Unfortunately, few DBMSs can provide that kind of total independence.

The degree of data independence provided depends on the thoroughness of the data base design phase. A thorough analysis of the enterprise's entities and their relationships minimizes the impact on other programs of changes in the data requirements of one program. This is what data independence is really all about.

One of the management tools supporting the development of a data base design is a data dictionary.

1.6   DATA DICTIONARY

A "data dictionary" is a central repository of information about entities: data elements representing entities, relationships between entities, their origins, meanings, uses, and representation formats.

In any enterprise, installation of a data base does not happen overnight. The data base expands as applications are developed and integrated. New data elements are introduced, and data elements used for the data base design may have to be modified. A facility that provides uniform and central information about all the data resources is called a data dictionary (DD).

The benefits of using a data dictionary are related to the effective collection, specification, and management of the total data resources of an enterprise. A data dictionary should help a data base user in:

- Communicating with other users
- Controlling data elements in a simple and effective manner, that is, introducing new elements into systems, or changing descriptions of elements
- Reducing data redundancy and inconsistency
- Determining the impact of changes to data elements on the total data base
- Centralizing control of data elements as an aid in data base design and in expanding the design.

In addition, an ideal data dictionary contains information about other entities. It stores information about groups of data elements, about data bases, and about cross-references between groups of data elements and data bases. It also indicates which programs use which data bases, and it keeps information regarding authorization and security codes. A detailed discussion of the data dictionary system is given in Chapter 3.

Design a conceptual model of a data base.	Data Analysis: Collect basic data (i.e., entities, relationships between entities).
	Existing Applications: Collect information about data in existing applications for determining the entities and their relationships. (Only the minimum functions fulfilled at present.)
	Potential Applications: Collect information about potential usage of the data. (Maximum functions that could be fulfilled.)

DBMS requirements and procedures imposed by a specific DBMS package

Design a logical model of a data base.

Estimate performance of the applications, considering frequency of usage and priorities

Design a physical model of a data base.

Evaluate the physical model of a data base.

If not satisfied with performance estimates

Implement the data base.

Figure 1.8. **Data base design steps.**

Let us study steps in the data base design that should deliver a data-independent design and satisfy performance requirements.

1.7 DATA BASE DESIGN AND PERFORMANCE—PREVIEW

The design starts with the end-users' views of the organization, called conceptual requirements. An end-user is a decision maker who uses information obtained by accessing the data base. End-users also provide data to be stored in the data base.

In considering the end-users' requirements, the following trade-offs have to be taken into account:

- It should satisfy today's needs for information.
- It should not only satisfy today's needs but also satisfy them in reasonable time, that is, it should satisfy the performance requirements.
- It should satisfy the anticipated as well as the unanticipated requirements of the end-users.
- It should be easily expandable with the reorganization and expansion of the enterprise.
- It should be easy to modify in changing software and hardware environments.
- Once correct data is stored in the data base, it should stay correct.
- Before inserting any data in the data base, the data should be checked for validity.
- Only authorized people should have access to the data stored in the data base.

Figure 1.8 shows the steps to be taken in designing a data base, considering the above trade-offs.

REFERENCES

1. Date, C. J., *An Introduction to Database Systems*, Vol. I, 4th ed., The Systems Programming Series, Reading, Massachusetts: Addison-Wesley, 1986.
2. Engels, R. W., "A Tutorial on Data Base Organization," *Annual Review in Automatic Programming*, Vol. 7, Part 1, edited by Halpern and McGee, Elmsford, N.Y.: Pergamon Press, July 1972.

QUESTIONS

1. Define the terms *enterprise, entity, attribute, key data element,* and *data value*. What are the relationships among them? Give examples.

2. What does it mean to say that application programs can have different views of the same data? What data processing approach was developed to replace the need for each application program to include data file handling routines?

3. Identify and explain the drawbacks of a conventional file environment. How does a data base management system (DBMS) handle these problems?

4. What is the difference between a data base and a DBMS?

5. A data base will integrate an organization's data into one central location. What possible problems and implications could such integration pose? How does a DBMS address such problems in its design?

6. What is the significance of data independence? Explain the two stages.

7. Define the terms *conceptual model*, *logical model*, *external model*, and *physical/internal model*. How are these models related?

8. In an enterprise with which you are familiar, identify several entities, their attributes, candidate key data elements, and data values. Construct a sample data record and sample data file.

9. Common Carrier Aircraft Co. plans to computerize its reservation service using a data base. Following is part of its schedule between Cleveland and New York.

Departure Time	Arrival Time	Flight No.	Aircraft Type	Max. Capacity	Meals Served	Intermediate Stops
8:00 AM	9:16 AM	572	737	110	Breakfast	0
9:20 AM	10:53 AM	326	737	110	Breakfast	1
11:05 AM	12:18 PM	582	727	80	Snack	0
11:45 AM	1:01 PM	438	707	100	Snack	0
4:10 PM	5:48 PM	840	727	80	None	1
5:30 PM	6:50 PM	688	737	110	Snack	0
9:00 PM	10:36 PM	888	737	110	None	1

9.1 Identify the most obvious entities represented by this table and list their attributes. Identify data values for each data element.

9.2 Construct a data record to show the number of snacks that may be needed on a given flight and the latest time at which they must be brought on board the aircraft. Identify the data elements used. What is the key attribute?

9.3 Construct a data file from question 9.2.

9.4 Construct a data record showing the maximum number of seats on a given flight. Identify the relevant data elements. What is the key attribute? (Create data values if necessary.)

PART 1

Data Administration

Converting the information processing of an enterprise to a data base technology or expanding an existing data base requires a tremendous investment. Therefore this process must be carefully planned and managed. The quantity of data to be converted to a data base and the applications are becoming more complex day by day. As a result, it is absolutely necessary that central control be established for decision making and monitoring through all the phases of the life cycle of the data base system.

CHAPTER 2

Data Administration

2.1 DATA ADMINISTRATION AND DATA BASE ADMINISTRATION FUNCTIONS

Today, the quantity of data stored for an enterprise increases in an almost geometric progression. The management decision-making process depends on the quality and quantity of information. The information that can be extracted from the data base is one of the most valuable resources of the enterprise. The data base must be properly designed, processed, and maintained to provide the right information at the right time to the authorized people. These responsibilities belong to the data administrator (DA) and his or her staff. The data administration function is made up of people and procedures. Hardware and software tools are used in performing this function. The expression "DA" will be used interchangeably to mean both the person and the function.

A fully developed DA function is not normally established all at once. The introduction of a data base management system (DBMS) into an enterprise requires highly technical personnel to oversee the day-to-day operations of implementation, backup and recovery, and performance and tuning. These responsibilities belong to the data base administrator (DBA) and his or her staff. (Again, the expression "DBA" is used interchangeably to mean both person and function.) The eventual need for data related functions to be represented at a higher level of the enterprise leads to the creation of the DA function, which encompasses that of the DBA. The DA establishes policy; the DBA implements it.

The DA function assists the enterprise in managing and controlling the data resource. This function is more that of a manager (DA) than that of a technician (DBA). The existence of the DA function signals a commitment to data as a resource; as such, it often begins with the introduction of a DBMS, but there is a distinction between DBMS and DA. In most environments, the DBMS is a vendor-supplied package and the DA is a function. The DA maintains the overall view of the enterprise, which we call a conceptual model. This view is the data model of the organization. As explained in Chapter 1, the one purpose of a data base is to provide information to different users in different functional areas of the organization. This often means that no one department feels responsible, however; and common ground is the last to be tended. The inevitable result is to make the job of the DA that of a coordinator. In many installations, management commits itself to a data base environment by going the technical route, that is, by deciding on the DBMS package first, rather than going the management route by establishing an administration function and investigating the viability of the data base approach.

The scope of the DA's position varies from enterprise to enterprise. In enterprises where the initial DBA function was assigned to a highly technical nonmanagement person (such as a systems programmer) instead of a person with middle management experience, the attempt to convert from a data file environment to a data base environment often failed, or did not achieve all the desired results. The following example illustrates this point.

In a large company, the DBA reported to the technical services manager and the technical services manager reported to the data processing manager. One of the initial meetings for designing a data base was attended by these two managers, the DBA, the application development managers, and the user-community managers. The first half of the meeting was spent in trying to resolve some departmental conflicts. During the second half of the meeting nobody paid any attention to the DBA's suggestions because he was on a lower level than the other managers attending the meeting. The whole effort was placed in jeopardy because the DBA lacked the authority to resolve differences between conflicting interests and reach a compromise.

If the DBA's role expands to that of a DA and is placed highly enough in the organization, he or she will have the necessary authority to insist that the proper strategies be implemented. Conversely, appointing a new senior manager out of the blue is unlikely to promote a spirit of fellowship and goodwill. The DA will have to foster cooperation by proving the worth of the function; thus this issue is related to that of choosing the first data base application. The importance of the DA is established relatively faster in an on-line than in a batch environment because of the visibility of the on-line applications.

2.1.1 DA's Responsibilities

The first important task of the DA at any level is to resolve differences between various functions of the organization to develop a conceptual and then a logical structure of the data base model for the enterprise. This individual must be the mediator among the different departments, not just to get *an* agreement from them, but also to get the *right* agreement about the entities of the enterprise. This may also require developing procedures and guidelines for data handling in addition to data definition and ownership. The implication is that the DA function must know exactly how the business runs and what the policies of the high level management and the future direction of the enterprise are. In the initial phase of designing the data base, the DA will concentrate on:

- Defining the data elements and the entities of the enterprise
- Determining the different names that will be used to refer to the same elements
- Defining the relationships between the data elements
- Establishing the textual description of data elements
- Knowing the departments or the users who will be responsible for keeping the data accurate (e.g., updating, data integrity)
- Determining the use of the data elements for control and planning purposes, that is, determining who is authorized to do what.

Collecting all this information from different departments and, at the same time, settling any differences that arise likens the job of a DA to that of a diplomat.

As previously mentioned, the sense of ownership of data does not exist in a data base environment. This occasionally makes the job of the DA extremely difficult. He or she may have to persuade some departments to give away their property for general use, or may find it necessary to control the access to sensitive information.

This idea of sharing not only may antagonize some departments but also may make them hostile to the whole data base development project. The DA has to be in a position to persuade some, convince some, comfort some, and, if nothing else works, coerce some. This means that the DA has to know how to use power and influence as needed, and implies that a DA should not be an individual hired off the street, but one knowledgeable about the intricacies of the politics within the organization. On the other hand, the DA should not be someone within the enterprise who has managed to turn a number of people into enemies.

In short, the selection of a DA should be taken very seriously by corporate management. The selection criteria for a DA's position should be the same as, or similar to, those used for filling other management positions within the enterprise. Management qualities are necessary, because the DA should place as much (or more) emphasis on the long-term needs of the enterprise as on the short-term goals. This responsibility becomes a weighty one, because a data base implies the integration of data across functional boundaries.

Implementation of guidelines can be successful only if everyone related to the data base is aware of, and is responsible for, the standards established by the DA. The application programmers' community, the operations staff, and the systems people must understand the procedures necessary for doing their jobs efficiently. This means that the DA has to establish effective two-way communication with all groups that have any involvement with the data base. (See Figure 2.1.)

The following sections give guidelines for the information flow along each of these paths.

2.1.2   DA and Management

Management is defined as that group of individuals to whom the DA reports either directly or indirectly. The DA desperately needs management's support and approval for managing the data base, and in return the DA has to establish credibility with management. To design a data base that can accommodate future changes in the mode of operation of the enterprise, ideally the DA should be supplied with the necessary information about future plans by management. The communication should take place as follows:

Management → DA

- Top priorities of the enterprise, if not directly through the organization then at least through newsletters, minutes, and other types of communication.

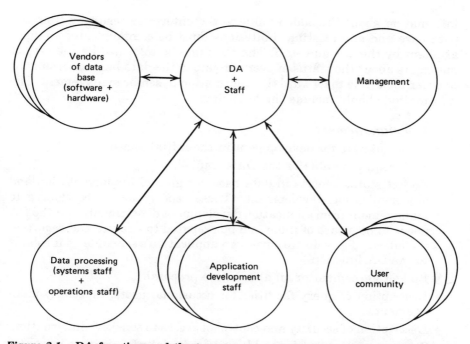

Figure 2.1. **DA function and the two-way communication paths with all groups that have any involvement with the data base.**

- Management's commitments with respect to time for the development of the new data base or for the expansion of it.
- Budgetary limitations for the project (including people, software, hardware).
- Commitment made to other parties (e.g., information availability, performance requirements).
- Future plans, for example, any changes that might affect the data base environment.
- Possibilities for restructuring the organization.

Some of the information that should be provided by management to the DA may be confidential. If the DA function operates at a substantially lower level than the top executives, it would be inappropriate to pass such information to this individual. But, if the data base is considered an extremely vital resource for the enterprise, the DA will be placed at least at the management level. Then, passing confidential information from the top executives to the DA will be appropriate.

In turn, the DA should communicate with management about the data, the data base design, its implementation, and its operation. Pertinent information about the added value to the enterprise resulting from the data base and any existing limitations must be communicated to management by the DA and staff. The DA must be informed by the project managers about the status of every project in the data base environment in order to be able to forward the information to senior management. The information should include the following:

DA → Management
- Time estimate for development in the initial phase.
- Staff requirements (for the DA's staff).
- Project status reports in data base design and implementation and any application development. (These reports should be coming to management from application development departments, but the DA needs to be aware of them and be prepared to analyze and report on the effects of any deviations in an application's schedule as it relates to the DA function.)
- Budget agreement or an alternative proposal.
- Description of query facilities for occasional users, especially management.
- Description of security and control of access to sensitive information.
- Space requirements (size and location, especially for any new hardware acquisitions for the data base).

2.1.3   DA and User Community

The data base will be designed for users. The DA's task is to design and maintain it in a proper fashion. The users should have full confidence in communicating with the DA; they should have the feeling that they are talking to an impartial authority who is going to help them to be more productive. To reflect all the needs of users that have to be satisifed by the data base, the following flow of information to the DA has to occur:

User Community → DA
- Data requirements of applications.
- Priorities of various applications in the data base environment.
- Ownership of data.
- Data elements for every application and their relationships.
- Relationships among different applications of the enterprise.
- Information about a quality assurance plan for contents of data elements.
- Data archiving requirements.

- Documentation.
- Data access restrictions (privacy and security).
- Possible future applications.
- Frequency of use and response requirements.

In a banking environment, for example, information regarding the interest paid to depositors must be saved for at least four years as required by the Internal Revenue Service. Information regarding frequency of access to this interest information should be provided to assist the DA in deciding how to store this information in the data base.

It may be a future requirement to notify customers of all inquiries concerning their accounts. The data base should be designed so that this possible future application can be added later without much difficulty. It is difficult, if not impractical, to try to anticipate all possibilities, however; and the DA must make trade-offs with current performance.

The DA has to tell the users how the data base will fulfill their needs, and the limitations as well. The following exchange of information is necessary between the DA and the user community:

DA → User Community

- Guidelines for changing any information regarding entities, data elements, and relationships between them in the data dictionary.
- Procedures for making such changes.
- Implementation and/or recommendations for:
  - Security controls
  - Privacy controls
  - Auditability controls
- Any changes, modifications, or compromises made in a specific user's requirements and the reasons for them.
- Status of development of data base design, implementation, and operations.
- Education and training suggestions.
- Any available tools that could make the user community more productive.
- Procedures regarding element synonyms.
- Cross-reference list of applications and data elements.
- Plan for phase-in of new data base systems.
- Performance objectives and their status, that is, whether they are met.
- Procedures for purging and archiving data.

2.1.4   DA and Application Development Staff

The DA communicates with all application development departments concerning the data base environment. He or she has an overall view of application development and therefore can communicate with individual application development departments effectively in the following areas:

DA → Application Development Staff

- Schedules for application development, showing data base-affected portions.
- Information about the data base required for application development (e.g., external model definitions such as data elements, symbolic names, contents, formats).
- Security controls as specified by user departments.
- Privacy controls as specified by user departments.
- Auditability controls as specified by management.
- Education and training suggestions.
- Cross-reference list of applications and data elements.
- Archival storage requirements.
- Rules and procedures for assuring accuracy and integrity of data.
- Specifications for data base maintenance programs.
- Interface rules for applications (external models).
- Aids available and ways to use them.
- Effective use of DBMS interface (remembering that powerful software is by definition easy to abuse).

The application development staff, by the same token, has to inform the DA and staff in the following areas:

Application Development Staff → DA

- Concurrence on the schedule for application development or alternative proposals. The application development staff should set the schedule, and the DA should concur.
- Requirements of application development staff.
- Procedures for implementing security, privacy, and access controls.
- Updating procedures.
- Storage of historical data and updates.
- Recovery procedures.
- Methods for implementing auditability controls.
- On-line and off-line data storage.
- Education and training requirements.

- Test plan, including any subset/test data bases.
  - Who should create test data bases, the DA's staff or the application development staff?
  - Who should maintain test data bases?
  - Who should verify proper operation vis-à-vis the data bases?
- Project status of the data base applications.

2.1.5 DA and Systems Staff

The data base will be physically established, preserved, and accessed in an environment provided by computer operations, together with systems programming. The DA and staff must inform the systems staff on the following issues. This is especially important during the process of designing the physical structure of the data base.

DA → Systems Staff
- Additional software and hardware, if any, required to support the data base.
- Performance constraints (e.g., response time) that affect the system.
- Security, privacy, and access control implementation plans.
- Any work that is expected to be performed by the systems staff in order to implement the data base.
- Changes in schedules and procedures.
- Off-site storage of historical data.
- Reliability, availability, and serviceability characteristics.
- Backup, recovery, and restart procedures.

The following information should be transferred by the systems staff to the DA:

Systems Staff → DA
- Incompatibility with any existing or planned software and hardware.
- Alternatives for handling any problems.
- Schedules for implementation of required hardware and software.
- Additional capacity requirements.

2.1.6 DA and Operations Staff

The information to be supplied to operations staff must be assembled by the DA, application development management, and user-community management. It may look as follows:

DA → Operations Staff

- Availability requirements for the data base (e.g., the data base should be accessible between 7:00 AM and 10:00 PM).
- Priorities of applications as set by users for batch jobs.
- Data base security procedures.
- Error recovery requirements for the data base.
- Archival requirements.
- Routine procedures to run the DBMS.
- Schedules and procedures for cutover of new applications in concurrence with users.
- Enabling/disabling of certain applications (if applicable) as suggested by users.
- Applications control: the proper execution of programs and delegation of responsibility for running abnormally ended programs.

To create and install a data base that operates optimally, the operations staff must inform the DA of the following areas:

Operations Staff → DA

- Procedures for updating the data base and hours of operation on a daily basis, set by the DA and concurred with by operations staff.
- Implementation of recovery and restart procedures of the data base as set by the DA.
- Security, privacy, and authorization mechanisms in place as suggested by the DA, who in turn concurred with users.
- Control mechanisms for scheduling as suggested by the DA.
- Reports of problems and errors encountered in data base systems.
- Reporting mechanisms for deviations from performance goals of data base applications.
- Procedures for keeping a log of all activities against the data base that were written up by the DA and staff.
- Recommendations for changes to data processing systems (cost savings, performance improvements, increased flexibility and reliability, etc.).
- Procedures for accessing and maintaining archived information.

2.1.7   DA and Software Vendors

The software vendors may be supplying the enterprise software packages in other data processing areas besides the DBMS. The DA, however, may be communicating with software vendors only regarding data base software and related packages.

DA → Software Vendors

- Education and training needs of the DA staff, users, and operations staff.
- The extent of security and authorization mechanisms needed.
- Performance bottlenecks in the data base area.

To gain credibility at the customer's location, software vendors should supply the following information to the DA:

Software Vendors → DA

- The best techniques for using software packages.
- Ways to think ahead for expansion purposes.
- Hardware requirements.
- Documentation for the DBMS.
- Program service support and maintenance.
- Potential application areas.
- Implications of the enterprise's future plans on current or planned software/hardware (e.g., potential problems, bottlenecks).
- Education provided.
- References to other, preferably similar, users.
- Ancillary packages (e.g., data dictionary, aids, applications, data communications interfaces, monitors).
- Hardware configurations supported.

2.1.8 DA and Hardware Vendors

In most enterprises the systems staff (also called technical services staff) communicates with the hardware vendor. The data base environment will use hardware resources substantially. As a result, the DA should be talking to hardware vendors regarding hardware requirements for the data base. This interface will be more or less direct as data base applications are more or less a part of the systems load.

Hardware Vendors → DA

- Capabilities of hardware.
- Procedures for using hardware effectively.
- Expansion possibilities.
- Any incompatibilities with existing hardware.
- Reliability factors.
- Servicing requirements.
- Software requirements when appropriate.

- Configurations needed to satisfy the enterprise's goals or needs.
- Training of personnel.
- Maintenance plan (e.g., preventive maintenance).

To prevent any bottlenecks due to insufficient hardware, it will be beneficial if the DA and the DA's staff can supply hardware vendors with the following information:

DA → Hardware Vendors
- Tentative future changes in information processing, including capacity and performance requirements.
- Equipment failures and any performance bottlenecks.

2.2   DATA BASE SYSTEM'S LIFE CYCLE

The six phases of the data base system's life cycle are as follows:

1. Design of the data base.
2. Physical creation of the data base.
3. Conversion of existing data sets and applications to match the newly created data base.
4. Integration of converted applications into the new data base.
5. Operations phase.
6. Growth, change, and maintenance phase.

In this diagram, <u>Path I</u> will be taken if existing data sets are to be converted to the newly created data base. <u>Path II</u> will be taken if existing data sets are <u>not</u> to be converted to the newly created data base. (See Figures 2.2 and 2.3.)

This section explains the DA's role during the six phases of the data base system's life cycle.

Before any data base is designed, it is necessary for an enterprise to take an inventory of all areas in which data exists, whether or not these areas are to be included in the total data base system. This is probably one of the important steps in data base system design. The DA must review the resources available and understand the data, its sources, dependencies, and relationships with other systems, to develop a picture of the total data resource of the enterprise and the way this information flows among various systems, and to create a written system design plan.

By performing a review of all systems, conflicts of data ownership, redundant data sources, and ambiguous or inconsistent data groupings can be identified early so system design will not have to be compromised at some later time. From this study, which should include detailed information of systems and operating procedures, a plan can be developed

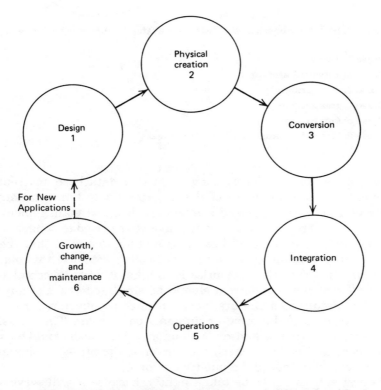

Figure 2.2. The main phases of the data base system's life cycle without overlap.

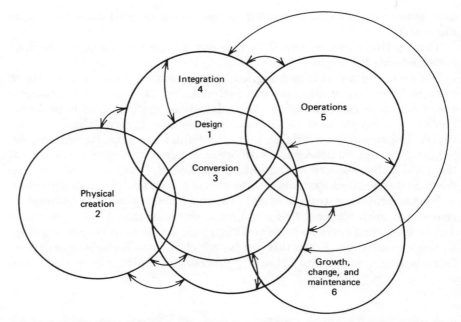

Figure 2.3. **The main phases of the data base system's life cycle with overlap (real world).**

- • **Phase 1: Design.**
- • **Phase 2: Physical creation.**
- • **Phase 3: Conversion.**
- • **Phase 4: Integration.**
- • **Phase 5: Operations.**
- • **Phase 6: Growth, change, and maintenance.**

that will allow for an orderly conversion to a data base environment. Depending on the complexity of the enterprise's system relationships, number of data entities, resource availabilities, and management commitment, this plan may extend over a five-year period or longer.

The system design plan will serve as a guide to assure that the data base system is developing in an orderly fashion. Because this plan will set the direction that the enterprise is to take, it must be complete and address *all* systems. The format should be similiar to that of any long-range plan, detailed for the first year, outlined by quarters for the next two to three years, and thereafter summarized by years. The plan should also be subject to review and revision on a periodic basis and be used by management and users to check the conversion progress. It should be a dynamic document, not just a one-time effort.

This first step is not to be taken lightly, because it will serve as the foundation for all future development. From this plan a logical approach may be taken toward determining which areas are to be converted first, and in what order this effort will proceed. These selections should not be made for visual effect. Most important, this primary step will allow for user involvement in (and, it is hoped, commitment to) the data base design process and will promote a feeling that the user is not just a helpless bystander but an active participant working with the DA.

2.2.1 Design of the Data Base
(Phase 1 from Figures 2.2 and 2.3)

The data base structure is a model of the enterprise and should represent it accurately and support its needs. The design process must have the support of all functional areas of the enterprise. These functional areas need to describe and define data elements from management's and users' viewpoints. The DA then must resolve any discrepancies and ambiguities in data definitions. The design of the data base will be only as good as the definitions of the data elements and their relationships. In fact, the design process is a definition of the organization in terms of its important entities and intrinsic relations.

In an educational environment, the important entities are students and instructors. Some other important entities are courses taught, enrollments, classroom scheduling, money received as tuition and fees, money spent, and special projects. These entities must be defined in the initial design phase, and the DA must be involved in the determination of these entities and their relationships.

A data dictionary (DD) is necessary to do this job effectively. A detailed explanation of the DD will be given in Chapter 3.

In the real world, it is not advisable to implement a data base at once for all the applications necessary for running the organization—in fact, it may be impossible. However, the effect upon the applications that cannot be implemented immediately must be considered, and a long-range plan should be established. It is definitely better to proceed in smaller steps. The aim in any project implementation is to finish the first part of the project successfully, and to demonstrate the potential of the data base approach as well as the ability of the DA to convert all functions of the enterprise to a data base environment. The initial applications chosen should be highly visible, but need not be the most vital. They should not be the least important either. The step-by-step implementation of all functions makes the design phase extremely important.

The design should be easily expandable. Few enterprises can afford to start all over again if a design proves too rigid. Since the data base will constantly need to change and grow, easy restructuring of it is mandatory as new data types and new applications are added. Some data base management systems provide a restructuring tool. With others, the user must write one (usually called a load/unload procedure). The DA must be mindful that two of the main reasons for abandoning the conventional data set era and implementing data base technology are to reduce maintenance costs and provide additional capabilities.

Figure 2.4 reflects the design steps. The major role of the DA in the logical design steps is to concentrate on *why* certain relationships between the entities exist and not on *how to* implement them.

2.2.2 Physical Creation of the Data Base (Phase 2 from Figures 2.2 and 2.3)

After the physical structure of the data base(s) has been adjusted to meet performance requirements, the next step is to present skeletal structure(s) of the physical data base(s) to the DBMS. These skeletons are sometimes placed in a data base description library. Also, logical views of users (also called external models) can be placed in similar libraries.

Before loading and exercising the completed full-scale data base, it is advisable that an experimental prototype of the data base be implemented or a model built. The prototype can give a reasonable estimate of the performance of the complete data base and can also be used for prediction purposes when expanding volume or functions. In no event should production runs be started immediately on the complete data base without any testing. This analysis phase can be overlapped with the conversion phase and with the integration phase. (See Figure 2.3.) It is feasible to go back to the design phase from this prototype phase if the performance requirements are not fulfilled.

After the prototype has been tested for satisfactory performance, the data base can be loaded. It must be remembered, however, that predicting performance with a prototype is very difficult and that it is very hard to tell when the job is done. In most cases, although a prototype is desirable, the model cannot reflect performance in an on-line environment satisfactorily. The reason is that no generalizable mathematical procedure exists to help someone judge whether the model is correct. Specifically, it is hard to do an adequate load test where there are 50 or 100 asynchronous transactions accessing the data base. Nor is it easy to replicate the quantity of information in the data base. Many things run fine on 1000 records but blow up on 100,000. It should be kept in mind that the performance of a data base is also dependent on the size of the data base. Some applications from the conversion phase (phase 3) and from the integration phase (phase 4) (see Figures 2.2, 2.3, and 2.5) can be run against the complete data base. The performance is verified on the basis of design requirements on the complete data base. If the results are unsatisfactory, the data base design must be modified. If the results are satisfactory, the security, privacy, and authorization controls are checked against the complete physical data base. If these controls pass the test, a green light can

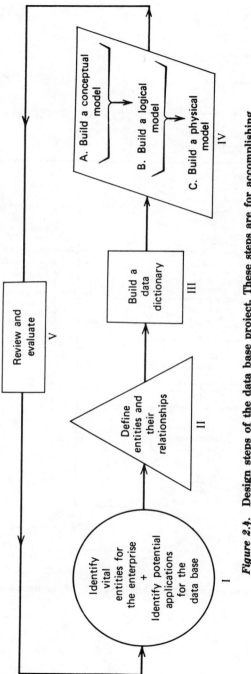

Figure 2.4. Design steps of the data base project. These steps are for accomplishing phase 1 from Figures 2.2 and 2.3.

41

Figure 2.5. **Phases of physical creation (phase 2) of the data base(s) from Figures 2.2 and 2.3.**

be given to the full scale phase (phase 3) of conversion. (See Figures 2.2, 2.3, and 2.5.)

2.2.3 Conversion of Existing Data Sets and Applications to Match the Newly Created Data Base (Phase 3 from Figures 2.2 and 2.3)

In many environments, the data base evolves from the existing information processing system. Existing data sets are converted to the data base. In the example discussed in Section 2.2.1, the educational institution might have data sets for courses taught, enrollment, and student information. Figure 2.6 shows decision paths taken in this phase.

2.2.4 Integration of Converted Applications and New Applications into the New Data Base (Phase 4 from Figures 2.2 and 2.3)

This phase may be heavily overlapped with phase 3. Ease of expansion of physical structure is absolutely necessary in this phase. It means supporting application development through proper management of the data

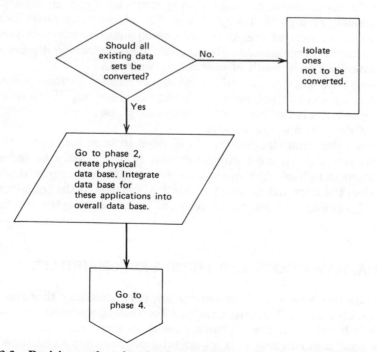

Figure 2.6. Decision paths taken in phase 3 of conversion from Figures 2.2 and 2.3.

base rather than scheduling application development. Application development is not the DA's responsibility. For example, in a banking environment, integrating a new type of credit card system should be possible. If the data base is not designed with this in mind, chances are very high that a return to the design phase will be required. This could be demoralizing for the DA's staff and disastrous for the application development staff.

2.2.5 Operations Phase
(Phase 5 from Figures 2.2 and 2.3)

In this phase all applications that are supposed to run using the data base are run full scale. Privacy, security, and access control procedures must be in place. Recovery and backup procedures must be established, and performance criteria met. There is heavy involvement on the part of the operations expert and the systems expert.

A detailed discussion of the DA's staff and the responsibilities of the various members is given in Section 2.3.

2.2.6 Growth, Change, and Maintenance Phase
(Phase 6 from Figures 2.2 and 2.3)

This is the last phase in the data base system's life cycle. In almost every environment, change is a way of life. The change can be in business practices, it can occur as a result of business expansion or business reduction, it can be due to reorganization. For example, if an environment is unionized, the change can be a result of new union contracts.

Coping with changes is the maintenance phase. In most situations, maintenance work is not necessarily very challenging. If the data base design is relatively flexible, the maintenance phase, most probably, is not the most difficult one to live with.

It is possible that the date base will need to be redesigned if changes are massive. But in most environments, it is a luxury to redesign a functioning data base. And in some environments, it is nearly impossible. Most often the approach taken, for practical reasons, is that of patchwork. The staff member with major involvement in this phase is the applications expert.

2.3 DA, DA'S STAFF, AND THEIR RESPONSIBILITIES

To pursue the interests of the enterprise, it is necessary that the DA be given an efficient staff. As the data base becomes operational and everyone begins to depend on it, the DA function will gain importance. Establishing a data base and running it is an ongoing process, not a one-time event. Upper level management of the enterprise must be convinced that the

DA function is valuable throughout the design phase, the implementation phase, and the operations phase.

The resources provided for the DA function should not reflect under-commitment. The DA organization cannot be expected to provide a satisfactory data base system and to meet schedules without adequate support. Before discussing the initial staffing of the DBA function, let us look again generally at the DA's placement in an organization.

2.3.1 DA's Placement in Organization

The placement of the DA in an organization depends on:

- The nature of the enterprise.
- The importance of existing applications the data base will serve.
- The importance of future applications the data base will serve.
- The management style of the enterprise.
- The maturity of the enterprise in regard to data processing.
- The personality of the DA.

Within each enterprise, the data processing function has its own unique nature, as defined by its purpose for existence. Certain basic interfaces and functional relationships with the data processing department, however, are common to all installations.

The data processing environment tries to serve the needs of the enterprise in terms of information. Most installations have an application development group that interacts with the users from various areas, such as finance, manufacturing, marketing, and personnel. The group develops and maintains application programs in such programming languages as COBOL, PL/I, ASSEMBLER, and FORTRAN for information processing for the user community. Another group, data processing systems and operations, tends the hardware schedules and runs the applications on it, maintains the tape library, takes care of physical security, and updates the operating system and other software necessary for running the applications. For the applications group the major source of data for running the applications may be the data base, and for the operations group the major maintenance activity may involve the hardware and software related to the data base. The DA's function is to develop a data base design that represents the entities and their relationships within the enterprise, and to maintain and expand these relationships as the enterprise grows.

In the initial phase of feasibility study, research, and startup, and before the emergence of a full DA function, the DBA may be reporting to the director of information processing. The applications and systems operations group may be at the same level as the DBA, as in Figure 2.7. Ideally, the DBA should be at least at the same level in the organization

Figure 2.7. **The DBA's placement in data processing. The DBA is independent of data processing function and applications development staff.**

as the managers of user departments for whom the data base is being developed and implemented.

The influence of the DBA increases as the data base starts to play a major role in the existence and normal running of the enterprise. The importance of the DBA depends on the maturity of the enterprise in the data processing area, the enterprise's confidence in the data base as a major resource for its continued existence, and the ability of the DBA and his or her staff to satisfy the user needs. As the enterprise matures and confidence and abilities increase, steps toward a full DA function can be taken.

The initial placement of the DBA will vary among enterprises. The organizational level of the DBA should be based on this individual's relative value and importance, which may vary among organizations, rather than on an artificial need to save face.

An organization where the DBA function has not been very successful is shown in Figure 2.8. In this organization, as in many others, the service function is blamed for any delays in delivering proper service. The data processing department, in turn, blames the application programmers for not maintaining the programs properly. There is finger pointing between line and staff departments. The line departments perform the day-to-day functions—running production jobs and providing a test environment for applications—while the staff departments develop the applications. The fact that the DBA reports to the data processing manager means that the DBA is part of the line function. Because of the tense relationships between line and staff, the application programmers do not cooperate well with the line, and vice versa.

An organization where the DA function has been extremely successful is shown in Figure 2.9. The DBA, whose responsibility is the operation of the data base, reports to the DA together with other groups that assist in the management, planning, and control of the data resources. The DA function, in turn, together with other data-related activities, reports at an even higher level in the organization.

Figure 2.8. The DBA reports to the data processing manager. The DBA is on the line side, and the application programmers are on the staff side.

2.3.2   DBA's Staff

In the earliest stages, soon after the acquisition of a DBMS, the DBA staff may consist of only two or three people capable of planning, organizing, and communicating with upper management and the user community. These skill requirements should be considered when staffing this function. More people can be added as the design progresses.

The size of the DBA's staff will depend on the size of the enterprise, the complexity of the applications to be run with the data base, the complexity of the DBMS chosen and its ability to generate the relationships required by the logical views, the level of the users' sophistication, and the phase of the data base project. The staff should consist of individuals who are able to define, organize, structure, and protect the data base and to communicate with people from various areas of the enterprise.

The DBA's function involves communication with such groups as management, non-DP users, DP programmers, and DP systems/operations. Ideally there should be at least one person on the DBA's staff who can communicate effectively with a group or a combination of groups. Figure 2.10 shows the functions of the DBA and his or her staff and their major interfaces. Figure 2.11 shows the DBA's staff at its full capacity and the responsibilities of its members. This staffing illustration is, of course, for a relatively large environment where 100 or more application programmers

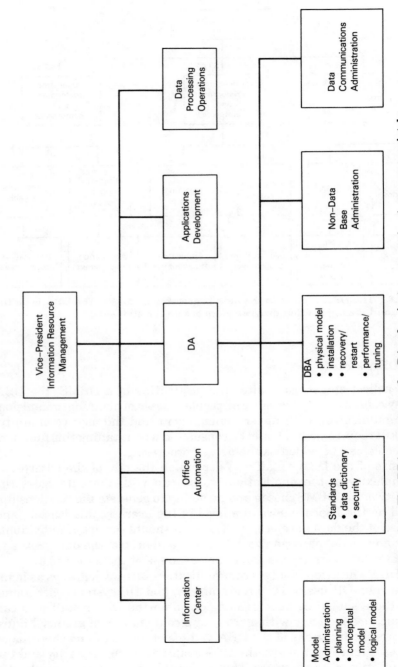

Figure 2.9. The DBA reports to the DA who, in turn, reports at an appropriately high level in the organization.

Function	Major Interface
DBA	Management DP programmers DP operations Non—DP users
Operations expert	DP operations
Systems expert	DP systems
Applications expert	DP programmers Non—DP users
Librarian	DP programmers Non—DP users
Query languages expert	DP programmers Non—DP users DP systems
Auditor	Non—DP users DP operations DP programmers

Figure 2.10. The DBA's staff and their major interfaces. The DBA's function involves communication with a number of different groups, such as management, non-DP users, DP programmers, DP systems/operations.

are employed. It is now ripe for a move to the DA function discussed earlier. If there is a relatively small application group, the DBA group will also be relatively small.

2.3.3 Responsibilities of the Individual Staff Members

The staff members have various duties in different stages of data base development. We distinguish between the following six phases, as in Figure 2.2.

1. Design phase.
2. Physical creation of the data base.
3. Conversion of existing data sets and applications to match the newly created data base.
4. Integration of converted applications and new applications into the data base.
5. Operations phase.
6. Growth, change, and maintenance phase.

Figure 2.11. **The DBA's staff at full capacity and their responsibilities. The size of the DBA's staff will depend on:**

1. **The size of the enterprise.**
2. **The complexity of the applications to be run with the data base.**
3. **The complexity of the DBMS chosen.**
4. **The level of the user's sophistication.**
5. **The phase of the data base project.**

Operations Expert. The operations expert is responsible for establishing effective communication between the DBA function and the operations staff of the data processing function.

1. Design Phase

- Evaluate impact on performance of several physical structure alternatives.
- If applications need operator intervention, develop operator interfaces that are easy to learn and to use.
- Evaluate credibility of backup, recovery, security, and privacy procedures.

2, 3, 4. Physical Creation, Conversion, and Integration Phases

- Supervise necessary operational preparations (e.g., checking the quality of auxiliary storage for the data base).
- Organize installation of the DBMS (e.g., defining libraries, establishing data sets).
- Assist operations manager in implementation plan.
- Reserve time slots for operations people, and arrange to have the most proficient operators from operations department for loading the data base.
- Establish procedures for starting up the DBMS every morning.
- Prepare procedures for logging data base operations.
- Set up procedures for recovery, backup, security, and authorization. Establish procedures also for information requirements for trouble-shooting and analysis of unexpected errors.
- Provide for operators' training, investigate their training programs, and make recommendations to the data processing manager.

5. Operations Phase

This phase is made up of day-to-day chores.

- Check that daily starting, logging, running, and stopping of any operations on the data base are done properly by operators.
- Supervise all restarts and recoveries after failure.
- Supervise all reorganizations of indexes and data bases.
- Check that all transactions and any activities against the data bases are logged.
- Establish a plan for periodic dumps of the data base, including initiating and supervising them. Control physical transfer of copies of the data base on auxiliary storage to locations other than the data center.
- Monitor recording of all malfunctions of hardware, and initiate regular preventive maintenance by operations staff.
- Obtain data base performance reports on a daily, weekly, and monthly basis, and track down any performance problems. Inform systems experts about problems. Use performance measurement tools.
- Continually evaluate and exercise backup/recovery plans.
- Evaluate data base quality (e.g., consistency of data, of pointers, etc.).

6. Growth, Change, and Maintenance Phase

- Evaluate impact of growth and changes to the data base on its performance.
- Check that backup and recovery procedures are intact before introducing any major changes.

Systems Expert. In a large data base environment, this is usually a group of experts who are knowledgeable in data base system languages and procedures. The DBA and the applications experts supply the system experts with the logical structure of the data base. The systems experts then have the following responsibilities in the various phases:

1. Design Phase
- Use logical structure for simulation with applications profiles and develop physical structure.
- Apply performance criteria against physical structure and make changes accordingly.
- Choose the right access methods and suitable physical organization to satisfy performance criteria and any future expansion requirements.
- Design software and hardware configuration necessary for the data base.
- Design recovery, backup, and restart procedures with operations staff.
- Select or create efficient randomizing modules for accessing the data base.
- Design security, privacy, and authorization routines.
- Make the DBA aware of all existing software and hardware constraints.

2, 3, 4. Physical Creation, Conversion, and Integration Phases
- Install the DBMS package.
- Coordinate implementation of applications with applications experts.
- Institute, along with operations experts, procedures for checking security, privacy, and access control violations.
- Set up procedures with operations experts for performance measurement and evaluation.
- Assist applications experts with any dumps of the data base system as a result of abnormal terminations.

5. Operations Phase
- Tune system as required because of performance problems.
- Periodically check auxiliary space utilization, and try to make it as efficient as possible.
- Try to project workload, based on past and present workloads, and make the DBA aware of any anticipated performance problems.
- Help application development people with any dumps of the data base system as a result of abnormal terminations.
- Analyze problems, dumps, traces, and so on. Often problems cannot be isolated to one application, or are not application problems at all.

6. Growth, Change, and Maintenance Phase

- Design software and hardware configurations necessary for growth of the data base.
- Coordinate implementation of the changed applications with applications experts.

Applications Expert. This group consists of experts in data base design and in data base programming techniques. Its responsibilities are as follows:

1. Design Phase

- Define data elements and their relationships.
- Develop logical structure of the data base with user community.
- Attempt to incorporate long-term goals of the enterprise in the logical structure of the data base.
- Determine data element synonyms with help of user community.
- Provide systems experts with information about usage frequency and changes to data elements. These numbers affect physical design and performance of the data base.
- Supply data element information and their relationships (i.e., which programs use which data elements) to the librarian, who will insert the information into the data dictionary.
- Control entry of new data elements into the data dictionary. The application programmer cannot perform insertions into or deletions from entries in the data dictionary.

2, 3, 4. Physical Creation, Conversion, and Integration Phases

- Assist application development staff in conversion and integration phases.
- Assist systems experts and operations experts in checking implementation of procedures for security, privacy, and auditability.
- Assist librarians in expansion of the data dictionary/directory system.

5. Operations Phase

- Check whether applications are following security, privacy, and access control restrictions.
- Check whether applications are storing historical data properly.
- Supervise proper sequence of running applications.

6. Growth, Change, and Maintenance Phase

- Evaluate results of changes to existing applications, and interactions between applications.

- Supply data element information and their relationships (i.e., which programs use which data elements) to the librarian, who inserts the information into the data dictionary.
- Control entry of new or changed data elements into the data dictionary.
- Assist application development staff in the "changing" phase.

Librarian.   One of the major responsibilities of a librarian is to establish the communication mechanisms for the data base administrator. Figure 2.1 shows the necessary communication paths in the data base environment. It is the librarian's function to set up meetings between the DBA and the different functions shown in Figure 2.1. This part of the librarian's responsibility is similar to the public relations function. The other responsibilities are as follows:

1. Design Phase
- Keep a record of changes in the data dictionary/directory system.
- Document and distribute results of design and outcome of meetings to those who need the information.

2, 3, 4, 5, 6. Physical Creation, Conversion, Integration, Operations, and Growth, Change, and Maintenance Phases
- Control data dictionary/directory system's libraries.
- Keep a record of any security, privacy, and/or authorization violations.
- Keep records for auditability mechanisms.
- Document and distribute results of these phases and outcome of meetings to those who need the information.

Query Languages Expert.   Since most data bases are used on-line, it is desirable to have a query facility for accessing the data base. A high level query language is better than a procedural one for unanticipated requests. For the occasional user, the chances of making mistakes in setting the query are higher with a procedural than with a high level query language. Also, a high level query language will be able to satisfy ad hoc queries from management. To support the function well, the DBA staff should include a query language expert.

The responsibilities in the various phases are as follows:

1. Design Phase
- Determine authorization levels for different types of queries.
- Establish formats for the queries.
- Design, in conjunction with systems experts, queries with adequate performance.
- Assist people with unanticipated queries. The ability to handle such queries is a prime benefit of a DBMS.

2, 3, 4, 5, 6. Physical Creation, Conversion, Integration, Operations, and Growth, Change, and Maintenance Phases

- Track performance of queries.
- Make DBA aware of queries that cannot be satisfied by the data base, and suggest alternative queries that retrieve the required information from the data base.
- Assist users in query development and maintenance.

Auditor. In a number of environments, it is possible for application programmers to circumvent security restrictions. More often than we think, they succeed in doing so. An auditor should be able to pinpoint possible places where security breaches may take place, as well as ones that have already occurred. Hardware as well as software security has to be considered.

Security and privacy issues go hand in hand. If security is at stake, privacy violations may follow immediately.

REFERENCES

1. *The Data Base Administrator,* prepared by the members of the Data Base Administration Project of the Information Management Group, Information Systems Division, GUIDE International Corporation, November 3, 1972.
2. Durrell, William, *Data Administration.* New York: McGraw-Hill Book Company, 1985.
3. Gerritsen, Rob, Howard Morgan, and Michael Zisman, "On some Metrics for Databases, or What Is a Very Large Database?" *ACM SIGMOD RECORD,* Vol. 9, No. 1 (June 1977).
4. Lyon, John K., *The Database Administrator.* New York: John Wiley & Sons, 1976.

QUESTIONS

1. What types of information should be gathered by the DA from the user community in planning for a DBMS?
2. The DA must relate to many groups. List the groups and discuss the information flow for at least one group.
3. What major factors should be considered by the DA when evaluating software packages?
4. List the major phases of a data base system's life cycle and illustrate concerns at each phase.
5. Why is it crucial to consider carefully the placement of the DA in the organization?
6. Should data base systems be designed on a top-down or bottom-up basis? Should they be implemented top-down or bottom-up? What are the advantages and disadvantages of each approach?

7. What would be the consequences of not having a DA or a DBA?

8. Write a job description for a DBA, including education, skills, background, and general characteristics.

9. You have been appointed a DBA in the following organization. The Data Processing Director of Information Processing is at the same level as the Manufacturing General Manager. You encounter the following conditions:

   a. A data base already exists and is supported by three application programmers.

   b. The only documentation is a DBMS manual and a sketch of how certain files are related, which was published by the last DBA who left two years earlier.

   c. Current information on the data base is through word of mouth from the senior applications programmers.

   d. Everybody is unhappy. Your own department manager dares not assign new applications programmers to access the data base since there is insufficient information about what is in the data base. The user department management wants more applications written but is not getting them. It is becoming less responsible for keeping the input data up to date. The senior application programmers (on whom you rely for data base information) are still debugging their

Figure 2.12.   Conditions for Question 9.

production programs and blame the data base for every program failure.

9.1. List your priorities in solving the above problems and suggest an appropriate course of action. You may hire two assistants. What would be their responsibilities and qualifications?

9.2. Suggest an alternate organizational structure. Justify your proposal.

Data Dictionary

3.1 WHAT IS A DATA DICTIONARY?

In a data base environment, one of the major objectives is the sharing of common data by multiple users. Another major objective is providing correct data to these users. To realize the objectives of correct data, minimum redundancy, and control of data usage, a centralized control mechanism is mandatory. A data dictionary is a likely vehicle to establish and to maintain these controls. An additional advantage is that systems established using a data dictionary tend to be more effective and less expensive to develop.

But the decision to acquire and implement a data dictionary should not be taken lightly. One aspect that should not be overlooked is that effective use of a data dictionary will probably require some organizational and procedural changes. Acquiring a data dictionary is a commitment, just as acquiring a data base management system is a commitment. Later in the chapter, we shall investigate the cost/benefit considerations. Let us first see where the data dictionary fits in the design process.

The first step in designing a data base is to collect information about the enterprise, that is, about the usage, relationships, and meaning of data. As the design process progresses, it is necessary to store information about conceptual, logical, internal, and external models at a central location. A tool that enables one to control and manage information about data in the design, implementation, operation, and expansion phases of a data base is called a "data dictionary."

In the beginning stage of collecting information regarding data, naming conventions for data elements must be established, conflicts between different departments regarding meanings, sources, and naming conventions resolved, descriptions of data elements agreed upon, and synonyms of data elements recognized. This process inevitably involves many iterations and many political struggles. Every department or other part of the organization considers its mission to be the most important one, and its perspective of the organization the right one. This results in conflicts regarding collection of information about data. In these situations the data administrator must assume the role of a tie breaker. To keep track of and to record information about data accurately, it is desirable for everyone involved with the data base to use an automated data dictionary.

The data dictionary stores such information about data as its origin, description, relationship to other data, usage, responsibility, and format. It is a data base itself, storing data about data. The data dictionary is a guide and contains road maps to the data base instead of raw data.

3.1.1 Basic Objectives of a Data Dictionary

One of the basic objectives of a data dictionary is to allow management of documentation about data. Since the data base serves a number of users, it is vital that every user understands precisely what the data is and what it means.

There are many aspects to data that a data base designer has to know. In the early stages of the design, the very first thing that should be recorded about each item of data is the English (or native language) definition. These definitions or descriptions should be such that every person who is going to use data understands exactly what each definition means and agrees with it.

There should be an understandable definition or description of every piece of data. If three different departments are using the same piece of data in three different contexts, however, it is not at all easy for the three departments to agree on one definition or one description of the shared item. Problems of this nature have to be resolved by the data administration function. The difficulties of finding solutions to problems of this type will serve as evidence that political disputes can be much more complicated to solve than technical issues in the data base environment.

At this stage, when an attempt is being made to arrive at a textual description of every piece of data, no attention need be given to actual physical representation. The designer does not have to determine whether data is going to be stored as packed, or in character form, or in some other format.

It is advisable to begin to collect information about data in a data dictionary on the day the project starts. As soon as the project is under way, the designer begins asking each user questions, such as what kind of system the user wants, what information the user wants to get from the system, and what type of input can be provided. As soon as user and designer start talking about the user's needs, they are going to use data element names; in a banking enterprise these may be account number, balance, and interest. The data base designer and the user have to be confident that when they use a term they mean precisely the same thing; otherwise the designer may build a system that is not what the user wanted. This points out another basic objective of a data dictionary, that is, helping to establish effective communication between designer and users and among users themselves.

Let us consider an example. In a banking environment, one of the important data elements is balance. What is the balance of a specific account? For most nonbankers, there is an obvious definition of what a balance means. But if an account master file for a commercial banking system is studied, it is possible that in one account's record there are as many as 25 fields with the word "balance" in their titles. It is extremely important, therefore, that when the designer talks to the user it is made very clear which balance the designer means: opening balance this morning, closing balance last night, book balance, available balance, and so on. Closing balance last night is not necessarily identical with opening balance this morning. Book balance goes up as soon as the customer makes a deposit, but if the deposit was made with a check, available balance rises only after the check has cleared. There are many more diverse balance fields. The data dictionary can be used to store information about all data elements in a central location to establish effective communication between all parties concerned.

In most enterprises, management does not have control over the data resource because there is no corporate view of data. To gain control over the data resource, information about data has to be collected at a central place. Management then can begin to impose controls over use of the data resource.

Thus the two basic objectives of a data dictionary are management and control of data as a resource at a central location through the phases of design, implementation, and operations, as well as establishment of effective communication between all those who are interested in the data base.

In the case of a distributed data base environment, data bases or portions of data bases may be physically stored in different locations on different computers, and connected via data communication facilities. It is possible that some installations may store and access data only at local places, whereas other installations may store and access local as well as remote data.

Let us take an example of a nationwide life insurance company. The insurance agents in the New York City area will request information about clients in the New York City area much more frequently than about clients in the San Francisco area, and vice versa. It may be advisable to store the data about New York City clients for on-line retrieval at some local places on the East Coast. If an agent from the East Coast needs information about a client on the West Coast, it can be retrieved in batch from the data base stored on the West Coast, and vice versa.

A data dictionary installed at every location may be loaded with the information about all physical locations where data is stored, access control, and security and privacy constraints. With the help of this information, the data dictionary may decide "intelligently" whether to satisfy a request from the local data base, or whether the user is authorized to access remote data, in which case the request is sent to the remote location.

In this book when we talk about a data dictionary it will be in the context of a DBMS. Some people argue that the data dictionary may also be put on paper, either handwritten or typewritten. But the problem with a manual data dictionary is that it will be difficult to satisfy the designer, who is going to need the definition of a data element sorted in a number of different ways. The same data element may be used by a number of different users in different contexts. In the beginning stage there will be a list of the data elements in some semirelated form. As the designer proceeds through the design phase, however, the data elements will be used in a number of different places. They will appear on input formats and on output formats in relationships to one another. In each place data elements will appear in a different context. Accomplishing all this will be a tedious undertaking, and soon listings will be difficult to manage. An automated version will be easier to control and manage.

In order for a data dictionary to be accepted and used in a data processing environment, it needs to have a central input. Information entered into this one source can be used through all the design phases and copied by programmers into their programs for data structures. If a manual dictionary is used, the information therein becomes inconsistent (over time) with what is actually in the system. A data dictionary may be referred to as a "meta data base" which stores information about the data base.

3.1.2 Data Base Management System and Data Dictionary

A data dictionary can also be used in a non-data base environment. A data dictionary is a central place for information about data description, such as meaning, relationships to other data, responsibility for keeping data up to date, and the origin of data. In a data base environment, the information stored in a data dictionary is about data stored in a data base, and in a non-data base environment the information stored in a data dictionary is about data stored in data files. It is also possible to use a data dictionary for DBMS and non-DBMS applications simultaneously.

It is necessary to install software to create and manage a data dictionary data base. The software is also called a data dictionary. The data dictionary may be dependent on a data base management system or it may be freestanding. A dependent data dictionary employs the underlying DBMS to manage its data; it is just another data base under the DBMS. A freestanding data dictionary effectively contains its own mini-DBMS to manage the meta data. A dependent data dictionary comes as part of the DBMS package, whereas a freestanding data dictionary is a separate package in addition to the DBMS package. Cullinet's Integrated Data Dictionary (IDD), IBM's DB/DC Data Dictionary, and Software AG's PRE-DICT are all dependent data dictionaries. MSP's Datamanager is an example of a freestanding data dictionary.

A data dictionary may be active, or it may be passive. In an active data dictionary, data descriptions exist only once in the system and are stored in the data dictionary. In a passive data dictionary, an option allows necessary data descriptions to be retrieved from the data dictionary or supplied otherwise. In the case of an active data dictionary, there is no option; it is necessary to check for currency of data descriptions prior to execution of a program. A passive data dictionary may or may not require a check for currency of data descriptions before a program is executed. A data dictionary is active with respect to a program or process if the program or process is wholly dependent on the data dictionary for its meta data. Otherwise it is, at least to some extent, passive. Even a totally passive data dictionary, however, can have value as a documentation and communication device.

Both approaches, a passive data dictionary package and an active data dictionary package, offer advantages and disadvantages.

Advantages of an Active Data Dictionary System

- Data descriptions are not stored redundantly. This reduces the occurrence of errors due to failure to update both places.
- The data dictionary has access to data in the data base. One potential use of the data dictionary may be in the area of data access tracking, to provide valuable statistics for improving performance.
- A data dictionary can serve as a much more powerful control tool when active, because data base designers and users will have to enforce the data dictionary as a tool for documentation and control of data.

Advantages of a Passive Data Dictionary

- There is less risk of commitment to a data base management system in implementing a passive data dictionary than an active data dictionary, especially one that is also dependent on the DBMS. Implementation of a passive dictionary is easier, because the dictionary does not have to adhere to the implementation idiosyncrasies of a DBMS.

- An active data dictionary needs all data descriptions required for a data base at one time, whereas data descriptions can be provided in stages to a passive data dictionary. In today's data processing environment, not all data files are converted to a data base at one time. A data base exists together with some conventional data files. A data dictionary package that can keep track of data in the data base as an active data dictionary, and of data in the data files as a passive data dictionary, would be desirable.

There is a recent trend among suppliers of software packages toward having the dictionary be the keystone for all of the related software packages, including a data base management system, a query language processor, and a teleprocessing monitor.

Whether a data dictionary is freestanding or dependent, active or passive, it is important to know about its interfaces in an ideal data base environment. The data dictionary packages available in the marketplace today do not necessarily provide all of the interfaces illustrated in the next section.

3.1.3 Data Dictionary and Its Interfaces

We will consider a data dictionary's interfaces in an environment with a single DBMS as in Figure 3.1.

In the beginning of the data base design process, the data administration function will be interacting with the data dictionary. With the help of a report generator (which probably is an integral part of the data dictionary package), management and users will be provided with reports tailored to individual users' needs.

The reports may contain information regarding the following:

- Data elements and entities.
- Relationships between data elements and between entities.
- Responsibilities of users for correctness of data.
- Frequency of usage and textual descriptions of data elements.
- Access control information.
- Audit reports.
- Predefined summary reports.
- User-defined ad hoc reports.
- Cross-reference reports.

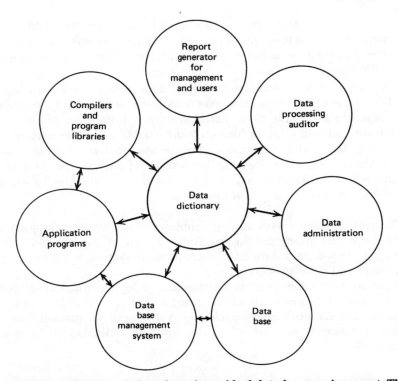

Figure 3.1. **Data dictionary's interfaces in an ideal data base environment. There are two types of interfaces:**

1. **The interface with the people involved, for example, data administrator, systems programmer, systems analyst, application programmer, management, end-user, and auditor.**
2. **The interface with the software, for example, data base management system, compilers, operating system, and report generators.**

- Change reports.
- Error reports.

A data dictionary may also generate appropriate data descriptions for high level languages to program libraries and to compilers. Information about cross-reference relationships between data elements and application programs can be stored in the data dictionary. The cross-reference list will enable any authorized person to inform any application programmer or department about an intended modification before it takes place, get concurrence if appropriate, and then implement the change. The change may involve content, format, or relationship to other data elements.

Ideally, the interface between the DBMS and the data dictionary should be such that the DBMS directories are readable by the data dictionary system in order to provide data on the current state of the DBMS. Data types in the data base should be updated after the data dictionary system makes note of changes, and data should be updated only when it is found acceptable to the DBMS. Thus data dictionary, DBMS, and data base should form a closed loop.

The data dictionary can be used as an effective tool by the data administration function in the design, implementation, and operations phases of the data base. It it the responsibility of the DA to protect the data dictionary by enforcing standards, security, and privacy constraints.

The auditing function has gained more importance in the last few years in the electronic data processing environment. In an environment where the data base is shared, auditing becomes mandatory. A data dictionary is the ideal place for finding answers to questions like where used, who used, and when used with regard to data elements and entities. It is also the ideal place to provide information for a cost/efficiency study of the organization's system, as well as to satisfy particular privacy and confidentiality requirements.

These interfaces show there are two types of uses of a data dictionary. One type of use is by people in their functions as data administrator, systems programmer, systems analyst, application programmer, manager, end-user, and auditor. The other type of use is by software in such areas as DBMS, compilers, operating system, and report generators.

These two types of interfaces enhance the management and control of the data base environment as a result of effective communication between the parties involved.

3.1.4　An Ideal Data Dictionary: Its Requirements and Organization

The following is a list of desirable requirements of a data dictionary data base. It does not imply that any single data dictionary package available today supports all these requirements.

Conceptual Model. Information about data needed in the design process of the conceptual model includes entities, data elements or attributes representing entities, and relationships between data elements. Also, the data dictionary should contain information about which departments and which users currently use or intend to use which data elements, and how frequently the data elements are used, together with textual descriptions giving meanings and purposes. Data elements, entities, and relationships should have appropriate labels, versions, status (proposed, concurred, approved, effective), textual descriptions, synonyms (other data dictionary entities with the same meaning but with different labels), memberships (entities of which a particular data element is a member or by which it is being referenced), and data element groupings with key data elements.

Logical Model. The following information about the logical model of the data base should be stored in the data dictionary: data element groupings with key data elements (these groupings may be subsets of groupings specified in the conceptual model), underlying data model, relationships of groupings based on the data model, external models supported by the logical model (i.e., different logical paths for information processing), logical transactions, programs, and modules. The interdependencies of transactions, programs, and modules should also be stored. The cross-reference information between transactions, programs, modules, and departments or functions that are served by them should be included. Other necessary information is programming language and program type (batch, teleprocessing) for programs and transactions.

Internal Model. The physical layout information about data elements—for example: length (characters); mode (bit string, character string, packed decimal, simple floating point); precision (for numerical elements); justification (right, left); picture (for display purposes only); edit rules (constant, range of values); derivation algorithm (for calculated elements); sequence (sequential position that a particular data element occupies in the membership); security (security code for read, update); medium (card, disk, tape, video); devices where data base(s) are stored; and access control information—all should be stored in the data dictionary.

An ideal data dictionary should be an integral part of the entire data base environment. The data administrator should be responsible for input to the data dictionary. Being the central part of the data base environment, a data dictionary has to be saved in backup copies to avoid disaster brought about by a system malfunction or any unintentional destruction of the production version of the data dictionary. The data administration function bears full responsibility for protecting the vital part of the data base environment—the data dictionary.

An ideal data dictionary package should also support the following features:

Retrieval and Reporting Facilities. Any communication and documentation tool can be effective only if it provides easy retrieval and reporting facilities. The facilities should support formal as well as ad hoc requests. Reports may include the following items:

- Element lists in alphabetical or any other desired sequence.
- Cross-reference listings between data elements, groups of data elements, programs using them, and department or people responsible for keeping contents valid.
- Data descriptions for host language programs, and logical views of external models supporting application programs.

The data dictionary should also contain sufficient information to provide some indication of any effect on programs or transactions as a result of a change to the data model. The provision of cost estimates for implementing the proposed change is a very desirable feature.

Capturing of Data as Input to Data Dictionary. Ideally the data dictionary should be used as a tool by the data administrator, application programmers, users, management, and any software interacting with the data base. The data stored in the data dictionary should be entered by people with some people-oriented input language, or by software from program definitions as in COBOL and PL/I, from data base management system definitions, and from program procedure statements.

Access Control Information. The data dictionary may contain information regarding access control, specifying who may have access to what part of the data base and in what way. The information can be used as follows:

- Before compiling any programs or printing any reports, a check for any contradictions between specifications for data retrieval given by the requestor and specifications provided by the data administrator should be made.
- To pinpoint any misuse of data for a part of the data base shared by multiple users, a stringent set of security restrictions has to be implemented.

If the data dictionary is to be used for access control, it must itself be subject to access control. The number of people eligible to make any modifications to the data dictionary must be restricted. Security restrictions on the contents of the data dictionary should be implemented.

Support of Utilities. Since the data dictionary is the central part of the data base environment, it should be able to support various utilities for editing, updating, and restructuring of data bases, report generators, and so on.

Generation of Program and Data Description Code. Storing information about data elements, about their physical layouts, about their relationships to other data elements, and about logical and internal models should enable a data dictionary to generate data description code, as well as some standard program modules such as input/output modules.

Consistency. The information contents of the data dictionary should be complete, correctly formatted, and properly cross-referenced. To satisfy these requirements, any input to the data dictionary should be checked for consistency. The checking should also be based on mapping information between conceptual, logical, external, and internal models stored in the data dictionary.

Ideal Data Dictionary System

1. The data dictionary should support conceptual, logical, internal, and external models.
2. The data dictionary should be active with respect to its environment.
3. The data dictionary should support various versions of documentation (e.g., test versions, production version).
4. The data dictionary should support efficient transfer of information to the DBMS. Ideally, binding between external models and internal models should be done at execution time, when the data dictionary should take information from the production version and create data base description and program description dynamically.
5. A data dictionary system should initiate reorganization of the production version of the data base as a result of changes to the data base description. Similarly, any changes to program descriptions should be reflected automatically in the program description library with the help of the data dictionary. This will happen when the data dictionary system is an active part of the DBMS.

3.2 IMPLEMENTATION STRATEGIES FOR A DATA DICTIONARY

Two types of data dictionary packages are available today. One type of package is freestanding and supports a varied number of DBMSs. The second type of package is dependent on a DBMS. For both types of packages, the data dictionary itself is implemented as a data base(s). Accordingly, the design of a data dictionary is subject to the same criteria as is that of any data base. The first study to be carried out concerns cost/benefit considerations. The second question that remains to be answered is how and when a data dictionary can be phased into the operations of the enterprise.

3.2.1 Cost/Benefit Considerations

As stated earlier, the data dictionary is not a dependent, active part of a data base management system in most of of the packages available today. As a result, the decision about buying a data dictionary package has to be made independently of the DBMS. The acquisition has to be cost justified for benefits to be expected. Let us first consider expenses that will be incurred as a result of using a data dictionary system. The issue here is not whether to have a data dictionary, but, first, whether to have a data administration function and, second, whether to provide the data administrator with a tool for control. From this perspective, we would like to compare a data base environment with and without a data dictionary. We shall not consider the conventional data set (data file) environment with or without a data dictionary.

The cost of an object or of a project can be measured in terms of resources required. Costs can usually be expressed in terms of dollars: package acquisition, personnel, creation and maintenance of the data dictionary data base, equipment costs, and so forth. Usually it is more difficult to measure benefits. A benefit is a consequence of an action that protects, aids, improves, or promotes the well-being of an individual or organization. Benefits may be expressed in terms of savings, cost avoidance, improved performance, and taking advantage of hidden opportunities. It is important in any cost/benefit analysis to list probable effects of the proposed project, positive as well as negative.

It remains an art to put price tags where benefits, costs, and savings are concerned. One school of thought holds that cost/benefit calculations simply do not work for most companies considering the acquisition of highly sophisticated software products like data dictionaries and data base management systems. The cost/benefit analysis is not done in the real world for the very practical reason that any relationship between calculations and the resulting real world environment is purely coincidental. Since this type of cost/benefit analysis is still an art, the following points are based more on intuition than on scientific research.

Costs

Personnel. The costs of personnel to install a data dictionary system, and to create and maintain the data dictionary data base, must be considered. These expenses will vary, depending on size and complexity of the enterprise, size of the data base, number of applications supported by the data dictionary, and sophistication of the personnel themselves. It should not be forgotten that there is a learning curve associated with the use of a data dictionary system, just as with any other system. The costs will be considerably higher if the enterprise is operating in a totally decentralized way. In this kind of environment, the change in organizational procedure will result in higher expenditure.

Creation of a data dictionary data base. This will be the main expense. The cost to create the data dictionary data base will depend on the following items:

1. The number of data elements to be recognized and to be entered with their textual descriptions and their attributes.

2. The task of locating and documenting relationships between data
    elements, between entities, and between applications, using data ele-
    ments, entities, and relationships between them.

The expenses for these two items depend, in turn, on the availability of
the data to be entered in the data dictionary data base at the time of the
initial creation of the data dictionary. For existing data base or data file
applications, the accumulation of data elements with their attributes and
descriptions will be relatively easy if documentation is at the disposal of
the data administration staff. For development of a new set of applications,
only a part of the cost has to be considered because documentation of a
similar nature should be done anyway.

Maintenance of a data dictionary data base. Although maintenance
expenses will be only a fraction of the cost of the original creation of the
data dictionary data base, they must be considered in a dynamic environment. The cost of maintaining a data dictionary data base will be
equal, in the worst situation, to the expenses without a data dictionary.

Equipment. The data dictionary, to be useful, should be stored on
random access storage for easy retrieval. Usually costs for random access
storage, central processing unit time, and memory use are low compared
to labor costs.

Let us now consider benefits to be expected from use of a data dictionary.

Benefits. Benefits vary from one enterprise to another. Savings with a
data dictionary system will be higher for a data base environment with
a larger number of data elements and relationships. Savings will also be
higher in an environment with a relatively high number of changes; that
is, a dynamic data base environment will benefit more from a data dictionary
than will a totally static one. A dynamic environment does not mean that
data structure is in a state of flux. Such an enterprise should not have a
data base. Any data base of real size cannot be restructured on a continuing
basis without incurring considerable expenses. Benefits from a data dictionary also increase as the sharing of data elements between programs
increases.

Data base design, development, creation, and maintenance. Use of the
data dictionary improves communications between designers and users
and among users themselves. This results in fewer iterations in the design
phase. Development costs are lower because of better documentation of
specifications and clearer understanding by all involved. Ideally, data
base creation should proceed at a faster pace because of faster data base
design. Also, maintenance of the data base should be less expensive with
the help of a data dictionary than in a nondictionary environment because
of better documentation, faster analysis of effects of proposed changes,
and better communication between maintenance personnel and people
requesting the changes.

Intangibles. There are also a number of intangible benefits as a result of using a data dictionary:

1. The ease of referencing a data base as a result of using a data dictionary, like the ease of referencing a book by using the index, cannot be expressed in terms of dollars.
2. A data dictionary makes possible more complete and systematic storage of information about data.
3. It is easier to implement standards for data element names, descriptions, usage, and so on, at a central location than in scattered places.
4. A data dictionary enables one to implement changes to the data base faster because of the cross-referencing capability.
5. A data dictionary improves the ability to create records of information accessed and persons accessing it.
6. It is also easier for auditors to audit the data base and its use because such information is centrally located.

In a data base environment with a data dictionary system, initial costs of implementation (i.e., populating the data dictionary with information about data elements, their interrelationships, their usage, etc.) are higher relative to those for a data base environment without a data dictionary system. But expenses for changes with the data dictionary system taper off with time, whereas without the data dictionary these expenses may continue to increase. Expenses in a data base environment without a data dictionary may also increase with time because of scattered documentation and loss of opportunity.

3.2.2 When to Implement a Data Dictionary

The choice of a reasonable time frame for phasing in the data dictionary is important because an incorrect estimate may jeopardize the entire data base project. At the same time, however, it should not be forgotten that there exists no single best cookbook recipe for every single enterprise. The implementation plan of the data dictionary depends on the environment of the enterprise, like anything else in data processing.

It may be ambitious to install a data dictionary for the data base of the entire enterprise, just as it is ambitious to install one data base for the entire enterprise. Data dictionary systems have a learning curve associated with them. The project of installing a data dictionary for the whole enterprise should not be undertaken before a high point on the curve is reached.

One of the following possibilities should be chosen for the first application with the data dictionary package.

A Conventional Application System. If it can be found, an application system that does not affect the other application systems to a large extent and that is also moderate in size may be considered as a possible candidate. At the same time this application system should have some visibility and be important to enterprise operations. Moreover, it should be a dynamic one with changes, because the data dictionary can then demonstrate its potential benefits and effectiveness in the changing environment.

A Set of Existing Data Base Management System Applications. Running data base management system applications seem to have high visibility in an enterprise and also tend to be dynamic. If it is intended to expand the given set of applications, introduction of a data dictionary system may be the right time to show the strengths of the data dictionary in the areas of communications between users, documentation, and storage of information about a number of applications at a centrally located place.

A New Set of Applications. If an enterprise is planning to expand its applications or convert its existing conventional applications to a data base environment, new applications would be an excellent choice. Programmers, analysts, and users do not necessarily like the idea of documenting applications that are already running. However, for new application systems to be developed, work has not been done before, and documenting applications for the first time is an incentive that should not be undermined.

The main point in selecting when and what to implement with a data dictionary is the advantage that will accrue to such people as managers, users, analysts, programmers, clerks, operators, and so on. A DBMS may provide support for an on-line system with high visibility to management. Typically a dictionary has no such visibility but is important as an internal control tool. Therefore one way of looking at the timing consideration and choosing which application to implement first is to regard the decision as a trade-off in the classic hare-and-tortoise tradition, with the dictionary being the tortoise.

In the process of answering the questions when and what about the data dictionary, objectives about its use must be set. One criterion of major importance is management commitment, and if it is not present, the whole management information system is in trouble. The design team has to research available products, keeping the following aspects in mind: ease of use, ease of changes, servicing by vendor, capability, expansion possibilities, and expenses. The design team also has to: (1) research specific needs of the enterprise and match them to features of various products available; (2) determine the plan for data collection; (3) train the people who are going to use the data dictionary; and finally (4) collect and review data to initiate building and analyzing the data dictionary.

The best time to start using a data dictionary is in the requirements definition phase. The user is there and eager to help the designer understand the system. A psychological edge mentioned earlier is that no one has spent time gathering data in his or her own way. Use of a data dictionary in the requirements definition phase will provide a solid baseline for project control and standards, as well as a common denominator for communications.

To get the biggest payback from a data dictionary, it should be implemented in the requirements definition phase for a new application system, for a major redesign of an existing application system, or for a merger of two or more application systems.

3.2.3 Data Definition Guidelines

If the data dictionary is to be an effective communications tool, there should be a common understanding among users about its building blocks. The following are the basic parts of the data dictionary data base(s):

Data Element.   An attribute describing an entity. Every data element has a unique name or label. The name or label should be descriptive and should consist of key words or abbreviations taken from authorized lists.

Group Data Element.   A grouping of logically related data elements. For a group data element, all subelements (elementary and group data elements) must be explicitly identified. For basic elements, all group data element memberships must be explicitly identified.

Derived Data Element.   A data element that originates as a result of a formula or calculation. For all derived data elements, the formula or calculation must be identified, along with all data elements used in the derivation. These data elements should also be defined in the dictionary.

Synonyms or Aliases.   A data element with a different designator but the same meaning as another data element. The description of a synonym must identify designators of other data elements with which this one is synonymous.

Homonyms.   Two data elements with the same designator but different meanings. By entering data element designators in the dictionary, synonym and homonym problems should be identified by the dictionary and resolved by the data base design team.

Conceptual Model Description.   The model describes entities of the enterprise, relationships between entities, and information structure.

Logical Model Description.   The logical model is possibly a subset of the conceptual model and is mapped to the DBMS package to be used.

External Models Descriptions.   External models describe the views of application programs, that is, ways in which relationships between entities are looked at by different applications.

Internal Model Description. The internal model is the physical mapping of the data base. It describes relationships between entities, access methods to be used, blocking factors, and other physical mapping details.

In addition to the foregoing building block descriptions, the following description of relationships between them should be provided:

Text. The text provides information that enables the dictionary user to decide whether a data element is applicable or potentially applicable to his or her needs. This description should be clear to all potential users of the dictionary but specific enough to distinguish a particular data element from similar ones. The following rules should be observed:

1. Use words that are specific and unambiguous.
   - Avoid phrases such as:
     Some employees
     Certain products
   - Instead of the above, use, for example:
     Retired employees
     Paper products
2. Abbreviate only where necessary because of space limitations. Be consistent with abbreviations.
3. Avoid language that has a limited audience (i.e., data processing, accounting, employee relations, etc.).
4. State units of measure (thousands of dollars, meters, centimeters, etc.) or frequencies of occurrence (per year, per shift, etc.) for quantities, averages, and the like where applicable.
5. Indicate source of data. The text should also specify document(s) where data is used, as well as program(s) and user department(s) requiring the data.

REFERENCES

1. Allen, Frank W., Mary E. S. Loomis, and Michael V. Mannino, "The Integrated Dictionary/Directory System," *ACM Computing Surveys*, Vol. 14, No. 2 (June 1982).
2. *The British Computer Society Data Dictionary Systems Working Party Report*, Vol. 9, No. 2 (Fall 1977).
3. King, J. L., and E. L. Schrems, "Cost-Benefit Analysis in Information Systems Development and Operation," *ACM Computing Surveys*, Vol. 10, No. 1 (March 1978).
4. Lefkovits, H. C., *Data Dictionary Systems*. Wellesley, Massachusetts: Q.E.D. Information Sciences, Inc., 1977.
5. Leong-Hong, Belkis W., and Bernard K. Plagman, *Data Dictionary/Directory Systems*. New York: John Wiley & Sons, 1982.

6. *Technical Profile of Seven Data Element Dictionary/Directory Systems*, National Bureau of Standards, Special Publication 500-3, U.S. Department of Commerce, Washington, D.C. 20234.

7. Uhrowczik, P. P., "Data Dictionary/Directories," *IBM Systems Journal*, Vol. 12, No. 4 (1973).

QUESTIONS

1. What are the major objectives of a data dictionary? Discuss their implications to the success of a data base system.
2. What is the difference between a dependent data dictionary and a freestanding one? What are the relative advantages of each?
3. What are the interfaces of a data dictionary in an ideal data base environment?
4. Should the primary responsibility for the data dictionary be assigned to the DA, a documentation group, or the Systems and Programming Department? Why?
5. How can a data dictionary be used as a device to implement the privacy and security requirements of an organization? How should the data dictionary itself be subject to these considerations?
6. Would a comprehensive data dictionary be expected to contain data elements not found in programs and files (i.e., those data elements found in procedures that are not currently programmed)?
7. A cost/benefit analysis of a data dictionary will surely take place prior to installation. What are the major points to be considered in such an evaluation? Why is the analysis difficult?
8. At what point in the system's life cycle is it best to start using a data dictionary? Explain your answer.
9. The following tables represent two views of an airline system. One view is that of the Reservation Department, which keeps track of the number of passengers on a given flight. The second view is that of the Food Preparation Department, which must deliver a certain number of meals to a given airplane by take-off time.

Reservation Department

Origin		Destination		Passenger Seats			Flight No.
Time	Airport	Time	Airport	Max	Booked	Available	
10 AM	Chicago	2 PM	Honolulu	400	300	100	273
9 AM	Los Angeles	5 PM	Newark	250	100	150	461
9 PM	JFK	12 AM	San Francisco	250	200	50	385

Food Preparation Department

Kitchen				
Deliver Before	Airport	Meal Type	Number of Meals	Trip No.
10 AM	Chicago	Lunch	400	273
10 AM	Chicago	Dinner	400	273
9 AM	Los Angeles	Breakfast	250	461
9 AM	Los Angeles	Lunch	250	461
9 PM	JFK	Dinner	250	385

Before designing a data base, a data dictionary is to be implemented and the difference between these views must be resolved.

- **9.1.** Identify one or more entities from each table and provide text relating them.
- **9.2.** Identify data elements and group elements. Provide text relating the elements.
- **9.3.** Identify any derived data elements, synonyms, and homonyms (if any). Provide text to describe the elements. Assign unique names to these elements.
- **9.4.** Reconstruct the tables (or views) using unique data element names obtained from the preceding three questions. Preferably set up one table and eliminate redundancies.

PART 2

Data Base Design (Conceptual Model and Logical Model)

Data Models

A data base management system (DBMS) uses one or more data models in its underlying structure. A data model embodies the relationships between the entities. Today many data base implementations use hierarchical and network data models. Another data model gaining importance is called a relational data model, for which a number of commercial packages have emerged.

In addition to these three data models available in today's market, there are many data base management systems that use file inversion on multiple keys. These DBMSs can frequently be categorized as either hierarchical or network, but in the real world they are used to construct simple files and use multiple key retrieval.

This chapter discusses the four data models: relational, hierarchical, network, and file inversion, and presents them using a hospital environment as an example.

4.1   WHAT IS A DATA MODEL?

One of the major responsibilities of the data administration function is the development of a conceptual model, also called an enterprise model, of the organization. The model embodies the entities and their relationships and is the tool used to represent the conceptual organization of data. The conceptual model is a tool for communications between the various users of data, so it is developed without any concern for physical representation. The conceptual model is used to organize, visualize, plan, and communicate ideas. It is (or should be) independent of a DBMS.

The entities of an organization and the relationships between them can be represented by a data model. The DBMSs available commercially today are based either on a hierarchical data model, a network data model, a relational data model, an inverted file data model, or some combination of two or more of them.

The conceptual, or enterprise, model has to be mapped to the logical model being used as the underlying structure for a DBMS; and the logical model must be mapped to the physical model (also called the internal model or the physical structure). The logical model is either a relational, a hierarchical, a network, or an inverted file data model. We use the term "data model" in the generic sense, that is, it may be a conceptual or a logical or an internal (physical) model.

The DBMS is not a factor in designing a conceptual model, but the design of a logical model is dependent on the DBMS to be used. In the real world, the DBMS is frequently a given, and the data administrator has no choice. Ideally, the choice of the DBMS should be made after the conceptual model is designed. The process of mapping from the conceptual model to the logical model should be examined while evaluating different DBMS packages.

The main difference among the four types of data models lies in the representation of the relationships between the entities. We would like to distinguish between a relationship among entities, and between a relationship among attributes of the same entity and among attributes of different entities. The next section deals with these relationships.

4.2 RELATIONSHIPS WITHIN A DATA MODEL

A relationship is a mapping or linkage between two sets of data. It can be one-to-one, one-to-many, or many-to-many. The following examples will illustrate these relationships.

In the hospital environment to be considered, a number of patients are admitted to the hospital. If the patient is new to the hospital, medical information about his or her history is recorded for the first time. If the patient has been admitted to the hospital previously, existing medical information is updated. The patient keeps the unique identification number regardless of the number of times he or she enters the hospital. The information about the patient will include name, assigned patient number, and an address. Thus the attributes of the entity PATIENT are patient number, patient name, and patient address.

Another entity we are interested in is SURGEON. The attributes representing the entity SURGEON in the example are surgeon license number and surgeon name.

The hospital environment in the example is only a surgical environment; that is, only surgeries are performed in the hospital, and the patients receive medical attention by the surgeons after surgery. The other entities we consider are BED and HOSPITAL ROOM.

4.2.1 One-to-One Relationship (between Two Entities)

At a given point in time, one patient is assigned to one bed. The relationship between PATIENT and BED is one-to-one. A one-to-one relationship can be denoted by single-headed arrows. (See Figure 4.1.)

4.2.2 One-to-Many Relationship (between Two Entities)

At any point, zero, one, or many patients are assigned to one hospital room (i.e., a hospital room may have zero, one, or many patients); but a patient is assigned to only one hospital room. A one-to-many relationship can be denoted by a single-headed arrow going in the one direction and a double-headed arrow going in the many direction. (See Figure 4.1.)

4.2.3 Many-to-Many Relationship (between Two Entities)

In the example we are using, a surgeon may have operated on several patients. On the other hand, a patient may have been operated on by several surgeons on several visits to the hospital. The relationship between PATIENT and SURGEON is many-to-many. We denote this relationship by double-headed arrows. (See Figure 4.1.)

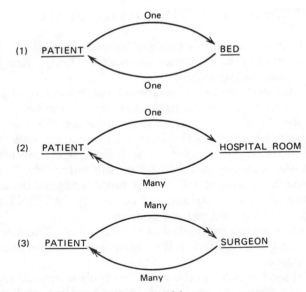

Figure 4.1. Relationships between two entities.

1. *One-to-One Relationship.* At a given point in time one patient is assigned to one bed.

2. *One-to-Many Relationship.* At a given point in time zero, one, or many patients are assigned to one hospital room; that is, a hospital room may have zero, one, or many patients, but a patient is assigned to only one hospital room.

3. *Many-to-Many Relationship.* A surgeon may have operated on several patients. A patient may have been operated on by several surgeons on several visits to the hospital.

The relationships between entities are part of the conceptual model, and they have to be represented in the data base. Any number of entities can participate in a relationship. On the other hand, the same entities can participate in any number of relationships.

There also exist mappings between the attributes of an entity. These mappings, too, can be classified as one-to-one, one-to-many, and many-to-many.

4.2.4 One-to-One Relationship (between Two Attributes)

We are assuming that the patient number is a unique identifier of a patient; that is, the patient number is reused at subsequent admittances. If, together with the patient number, another unique identifier of the patient is stored in the data base, the relationship between the two unique identifiers is one-to-one. The one-to-one relationship can be denoted by single-headed arrows. (See Figure 4.2.)

4.2.5 One-to-Many Relationship (between Two Attributes)

The patient name and number exist together. There can be many patients with the same name, but their numbers will be different. Every patient is assigned a unique patient number; that is, to a given patient number there corresponds only one name. The one-to-many relationship can be denoted by a single-headed arrow in the one direction and a double-headed arrow in the many direction. (See Figure 4.2.)

4.2.6 Many-to-Many Relationship (between Two Attributes)

A number of patients with the same name may have been operated on by many surgeons. A number of surgeons with the same name may have operated on many patients. The relationship between the attributes patient name and surgeon name is many-to-many. We denote this relationship by double-headed arrows. (See Figure 4.2.)

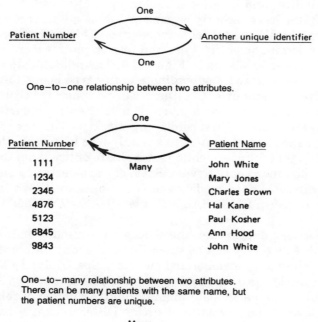

One

Patient Number — Another unique identifier

One

One–to–one relationship between two attributes.

Patient Number		Patient Name
1111		John White
1234		Mary Jones
2345		Charles Brown
4876		Hal Kane
5123		Paul Kosher
6845		Ann Hood
9843		John White

One (Many)

One–to–many relationship between two attributes.
There can be many patients with the same name, but
the patient numbers are unique.

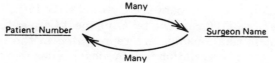

Many

Patient Number — Surgeon Name

Many

Many–to–many relationship between two attributes.

Figure 4.2.

4.2.7   Overview of the Data Models

The hierarchical, network, and inverted file data models have been in use as underlying structures for data base management systems since the early 1960s, whereas the relational data model was proposed as an underlying structure for a DBMS in the early 1970s. The main difference between the four data models is the way they represent the relationships of entities.

In the relational data model, the entities and their relationships are represented with two-dimensional tables, as in Figure 4.3a. Every table represents an entity and is made up of rows and columns. Relationships between entities are represented through common columns containing values from a common pool or domain. Relational data base management systems have been in use for some time in universities and research laboratories. Some of the commercial packages available are IBM's Database 2 (DB2) and SQL/DS, Tymshare's MAGNUM, Honeywell's MRDM provided with MULTICS, National CSS's NOMAD, Oracle Corporation's ORACLE, Cincom's SUPRA, and Relational Technology's INGRES. Also, many relational DBMSs have recently become available on microcomputers.

The hierarchical data model is made up of a hierarchy of entity types involving a dominant entity type and one or more subordinate entity types at the lower levels, as in Figure 4.5. The relationship established between a dominant and a subordinate entity type is one-to-many, that is, for a given dominant entity there can be many subordinate entity types. At the same time, for a given dominant entity occurrence, there can be many occurrences of a subordinate entity type. Thus the relationships between the entities are similar to a family-tree hierarchy, the only difference being that for every child (subordinate entity type) there is only one parent (dominant entity type). Some of the oldest systems are based on the hierarchical data model, some examples are IBM's Information Management System (IMS), SAS Institute's System 2000, and Informatics' Mark IV.

In the network data model, the concept of dominant and subordinate is expanded: Any entity can be subordinate to many different dominant entities (referred to as member and owners, respectively). In addition, an entity can function as owner and/or member simultaneously. This means that any entity can participate in an unlimited number of relationships. There are several commercially available DBMS packages based on the network data model. Some of them are Cullinet's IDMS/R, Honeywell's IDS/II, UNIVAC's DMS 1100, and Digital Equipment Corporation's DBMS.

Entities and their relationships are represented in the inverted file data model much as in the relational data model. Files represent entity types and fields their data elements. Relationships between entities are once again represented through common fields having common values. Multiple fields can be inverted upon to allow easy access. Some DBMS packages based on the inverted file data model are Software AG's ADABAS, Applied Data Research's DATACOM/DB, and Computer Corporation of America's MODEL 204.

Sections 4.3 through 4.6 show in more detail how the four data models represent the relationships between the entities and between the data elements. These four data models are the user's view of data and not necessarily the physical mapping.

4.3 THE RELATIONAL DATA MODEL

We shall use the example of a hospital to discuss the various relationships between the entities of an enterprise. A hospital has data requirements for medical and insurance purposes, peer review, and research study of drug reactions. It has patients, physicians, facilities, drugs, and so on. The hospital example will serve also to illustrate the various approaches to creating a data model.

Consider the sample shown in Figure 4.3a. This data is represented in a two-dimensional table, which is called a relational model of the data. In the relational data model terminology, a table like the one in Figure 4.3a is called a "relation." But to avoid confusion between a relation and a relationship between the entities, sometimes a relation is called a table. Every column in a relation is an "attribute." The values in the column

PATIENT TABLE		Attribute
Patient Number	Patient Name	Patient Address
1111	John White	15 New Street, New York, N.Y.
1234	Mary Jones	10 Main Street, Rye, N.Y.
2345	Charles Brown	Dogwood Lane, Harrison, N.Y.
4876	Hal Kane	55 Boston Post Road, Chester, Conn.
5123	Paul Kosher	Blind Brook, Mamaroneck, N.Y.
6845	Ann Hood	Hilton Road, Larchmont, N.Y.

Figure 4.3a. Representation of data using relational data model. Primary key is patient number; that is, the patient number is unique. The PATIENT table has three attributes and at this point in time has six tuples. We do not intend to split the entries in the column headed "Patient Address" any further into more columns. We are considering the house number, the street, the name of the city, and the name of the state as a single attribute.

are drawn from a "domain"; that is, a domain is a set of all the values an attribute may have. For example, the domain for patient number is made up of all the four-digit integers (0000, 0001, 0002, . . . , 9999), but the actual values taken in the PATIENT table at this time are 1111, 1234, 2345, 4876, 5123, and 6845. (See Figure 4.3a.) The rows of the table are called "tuples."

We could say that the columns of the table roughly represent data elements and the rows of the table represent the data records in conventional terminology.

The SURGEON table in Figure 4.3b represents the entity SURGEON. The PATIENT-AND-SURGEON table in Figure 4.3c represents the entity connecting the patient, the surgeon, and the date of surgery, whereas the table in Figure 4.3d represents the entity DRUG with its side effect.

A column or set of columns is called a "candidate key" (often shortened to "key") when its values uniquely identify the rows of the table. (A brief summary of the relational data model terminology is given in Figure 4.3e.) It is possible for a relation to have more than one key, in which case it is customary to designate one as the "primary key." In the PATIENT relation, given the patient number, 1234, which is the value of the key, the patient name, Mary Jones, and the patient address, 10 Main Street, Rye, N.Y., are both uniquely determined.

In a table with uniquely assigned names for the columns, the ordering of columns and the ordering of rows are insignificant. No two rows in a table are identical. Null key values are prohibited to guarantee a unique

SURGEON TABLE	
Surgeon License Number	Surgeon Name
145	Beth Little
189	David Rosen
243	Charles Field
311	Michael Diamond
467	Patricia Gold

Figure 4.3b. **Representation of data using relational data model. Primary key is surgeon license number.**

PATIENT—AND—SURGEON TABLE

Patient Number	Surgeon License Number	Date of Surgery	Surgery	Postoperative Drug Administered
1111	145	Jan. 1, 1985	Gallstones removal	Penicillin
1111	311	June 12, 1985	Kidney stones removal	— — —
1234	243	April 5, 1984	Eye cataract removal	Tetracycline
1234	467	May 10, 1985	Thrombosis removal	— — —
2345	189	Jan. 8, 1986	Open heart surgery	Cephalosporin
4876	145	Nov. 5, 1985	Cholecystectomy	Demicillin
5123	145	May 10, 1985	Gallstones removal	— — —
6845	243	April 5, 1984	Eye cornea replacement	Tetracycline

Figure 4.3c. **Representation of data using relational data model. Primary key is patient number + surgeon license number + date of surgery. One assumption made here is that a patient may receive only one postoperative drug, if any, for a given specific surgery performed.**

DRUG TABLE

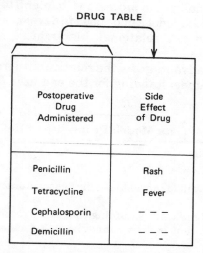

Postoperative Drug Administered	Side Effect of Drug
Penicillin	Rash
Tetracycline	Fever
Cephalosporin	— — —
Demicillin	— — —

Figure 4.3d. **Representation of data using relational data model. Primary key is postoperative drug administered. One assumption made here is that there can be only one side effect of a drug, if any. Another assumption is that the side effect of a drug depends only on the drug having been administered.**

Terminology: Summary for Relational Data Model

Term	Alternative	Approximate Equivalent
Relation	Table	File (1 record type, fixed number of field types)
Attribute	Column	Field (type, not occurrence)
Tuple	Row	Record (occurrence, not type)
Primary key		Record key, record identifier
Domain		

Figure 4.3e. **These are only some of the terms used with the relational data model. Anyone interested in other terms used with the relational data model should refer to the bibliography at the end of the chapter.**

identifier. The ordering of tables is insignificant too. Properties of relations are given in Table 4.1.

The notion of using a relational data model as an underlying structure of a DBMS was introduced by Dr. E. F. Codd in 1970. (See the reference at the end of the chapter.) The process of crystallizing the entities and their relationships in table formats using relational concepts is called the "normalization process." The normalization theory is based on the observation that a certain set of relations has better properties in an updating environment than do other sets of relations containing the same data. We will use the normalization process in Chapter 5 to build the conceptual model. The conceptual model can be used to develop a logical model, which can then be mapped to a relational, hierarchical, network, or inverted file data model.

One of the major advantages of the relational approach is its simplicity, that is, the ease of understanding for the end-user. The end-users do not

Table 4.1. Relational Data Model: Properties of Relations

Within any one relation:

1. No duplicate rows.[a]
2. Row order insignificant (a conventional file has some ordering sequence, especially for performance).
3. Column order insignificant (assuming that every column has a unique name).
4. All values atomic; that is, they cannot be split further (without loss of information).
5. No undefined key values.

[a] Relation is a set with tuples as elements, and by definition a set is not supposed to have any duplicate elements. In a conventional file there is no reason why two identical records cannot exist.

have to be concerned about the physical storage structure; they can be oriented toward the information content of their data and need not worry about the physical representation details. (See Figure 4.3f.) The ability to use the data base without knowing the representation details is called "data independence." We saw the advantages of data independence in Chapter 1.

To establish linkage between tables, some tables must keep some common attributes. For example, the PATIENT table and the PATIENT-AND-

Figure 4.3f. A relational data base. The end-user is concerned with the end-user's views supported by the data base management system. The end-user is not concerned with how the data is stored, how it is accessed, and in what format it is stored. The data base designer, however, is concerned with the whole spectrum, with the addition of the mapping between the storage and the end-user's views.

SURGEON table have redundancy in the attribute patient number. As a result, we have key redundancy between some tables. But the tables are user's view of data and do not necessarily reflect the physical mapping.

4.3.1 Advantages of a Relational Data Model

Simplicity

The end-user is presented with a simple data model. His or her requests are formulated in terms of the information content and do not reflect any complexities due to system-oriented aspects. A relational data model is what the user sees, but it is not necessarily what will be implemented physically.

Nonprocedural Requests

Because there is no positional dependency between the relations, requests do not have to reflect any preferred structure and therefore can be non-procedural.

Data Independence

This should be one of the major objectives of any DBMS. The relational data model removes the details of storage structure and access strategy from the user interface. The model provides a relatively higher degree of data independence than do the next two models to be discussed. To be able to make use of this property of the relational data model, however, the design of the relations must be complete and accurate.

Theoretical Foundation

The relational data model is based on the well developed mathematical theory of relations. The rigorous method of designing a data base (using normalization, discussed in Chapter 5) gives this model a solid foundation. This kind of foundation does not exist for the other data models.

4.3.2 Disadvantages of a Relational Data Model

Although some data base management systems based on the relational data model are commercially available today, the performance of a relational DBMS has not been comparable with the performance of a DBMS based on a hierarchical data model, network data model, or an inverted file data model. As a result, the major question yet to be answered concerns performance. Can a relational data model be used for a DBMS that can provide a complete set of operational capabilities with required efficiency on a large scale? It appears today that technological improvements in providing faster and more reliable hardware may answer the question positively.

4.4 THE HIERARCHICAL DATA MODEL

It is quite easy to understand what a hierarchy is, because we have to deal with a number of hierarchies on a daily basis. Almost every organization has a chief executive officer with a number of executives reporting to him or her. As this hierarchy reaches lower and lower levels, fewer and fewer responsibilities are delegated to the people on these levels.

Consider a family tree, in which the parents can have none, one, or more than one child. If there are children, the children themselves can have their own children. The family tree is a hierarchical tree if we ignore one parent at each node. It is no accident that the hierarchical data model derives much of its terminology from this analogy.

The components of a data base using a hierarchical data model as the underlying structure are shown in Figure 4.4.

4.4.1 A Hierarchical Tree Structure

A hierarchical tree structure is made up of nodes and branches. A node is a collection of data attributes describing the entity at that node. The highest node of a hierarchical tree structure is called a "root" (e.g., the chief executive officer of an organization). The dependent nodes are at lower levels in the tree. The level of these nodes depends on the distance from the root node. (See Figure 4.5.) (The hierarchical tree is the reverse of an organic tree, which has its root at the bottom and its branches going up.)

A hierarchical data model is one that organizes data in a hierarchical tree structure. Every occurrence of the root node begins a logical data base record; that is, a hierarchical data base is made up of a number of trees. In a hierarchical data model, the nodes at level 2 are called the children of the node at level 1; and the node at level 1 is called the parent of the nodes at level 2. The nodes at level 3 for a corresponding node at level 2 are called the children of the node at level 2, and the node at level 2 is called the parent, and so on.

A hierarchical tree structure has to satisfy the following conditions:

1. A hierarchical data model always starts with a "root node."
2. Every node consists of one or more attributes describing the entity at that node.
3. Dependent nodes can follow the succeeding levels. The node on the preceding level becomes the "parent node" of the new "dependent nodes." The dependent nodes can be added horizontally as well as vertically with no limitation. (See Figure 4.4.) (Exception: Level 1 can have only one node, which we called the root node.)
4. Every node occurring at level 2 has to be connected with one and only one node occurring at level 1. Every node occurring at level 3 has to

Figure 4.4. The data of an enterprise may be stored in a number of data bases. Every data base has an underlying hierarchical tree model. A number of trees or records form a data base. A tree is composed of a number of branches or nodes. Every branch has a number of leaves or fields.

be connected with one and only one node occurring at level 2, and so on. Because there can be at most one arc (i.e., connection) between any two nodes, the arcs do not need any labels.

5. A parent node can have one child node as a dependent or many children nodes. If it does not have any node as its dependent, it is not a parent node.

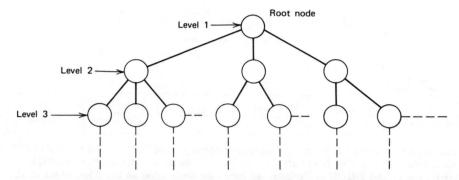

Figure 4.5. A hierarchical tree structure is made up of nodes and branches. A node is a collection of data attributes describing the entity at that node. The highest node of a hierarchical tree structure is called a "root" node (dominant entity type). A root node is at the first level. The dependent nodes (subordinate entity types) are at the second, third, ... levels.

Parent node $\overset{\text{one}}{\underset{\text{many}}{\rightleftarrows}}$ children nodes (one-to-many relationship).

6. Every node except, of course, the root has to be accessed through its parent node. The node represented in a true hierarchy should be retrieved only through its parent, as this is where the true meaning of that data exists. Therefore the access path to every node within a hierarchical data model is unique. (See Figure 4.6.) (For example, node I can be reached only through the path A to G to H to I. Node D can be accessed only through the path A to B to D.) Hence a hierarchical data model consists of linear paths.

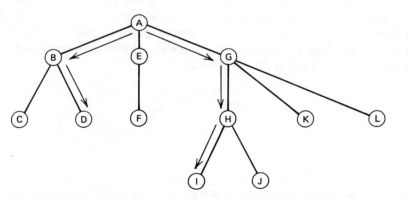

Figure 4.6. The access path to every node within a hierarchical data model is unique. For example, node I can be reached only through the path A to G to H to I. Node D can be accessed only through the path A to B to D. Hence a hierarchical data model consists of linear paths.

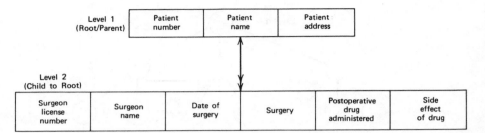

Figure 4.7. Representation of data using hierarchical data model for PATIENT data base. The entity PATIENT is the root node type. The entities SURGEON, SURGERY, and DRUG are combined into one node type as the dependent of the root.

7. There can be a number of occurrences of each node at each level. Each node occurrence (except the root node occurrence) has to be connected with a parent node occurrence; that is, there can be many occurrences of node A. Every node occurrence of A starts a logical record. There can be zero, one, or many occurrences of node B for every node occurrence of A, and so on.

Consider the example with information from the PATIENT relation, SURGEON relation, PATIENT-AND-SURGEON relation, and DRUG relation as shown in Figures 4.3a, 4.3b, 4.3c, and 4.3d, respectively. A hierarchical data model can represent the information in a number of ways. One possibility is shown in Figure 4.7. The entity PATIENT is the root node, and every patient has a root node occurrence. The data base has, at this time, records for the patients John White (1111), Mary Jones (1234), Charles Brown (2345), Hal Kane (4876), Paul Kosher (5123), and Ann Hood (6845). The data base record for John White (1111) is shown in Figure 4.8. The node at level 2 from Figure 4.7 has two occurrences in Figure 4.8. The hierarchical data model enables us to represent many surgeries and surgeons for a patient.

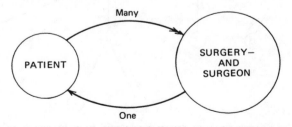

For the hierarchical data model in Figure 4.7, there are five more data base records, for the patients Mary Jones, Charles Brown, Hal Kane, Paul Kosher, and Ann Hood. The data base record for the patient Hal Kane is shown in Figure 4.9.

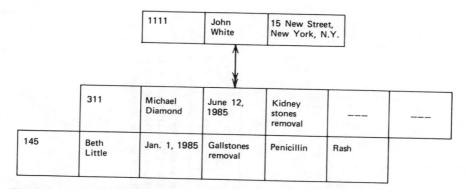

Figure 4.8. A hierarchical data base record occurrence for the hierarchical data model in Figure 4.7. The data base record is for the patient John White. The dependent node type (child to root in this case) has two occurrences for the surgeries "gallstones removal" and "kidney stones removal."

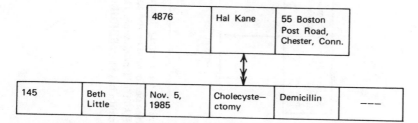

Figure 4.9. A hierarchical data base record occurrence for the hierarchical data model in Figure 4.7. The data base record is for the patient Hal Kane. The dependent node type (child to root in this case) has one occurrence for the surgery cholecystectomy.

The information about PATIENT, SURGEON, PATIENT-AND-SURGEON, and DRUG can also be represented with another version of a hierarchical data model, which is shown in Figure 4.10. The entity SURGEON is the root node. Every surgeon has a root node occurrence. The data base has, at this time, records for the surgeons Beth Little (145), David Rosen (189), Charles Field (243), Michael Diamond (311), and Patricia Gold (467). The data base record for Beth Little (145) is shown in Figure 4.11. The node at level 2 from Figure 4.10 has three occurrences in Figure 4.11. The hierarchical data model makes possible the representation of many patients for a surgeon.

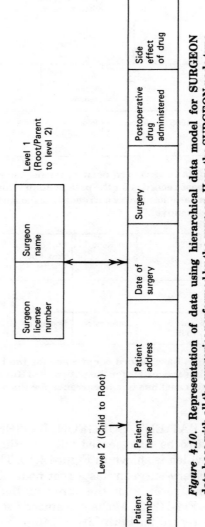

Figure 4.10. Representation of data using hierarchical data model for SURGEON data base with all the surgeries performed by the surgeon. Here the SURGEON node type is at a higher level than the PATIENT node type. This structure shows the DA's intention of implementing the relationship between SURGEON and PATIENT as one-to-many.

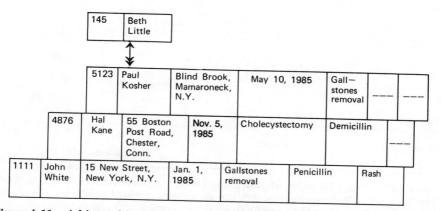

Figure 4.11. A hierarchical data base record occurrence for the hierarchical data model in Figure 4.10. The data base record is for the surgeon Beth Little. The dependent node type (child to root in this case) has three occurrences for the patients John White, Hal Kane, and Paul Kosher.

The hierarchical data models in Figures 4.7 and 4.10 are different, although they are data models of the same hospital environment. The difference is the result of the two ways of looking at the entity relationships. Figure 4.7 has the PATIENT at a higher level than the SURGEON, reflecting the fact that the data administrator intends to implement the relationship between PATIENT and SURGEON as one-to-many. Figure 4.10 has the SURGEON at a higher level than the PATIENT, showing the data administrator's intention of implementing the relationship between SURGEON and PATIENT as one-to-many. The choice of the hierarchical data model should be made with performance issues in mind. A detailed discussion of these issues is given in Part 3.

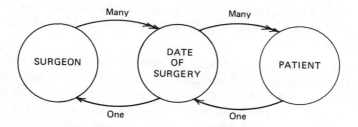

The same information can be represented in a different relationship with the help of the data model in Figure 4.12. A data base record occurrence using the data model in Figure 4.12 is shown in Figure 4.13. In this example there is only one occurrence of the node at level 3 for every occurrence of the node at level 2. But there is a possibility that on a specific day a surgeon operated on more than one PATIENT. This hierarchical data model is a simple version with only one node at level 2 and

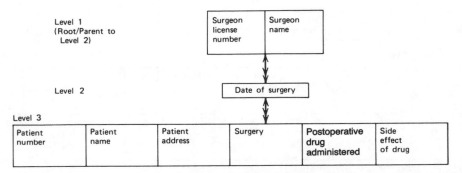

Figure 4.12. **Representation of data using hierarchical data model for SURGEON data base with all the days on which the surgeon performed surgeries and all the surgeries performed on the specific day.**

one node at level 3. The hierarchical data model makes possible the representation of many dates of surgery for a surgeon and many patients on whom surgeries were performed on a specific date.

4.4.2   Storage Operations with a Hierarchical Data Model

In the hierarchical data model in Figure 4.7, the PATIENT node is the parent node, and the SURGEON node with the medical information of the patient is the child node. If the same surgeon has operated on more than one patient, the information on the surgeon will be repeated for every patient he or she is treating; for example, in the data base records from Figures 4.8 and 4.9, the information about the surgeon with license number 145 (Beth Little) is redundant.

Insertion.   A child node occurrence cannot exist without a parent node occurrence. If the hierarchical data model is like the one in Figure 4.7, no new surgeon can be added to the data base unless he or she is treating a patient.

Deletion.   When a parent node occurrence is deleted, the child occurrences are deleted too. For example, in the hierarchical data model in Figure 4.10, when a SURGEON node occurrence is deleted, all the node occurrences of the patients operated on by the surgeon are also deleted. This results in the loss of information about those patients.

The reason for the storage and update anomalies is that a many-to-many relationship cannot be efficiently represented with one hierarchical data model, which always represents a one-to-many relationship. The anomalies can be partly resolved by introducing two hierarchical data models with a relationship established between the two, as in Figure 4.14. Data model 1 has PATIENT as its root node and SURGERY as the second level node. The second level node is interconnected with the SUR-

Figure 4.13. A hierarchical data base record occurrence for the hierarchical data model in Figure 4.12. The data base record is for the surgeon Beth Little. It just so happens that on Jan. 1, 1985, on May 10, 1985, and on Nov. 5, 1985, Beth Little performed one surgery each day. On Jan. 1, 1985, the patient was John White; on May 10, 1985, the patient was Paul Kosher; and on Nov. 5, 1985, the patient was Hal Kane.

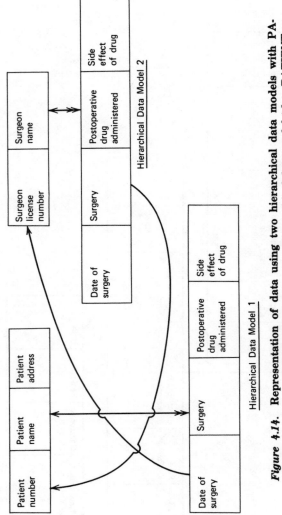

Figure 4.14. Representation of data using two hierarchical data models with PA-TIENT data base and SURGEON data base. Hierarchical data model 1 has PATIENT as its root node and SURGERY as the second level node type. The SURGERY node from hierarchical data model 1 is interconnected with the SURGEON node from hierarchical data model 2. In hierarchical data model 2, SURGEON is the root node and SURGERY is the second level node, which is interconnected with the PATIENT node from hierarchical data model 1.

GEON node from data model 2. In data model 2, SURGEON is the root node and the SURGERY node is the second level node, which is interconnected with the PATIENT node from data model 1. As a result of these two data models, the information regarding the date of surgery, SURGERY, still will be stored redundantly, but the anomalies of insertion and deletion of PATIENT and SURGEON are removed. The problem of redundancy is solved in data base management systems using a hierarchical data model as the basic data model in different ways.

4.4.3 Advantages of a Hierarchical Data Model

- The major advantage of the hierarchical data model is the existence of proven data base management systems that use the hierachical data model as the basic structure.
- The relative simplicity and ease of use of the hierarchical data model and the familiarity of data processing users with a hierarchy are major advantages.
- There is a reduction of data dependency. When the two hierarchical data models from Figure 4.14 are used, a number of different views can be provided to the application programmers, as in Figure 4.15.
- Performance prediction is simplified through predefined relationships.

4.4.4 Disadvantages of a Hierarchical Data Model

- The many-to-many relationship can be implemented only in a clumsy way. This may result in redundancy in stored data. We know that redundancy at the logical level is not necessarily bad—on the contrary, it promotes simplicity. Redundancy at the physical level, however, is undesirable.
- As a result of the strict hierarchical ordering, the operations of insertion and deletion become unduly complex.
- Deletion of parent results in the deletion of children. As a result, users have to be careful in performing a DELETE operation.
- Hierarchical commands tend to be procedural because of the strictness of the structure.
- "Root" is the dominant node type. Any child node is accessible only through its parent node.

4.5 THE NETWORK DATA MODEL

Much of today's awareness of the concepts of the data base can be credited to the work of CODASYL (Conference On Data Systems Languages) and its committees.

Application Programmer's View 1, Using the Hierarchical Data Models in Figure 4.14

| Date of surgery | Surgery | Postoperative drug administered | Side effect of drug |
| | | | Surgeon license number | Surgeon name |

$\longleftrightarrow$

| Patient number | Patient name | Patient address |

Application Programmer's View 2, Using the Hierarchical Data Models in Figure 4.14

| Date of surgery | Surgery | Postoperative drug administered | Side effect of drug |
| | | | Surgeon license number | Surgeon name |

$\longleftrightarrow$

| Patient number | Patient name | Patient address |

Figure 4.15. Application programmer's view is called "external model" in ANSI (American National Standards Institute) terminology, as in Figure 1.7.

CODASYL was established in 1959 in Washington, D.C., at a meeting of the representatives of 40 major computer users, manufacturers, and government departments. It is a voluntary organization and is supported by the enterprises represented. It is not an official government body responsible for standards, nor does it develop standards. The aim of the committee is to develop, design, and recommend techniques and languages for data processing systems, analysis, implementation, and operation, and to provide these specifications to the Standards Groups in the form of a *Journal of Development*.

CODASYL's first project was to develop specifications for a Common Business Oriented Language, acronymed as COBOL. In 1966 CODASYL started a new task force, the List Processing Task Force, to extend COBOL for handling data bases. The name of this group was later changed to the Data Base Task Group (DBTG).

The initial specifications of the DBTG were made semipublic in 1969, and were reviewed by a number of interested parties. After their suggestions had been considered, a new report was published in 1971. The DBTG has continued since that date to issue reports. However, because the major implementations of the model are based on the 1971 report, our emphasis will be on it.

After the 1971 report, CODASYL formed a new committee, the Data Description Language Committee (DDLC), to deal with the issues of data description, and replaced the DBTG with the Data Base Language Task Group (DBLTG) for dealing with COBOL extensions to the data base area. These extensions were included in the CODASYL COBOL *Journal of Development*.

The DBLTG's task was to make the DBTG's 1971 report consistent with CODASYL's COBOL specifications. This was accomplished with a report in 1973.

The basic underlying data model in the 1969, 1971, and 1973 reports is a network data model. Implementations conforming to CODASYL are UNIVAC's DMS 1100 for UNIVAC 1108 and 1110 series computers, Cullinet's IDMS/R for IBM hardware, DEC's DBMS-11 for DEC's PDP11/70, and Honeywell's IDS/II, to name just a few.

The components of a data base with a network data model as the underlying structure are shown in Figures 4.16 and 4.17. Let us study the major components of a network data model, a set and a record, in more detail.

The network data model interconnects the entities of an enterprise into a network. The graphic notation for this data model uses blocks and arrows. This notation was introduced by C. W. Bachman ["Data Structure Diagrams," *Database*, Vol. 1, p. 2 (Summer, 1969)]. A block represents an entity or record type. Each record type is composed of zero, one, or more attributes (also called data elements or fields).

Figure 4.16. A data base consists of a number of areas. An area contains records. In turn, a record may consist of fields. A set, which is a grouping of records, may reside in an area or span a number of areas.

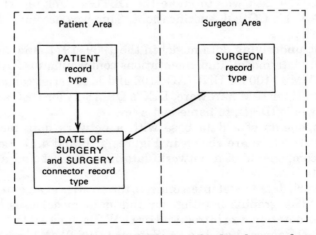

Figure 4.17. An area is a named subdivision of a data base and may contain occurrences of records and sets or parts of sets. Each area can have its own unique physical attributes. Areas can be operated independently of, or in conjunction with, other areas.

Figure 4.18. A set type PATIENT-HAS-SURGERY based on the owner record type PATIENT and the member record type SURGERY.

- A set type is a named grouping of related records.
- There is only a single "owner" occurrence in a set occurrence.
- There may be zero, one, or many "member" occurrences in a set occurrence.
- A set occurrence is said to be "empty" when no member record occurrence is associated with the corresponding owner record occurrence.
- A set occurrence exists when an owner record occurrence is stored.

Let us distinguish between a record type and a record occurrence. PATIENT is a record type, and "1111   John White   15 New Street, New York, N.Y." is a record occurrence of the record type PATIENT (see Figures 4.18 and 4.19). Thus a record type has one or more occurrences in the data base.

A directed arrow connects two or more record types and is used to represent a set type. The record type located at the tail of the arrow

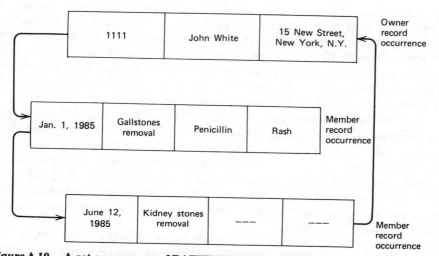

Figure 4.19. A set occurrence of PATIENT-HAS-SURGERY with an owner record occurrence and two member record occurrences implemented as a ring structure. The set occurrence could be implemented in a number of other ways.

functions as the owner record type, and the record type located at the head of the arrow as the member record type. The arrow from owner to member is called a set type. A set type shows a logical one-to-many relationship between an owner and a member (Figure 4.18). Physical storage, that is, closeness between owner and member, is not implied; although, as we shall see in Chapter 9, it can occur.

Every set type is named. The naming of a set type enables the same pair of entities to appear in more than one relationship. (This will be elaborated on as we move along.) The term "set type" has nothing to do with set theory in the mathematical sense.

Let us distinguish between a set type and a set occurrence. In our example from Figure 4.19, PATIENT-HAS-SURGERY is a set type with an occurrence of the owner record type PATIENT "1111   John White   15 New Street, New York, N.Y." The occurrences of the member record type SURGERY are "Jan. 1, 1985   Gallstones removal, Penicillin, Rash" and "June 12, 1985   Kidney stones removal - - -." This is a set occurrence. Thus a set occurrence is one occurrence of the owner record type, together with zero or more occurrences of the member record type, from a given set type. The relationship between the owner record occurrence and the member record occurrence(s) is one-to-many. A given member record occurrence cannot simultaneously belong to two or more owner record occurrences of the same set type; that is, a member record occurrence cannot violate the rule of unique ownership for a given set type.

4.5.1   Representation of One-to-Many Relationship

In a data model representing a one-to-many relationship, an owner record type owns zero to n occurrences of a member record type. A member record type, in turn, can play the role of an owner record type with zero to n member record occurrences in a set occurrence. An owner record type can be an owner record type in a number of set types. This type of data model is a hierarchical data model; that is, a hierarchical data model is a special case of a network data model.

The CODASYL model does not allow direct implementation of a many-to-many relationship. Using the notation developed earlier, we would like to model the structure as shown in Figure 4.20. We would like to represent the information of one patient having undergone many surgeries and a specific kind of surgery performed on many patients. According to Figure 4.20, a surgery with more than one patient would simultaneously be a member in two or more occurrences of the same set type, violating the rule of unique ownership.

A many-to-many relationship can be implemented by creating two one-to-many relationships. As we shall see later, this is only one example of the need to alter a conceptual design because of constraints imposed by the DBMS. Let us look at this on the basis of the example.

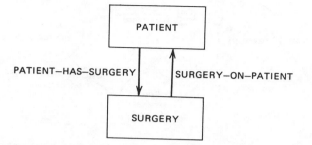

Figure 4.20. A structure of this type would violate the rule of unique ownership because a surgery with more than one patient would simultaneously be a member in two or more occurrences of the same set type.

The entity types here are PATIENT, SURGEON, and SURGERY. A given surgeon may have operated on several patients, and a given patient may have been operated on by several surgeons. PATIENT, SURGEON, and SURGERY form a network. The relation between PATIENT and SURGEON is many-to-many. PATIENT can be considered a record type, and SURGEON as well can be considered a record type. To transform the many-to-many relationship between PATIENT and SURGEON into two one-to-many relationships, we will use the surgery with date of surgery, surgery, drug, and side effect of drug, which we will call SURGERY, as a "link" or "connector" record type. Note that this is called a connector record type even if it contains no data itself. In many instances, however, the link record contains information describing the relationship between the other two records.

Figure 4.21 represents two record types, namely, PATIENT record type, and the record type SURGERY.

In the network data model of Figure 4.22, a set is constructed with two record types. PATIENT and SURGERY record types create a PATIENT-HAS-SURGERY set. PATIENT record type is called an owner record type, and SURGERY record type a member record type. SURGEON and SURGERY record types are related by the SURGERY-ON-PATIENT set type. SURGEON record type is called an owner record type, and SURGERY a member record type.

Each occurrence of the set type PATIENT-HAS-SURGERY represents a hierarchical relationship between the patient and the surgery. The significant difference between the hierarchical data model and the network data model is that in the latter any record type can participate in any number of sets, playing the role of an owner record type or of a member record type.

Figure 4.23 shows the set occurrences of PATIENT-HAS-SURGERY and SURGERY-ON-PATIENT at this time for the hospital environment.

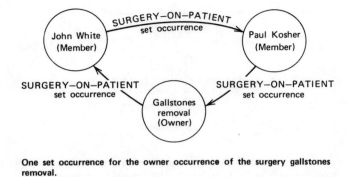

One set occurrence for the owner occurrence of the surgery gallstones removal.

Two set occurrences for the owner occurrence of patient John White and for the owner occurrence of patient Paul Kosher with the same member occurrence, gallstones removal.

Figure 4.21.

4.5.2 Three More Classes of Set Types

The set types defined in Figure 4.24 are made up of two record types, PATIENT and SURGERY.

A second class of set type is made up of three or more record types, as in Figure 4.25, and is called a "multimember" set type. The owner record type is PATIENT, and the member record types are SURGERY and ILLNESS.

The third class of set type is called a "singular" set type. It is also defined on the basis of an owner record type and a member record type. The difference between this set type and the types previously discussed is that only one occurrence of the set can exist in the data base. This structure is used in two ways:

1. It can join records together into a set where no natural owner record exists.

2. It can hold record occurrences that do not have an owner when they are entered into the data base but will have an owner at some later time. (See Figure 4.26.) When it is time to join the record to its final owner, it is disconnected from the system record and connected into the new owner record's set occurrence.

The following cases describe the various structures that can be built using the set type as a building block.

Case I. A patient may be admitted to the hospital for observation before surgery is performed. (See Figure 4.24.) The set type SURGERY-PLANNED between the record types PATIENT and SURGERY is not the same as the set type SURGERY-PERFORMED between the same record types, PATIENT and SURGERY, because of a different perspective.

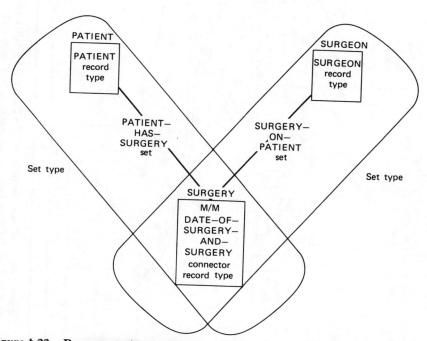

Figure 4.22. **Representation of data using network data model. Many-to-many relationship implemented with two set types:**

1. **PATIENT-HAS-SURGERY with PATIENT as owner record type and SURGERY as member record type.**
2. **SURGERY-ON-PATIENT with SURGEON as owner record type and SURGERY as member record type.**

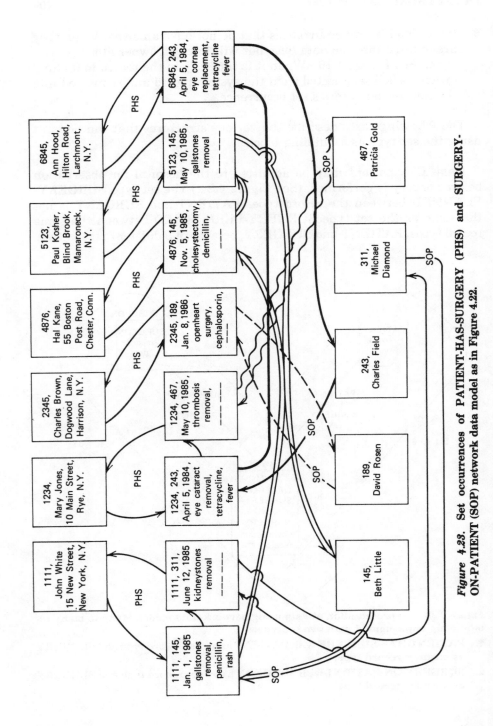

Figure 4.23. Set occurrences of PATIENT-HAS-SURGERY (PHS) and SURGERY-ON-PATIENT (SOP) network data model as in Figure 4.22.

110

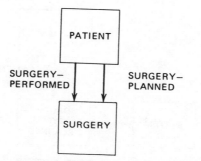

Figure 4.24. Two set types defined on two record types to imply two different contexts. One set type is SURGERY-PLANNED between the two record types PATIENT and SURGERY. Another set type is SURGERY-PERFORMED between the same record types.

Case II. A hierarchical structure can be constructed using a number of set types. (See Figure 4.27.)

Case III. A Y-structure can be built with the help of a number of set types. (See Figure 4.28.)

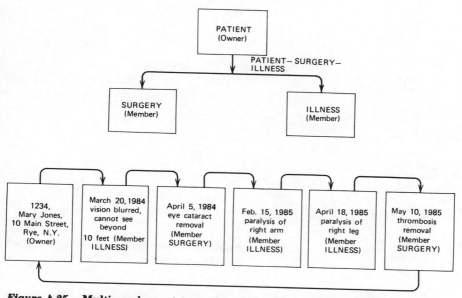

Figure 4.25. Multimember set type. An owner occurrence with five member occurrences.

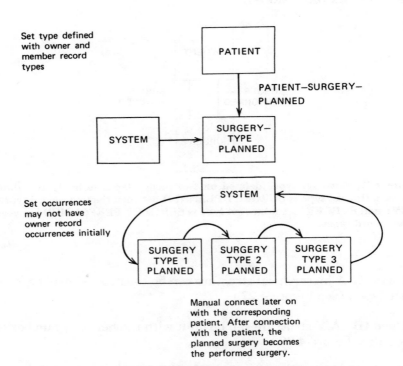

Set type defined
with owner and
member record
types

PATIENT

PATIENT—SURGERY—
PLANNED

SYSTEM

SURGERY—
TYPE
PLANNED

SYSTEM

Set occurrences
may not have
owner record
occurrences initially

SURGERY
TYPE 1
PLANNED

SURGERY
TYPE 2
PLANNED

SURGERY
TYPE 3
PLANNED

Manual connect later on
with the corresponding
patient. After connection
with the patient, the
planned surgery becomes
the performed surgery.

Figure 4.26. **System-owned set type or singular set type.**

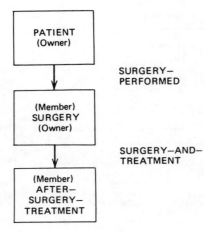

PATIENT
(Owner)

SURGERY—
PERFORMED

(Member)
SURGERY
(Owner)

SURGERY—AND—
TREATMENT

(Member)
AFTER—
SURGERY—
TREATMENT

Figure 4.27. **Hierarchical structure defined
with the help of set types.**

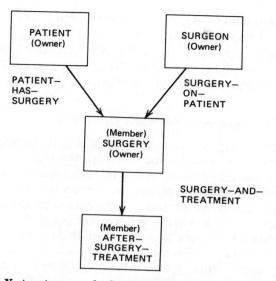

Figure 4.28. **A Y-structure can be built with the help of a number of set types.**

4.5.3 Storage Operations with a Network Data Model

Insertion. A new surgeon can be added as an owner occurrence of a SURGERY-ON-PATIENT set occurrence without a member SURGERY occurrence, that is, without having a corresponding patient to operate on. Similarly, the information about a patient can be entered without an assigned surgeon.

Deletion. If an owner occurrence of a surgeon is deleted, all the pointers connecting the surgeries performed by the surgeon may be deleted for the occurrence of the set type SURGERY-ON-PATIENT. But the information about all the patients operated on by the surgeon remains intact. Only the corresponding surgeon's information is deleted.

Similarly, when an owner occurrence of a patient is deleted, all the pointers connecting the surgeries performed on the patient may be deleted for the occurrence of the set type PATIENT-HAS-SURGERY. But the information about all the surgeons who performed surgeries on the patient remains intact.

4.5.4 Advantages of a Network Data Model

- The major advantage of the network data model is, as for the hierarchical data model, there are successful data base management systems that use the network data model as the basic structure.

- The many-to-many relationship, which occurs quite frequently in real life, can be implemented easily.
- The network data model is backed by the CODASYL Data Base Task Group (DBTG). The reports of DBTG in 1971 and 1973 will certainly influence future national and international standards for data bases.

4.5.5 Disadvantages of a Network Data Model

The main disadvantage of the network model is its complexity. The application programmer must be familiar with the logical structure of the data base, because he or she has to navigate through different set occurrences with the help of connector record type occurrences. The connector record types are not invisible to the application programmer. In other words, the programmer has to know his or her position in set occurrences when moving through the data base. Although this can be quite complicated if all operations involve movement through sets, the CODASYL model gives the programmer entry points into occurrences that greatly simplify the programming effort.

An added complication is that, unless great care is taken when the data base is reorganized, it is possible to lose data independence. This occurs when sets are removed. Also, because the views supplied to the application programmers are less simple than the views based on the hierarchical data model, the programming may become complex.

Remedy to Gain More Data Independence.   The remedy is to have a series of predefined routines that actually navigate the data base. Application programming, then, reduces to calls to these routines.

4.6 THE INVERTED FILE DATA MODEL

In the inverted file data model, each entity is represented by a file. Each attribute becomes a field in the file and, of course, each record in the file represents an occurrence of the entity. The data from our hospital environment could be stored in four files, PATIENT, SURGEON, PATIENT-AND-SURGEON, and DRUG, which would look exactly like the tables in Figures 4.3a, 4.3b, 4.3c, and 4.3d, respectively.

If two files have one or more fields in common, then a relationship exists between the entities represented by these files. The names of the fields need not be identical, but their data values must come from a common pool of values. The relationship is meaningless unless the fields arise from a single attribute. The exact nature of the mapping (one-to-one, one-to-many, or many-to-many) is determined only by looking at the data values. For instance, the PATIENT and PATIENT-AND-SURGEON files have the common field patient number; thus there is a relationship.

Further examination reveals that this relationship is one-to-many. Similarly, there is a one-to-many mapping between DRUG and PATIENT-AND-SURGEON through the common field postoperative drug administered.

To allow the user to take advantage of these relationships (i.e., to present them in an external model) and to allow efficient access to individual files, fields are inverted. To do this, an index file is created containing all the values taken by the inverted field. These values are maintained in order for easy access to the index file. With each value are kept pointer(s) to the record(s) containing that value in that field. (See Figure 4.29.) The inverted file data model allows zero, one, or many fields in each file to be inverted.

An appropriate question here is: Why is file inversion treated as a data model when it is really an access method and is discussed as such in

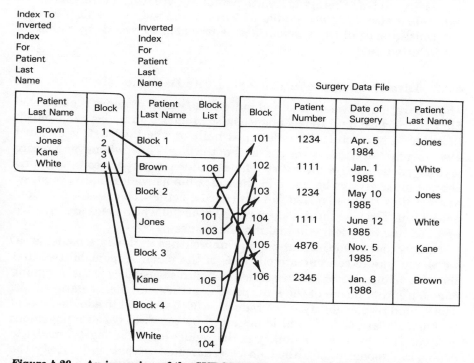

Figure 4.29. **An inversion of the SURGERY file on the field patient last name.**
- **For each inverted field an index file is built with entries containing:**
  - **A field value**
  - **Pointers to all records in the file containing that value in that field.**
- **Entries are ordered by field value.**
- **A separate index file is built for each field to be inverted.**
- **Higher levels of index are added if needed.**

Section 7.2.4? The answer is that several widely used DBMSs, among which are Software AG's ADABAS, ADR's DATACOM/DB, and CCA's MODEL 204, have file inversion as their dominant underlying feature. Further, many DBMSs based on other data models contain strong elements of inverted file. For these reasons, inverted file is also distinguished as a data model.

4.6.1 Advantages of an Inverted File Data Model

One of the major advantages the inverted file data model shares with the relational data model is simplicity. In contrast, however, inverted file DBMSs have been performance tested through many years of use in large and small environments. The inverted file data model also allows data independence. New entities and attributes in the form of files and fields are easily added. Changing relationships by creating or removing an index file is also easily accomplished. Finally, the wide use of file inversion is a consequence of the efficient access provided to records by values of the inverted field.

4.6.2 Disadvantages of an Inverted File Data Model

The separation between data and index files, which provides the inverted file DBMSs with data independence, also produces an undesirable effect. In order to be useful, the index files built on the inverted fields must always reflect accurately the contents of the files. Thus, whenever a record is inserted, deleted, or an inverted field's value is altered, a corresponding change must always be made in the index file as well. Finally, requests against files in an inverted file data model cannot be classified as non-procedural. The user must, in general, be aware of which fields are inverted and use this knowledge in making the requests.

Having discussed the four popular approaches in the data model area, we would like to concentrate on three of the major responsibilities that the data administrator has to fulfill. The first responsibility is the designing of a conceptual model of the enterprise's entities and their relationships. The second responsibility is the reduction of that model to a logical model that is compatible with and is managed by the data base management system. The third responsibility is the reduction of the logical model to a physical model (also called an internal model) that will satisfy the performance requirements. The methodology for fulfilling the first and second responsibilities is discussed in Chapters 5 and 6, and the third responsibility is covered in Part 3.

REFERENCES

1. Atre, S., *Data Base Management Systems for the Eighties*. Wellesley, Massachusetts: Q.E.D. Information Sciences, Inc., 1983.

2. Atre, S., "End-User Designed/Driven Data Bases," *Computerworld/Extra* (September 1, 1982).

3. Atre, S., "Spreading the Wealth of DBMS," *Computerworld Buyer's Guide Software* (December 14, 1983).

4. Bachman, C. W., "The Programmer as Navigator," *Communications of the ACM*, Vol. 16, No. 11 (November 1973).

5. "COBOL Extensions to Handle Data Bases" (PB 177 682). Unpublished report of CODASYL Data Base Task Group, January 1968.

6. Codd, E. F., "A Relational Model of Data for Large Shared Data Banks," *Communications of the ACM*, Vol. 13, No. 6 (June 1970).

7. Codd, E. F., "Further Normalization of the Relational Model," *Data Base Systems*, Courant Computer Science Symposia 6. Englewood Cliffs, New Jersey: Prentice-Hall, 1972.

8. Date, C. J., *An Introduction to Database Systems*, Vol. 1, 4th ed., The Systems Programming Series. Reading, Massachusetts: Addison-Wesley, 1986.

9. Fry, J. P., and E. M. Sibley, "Evolution of Data-Base Management Systems," *ACM Computing Surveys*, Special Issue: *Data-Base Management Systems*, Vol. 8, No. 1 (March 1976).

10. Knuth, Donald E., *The Art of Computer Programming*, Vol. 3: *Sorting and Searching*. Reading, Massachusetts: Addison-Wesley, 1973.

11. Martin, James, *Principles of Data-Base Management*. Englewood Cliffs, New Jersey: Prentice-Hall, 1976.

12. *The National Symposium on Comparative Data Base Management Systems*, Advanced Management Research International, Inc., Vol. I (June 26–28, 1978).

13. Olle, T. William, *The CODASYL Approach to Data Base Management*. New York: Wiley-Interscience, 1978.

14. Palmer, Ian R., *Data Base Systems: A Practical Reference*. Wellesley, Massachusetts: Q.E.D. Information Sciences, Inc., 1978.

15. Report, CODASYL Data Base Task Group, April 1971 (available from Association for Computing Machinery, 1133 Avenue of the Americas, New York, New York 10036).

16. Tsichritzis, Dionysios C., and Frederich H. Lochovsky, *Data Base Management Systems*. New York: Academic Press, a subsidiary of Harcourt Brace Jovanovich, 1977.

17. Ullman, J. D., *Principles of Database Systems*, 2nd ed. Rockville, Maryland: Computer Science Press, 1982.

18. Vetter, M., "Principles of Data Base Systems," unpublished paper presented at the International Computing Symposium, Liege, Belgium, April 1977.

QUESTIONS

1. Define the purpose of a conceptual model and describe the extent to which it depends on a DBMS to achieve its objective.

2. What are the four types of data models? What are the main differences among them?

3. Describe the differences between one-to-one, one-to-many, and many-to-many relationships as they apply to entities and attributes. Give examples of each.

4. As they apply to a relational data model, define the terms "relation," "tuple," "attribute," "candidate key," "domain," and "normalization."

5. Define tree structure in the context of the hierarchical data model and describe how records and fields manifest themselves in this structure.

6. In a hierarchical system, distinguish between the generic model and a data base record occurrence.

7. What relationship can a parent node have to a dependent node in the pure hierarchical data model? Identify the limitations, if any, that exist in this relationship.

8. Define and illustrate the terms "set type," "set occurrence," "owner," and "member" in a network data model. What is the limitation imposed on a member record occurrence?

9. What is the function of a singular set type in a network data model?

10. Define and illustrate the terms "file," "field," "record," "inverted field," and "index" in an inverted file data model. How are relationships between entities represented?

11. Can you think of times when it might be advantageous and/or necessary to carry some redundant data in a data base?

12. How is a many-to-many relationship implemented in both a hierarchical and a network data model?

13. How do the four data models support data independence?

14. Discuss the major advantages and disadvantages of the four data models.

15. Reservation clerk #31A has booked passengers on the following flights.

Start Time	Arrival Time	Flight No.	Origin Airport	Destination Airport	Plane Type	Capacity	Meals Served	Movie in Flight
10:15 AM	2:05 PM	1	Chicago	Honolulu	747	442	Lunch Supper	Yes
9:15 AM	5:20 PM	4	Los Angeles	Newark	DC-10	250	Breakfast Lunch	No
9:30 PM	11:20 AM	21	JFK	San Francisco	DC-10	250	Supper	Yes
8:30 AM	4:25 PM	40	Seattle	JFK	DC-10	250	Breakfast Lunch	No
1:05 PM	3:10 PM	107	Chicago	Los Angeles	DC-10	250	Lunch	No
8:40 AM	10:49 AM	112	Chicago	Cleveland	DC-10	250	Supper	No
6:00 PM	7:50 PM	331	Seattle	Oakland	737	145	· · ·	No

15.1. For a given airport (point of origin of a flight) construct a hierarchical data model showing the types of airplanes that will be needed and at what times each type will be needed.

15.2. To determine the kitchen facilities needed on board an airplane, construct a relation using the plane type and meal served. What is the domain of each attribute? If a key attribute is part of the relation, identify it; otherwise select a suitable key attribute.

15.3. Assume that start time is an entity with two data values or occurrences: AM and PM. Construct a network set type using a Bachman Diagram relating start time to origin airport. Start time will be the owner.

15.4. Construct set occurrences using the values AM and PM and the appropriate airports. The set type is from Part 3.

CHAPTER 5

Data Base Design (Conceptual Model)

To develop a data base that satisfies today's as well as tomorrow's information needs, a conceptual model must be designed. This conceptual model reflects the entities and their relationships and is based on the data processing needs of the organization. When determining the entities and their relationships, a data analysis is necessary. This analysis can be based on the information about data for existing, as well as future, applications.

For developing the conceptual model, some concepts from the relational approach are used. However, this methodology yields a data base design that is independent of the implementation approach; that is, the conceptual model can be mapped to a relational, hierarchical, network, or inverted file data model. Unfortunately, it appears that the people implementing hierarchical and CODASYL-DBTG-type systems do not necessarily practice the kind of relational normalization process discussed in this chapter. Perhaps data base design would be easier if people did.

DESIGN A CONCEPTUAL MODEL OF A DATA BASE

One major responsibility of a data administrator is designing a conceptual model of the enterprise. This model should represent the entities of the enterprise and the relationships between them.

The conceptual model is not the approach by which an individual application programmer processes the information. Instead, it is a combination of several ways used to process the data for several applications. The view of an individual application programmer is called an "external model." The conceptual model is independent of individual applications, independent of the data base management system, independent of the hardware used for storing the data, and independent of the physical model of the data in the storage media.

When designing the conceptual model, efforts should be concentrated on structuring the data and the relationships between data elements of the enterprise. At this stage, there should be no concern for the implementation and operation phases of the data base.

The first step in designing a conceptual model is data analysis, which will provide information about the data elements and the relationships between them.

5.1 DATA ANALYSIS

5.1.1 Collecting Information about Data for Existing Applications

Collecting information about data is very time consuming and requires patience on the part of management. The data administrator should initiate a plan to complete this task. First, the DA should use a questionnaire or similar vehicle to obtain from each level of management (executive, functional, and operational) a composite list of the data it needs. The various levels may process the data, or they may store it. Second, the DA should investigate all the clerical, operational, and data processing uses of the enterprise's data.

One fact not to be overlooked is that forms, bills, reports, existing data files, and old programs are starting points for data collection. The real question, however, is what data is needed in the new data base to support the applications, and the needed data is seldom in a one-to-one correspondence with the data seen on forms and reports.

The questionnaire or data survey form should be addressed to every manager and supervisor within the enterprise who has need of data or supplies data to the repository. It is imperative that the survey be completed by management and not by subordinate personnel. The survey should reflect management's perspective of what it needs. Additional survey forms should be made available to the initial subscribers so that they can add to the survey's breadth if the initial list does not include all data users. A point should be made here: If the initial subscription list to the survey is not complete, the model of the enterprise should be reviewed to determine why omissions occurred in the survey subscription.

The questionnaire should ask for the following information: data entity name, data element name, description, attributes, source and sensitivity (security), value or importance of the data, and relationships of the elements and entities. Every individual supplying information on the questionnaire may not be able to answer all of the entries, but each should provide as much of the information as possible. No one filling out the form should assume that someone else will supply information he or she has omitted. The prime motivational factor to be emphasized is that an accurate perception of the enterprise's data can be obtained only if everyone answers the questionnaire completely.

A brief description of the entries on the questionnaire follows. There is no best format for the questionnaire; it is important only that the items listed below be included. The format may be dictated by particular data dictionary applications to make the eventual entry to these applications less cumbersome. The enterprise may have data definition standards that it may revise to complete the questionnaire. The specific form the DA chooses is irrelevant to the actual purpose of the questionnaire.

Questionnaire/Survey Content

1. **Data Entity Name and Description.**   List the name and any synonyms by which the data elements (see below) are called. Examples are orders, weekly time card, production log, and accounts receivable form. Give a description of what the name means even though the name seems to be self-defining or self-explanatory. Describe in general the use or function of the entity, the purpose it serves within the operational or functional unit, and any users outside the unit.

2. **Data Elements.**   For each piece of information in the entity, provide the following information:

    a. *Element Name and Description.*   List the names, acronyms, and mnemonics. Give a full description of the element in prose.

    b. *Element Source.*   List the originating source(s) as perceived by the functional or operating unit. Examples include such entries as these: from the customer, from interoffice memos, from the shipping department.

    c. *Element Attributes.*   List attributes such as numeric, alphabetic, and textual. Give the unit of measure associated with the data, such as pieces, dollars, and feet. If there are boundaries to the acceptable value ranges for the element, list them (e.g., the value cannot be less than 100 or greater than 500).

    d. *Element Use.*   Describe the use. Examples include the following: to provide addressing information, to determine quantity, to establish the payroll scale rate.

e. *Element Security/Sensitivity.* List any constraints associated with the element name. These constraints are generally relative to audience restrictions, that is, who may use, access, read, and/or publish the data.

f. *Importance/Value.* List the importance of the data. Of what value is it in terms of the enterprise's continuing or expanding its functioning? It is no sin to state the value of the data in a negative way (i.e., "We couldn't do business without it!"). Correspondingly, though, the statement relative to the element's use (item d above) should support and elaborate on the value of the element.

g. *Element Relationship(s).* List the way(s) in which this element is used or paired with other elements. These elements need not be limited to the specific entity being discussed. Such relationships are part number/name, employee number/name/social security number, production code/job lot, and order number/shipping number.

3. **Retention Criteria and Archiving.** Describe the length of time and the manner in which the data is to be kept. List also, if known, the reason or cause for the retention (e.g., government regulation, company policy).

In conjunction with the completion of the survey, the DA should investigate the clerical, administrative, and data processing flows of data in the enterprise. The investigation should not be viewed as a "policing" to insure the correctness of the questionnaire, but rather as an adjunct to the model of the enterprise. The survey should also help the DA to follow the flow of paper through the enterprise, noting the paths and means of data communication, its use, and its purpose.

The next, and by far the most important, process performed by the DA is analysis of the data repository, which is built from the questionnaire and the data flow investigation. The analysis itself is easily described, but the process of the analysis is not routine or simplistic. The DA will now create a data map of the entities and elements, showing functional sources and entities and receiving or using functions and their functional entities and elements, as in Figure 5.1.

The diagrams show the flow, although oversimplified from any real situation, as it would be initially mapped from the data collection steps, and the ultimate data map structured from the source to the end-user. In the construction of the data map, the DA will invariably encounter discrepancies, errors, and omissions. He or she must resolve these matters before an accurate picture can be constructed. A handy tool that should be used during the process of data analysis is a data dictionary.

During the reconciliation process, the DA must determine the value of the data to the end-user. The DA will become aware of the end-user's perceived need and the real need for specific entities and elements in the

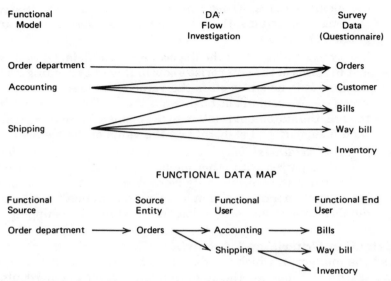

Figure 5.1. **The DA should create a data map of the entities and elements showing:**
1. **The functional source.**
2. **The receiving or using functions.**

repository. It is important now that the DA has as much authority and management leverage as possible to implement the elimination, reduction, or redirection of data in the functional units in order to manage the data resource properly.

After the process has been completed, the DA should review with the functional, operational, and executive levels the data relationships, the functional sources, and the user requirements. Again, it is important that all data users agree with the DA's perspective of the data.

The DA may now begin to build a data model or conceptual model of the data base.

5.1.2 Collecting Information about Data for Future Applications

One of the most important and most difficult tasks of the data administrator is collecting information about the future use of the data base. Once the data base is put in place, and the users see its value in information processing and decision making, they are going to ask for more in terms of better responsiveness, more functions, more applications, or more cross referencing of the enterprise's data. If the data base was designed based on knowledge of only the current use of data, it may be difficult to implement new relationships, new entities, and new data elements. To minimize the problems of this nature, the data administrator must determine other ways in which the information can be used. This is definitely a difficult task to perform, but the DA has to watch for any overlooked entities, entity relationships, and intrinsic data relationships regardless of functions, and discuss them with the users. Information about the future use of data not only is necessary for designing the conceptual and logical models but also may have an impact on the physical model. The information about the volume of data anticipated in the future may be an important determinant in the decision regarding the physical model.

5.2   RELATIONAL CONCEPTS FOR THE DESIGN PROCESS

The underlying model of an enterprise, representing entities and relationships between them, is more stable than the different ways in which information stored in a data base is retrieved. An effective way of developing a model, which we would like to call a conceptual model, is by applying concepts from the relational data model. These concepts are applied to analysis of data and relationships information provided by end-users. *The conceptual model need not be implemented with a relational data base management system. Rather, the model can be used as a basis to develop a logical model, which can be implemented with a relational, hierarchical, network, or inverted file data base management system.*

The major concept from the relational data model used in developing the conceptual model is the "normalization process," that is, the process of grouping data elements into tables representing entities and their relationships. Normalization theory is based on the observation that a certain set of relations has better properties in an inserting, updating, and deleting environment than do other sets of relations containing the same data.

The reason one would use the normalization process is to insure that the conceptual model of the data base will work. This means not that an unnormalized structure will not work, but only that it may cause some problems when application programmers attempt to modify the data base. The data administrator must decide, after locating violations of normalization, whether modifications will affect how the data base will function.

An unnormalized data model consists of records as they are used by application programs. The first step in normalization consists of transforming the data values into a two-dimensional table. All that is usually required at this step is removal of repeated occurrences of data values so that a flat file is obtained. For example, if a record includes space for an employee name, employee number, spouse, and up to ten children, the result will be a table with four columns and ten rows. Every row will have the employee name, employee number, spouse, and the name of one of the ten children. Ten rows will have the names of ten children. This step is just a preliminary one that makes it possible to move to second normal form.

The second step in normalization is to state what the keys are and to relate data elements to keys. In first normal form, the entire row (or tuple) of the table is dependent on all key attributes. In second normal form, an attempt is made to state what data elements are related to parts of the total key. If data elements depend only on part of the key, the key and the data elements connected to the partial key are candidates for removal into separate records. Breaking apart the first normal form table into a series of tables in which each element depends only on the entire key is called second normal form.

The third step is to separate out data elements from second normal form relations that, while dependent only on the key, may have an independent existence in the data base. This is done so that information about these data elements can be entered separately from relationships in which they are involved.

In every data model, one or more data elements are grouped to represent entities and their relations. In the groupings of data elements, three general types of problems can occur, and the removal of each gives rise to the three normal forms of relations (tables). Thus, the normalization process is a discipline of grouping data elements into a set of relations (tables). Figure 5.2 shows the three normal forms.

All normalized relations are in first normal form; some first normal form relations are in second normal form; and, finally, some second normal form relations are in third normal form. The normalization process yields third normal form relations. Third normal form relations represent entities and relationships between entities of an enterprise.

First, second, and third normal forms provide successive improvements in the insertion, deletion, and update operations against the data base. As we shall see, the normalization process makes the designer understand the semantics of attributes and their relationships and as a result mandates the thought process for data analysis.

The preceding paragraphs have given an overview of the steps involved in taking an unnormalized structure and transforming it into third normal form. The rest of this section shows how to go about doing this.

Consider the example in Figure 5.3. The data elements or attributes are patient number, patient name, patient address, surgeon license number, surgeon name, date of surgery, surgery, postoperative drug administered, and side effect of drug. Some restrictive assumptions for the hospital environment are made here for illustration purpose only, and are specified as we proceed.

A column or set of columns is called a "candidate key" when its values uniquely identify the row of the relation. Given the patient number (1234), the surgeon license number (243), and the date of surgery (Apr. 5, 1984), the row (or the tuple) "1234 243 Apr. 5, 1984, Mary Jones, 10 Main Street,

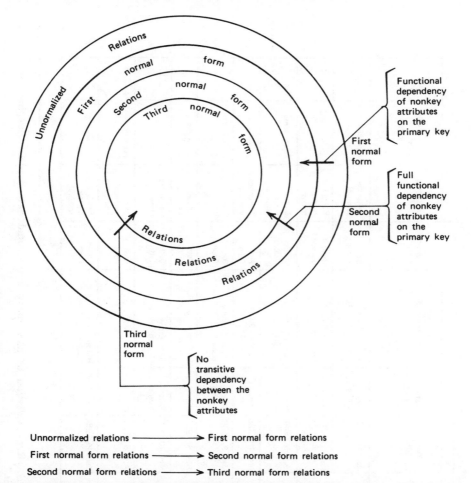

Unnormalized relations ⟶ First normal form relations

First normal form relations ⟶ Second normal form relations

Second normal form relations ⟶ Third normal form relations

Figure 5.2. **Every relation in first normal form is a special case of an unnormalized relation. But every unnormalized relation is not in first normal form. Every relation in second normal form is a special case of a first normal form relation, but not vice versa. Every relation in third normal form is a special case of a second normal form relation, but every second normal form relation is not necessarily in third normal form.**

Rye, N.Y. Charles Field Eye cataract removal Tetracycline Fever" is uniquely determined. Since this is the only candidate key, it becomes the primary key.*

* For simplicity we will assume throughout this section that every relation has only one candidate key. The only candidate key is then the primary key, and every attribute that does not participate in the primary key is a nonkey attribute. In practice, most of the time the primary key identifying an entity is obvious.

Patient Number	Surgeon License Number	Date of Surgery	Patient Name	Patient Address	Surgeon Name	Surgery	Postoperative Drug Administered	Side Effect of Drug
1111	145	Jan. 1, 1985	John White	15 New Street, New York, N.Y.	Beth Little	Gallstones removal	Penicillin	Rash
1111	311	June 12,1985	John White	15 New Street, New York, N.Y.	Michael Diamond	Kidney stones removal	---	---
1234	243	Apr. 5, 1984	Mary Jones	10 Main Street, Rye, N.Y.	Charles Field	Eye cataract removal	Tetracycline	Fever
1234	467	May 10,1985	Mary Jones	10 Main Street, Rye, N.Y.	Patricia Gold	Thrombosis removal	---	---
2345	189	Jan. 8, 1986	Charles Brown	Dogwood Lane, Harrison, N.Y.	David Rosen	Open heart surgery	Cephalosporin	---
4876	145	Nov. 5, 1985	Hal Kane	55 Boston Post Road, Chester, Conn.	Beth Little	Cholecy—stectomy	Demicillin	---
5123	145	May 10, 1985	Paul Kosher	Blind Brook, Mamaroneck, N.Y.	Beth Little	Gallstones removal	---	---
6845	243	Apr. 5, 1984	Ann Hood	Hilton Road Larchmont, N.Y.	Charles Field	Eye cornea replacement	Tetracycline	Fever
6845	243	Dec. 15,1984	Ann Hood	Hilton Road, Larchmond, N.Y.	Charles Field	Eye cataract removal	---	---

Primary Key

Tuple

Attribute

Figure 5.3. Representation of data using a relational data model: "Hospital Environment."

First Normal Form. A relation in first normal form is a table. At every intersection of a tuple (row) and a column there can be only one value in the table. No groups of values are permitted at the intersections.

Consider Figure 5.4. This is an unnormalized relation. At the crossings of some rows and columns more than one value is present. This implies that in this environment, for a given value of the primary key, the values of the nonkey attributes cannot be determined uniquely.

We transfer the unnormalized relation from Figure 5.4 to a normalized relation in Figure 5.5. In this transformation, we repeated the values taken by patient number, patient name, patient address, and, in one instance, surgeon license number and surgeon name. Figure 5.5 represents a relation in first normal form. At every intersection of a tuple (row) and a column, there is only one value in the table—no groups of values. Figure 5.6 shows the relation in pictorial format.

When the values taken by the patient number and the surgeon license number and the date of surgery are known, the values taken by the patient name, patient address, surgeon name, surgery, postoperative drug administered, and side effect of drug are also known. The primary key is thus made up of the patient number, the surgeon license number, and the date of surgery. There is no other candidate key for this relation. All the nonkey attributes in the relation are functionally dependent on the primary key, that is, given the value of the primary key, the values taken by the nonkey attributes are uniquely determined.

Storage Anomalies of First Normal Form. The following anomalies will result if we leave our data in first normal form. (See Figure 5.5.)

Insertion anomaly. It is possible that a new patient has not undergone any surgery at the hospital and no surgeon has been assigned to the patient. As a result of not assigning a surgeon, the patient tuple cannot be entered, that is, no information about the patient can be stored in the first normal form in Figure 5.5.

Suppose that we would like to insert the data about patient name and patient address. It should not be necessary to know the surgeon license number and date of surgery. This means that, to uniquely identify patient name and patient address, two components of the primary key, that is, surgeon license number and date of surgery, are superfluous. If we separate patient name and patient address, together with patient number, in a different relation, as in Figure 5.7a, this insertion anomaly will be rectified.

Insertion anomaly. It is possible that the hospital has appointed a new surgeon who has not yet operated on any patient at this hospital. As a result, in a tuple for this surgeon, there will not be any value assigned either to the patient number or to the date of surgery. Only part of the primary key is made up of the surgeon license number; the rest consists of the patient number and the date of surgery. As a result, a new tuple

Patient Number	Surgeon License Number	Date of Surgery	Patient Name	Patient Address	Surgeon Name	Surgery	Postoperative Drug Administered	Side Effect of Drug
1111	145	Jan. 1, 1985	John White	15 New Street, New York, N.Y.	Beth Little	Gallstones removal	Penicillin	Rash
	311	June 12, 1985			Michael Diamond	Kidney stones removal	---	---
1234	243	Apr. 5, 1984	Mary Jones	10 Main Street, Rye, N.Y.	Charles Field	Eye cataract removal	Tetracycline	Fever
	467	May 10, 1985			Patricia Gold	Thrombosis removal	---	---
2345	189	Jan. 8, 1986	Charles Brown	Dogwood Lane, Harrison, N.Y.	David Rosen	Open heart surgery	Cephalosporin	---
4876	145	Nov. 5, 1985	Hal Kane	55 Boston Post Road, Chester, Conn.	Beth Little	Cholecystectomy	Demicillin	---
5123	145	May 10, 1985	Paul Kosher	Blind Brook Mamaroneck, N.Y.	Beth Little	Gallstones removal	---	---
6845	243	Apr. 5, 1984	Ann Hood	Hilton Road Larchmont, N.Y.	Charles Field	Eye cornea replacement	Tetracycline	Fever
		Dec. 15, 1984				Eye cataract removal	---	---

Figure 5.4. An unnormalized relation. Given a value of an assumed primary key, for example patient number = 1111, there are a number of values at the crossings with surgeon license number (145 and 311), date of surgery (Jan. 1, 1985 and June 12, 1985), and so on.

Patient Number	Surgeon License Number	Date of Surgery	Patient Name	Patient Address	Surgeon Name	Surgery	Postoperative Drug Administered	Side Effect of Drug
1111	145	Jan. 1, 1985	John White	15 New Street, New York, N.Y.	Beth Little	Gallstones removal	Penicillin	Rash
1111	311	June 12, 1985	John White	15 New Street, New York, N.Y.	Michael Diamond	Kidney stones removal	---	---
1234	243	Apr. 5, 1984	Mary Jones	10 Main Street Rye, N.Y.	Charles Field	Eye cataract removal	Tetracycline	Fever
1234	467	May 10, 1985	Mary Jones	10 Main Street Rye, N.Y.	Patricia Gold	Thrombosis removal	---	---
2345	189	Jan. 8, 1986	Charles Brown	Dogwood Lane, Harrison, N.Y.	David Rosen	Open heart surgery	Cephalosporin	---
4876	145	Nov. 5, 1985	Hal Kane	55 Boston Post Road, Chester, Conn.	Beth Little	Cholecystectomy	Demicillin	---
5123	145	May 10, 1985	Paul Kosher	Blind Brook, Mamaroneck, N.Y.	Beth Little	Gallstones removal	---	---
6845	243	Apr. 5, 1984	Ann Hood	Hilton Road, Larchmont, N.Y.	Charles Field	Eye cornea replacement	Tetracycline	Fever
6845	243	Dec. 15, 1984	Ann Hood	Hilton Road, Larchmont, N.Y.	Charles Field	Eye cataract removal	---	---

Primary Key

Figure 5.5. Representation of data using a relational data model. First normal form relation.

131

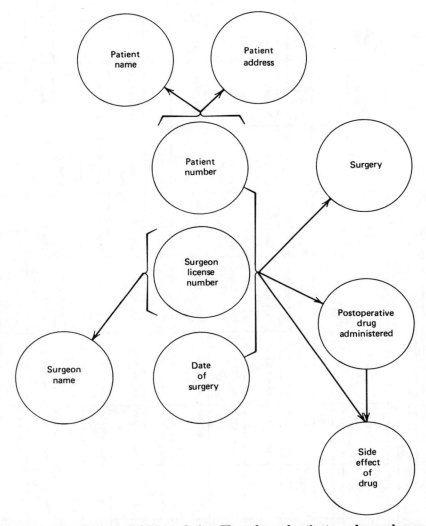

Figure 5.6. **One first normal form relation. The values of patient number and surgeon license number and date of surgery uniquely identify any of the perimeter values.**

for a new surgeon cannot be entered; that is, no information about the surgeon can be stored.* Here the nonkey attribute surgeon name is uniquely identified by the primary key patient number + surgeon license number + date of surgery. But for the unique identification of surgeon name, the only part of the primary key necessary is surgeon license number. If

---

* The reader might suggest the use of null keys or fictitious keys to avoid the problems of insertion. But in relational concepts null or fictitious key values are not permitted, since key values play an important role in insuring the integrity of the data base.

PATIENT Table

Patient Number	Patient Name	Patient Address
1111	John White	15 New Street, New York, N.Y.
1234	Mary Jones	10 Main Street, Rye, N.Y.
2345	Charles Brown	Dogwood Lane, Harrison, N.Y.
4876	Hal Kane	55 Boston Post Road, Chester, Conn.
5123	Paul Kosher	Blind Brook, Mamaroneck, N.Y.
6845	Ann Hood	Hilton Road, Larchmont, N.Y.

Figure 5.7a. Second normal form relation. The primary key is patient number. The nonkey attributes patient name and patient address need the full primary key, which is patient number, for unique identification. Patient name and patient address appear only in this relation.

we separate surgeon name with surgeon license number, as in Figure 5.7*b*, this insertion anomaly is rectified.

These anomalies occur because some columns depend on only part of the primary key, whereas the entire primary key is necessary to uniquely identify the tuple.

Update anomaly. If John White enters the hospital for the third time, and if between his second and third visits he has moved, we would like to update his address in all the tuples where he appears. (We want to

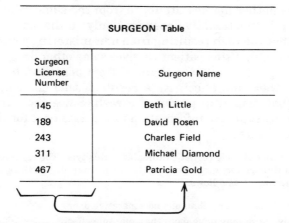

SURGEON Table

Surgeon License Number	Surgeon Name
145	Beth Little
189	David Rosen
243	Charles Field
311	Michael Diamond
467	Patricia Gold

Figure 5.7b. Second normal form relation. The primary key is surgeon license number. The nonkey attribute surgeon name needs the full primary key, which is surgeon license number, for unique identification. Surgeon name appears only in this relation.

keep only up-to-date information about the names and addresses for the sake of consistency. We assume that the hospital does not want to keep the old address.) This example shows that it is difficult to update a first normal form relation, because the number of tuples where the change has to be reflected is time-varying. The worst thing could be to have some tuples with the old address and some tuples with the new one.

This update anomaly will be taken care of if patient address appears only once. If we separate patient name and patient address, together with patient number, as in Figure 5.7a, the anomaly disappears. John White's address will appear only once in the PATIENT table, as in Figure 5.7a.

Deletion anomaly (type 1). Suppose that we wish to delete the information about a patient after he or she is deceased. Let us assume that the patient Charles Brown dies. (See Figure 5.5.) But when we delete the Charles Brown tuple, all facts about the surgeon David Rosen are lost because this was the only surgery that he performed. In some applications, the loss of information of this type could have serious effects. Since the tuple deleted might be the only source of information about David Rosen in our data base, we risk losing all the information about this surgeon. To prevent something like this from happening, we would have to burden the user with the responsibility of checking that the tuple to be deleted is not the only source of information for that category.

One possibility of resolving a problem of this kind is separating the information about the surgeon that is not dependent on the patient and vice versa. This can be achieved by having two relations, as in Figures 5.7a and 5.7b, for PATIENT and SURGEON, respectively.

Deletion anomaly (type 2). Another type of deletion anomaly is the result of a nonkey attribute from the relation in Figure 5.5 being functionally dependent on another nonkey attribute from the same relation. The side effect of a drug is functionally dependent only on the drug administered. It is possible that the rash resulting from administering penicillin to John White is so severe that this patient receives some other drug. The attribute values for the specific tuple are changed from penicillin to another drug and to some other side effect. As a result of this change, we lose the information that penicillin produced a rash. Since the particular tuple might be the only source of information in the data base for that category, this loss is not desirable.*

---

* The reader can think of some realistic examples of this type. The restrictive assumptions made here are for illustration purposes only. The reader may change the assumptions about the hospital environment as follows:

1. A patient may receive more than one postoperative drug.
2. A postoperative drug may have more than one side effect.
3. The side effect depends not only on the drug administered but also on the patient.

With the changed assumptions the reader will develop a different set of third normal form relations.

PATIENT—and—SURGEON Table

Patient Number	Surgeon License Number	Date of Surgery	Surgery	Postoperative Drug Administered	Side Effect of Drug
1111	145	Jan. 1, 1985	Gallstones removal	Penicillin	Rash
1111	311	June 12, 1985	Kidney stones removal	---	---
1234	243	Apr. 5, 1984	Eye cataract removal	Tetracycline	Fever
1234	467	May 10, 1985	Thrombosis removal	---	---
2345	189	Jan. 8, 1986	Open heart surgery	Cephalosporin	---
4876	145	Nov. 5, 1985	Cholecystectomy	Demicillin	---
5123·	145	May 10, 1985	Gallstones removal	---	---
6845	243	Apr. 5, 1984	Eye cornea replacement	Tetracycline	Fever
6845	243	Dec. 15, 1984	Eye cataract removal	---	---

Figure 5.7c. Second normal form relation. The primary key is patient number + surgeon license number + date of surgery. Every nonkey attribute (i.e., surgery, postoperative drug administered, and side effect of drug) requires the full primary key patient number + surgeon license number + date of surgery for unique identification.

To take care of these anomalies, we will separate the patient's information into a PATIENT relation, as in Figure 5.7a, and the surgeon's information into a SURGEON relation, as in Figure 5.7b. The primary key in the PATIENT relation from Figure 5.7a is the patient number, and the primary key in the SURGEON relation from Figure 5.7b is the surgeon license number. The remaining attributes comprise the PATIENT-AND-SURGEON relation shown in Figure 5.7c, with the primary key composed of patient number, surgeon license number, and date of surgery.

The relations in Figures 5.7a, 5.7b, and 5.7c are said to be in second normal form. These three second normal form relations for our data are more desirable than the one first normal form relation in Figure 5.5, because a second normal form relation removes some of the storage anomalies encountered with a first normal form relation. Figure 5.8 represents the three second normal form relations in a pictorial format.

Second Normal Form. A relation is said to be in second normal form when every nonkey attribute is fully functionally dependent on the primary key; that is, every nonkey attribute needs the full primary key for unique

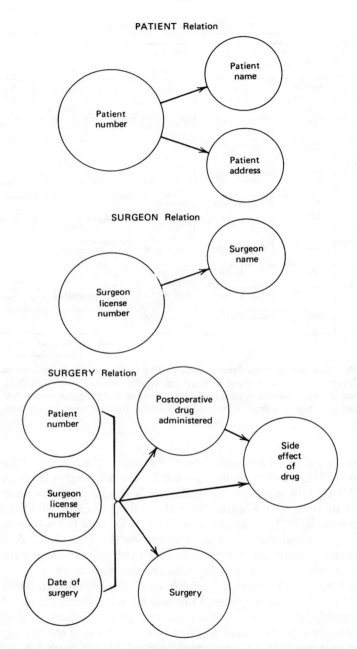

Figure 5.8. **Three second normal form relations. The primary key of the PATIENT relation is patient number. The primary key of the SURGEON relation is surgeon license number. The primary key of the SURGERY relation is patient number + surgeon license number + date of surgery.**

136

identification. Conversely, a relation is not in second normal form if there is a nonkey attribute that is not fully functionally dependent on the primary key. Every relation in second normal form is also in first normal form.

Storage Anomalies of Second Normal Form. Figures 5.7a, 5.7b, and 5.7c represent three second normal form relations. Some of the anomalies with first normal form, as in Figure 5.5, have been removed with the second normal form relations.

Insertion. We can enter a new patient who has not undergone any surgery at the hospital and to whom no surgeon has been assigned by simply entering the patient's information in the relation in Figure 5.7a.

Insertion. The information regarding a new surgeon who has not yet operated on any patient at the hospital can be entered by simply introducing a new tuple into the relation in Figure 5.7b.

Deletion (type 1). If Charles Brown dies, the corresponding tuple from the relations in Figures 5.7a and 5.7c can be deleted. The information about the surgeon David Rosen will remain in the relation in Figure 5.7b.

Update. If John White enters the hospital for the third time with a new address, the only place where the address change will have to take place will be in the relation in Figure 5.7a and *not* in Figure 5.7c. However, there still seem to be some storage anomalies with the relation in Figure 5.7c.

Insertion anomaly. We cannot enter the fact that a particular drug has a particular side effect unless that drug is given to a patient. We cannot enter a tuple in the relation of Figure 5.7c until we have a patient who is operated on and to whom the particular drug can be given.

Deletion anomaly. The deletion anomaly where a nonkey attribute from a relation is functionally dependent on another nonkey attribute remains. If John White receives some other drug as a result of the severe rash due to penicillin and the attribute values for the drug administered and the side effect of the drug are updated, we lose the information that penicillin produced a rash. Since that particular tuple was the only source of information in the data base for that category, this loss is not desirable.

Update anomaly. The side effect of a drug appears in the relation in Figure 5.7c many times. If the manufacturer of a particular drug changes the formula so that the side effect of the drug changes, we are faced with two approaches: (1) either search through the whole relation in Figure 5.7c and change the side effect value every time the drug was administered, or (2) live with some inconsistency as a result of changing the value in some tuples and not changing it in others. (This example is for illustration purposes only.) The insertion, deletion, and updating anomalies are the results of the dependency of the nonkey attribute side effect of drug on another nonkey attribute, postoperative drug administered. This type of dependency is called a "transitive" dependency. (See Figure 5.9.)

The solution to these problems with the relation in Figure 5.7c is to replace it with two relations, as in Figures 5.10c and 5.10d.

Since there are no storage anomaly problems with the relations in Figures 5.7a and 5.7b, we keep them untouched in Figures 5.10a and 5.10b, respectively.

It should be noted that the transformation from second to third normal form is similar to the transformation from first to second normal form except for dealing with nonkey attributes. In transforming from 1NF to

Transitive Dependency

Patient Number	Surgeon License Number	Date of Surgery	Surgery	Postoperative Drug Administered	Side Effect of Drug
1111	145	Jan. 1, 1985	Gallstones removal	Penicillin	Rash
1111	311	June 12, 1985	Kidney stones removal	---	---
1234	243	Apr. 5, 1984	Eye cataract removal	Tetracycline	Fever
1234	467	May 10, 1985	Thrombosis removal	---	---
2345	189	Jan. 8, 1986	Open heart surgery	Cephalosporin	---
4876	145	Nov. 5, 1985	Cholecystectomy	Demicillin	---
5123	145	May 10, 1985	Gallstones removal	---	---
6845	243	Apr. 5, 1984	Eye cornea replacement	Tetracycline	Fever
6845	243	Dec. 16, 1984	Eye cataract removal	---	---

Patient number + Surgeon license number + Date of surgery ⟶ Postoperative drug administered ⟶ Side effect of drug

Postoperative drug administered, which is not a part of the primary key, uniquely identifies the nonkey attribute side effect of drug. This type of dependency between the nonkey attributes is called "transitive" dependency.

Figure 5.9. Representation of data using a relational data model:

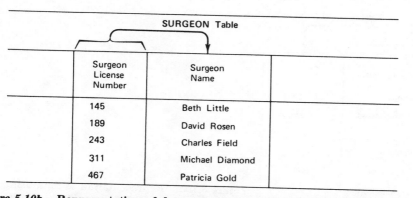

PATIENT Table

Patient Number	Patient Name	Patient Address
1111	John White	15 New Street, New York, N.Y.
1234	Mary Jones	10 Main Street, Rye, N.Y.
2345	Charles Brown	Dogwood Lane, Harrison, N.Y.
4876	Hal Kane	55 Boston Post Road, Chester, Conn.
5123	Paul Kosher	Blind Brook, Mamaroneck, N.Y.
6845	Ann Hood	Hilton Road, Larchmont, N.Y.

Figure 5.10a. **Representation of data using relational data model. Third normal form relation. The primary key is patient number.**

2NF, we look at relationships between key attributes and nonkey attributes. In transforming from 2NF to 3NF, however, we look at relationships between nonkey attributes.

The relations PATIENT, SURGEON, PATIENT AND SURGEON, and DRUG, as in Figures 5.10a, 5.10b, 5.10c, and 5.10d, respectively, are in third normal form. Figure 5.11 shows the four third normal form relations in pictorial format.

Note, also, that a value of postoperative drug administered can be used to enter the table in Figure 5.10c to answer questions such as, "Who is taking or took tetracycline?"

Third Normal Form. A relation is said to be in third normal form if *there is no transitive functional dependency between nonkey attributes.* (When one nonkey attribute can be determined with one or more nonkey

SURGEON Table

Surgeon License Number	Surgeon Name	
145	Beth Little	
189	David Rosen	
243	Charles Field	
311	Michael Diamond	
467	Patricia Gold	

Figure 5.10b. **Representation of data using relational data model. Third normal form relation. The primary key is surgeon license number.**

PATIENT—and—SURGEON Table

Patient Number	Surgeon License Number	Date of Surgery	Surgery	Postoperative Drug Administered
1111	145	Jan. 1, 1985	Gallstones removal	Penicillin
1111	311	June 12, 1985	Kidney stones removal	----
1234	243	Apr. 5, 1984	Eye cataract removal	Tetracycline
1234	467	May 10, 1985	Thrombosis removal	----
2345	189	Jan. 8, 1986	Open heart surgery	Cephalosporin
4876	145	Nov. 5, 1985	Cholecystectomy	Demicillin
5123	145	May 10, 1985	Gallstones removal	----
6845	243	Apr. 5, 1984	Eye cornea replacement	Tetracycline
6845	243	Dec. 15, 1984	Eye cataract removal	----

Figure 5.10c. **Representation of data using relational data model. Third normal form relation. The primary key is patient number + surgeon license number + date of surgery. The nonkey attributes are surgery and postoperative drug administered.**

attributes, there is said to be transitive functional dependency between the two. The side effect of a drug can be determined from the drug administered. The side effect of a drug is thus transitively functionally dependent on the drug administered.) Alternatively, if there are any nonkey attributes with functional dependency between them, the relation is not in third normal form.

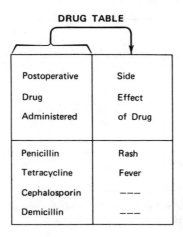

DRUG TABLE

Postoperative Drug Administered	Side Effect of Drug
Penicillin	Rash
Tetracycline	Fever
Cephalosporin	----
Demicillin	----

Figure 5.10d. **Representation of data using relational data model. Third normal form relation. The primary key is postoperative drug administered.**

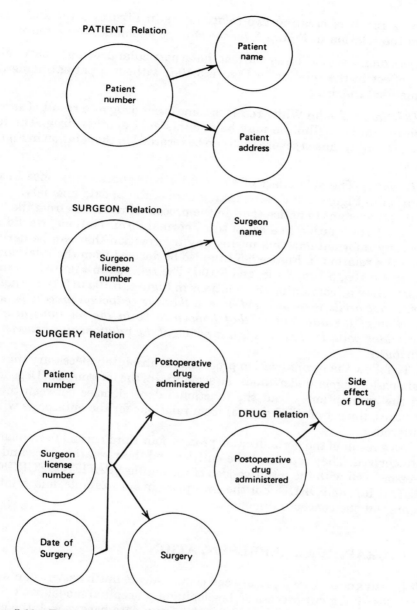

Figure 5.11. Four third normal form relations.
1. PATIENT relation. The primary key is patient number.
2. SURGEON relation. The primary key is surgeon license number.
3. SURGERY relation. The primary key is patient number + surgeon license number + date of surgery.
4. DRUG relation. The primary key is postoperative drug administered.

As a result of creating two relations, as in Figures 5.10*c* and 5.10*d* from the relation in Figure 5.7*c*, the storage anomalies are removed.

Insertion.   We can enter the fact that a particular drug has a particular side effect in the relation in Figure 5.10*d*, without a patient being administered the drug.

Deletion.   If John White receives some other drug as a result of severe rash due to penicillin, he may be administered another drug. The fact that penicillin caused severe rash can be recorded in the relation in Figure 5.10*d*.

Update.   The side effect of every drug will appear only once in the relation in Figure 5.10*d*, thus taking care of the update anomaly.

It is important to notice that, in the process of reduction from the first normal form relation to a set of third normal form relations, we did not lose any information. This means any information that can be derived from the relation in Figure 5.5 can also be derived from the relations in Figures 5.10*a*, 5.10*b*, 5.10*c*, and 5.10*d*. The relation in Figure 5.5 can be constructed by combining the relations in Figures 5.10*a* to 5.10*d*. *Another point that needs to be stressed here is that the reduction process is not a function of the data values that happen to be in the relations at some particular point in time, but is a function of the relationships between the attributes.*

To follow the normalization process, it is absolutely necessary that the data base designer understands the semantics of the information. Depending on the assumptions about the functional dependencies between the attributes, the set of third normal form relations for the enterprise will be different.*

As a result of the normalization process, four third normal form relations are derived. They represent the entities and their relationships and correspond well with the intuitive idea of the entities: PATIENT, SURGEON, SURGERY, and DRUG. For the enterprise in our example, four relations represent the conceptual model.

5.3   GRAPHICAL REPRESENTATION

It is well known that a picture can communicate much better than words. For describing our process of developing a conceptual model, we will use a notation for the two basic elements of any data base model: the entity and the mapping.

---

* There have been some publications about fourth and fifth normal forms, which should eliminate the problem of multivalued dependence. The author considers the normalization process up to third normal form of sufficient practical value and refers any interested reader to the bibliography for the literature on higher normal forms.

Consider the following example.

In a university environment a student can take many courses, and a course can be taken by many students. For every course taken, a student will receive some grade. The information about only the student and the grade is insufficient because it is not clear in which course the student received the specific grade. On the other hand, the information about only the course and the grade is not sufficient either. We would like to know which student received the specific grade in which course. (See Figure 5.12.)

Figure 5.13 represents the underlying conceptual model of Figure 5.12 and can be interpreted as follows:

- Any STUDENT may take any number of courses.
- Any one COURSE can be taken by any number of students.
- A specific GRADE can, and must, be related to one and only one student *and* to one and only one course.
- The double-headed arrow joining STUDENT and GRADE represents the fact that a student may have zero, one, or many grades, depending on none, one, or many courses taken by the student.

The double-headed arrow will be used to denote this type of relationship, which is described as many, throughout the book.

Course / Student	CS601	MA123	GY456	PH387	CH890
Robert Braun	A	B	A		
Helen Plain		A		A	
Harry Klein		A	B		
Jim White	A				A
John Flunk	C			C	

Many

STUDENT ⟷ COURSE

Many

Figure 5.12. Relationships between STUDENT, COURSE, and GRADE. A given student may taken many courses. A given course may be taken by many students. A specific grade tells more about the student and the course.

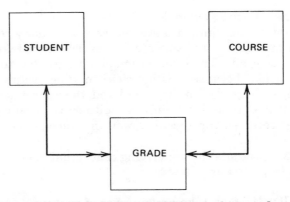

Figure 5.13. Graphical representation of entities. A given student may be taking many courses. A given course may be taken by many students.

The schematic representation for the conceptual model will be used in this chapter. We must determine how to extract entities, relationships between data elements representing entities, and relationships between entities themselves. The next section will discuss these issues.

5.4 DESIGN PROCESS

It is desirable to examine systematically the purpose, the inputs, and the desired outputs of the application that will use the data base as a repository of information. The approach of the design procedure is outside-in.

Here the application of the normalization process is demonstrated with a subset of a university environment. A complete treatment is given in Appendix B as a case study.

Elements and relationships between elements will be extracted from conceptual requirements, and it will be determined which elements can be considered as key data elements. This determination will help the data administrator to develop the model of the enterprise.

In this section we will apply relational concepts to designing a data base with the help of only one end-user's view in the university environment of Appendix B. The end-user's view is represented in Figure 5.14. Data base design for the university environment is done for all the end-users' views in Appendix B.

The data elements referenced in the conceptual requirement of Figure 5.14 are represented in Figure 5.15.

The assumptions about the conceptual requirement in Figure 5.14 are as follows:

1. A student has one student identification number.

STUDENT SCHEDULE LIST/SEMESTER

DATE: SEPTEMBER 7, 1987

SEMESTER: FALL 1987: SEPTEMBER 10, 1987
                       TO DECEMBER 22, 1987

SCHOOL: STATE UNIVERSITY
STUDENT: 123456789
NAME: JOHN F. SMITH
STATUS: UNDERGRADUATE
MAJOR: COMPUTER SCIENCE
MINOR: GYMNASTICS
FACULTY—   JOSEPH A. CORRIGAN
ADVISOR:

NO—COURSE	COURSE—TITLE	NAME—INSTR	CREDITS	CAMPUS	DAY—TIME	BLDG—NO—ROOM
CS601	INTRO TO COMP SCIENCE	A.B. ADAMS	3	WHITE PLAINS	W6—8 P.M.	AL201
CS605	INFO STRUCT ALGORITHMS	J.S. FINK	3	BROOKLYN	TH8—10 A.M.	MAIN 605

Figure 5.14. **Every registered student at the school receives the report at the beginning of every semester. It is a confirmation of the courses for which the student has registered. This report is a conceptual requirement of an end-user.**

2. The student identification number uniquely determines the student name, the student status, the major discipline, the minor discipline, and the faculty advisor.

3. A course with the same number can be offered in different semesters and at different campuses. At the time of an offering, the title of the course may be changed. Also, the instructor teaching the course may be changed from one semester to another. The campus, the period, and the room may be changed from one semester to another.

4. In a specific semester a specific course will be taught by a specific instructor, at a specific campus, in a specific period, and in a specific room for a specific number of credits.

5. A student may choose the number of credits to be taken for a specific course in a specific semester. Auditors, that is, the students who will appear for examinations, will receive fewer credits.

The purpose of stating the assumptions is not to solve the environment's problems regarding these assumptions but to reflect them in our conceptual model.

SEMESTER	
DSTRTSEM	Date of start of semester.
DENDSEM	Date of end of semester.
NO-STUDENT	Number of student.
NAME-STUDENT	Name of student.
STATUS	Status of student.
MAJOR	Major discipline.
MINOR	Minor discipline.
FACULTY-ADVISOR	Faculty advisor.
NO-COURSE	Number of course.
COURSE-TITLE	Course title.
NAME-INSTR	Name of instructor.
CREDITS	Credits for which the student has registered.
CAMPUS	Campus where the course will be taught.
DAY-TIME	Which day and what time the course will be taught.
BLDG-NO-ROOM	Building number and room number where the course will be taught.

Figure 5.15. **The data elements representing the entities of the conceptual requirement in Figure 5.14.**

The relationships between the data elements from Figure 5.15 are as follows:

1. SEMESTER ⟷ DSTRTSEM, DENDSEM. For a given SEMESTER there is only one date of start of semester (DSTRTSEM) and also only one date of end of semester (DENDSEM) and vice versa. This is a one-to-one mapping, represented as ⟷ or as $\overset{one}{\underset{one}{\rightleftarrows}}$. The primary key picked is SEMESTER from the candidate keys SEMESTER, DSTRTSEM, and DENDSEM.

2. NO-STUDENT ⟷ NAME-STUDENT, STATUS, MAJOR, MINOR, FACULTY-ADVISOR. For a given number of student (NO-STUDENT) there is only one NAME-STUDENT, STATUS (of the student), MAJOR (discipline of the student), MINOR (discipline of the student), and FACULTY-ADVISOR. But for a given status there can be many students. There can be many students with the same

major and minor disciplines. And a faculty advisor may be advising more than one student. This is a one-to-many mapping, represented as ◄◄——► or $\overset{\text{one}}{\underset{\text{many}}{\rightleftarrows}}$.

3. SEMESTER*NO-COURSE ◄◄——► COURSE-TITLE, NAME-INSTR, CAMPUS, DAY-TIME, BLDG-NO-ROOM. In a given SEMESTER and for a given number of course (NO-COURSE) there is only one COURSE-TITLE, one instructor teaching the course (NAME-INSTR) (if more than one instructor is teaching the course, we consider it one team of instructors), one CAMPUS, and one DAY-TIME and one BLDG-NO-ROOM where the course will be taught.

But there may be a number of courses with the same course title (e.g., Introduction to Computer Science, taught in different sections with course numbers CS601.1, CS601.2, etc.). The same instructor may be teaching a number of courses in a semester. A number of courses in a specific semester may be taught on a specific campus, at the same time, on the same day, in the same room, or in the same building.

This is a one-to-many mapping with SEMESTER and NO-COURSE being the compound key and represented as ◄◄——► or $\overset{\text{one}}{\underset{\text{many}}{\rightleftarrows}}$.

3a. NO-STUDENT*SEMESTER ◄◄——►► NO-COURSE, CREDITS. A given student (NO-STUDENT) may be taking in a given SEMESTER many courses (NO-COURSE) and also a set of CREDITS. A given course may also be taken by many students in a specific semester, and a given number of credits may be taken by many students as well. This is a many-to-many mapping, represented as ◄◄——►► or $\overset{\text{many}}{\underset{\text{many}}{\rightleftarrows}}$.

Relations 1, 2, and 3 are in third normal form, because nonkey data elements from these relations require full keys for their identification. There is no transitive dependency between nonkey data elements as well. But relation 3a is not even in first normal form, because the mapping is many-to-many. First normal form requires the mapping between primary key and nonkey data elements to be one-to-many (◄◄——►) or one-to-one (◄——►). Second normal form requires that nonkey data elements have the full primary key for their unique identification. And third normal form requires that there be no transitive dependency between nonkey data elements.

Relation 3a can be transferred into a third normal form relation if the primary key is further qualified, that is, if the primary key is further compounded with NO-COURSE.

3b.   NO-STUDENT*SEMESTER*NO-COURSE ◄──── ► CREDITS.
Relation 3b is now in third normal form. A given student (NO-STUDENT), in a given SEMESTER and for a given course (NO-COURSE), takes a specific number of CREDITS.

Drawing the Conceptual Model. Relations 1, 2, 3, and 3b are re-numbered as 4, 5, 6, and 7. Relations 4, 5, 6, and 7 (Figure 5.16) can be represented in a pictorial format as follows:

1. Each relation for which the primary key consists of only one data element represents an entity. Relations 4 and 5 represent the entities SEMESTER and STUDENT, respectively. All entities of this type are placed on level 1. In Figure 5.17 the boxes SEMESTER and STU-DENT on level 1 represent the entities in relations 4 and 5. The data elements are written inside the boxes. The primary keys of the entities are underlined. If a box cannot hold all the data elements representing an entity, the omissions are shown by three dashes, - - -.

2. Relations with a primary key of two data elements represent rela-tionships between two entities. Relations of this type are placed on the second level. If a part of a primary key is not represented as an entity, a new entity relation will be generated; for example, the com-pound key of relation 6 is SEMESTER*NO-COURSE. This key rep-resents the relationship between the two entities SEMESTER and COURSE. There is a box for the entity SEMESTER on level 1, but no box for the entity COURSE on level 1. To represent the relationship between the entities SEMESTER and COURSE on level 2, a new entity relation for COURSE will be created on level 1, because no relation in Figure 5.16 is defined only with number of course (NO-COURSE) as the primary key. The box with relation 6 on level 2 interconnects the relation SEMESTER and the newly created relation

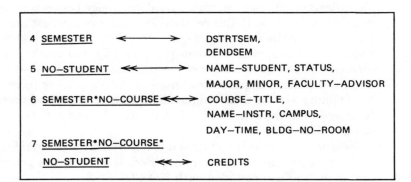

Figure 5.16. **Third normal form relations for the end-user's view from Figure 5.14.**

Figure 5.17. Conceptual model for the end-user's view from Figure 5.14. Created relations are shown in dashed boxes.

COURSE on level 1. The newly created box is represented with dashed lines.

The single-headed and double-headed arrows between relations 4 and 6 and the dashed box COURSE from Figure 5.17 indicate that in a given semester many courses may be taught, and a given course may be taught in many semesters.

3. The procedure for level 2 will be repeated for level 3 with relations with a primary key of three data elements, and so on.

The resulting diagram for relations 4, 5, 6, and 7 is shown in Figure 5.17.

After the conceptual model is determined, the data administrator can develop a logical model with the underlying structure of a relational, hierarchical, network, or inverted file data model. Designing a logical model is presented in the next chapter, and the determination of a physical model on the basis of cost, size, and performance is treated in Part 3.

REFERENCES

1. Atre, S., "End-User Designed/Driven Data Bases," *Computerworld/Extra* (September 1, 1982),
2. Atre, S., *Information Center: Strategies and Case Studies.* Atre International Consultants, Inc., P.O. Box 727, Rye, N.Y. 10580, 1986.
3. Atre, S., "Spreading the Wealth of DBMS," *Computerworld Buyer's Guide:Software* (December 14, 1983).
4. Date, C. J., *An Introduction to Database Systems*, Vol. 1, 4th ed. Reading, Massachusetts: Addison-Wesley, 1986.
5. Kent, William, "A Simple Guide to Five Normal Forms in Relational Database Theory," *Communications of the ACM*, Vol. 26, No. 2 (February 1983).
6. Lyon, John K., *An Introduction to Data Base Design*, The Wiley Communigraph Series in Business Data Processing. New York: John Wiley & Sons, 1971.

QUESTIONS

1. Identify and describe the major components of a questionnaire to be used to collect information for the construction of a new data base. Who should be responsible for completing the questionnaire? Why?
2. In evaluating and analyzing the responses to the questionnaire, the DA will often construct a data map to aid him or her in this process. What does a data map consist of and what can a DA realistically hope to achieve by using this tool? Give an example of a data map.
3. Is it reasonable to expect that all entities, attributes, and relationships within an enterprise can be anticipated during the conceptual model design phase of data base system development? What can be done to minimize future revisions to the data base?
4. Why can the normalization process developed by the relationalists be used regardless of the DBMS to be utilized?
5. What does it mean to say that a relation is unnormalized? How does this form differ from relations in first normal form? How does one make the transition from unnormalized to first normal form?
6. Describe potential anomalies in first normal form as they relate to updating, insertion, and deletion of records in a data base. Give specific examples to support your answer.
7. Define what is meant by second normal form. How are storage anomalies of first normal form overcome at this stage of the normalization process?

8. Anomalies in second normal form are most often caused by transitive dependencies. Define this problem and explain how it manifested itself in the hospital environment.

9. Define third normal form and describe how the transitive dependency anomaly of second normal form is resolved. Give an example.

10. Why must the data base designer understand the semantics of the information in the data base?

11. Given the following table of third normal form relations from the hospital environment, draw the conceptual model for the end-user's view:

Patient Relation	PAT-NO (Patient Number)
	PAT-NA (Patient Name)
	PAT-AD (Patient Address)
Surgeon Relation	SUR-NO (Surgeon License Number)
	SUR-NA (Surgeon Name)
Drug Relation	DRU-AD (Drug Administered)
	SID-EF (Side Effect)
Surgery Relation	PAT-NO (Patient Number)
	SUR-NO (Surgeon License Number)
	DAT-SU (Date of Surgery)
	DRU-AD (Drug Administered)
	SURGER (Surgery Performed)

12. Given the data in Chapter 4, question 14, and the following assumptions, show first, second and third normal form relations. Identify primary keys.

   a. Origin, destination, start and arrival times, and plane type are determined by the flight number.
   b. The capacity is determined by the plane type.
   c. The type of meal served is determined by the time of the flight.
   d. Showing of a movie is determined by the length of the flight.

CHAPTER 6

Data Base Design (Logical Model)

This chapter demonstrates a procedure for mapping a conceptual model into a logical model. Because today's data base management systems use a relational, a hierarchical, a network, or an inverted file data model, or a combination of these data models, the steps for mapping the conceptual model to each of these data models are given.

DESIGN A LOGICAL MODEL OF A DATA BASE

In developing a logical model of the data base, the first consideration is deciding which data model will be the best one for the particular conceptual model. Commercial DBMSs are based on one data model or on a combination of data models. The four major data models are known as relational, hierarchical, network, and inverted file, and a detailed discussion of these data models was given in Chapter 4.

The conceptual model of Chapter 5, Figure 5.17, is shown here for convenience as Figure 6.1. The boxes at the first level, STUDENT, COURSE, and SEMESTER, represent the basic entities. As explained in Chapter 5, the primary key of an entity at the first level consists of only one attribute. For example, the key of the STUDENT entity is NO-STUDENT. The box SEMESTER + COURSE at the second level has a primary key composed of SEMESTER and NO-COURSE. This box connects the basic entities SEMESTER and COURSE. The primary key of the box at the third level, SEMESTER + COURSE + STUDENT, is made up of three attributes: SEMESTER, NO-COURSE, and NO-STUDENT.

The following discussion gives versions of the logical model using a relational, a hierarchical, a network, and an inverted file data model.

Figure 6.1. Conceptual model to be used to map to a logical model. This conceptual model is taken from Figure 5.17.

6.1 MAPPING TO A RELATIONAL DATA MODEL

A relational data model consists of a number of relations (tables). In mapping the conceptual model from Figure 6.1 to a logical model, we will be defining the relations and their attributes. An attribute, or a number of attributes from these relations, will represent the primary key.

Every box in Figure 6.1 represents a relation. The five relations illustrated are STUDENT, COURSE, SEMESTER, SEMESTER + COURSE, and SEMESTER + COURSE + STUDENT. These could be specified as tables for IBM's DB2.

In Figure 6.1 the boxes are the relations, and the attributes are written inside the boxes. Figures 6.2*a*, 6.2*b*, and 6.2*c* show the relations with the corresponding attributes.

The user view of the STUDENT table is shown in Figure 6.2*a*. The table is made up of the attributes NO-STUDENT, NAME-STUDENT,

STUDENT RELATION

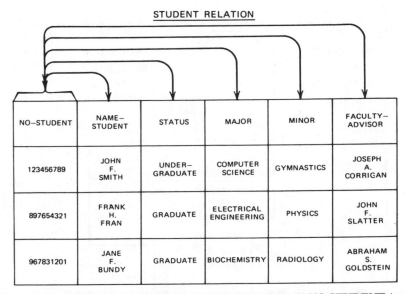

NO—STUDENT	NAME—STUDENT	STATUS	MAJOR	MINOR	FACULTY—ADVISOR
123456789	JOHN F. SMITH	UNDER—GRADUATE	COMPUTER SCIENCE	GYMNASTICS	JOSEPH A. CORRIGAN
897654321	FRANK H. FRAN	GRADUATE	ELECTRICAL ENGINEERING	PHYSICS	JOHN F. SLATTER
967831201	JANE F. BUNDY	GRADUATE	BIOCHEMISTRY	RADIOLOGY	ABRAHAM S. GOLDSTEIN

Figure 6.2a. STUDENT relation (table). The key attribute is NO-STUDENT (number of student). The nonkey attributes are NAME-STUDENT, STATUS, MAJOR, MINOR, and FACULTY-ADVISOR.

STATUS, MAJOR, MINOR, and FACULTY-ADVISOR. The primary key of this relation is NO-STUDENT. The values of the primary key are unique, that is, there are no two tuples (rows) with the same NO-STUDENT (number of student).

The COURSE relation in Figure 6.2b consists only of the attribute NO-COURSE (number of course), which is the key attribute. This table shows the numbers of all the courses taught at the university. Every course number appears only once.

The SEMESTER relation from Figure 6.2b has the attributes SE-MESTER (number of semester), DSTRTSEM (date of start of semester), and DENDSEM (date of end of semester), with SEMESTER being the primary key. Given the value of SEMESTER, there is only one tuple with that value; that is, there is only one DSTRTSEM and only one DENDSEM. The semester FALL, 1987 starts on September 10, 1987, and ends on December 22, 1987.

The relation that links the two relations SEMESTER and COURSE is SEMESTER + COURSE. The key attributes of that relation are SE-MESTER and NO-COURSE, and the nonkey attributes are COURSE-TITLE, NAME-INSTR, CAMPUS, DAY-TIME, and BLDG-NO-ROOM. The key is called a compound key because it is composed of more than one attribute. For a given SEMESTER and for a given NO-COURSE, there is only one COURSE-TITLE and one NAME-INSTR, CAMPUS,

COURSE Relation

NO-COURSE
CS601
CS603
CS605
CS618
CS623
EE101
PH500
⋮

SEMESTER Relation

SEMESTER	DSTRTSEM	DENDSEM
SPRING, 1986	JANUARY 12, 1986	APRIL 29, 1986
SUMMER, 1986	MAY 11, 1986	AUGUST 16, 1986
FALL, 1986	SEPTEMBER 9, 1986	DECEMBER 21, 1986
SPRING, 1987	JANUARY 10, 1987	APRIL 30, 1987
SUMMER, 1987	MAY 12, 1987	AUGUST 15, 1987
FALL, 1987	SEPTEMBER 10, 1987	DECEMBER 20, 1987
⋮	⋮	⋮

SEMESTER + COURSE Relation

SEMESTER	NO-COURSE	COURSE-TITLE	NAME-INSTR	CAMPUS	DAY-TIME	BLDG-NO-ROOM
SUMMER, 1987	CS608	COMPILER	A.B. ADAMS	BROOKLYN	THU 8–10 pm	MAIN601
SUMMER, 1987	CS623	SWITCHING AND DIGITAL SYSTEMS	J.N. DOLM	WHITE PLAINS	TU 6–8 pm	ACCT389
SUMMER, 1987	PH500	FIELD & WAVES	A.T. FRIEDMAN	BROOKLYN	MO 8–10 pm	AL302
FALL, 1987	CS601	INTRO TO COMP SCIENCE	A.B. ADAMS	WHITE PLAINS	W 6–8 pm	AL201
FALL, 1987	CS605	INFO STRUCT & ALGORITHMS	J.S. FINK	BROOKLYN	THU 8–10 pm	MAIN605
FALL, 1987	CS623	SWITCHING & DIGITAL SYSTEMS	A.M. JONES	LONG ISLAND	TU 6–8 pm	MAIN238
FALL, 1987	PH500	FIELD & WAVES	A.B. ADAMS	BROOKLYN	THU 8–10 am	ACCT389
⋮	⋮					⋮

Figure 6.2b. **Three relations are shown.**

155

SEMESTER	NO–COURSE	NO–STUDENT	CREDITS
SUMMER, 1987	CS608	967831201	4
SUMMER, 1987	CS608	897645123	2
SUMMER, 1987	CS623	967831201	3
SUMMER, 1987	PH500	967831201	4
FALL, 1987	CS601	123456789	3
FALL, 1987	CS601	897645123	2
FALL, 1987	CS605	123456789	2
FALL, 1987	CS623	967831201	3
FALL, 1987	PH500	897645123	3

Figure 6.2c. SEMESTER + COURSE + STUDENT relation. SEMESTER, NO-COURSE, and NO-STUDENT comprise the primary key. The nonkey attribute is CREDITS.

DAY-TIME, and BLDG-NO-ROOM. This table gives a user view of all the courses taught in a given semester and all the semesters where a given course is taught. For example, in FALL, 1987, the courses taught are CS601, CS605, CS623, and PH500, whereas the course CS623 is taught in the semesters SUMMER, 1987 and FALL, 1987. The combination of the values of NO-COURSE and SEMESTER uniquely identifies the values taken by the nonkey attributes.

Finally, the SEMESTER + COURSE + STUDENT relation in Figure 6.2c establishes the linkage at the third level in Figure 6.1 between SEMESTER, COURSE, and STUDENT. The primary key is composed of SEMESTER, NO-COURSE, and NO-STUDENT. The nonkey attribute is CREDITS. In one semester many courses may be taught, and one course may be taken by many students. On the other hand, a student may take many courses in a specific semester. This table reflects the many-to-many relationships between SEMESTER, NO-COURSE, and NO-STUDENT. In a given semester (e.g., FALL, 1987), a given student, 123456789 (JOHN F. SMITH), has elected three credits for a specific course, CS601.

The five relations from Figures 6.2a, 6.2b, and 6.2c are the user views or the logical model of the data base. This logical model is derived from the conceptual model in Figure 6.1. The key attributes are redundant in some of the user views. For example, NO-COURSE appears in three of the five relations. However, the relations in Figures 6.2a, 6.2b, and 6.2c are user views, and are not necessarily implemented physically in that way.

The mapping of the conceptual model onto a relational data model is a relatively easy process. Every box from the conceptual model becomes a relation or a table, and the user is supplied with the user view, which is in a table format. This is due to using a relational approach to designing the conceptual model.

6.2 MAPPING TO A HIERARCHICAL DATA MODEL

Deriving a logical hierarchical data model from a conceptual model is not a straightforward process in that many seemingly arbitrary choices can be made, and there is no one right result. However, the steps to be followed can be grouped into categories with rules and guidelines for the choices to be made within each category. These categories are as follows:

A. Derive a hierarchical data model without regard for a particular data base management system (DBMS).
B. Modify the data model to eliminate conflicts with the rules of the DBMS to be used.
C. Refine the modified data model according to some obvious performance considerations.
D. Simplify key names.
E. Add relationships that exist between data but have not surfaced in the logical model so far.

A. Derive a hierarchical data model without regard for a particular DBMS.

A.1. Eliminate superfluous relationships.

The relationship between A and C (Figure 6.3) is superfluous if it can be removed without any loss of essential information. The

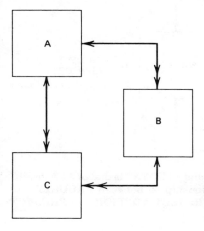

Figure 6.3. **The relationship between A and C is superfluous if the same relationship can be derived from the relationships between A, B and B, C.**

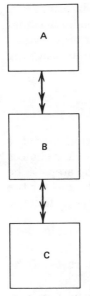

Figure 6.4. Direct relationship between A and C was removed from Figure 6.3. The relationships between A, B and B, C are intact, and the relationship between A and C can be derived through B.

relationship between A and C can be derived from the relationships between A, B and B, C.

After removal of the relationship between A and C, Figure 6.3 can be redrawn as Figure 6.4.

Before the removal of any relationship, it should be examined to determine whether any information could be lost. For example, consider Figure 6.5, where relationship ① between FACULTY

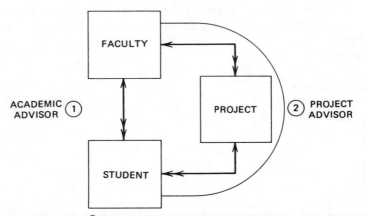

Figure 6.5. Relationship ① between FACULTY and STUDENT is that of ACADEMIC ADVISOR and ACADEMIC ADVISEE. Relationship ② between FACULTY and STUDENT is over PROJECT, that is, that of PROJECT ADVISOR and PROJECT ADVISEE.

and STUDENT is that of ACADEMIC ADVISOR and ACADEMIC ADVISEE. Relationship ② between FACULTY and STUDENT is over PROJECT. A faculty member may be an academic advisor or counselor for one group of students and also a project advisor for a specific project of another group of students. In this situation relationship ① is not superfluous and cannot be removed.

A.2. Derive parent-child relationships.

In the conceptual model, the boxes represent node types and the arrows represent parent-child relationships between these node types. In Figure 6.1 the root node types are the boxes at the first level, that is, STUDENT, COURSE, and SEMESTER. The box at the second level is SEMESTER + COURSE, which can be a child node type of SEMESTER or of COURSE. Here we have two root node types, that is, two hierarchical trees with the interconnecting node type SEMESTER + COURSE, as in Figure 6.6. A decision has to be made whether SEMESTER + COURSE should be a child of SEMESTER or of COURSE.

Let us further take a part of Figure 6.1 with the node types STUDENT, SEMESTER + COURSE, and SEMESTER + COURSE + STUDENT, as in Figure 6.7. The node type SEMESTER + COURSE + STUDENT could be a child of SEMESTER + COURSE at the second level or of STUDENT at the first level.

In this stage, the possible parent-child relationships are identified. These relationships are resolved in the next stage.

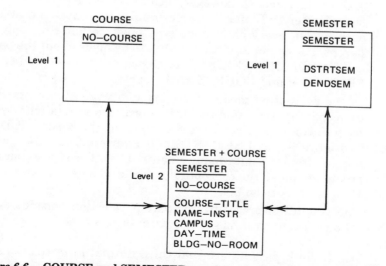

Figure 6.6. COURSE and SEMESTER are the two root node types. SEMESTER + COURSE is a node type that could be a child of either SEMESTER or COURSE.

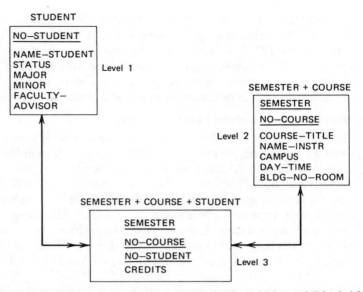

Figure 6.7. **SEMESTER + COURSE + STUDENT could be a child of either STU-
DENT or SEMESTER + COURSE.**

A.3. Resolve multiple parentage.

In the conceptual model as presented in Figure 6.1 and as seen
in its subsets as in Figures 6.6 and 6.7, there may be several
nodes with two or more parents. In Figure 6.6, SEMESTER +
COURSE has SEMESTER and COURSE as parents. In a hierarchical data model, however, a child can have only one parent
(see Chapter 4). To map the conceptual model onto a hierarchical
data model, every child node type must be left with only one
parent. For example, a decision has to be made about the parent
of SEMESTER + COURSE. A choice must be made between
SEMESTER and COURSE as the parent.

In the conceptual model, there are two types of parents. Some
of the parents represent real third normal form relations derived
from the data requirements. For example, the boxes STUDENT
in Figure 6.7 and SEMESTER in Figure 6.6 are the parents
derived from the data requirements. The other type of parent is
created to make the conceptual model complete, as explained in
Chapter 5, Section 5.4.

The resolution procedure for parent selection depends on the
following combinations of two parents at a time.

A.3.1. Both parents are real third normal form relations and
not the created ones. In Figure 6.8, the parents are X and

Y, and Z is the child. The resolution of multiple parentage may take place in either of two ways: X as a parent, Y and Z combined as a child; or Y as a parent, X and Z combined as a child. In both cases, redundancy may be introduced by making Y a part of a child of X, or, in the alternative solution, X a part of a child of Y. Thus, in resolving the multiple parentage of real parents, it must be decided whether both parents are necessary or whether one of them can be integrated into the child node at the cost of some redundancy. The third possibility is to integrate both parents and child in one node type, for example, X, Y, and Z combined as in Figure 6.8.

A.3.2. One parent is a real third normal form relation, and the other parent is a created one. The most probable candidate for removal may be the created parent. In Figure 6.9*a*, the child at the second level, SEMESTER + COURSE, has SEMESTER, which is a result of a real third normal form relation, as one parent, whereas the other parent is COURSE, which is a created one. The box COURSE has only one attribute, NO-COURSE. The same attribute is represented also in SEMESTER + COURSE. There will not be any loss of data or of relationships if we eliminate the box COURSE and make SEMESTER the only parent of SEMESTER + COURSE, as in Figure 6.9*b*. One precaution to be taken while eliminating the boxes is that no other relationships with the other boxes are left unresolved, as in Figure 6.9*c*.

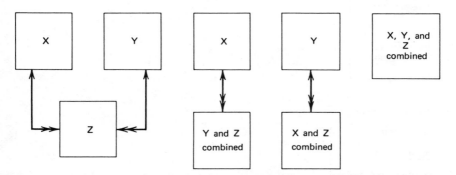

Figure 6.8.   Resolution of multiple parenthood. X and Y are the parent node types. Z is the child node type. The resolution of multiple parentage may take place with X as the parent, Y and Z combined as a child. It may take place with Y as the parent, X and Z combined as a child. It may also take place with X, Y, and Z combined into one node.

Figure 6.9a. **SEMESTER is a real parent, whereas COURSE is a created parent of SEMESTER + COURSE.**

After making the change indicated in Figure 6.9b to Figure 6.1, the logical model at this stage appears as in Figure 6.10.

A.3.3. Both parents are created ones. The most probable candidates for removal may be both parents. In Figure 6.10a, the created parents are X and Y, and the child is Z. X, Y, and Z may be integrated into one node type. Because both X and Y are removed, the combined node X, Y, and

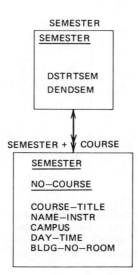

Figure 6.9b. **The created parent is removed, and the only parent left of SEMESTER + COURSE is SEMESTER.**

Figure 6.9c. **X is a good candidate for removal, as a parent of Z, because it is a created parent. Before removing the parent X, however, the other relationships indicated by the arrows pointing to X must be taken care of.**

Z moves one level higher in the hierarchy, as in Figure 6.10*b*.

A.3.4. If no decision can be reached with A.3.1 to A.3.3, the choice is arbitrary. The remaining parents of the child can be considered in the same way until either only one parent per child node is left, or a decision is made that the multiple parents are necessary. In such a situation, a DBMS has to be chosen that will support multiple parentage. The node SEMESTER + COURSE + STUDENT has two parents. We decide to leave that node with two parents, and the logical model remains the same as in Figure 6.10.

Steps A.3.1 to A.3.3 can be repeated in resolving multiple parentage with parents at the lower levels, for example, with parents at the second level and children at the third level, or with parents at the third level and children at the fourth level.

We are now ready to apply the rules of the DBMS to be used.

B. Modify the data model to eliminate conflicts with the rules of the DBMS to be used.

A number of data base management systems use a hierarchical data model. One of them is IMS (Information Management System), marketed by IBM. IMS also provides some network capabilities. When IMS is

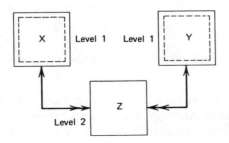

Figure 6.10. **Multiple parentage of SEMESTER + COURSE from Figure 6.1 is resolved. Multiple parentage of SEMESTER + COURSE + STUDENT is not yet resolved.**

used as the DBMS, some constraints are imposed on the model that may require modifications.

1. There can be no more than 255 node types (called "segment types" in IMS).
2. There can be no more than 15 hierarchical levels.
3. A child segment type can have at the most two parents. (A more detailed discussion of IMS will be given in Chapter 8.) One parent,

Figure 6.10a. **X and Y are the created parents. Both are candidates for removal for parent resolution.**

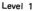

Level 1 | X, Y, and Z combined

Figure 6.10b. X and Y are combined with Z. The combined node goes one level higher than the previous level of Z.

in whose hierarchy the child is placed, is called a "physical" parent, and the other parent is called a "logical" parent. In Figure 6.10c, X is the physical parent, Y is the logical parent, and Z is the logical child. A constraint based on the logical child is as follows.

4. A logical child cannot have a logical child. In Figures 6.10c and 6.10d, Z is a logical child. Z cannot have M as a physical child that has a logical parent N, as in Figure 6.10c. Z cannot have M as a logical child whose physical parent is N, as in Figure 6.10d.

In Figure 6.10, none of the constraints listed above is violated; hence no modifications are required. The logical model to be used for IMS is thus as shown in Figure 6.10. The only decision yet to be made concerns the placement of the logical child SEMESTER + COURSE + STUDENT. This logical child has to be placed as the physical child of either STUDENT or SEMESTER + COURSE.

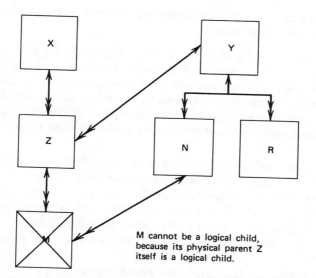

M cannot be a logical child, because its physical parent Z itself is a logical child.

Figure 6.10c. One hierarchical tree is composed of the nodes X, Z, and M. Another hierarchical tree consists of the nodes Y, N, and R. The node Z has X as its physical parent and Y as its logical parent; that is, Z is a logical child. The node M cannot be a logical child; that is, it cannot have two parents, Z and N. Z, being a logical child, cannot have a physical child M that has another parent, N.

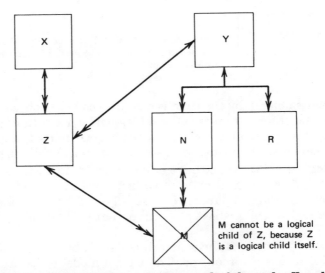

M cannot be a logical child of Z, because Z is a logical child itself.

Figure 6.10d. **One hierarchical tree is composed of the nodes X and Z. Another hierarchical tree consists of the nodes Y, N, R, and M. The node Z has X has its physical parent and Y as its logical parent; that is, Z is a logical child. The node M cannot be a logical child; that is, it cannot have two parents, N and Z. Z, being a logical child, cannot have a logical child M.**

C. Refine the modified data model according to some obvious performance considerations.

We are still working with the view of Figure 6.11 which is identical to Figure 6.10. This view will provide the functional capabilities required. The question now is, can performance capabilities be enhanced by combining segments to reduce the number of levels, splitting segments to provide more efficient data transfer or more security, combining hierarchies, splitting hierarchies, or making other types of arrangements?

Considerations of this type cannot be fully resolved without quantitative performance information, such as frequency of use of the various hierarchical paths, average number of occurrences of each segment type, and segment length. Thus a thorough treatment of these considerations belongs to physical design rather than to logical design. However, a few obvious choices can be made as part of the logical design process.

C.1. Parents having only one child segment type are potential candidates for combination with their children.

In Figure 6.11, SEMESTER has only one child, SEMESTER + COURSE. The trade-off is between redundancy and performance. Here SEMESTER has only two fields, DSTRTSEM (date of start of semester) and DENDSEM (date of end of semester). If we keep the segment SEMESTER as the parent of SEMESTER + COURSE, there will be only one occurrence of the SEMESTER segment per semester, that is, date of start of semester and date of end of semester will be stored only once each semester. But there will be at least one pointer from the semester occurrence to its first course occurrence. There will also be pointers between the semester occurrences. The time required for updating the pointers and the time required for accessing separate segments, SEMES-TER and SEMESTER + COURSE, have to be considered.

The alternative here is to combine the SEMESTER segment with the SEMESTER + COURSE segment, as in Figure 6.12. By combining the two segments, we are introducing redundancy on DSTRTSEM (date of start of semester), and DENDSEM (date of end of semester). If 50 courses are offered in a specific semester, there will be 50 occurrences of the SEMESTER + COURSE segment, and in each occurrence the fields DSTRTSEM (date of start of semester), and DENDSEM (date of end of semester) will

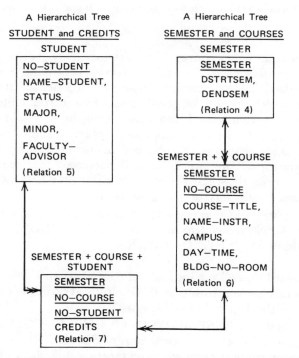

Figure 6.11. **Logical model with two hierarchical trees for the conceptual model from Figure 6.1.**

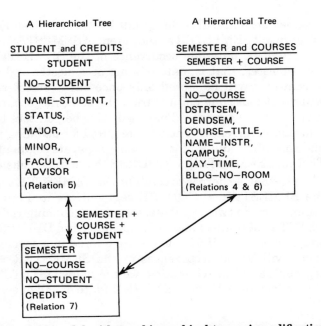

Figure 6.12. Logical model with two hierarchical trees. A modification of Figure 6.11.

appear for every course. This is redundancy of data, that is, more space will be used. The real problem could be maintaining integrity of data if the same data is stored more frequently than necessary. The major issue to be considered when introducing redundancy of data is volatility. If the data is volatile, it should not be stored redundantly. In this case, date of start of semester and date of end of semester are not volatile data elements for a given semester. Updating of the two fields will not occur too frequently. Thus combining SEMESTER with its child SEMESTER + COURSE seems intuitively to be a good move.

We have decided to make the segment SEMESTER + COURSE + STUDENT a physical child of the parent STUDENT and a logical child of SEMESTER + COURSE.

C.2. Should there be a logical relationship, or should the logical parent be combined with the logical child in order to eliminate the logical relationship?

In Figure 6.12 SEMESTER + COURSE + STUDENT is the logical child of the logical parent SEMESTER + COURSE. In IMS every root segment type starts a new data base. We have two hierarchical trees and two data bases. Every time an application program needs information about courses taken by a student, IMS will have to access two separate data bases, the STUDENT and CREDITS data base and the SEMESTER and COURSES data base. If we combine the logical child SEMESTER + COURSE + STUDENT with the logical parent SEMESTER + COURSE, the hierarchical tree will appear as in Figure 6.13.

The major consideration here for not having the hierarchical tree as in Figure 6.13 is the redundancy of volatile data about courses. A data base with this hierarchical tree will have redundancy of course occurrences for every student who has taken a particular course. For example, if students FRANK H. FRAN and JANE F. BUNDY have taken the same course, CS608, the course, with all the data about COURSE-TITLE, NAME-INSTR, and so on, will appear twice in the same data base. This type of redundancy may have adverse effects on data integrity. We do not choose to have one hierarchical tree, as in Figure 6.13, but prefer to have two hierarchical trees, as in Figure 6.12.

If we have a choice of having one hierarchical tree, as in Figure 6.13, we will have eliminated one physical data base, SEMESTER

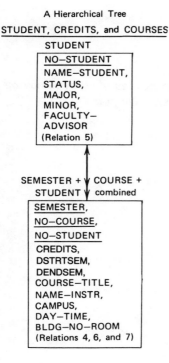

A Hierarchical Tree
STUDENT, CREDITS, and COURSES

STUDENT

| NO—STUDENT |
| NAME—STUDENT, STATUS, MAJOR, MINOR, FACULTY— ADVISOR (Relation 5) |

SEMESTER + COURSE + STUDENT combined

| SEMESTER, |
| NO—COURSE, |
| NO—STUDENT |
| CREDITS, DSTRTSEM, DENDSEM, COURSE—TITLE, NAME—INSTR, CAMPUS, DAY—TIME, BLDG—NO—ROOM (Relations 4, 6, and 7) |

Figure 6.13. Logical model with one hierarchical tree. Logical child and logical parent from Figure 6.12 are combined into one segment type.

and COURSES, as in Figure 6.12. Elimination of a physical data base is a strong consideration from the viewpoint of performance. Further performance considerations are discussed in more detail in Chapter 8, with quantitative information such as frequency of use of the various hierarchical paths, average number of occurrences of each segment type, and segment length.

D. Simplify key names.

Segments in a hierarchical path may now have key names as follows:

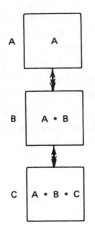

For each child segment, these key names may be simplified by removing the subsets that occur in the parent segment. We get:

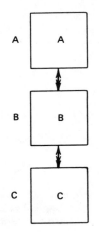

In a hierarchy the key of a child (called a physical child) is implied. But compound keys that represent logical children, which relate parents in different paths, are retained:

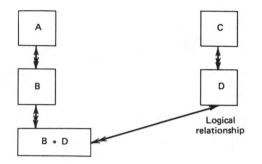

In Figure 6.12 the only segment where the key can be simplified is SEMESTER + COURSE + STUDENT. The segment is a logical child and relates parents in different paths. As a result we would like to keep the compound key SEMESTER, NO-COURSE, and NO-STUDENT.

E. Add relationships that exist between data but have not surfaced in the logical model so far.

The refined logical model in Figure 6.12 satisfies the functional data requirements, and it possesses intuitively better performance characteristics than the original conceptual model of Figure 6.1. At this point, the logical design with mapping to a hierarchical data model could be considered complete.

However, the designers may want to strengthen the logical design by adding some inherent (also called intrinsic) data relationships. These are data relationships that exist intrinsically because of the organizational or physical characteristics of the enterprise being modeled or because of the working relationships within the enterprise, but that were not explicitly requested in the data requirements. The reason for adding intrinsic relationships is to obtain a data base that is more likely to support ad hoc queries as well as additional future functions.

It is not necessary to add any relationships to the logical model in Figure 6.12.

The logical model for IMS may look as in Figure 6.12, and an external model that enables an application programmer to generate the report in Student Schedule List/Semester may look like the one in Figure 6.14.

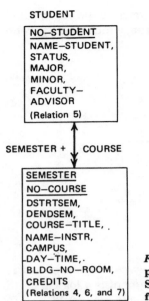

STUDENT

| NO—STUDENT |
| NAME—STUDENT, |
| STATUS, |
| MAJOR, |
| MINOR, |
| FACULTY— |
| ADVISOR |
| (Relation 5) |

SEMESTER +   COURSE

| SEMESTER |
| NO—COURSE |
| DSTRTSEM, |
| DENDSEM, |
| COURSE—TITLE, |
| NAME—INSTR, |
| CAMPUS, |
| DAY—TIME, |
| BLDG—NO—ROOM, |
| CREDITS |
| (Relations 4, 6, and 7) |

Figure 6.14. **An external model that enables an application programmer to generate the report Student Schedule List/Semester is based on the logical model from Figure 6.12 for IMS.**

6.3   MAPPING TO A NETWORK DATA MODEL

Mapping the conceptual model to a network data model is also not a straightforward process. Many arbitrary choices have to be made, and there is no one right result. The following major steps, similar to those used in mapping to a hierarchical data model, may be taken:

A. Derive a network data model without regard for a particular data base management system (DBMS).

B. Modify the data model to eliminate conflicts with the rules of the DBMS to be used.

C. Refine the modified data model according to some obvious performance considerations.

D. Simplify key names.

E. Add relationships that exist between data but have not surfaced in the logical model so far.

A.   Derive a network data model without regard for a particular DBMS.

A.1.   Derive owner-member relationships.

In the conceptual model, the boxes represent record types and the arrows ◄——►► represent mappings between the record types. We would like to use the "Bachman arrow" while discussing the network data model. If we redraw the conceptual model from Figure 6.1 with Bachman arrows, it will look like Figure 6.15. We also have named the set types as follows:

Set Type I. STUDENT-HAS-CREDITS with owner STUDENT and member SEMESTER + COURSE + STUDENT.

Set Type II. STUDENT-COURSE-CREDITS with owner SE-MESTER + COURSE and member SEMESTER + COURSE + STUDENT.

Between set types I and II, the member record type SEMESTER + COURSE + STUDENT is the link.

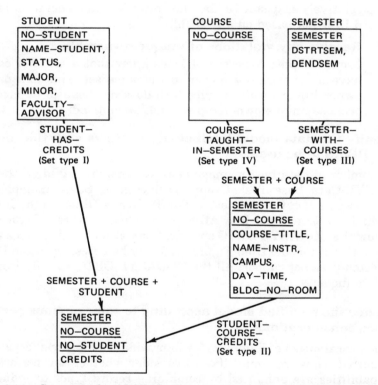

Figure 6.15. Conceptual model from Figure 6.1, redrawn using Bachman arrows. This figure could be used as a starting point for drawing a logical model. The following assumptions are made:

1. COURSE-TITLE is accompanied by SEMESTER and NO-COURSE. It is possible that for the same NO-COURSE the COURSE-TITLE may vary from one semester to another.
2. CREDITS is accompanied by SEMESTER, NO-COURSE, and NO-STUDENT. A student has a choice of selecting the number of credits in a semester and for a course.

Set Type III. SEMESTER-WITH-COURSES with owner SE-MESTER and member SEMESTER + COURSE.

Set Type IV. COURSE-TAUGHT-IN-SEMESTER with owner COURSE and member SEMESTER + COURSE.

Between set types III and IV, the member record type SEMES-TER + COURSE is the link.

The record type SEMESTER + COURSE is the member record type in set types III and IV and is simultaneously the owner record type in set type II.

Translating the conceptual model from Figure 6.1 into a logical model that is based on a network data model seems to be a relatively easy step so far. The network data model from Figure 6.15 is not based on any DBMS.

A.2. Resolve any violations of unique ownership.

From Chapter 4, Section 4.5, we know that a member cannot have more than one owner in the same set. This is a unique ownership criterion. Figure 6.15 does not have to be modified because unique ownership will not be violated.

B. Modify the data model to eliminate conflicts with the rules of the DBMS to be used.

A number of data base management systems are based on the CO-DASYL-Data Base Task Group specifications. Some examples are Honeywell's IDS/II, Cullinet's IDMS/R, DEC's DBMS, and Univac's DMS 1100, to name a few. All four set constructs from Figure 6.15 follow the CODASYL-DBTG specifications. Some modifications to the network data model from Figure 6.15 may be necessary if the DBMS selected does not support all the CODASYL-DBTG specifications for a data model.

C. Refine the modified model according to some obvious performance considerations.

The logical model of Figure 6.15 will provide the functional capabilities required. Now we would like to consider whether the performance capabilities are enhanced by combining record types to reduce the number of set types, whether more security can be provided by splitting the record types and increasing the number of set types, or whether some other type of arrangement will be more beneficial for the data base to be implemented.

With the network data model, unlike the other data models, the DA should be aware of how record occurrences will be stored, because the record definition must say how this is done. Choices made at this time can have a profound impact on the data base performance. For example, we could specify that the SEMESTER + COURSE + STUDENT record will be stored via the STUDENT-HAS-CREDITS set or the STUDENT-COURSE-CREDITS set. The choice is determined by which way access will be faster. (No matter which one is chosen, occurrences still can be accessed through either set.) See Chapter 9 for more information.

Considerations of this type can be resolved more effectively with the help of quantitative performance information, such as frequency of use of the various sets, average number of occurrences of each record type, and record length. Thus a thorough treatment of these considerations belongs to physical design rather than logical design. There are, however, some obvious performance considerations, as follows.

C.1. Don't overstructure.

STEP 1. Owners or members that are not providing any data in their own right may be removed. The best candidates for this consideration are the created record types. In Figure 6.15, the owner record type from set type IV is not providing any data in its own right. The data provided by the COURSE record type is NO-COURSE. The same data can be found in the member SEMESTER + COURSE. The resulting diagram after removal of the owner COURSE from set type IV is shown in Figure 6.16. The three set types left are:

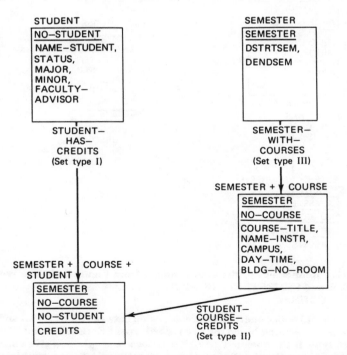

Figure 6.16. Refinement of the logical model from Figure 6.15. The owner COURSE from Figure 6.15 is removed. Only three set types are left.

Set Type I.   STUDENT-HAS CREDITS with owner STUDENT and member SEMESTER + COURSE + STUDENT.

Set Type II.   STUDENT-COURSE-CREDITS with owner SEMESTER + COURSE and member SEMESTER + COURSE + STUDENT.

Between set types I and II, the member record type SEMESTER + COURSE + STUDENT is the link.

Set Type III.   SEMESTER-WITH-COURSES with owner SEMESTER and member SEMESTER + COURSE.

STEP 2. Owners providing only trivial data and participating in only a small number of set types as owners are candidates for combination with their members if their contents are not volatile, that is, are not subject to much change. The owner record type SEMESTER from set type III in Figure 6.16 provides only DSTRTSEM (date of start of semester) and DENDSEM (date of end of semester) and participates in only one set type, III. SEMESTER from Figure 6.16 seems to be a good candidate for combination with the member record type SEMESTER + COURSE. The resulting diagram is shown in Figure 6.17. (In reality, semester dates would not be part of a

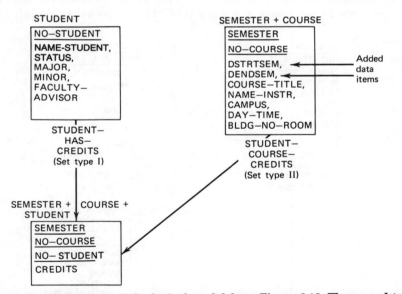

Figure 6.17.   **Refinement of the logical model from Figure 6.16. The record types SEMESTER and SEMESTER + COURSE are combined into one record type, SEMESTER + COURSE.**

The reader should notice one fact. The relationship between SEMESTER and COURSE is many-to-many. We combined the two record types SEMESTER and COURSE into one record type. If the question "Which courses are taught in a given semester?" is asked quite frequently, the designer must give thought to not combining the two record types into one record type.

data base because they are not used very frequently. The dates may be stored in a separate table.) The owner record type STUDENT does not seem to be a good candidate for combination with the member SEMESTER + COURSE + STUDENT in set type I. The STUDENT record type provides data in its own right about STUDENT.

The combined record type SEMESTER and SEMESTER + COURSE from Figure 6.17 is also not a good candidate for combination with the member SEMESTER + COURSE + STUDENT in set type II.

Figure 6.17 has two set types.

Set Type I. STUDENT-HAS CREDITS with owner STUDENT and member SEMESTER + COURSE + STUDENT.

Set Type II. STUDENT-COURSE-CREDITS with owner SEMESTER + COURSE and member SEMESTER + COURSE + STUDENT.

Between set types I and II the member record type SEMESTER + COURSE + STUDENT is the link.

D. Simplify key names.

Record types in a set construct may have key names as follows:

For each member, these names may be simplified by removing the subsets that occur in the owner record. We get:

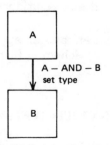

After simplifying the key names from Figure 6.17, the logical model is reflected in Figure 6.18.

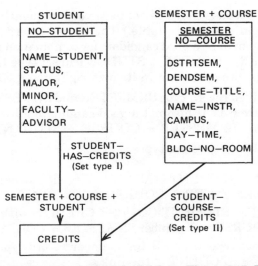

Figure 6.18. Refinement of the logical model from Figure 6.17. The elements <u>SE-MESTER, NO-COURSE</u>, and <u>NO-STUDENT</u> have been removed from the record type SEMESTER + COURSE + STUDENT.

The resulting logical model has two set types:

Set Type I. STUDENT-HAS-CREDITS with owner STUDENT and member SEMESTER + COURSE + STUDENT.

Set Type II. STUDENT-COURSE-CREDITS with owner SEMESTER + COURSE and member SEMESTER + COURSE + STUDENT.

Between set types I and II the member record type SEMESTER + COURSE + STUDENT is the link with the data item CREDITS.

E. Add relationships that exist between data but have not surfaced in the logical model so far.

It is not necessary to add any relationships to the logical model in Figure 6.18.

An external model that enables an application programmer to generate the report in Student Schedule List/Semester is identical to the logical model in Figure 6.18.

6.4 MAPPING TO AN INVERTED FILE DATA MODEL

Mapping the conceptual model to an inverted file data model is more straightforward than mapping to a hierarchical or to a network data model. But still many arbitrary choices must be made and there is no one right answer. Once again there are five steps to be followed:

A. Derive an inverted file data model without regard for a particular data base management system (DBMS).
B. Modify the data model to eliminate conflicts with the rules of the DBMS to be used.
C. Refine the modified data model according to some obvious performance considerations.
D. Select the attributes to be inverted.
E. Add relationships that exist between data but have not surfaced in the logical model so far.

A. Derive an inverted file data model without regard for a particular DBMS.

There are five boxes in Figure 6.1, each representing a relation in the conceptual model. In mapping to a logical model for inverted file, each of these relations becomes a file and each attribute becomes a field within the file. The five files resulting are as follows (see Figure 6.19):

The STUDENT file with fields NO-STUDENT, NAME-STUDENT, STATUS, MAJOR, MINOR, and FACULTY-ADVISOR.

The COURSE file with the single field NO-COURSE.

The SEMESTER file with fields SEMESTER, DSTRTSEM, DENDSEM.

The SEMESTER + COURSE file with fields SEMESTER, NO-COURSE, COURSE-TITLE, NAME-INSTR, CAMPUS, DAY-TIME, and BLDG-NO-ROOM.

The SEMESTER + COURSE + STUDENT file containing the fields SEMESTER, NO-COURSE, NO-STUDENT, and CREDITS.

The one-to-many relationships between the entities these files represent exist because the files contain common fields having common values. The primary keys in the relations of the conceptual model have not been implemented in the logical model at this stage.

B. Modify the data model to eliminate conflicts with the rules of the DBMS to be used.

Several data base management systems have the inverted file data model as their basic underlying data model. One of them is ADABAS (Adaptable Data Base System) marketed in the United States by Software AG of North America, Inc. ADABAS will be discussed in more detail in Chapter 10. We note here that the ADABAS term for an

STUDENT FILE

NO-STUDENT	NAME-STUDENT	STATUS	MAJOR	MINOR	FACULTY-ADVISOR
123456789	John F. Smith	Undergraduate	Computer Science	Gymnastics	Joseph A. Corrigan
"	"	"	"	"	"
"	"	"	"	"	"

COURSE FILE

NO-COURSE
CS601
CS603
"
"

SEMESTER FILE

SEMESTER	DSTRTSEM	DENDSEM
Spring, 1986	Jan. 12, 1986	April 29, 1986
"	"	"

SEMESTER + COURSE FILE

SEMESTER	NO-COURSE	COURSE-TITLE	NAME-INSTR.	CAMPUS	DAY-TIME	BLDG-NO.-ROOM
Summer, 1987	CS608	Compiler	A. B. Adams	Brooklyn	THU 8-10 PM	MAIN 601
"	"	"	"	"	"	"
"	"	"	"	"	"	"
"	"	"	"	"	"	"

SEMESTER + COURSE + STUDENT FILE

SEMESTER	NO-COURSE	NO-STUDENT	CREDITS
Summer, 1987	CS608	967831201	4
"	"	"	"
"	"	"	"

Figure 6.19. An inverted file logical model consisting of five files.

inverted field is "descriptor" and that ADABAS compresses all records stored in order to conserve physical storage space. The restrictions imposed by ADABAS are the following:

1. An ADABAS data base may contain up to 255 files.
2. Each file may contain up to 16.7 million records.
3. Each record may contain up to 926 fields.
4. A file may contain up to 200 descriptors.
5. A field may contain up to 253 bytes alphanumeric.
6. The maximum compressed record length is device dependent, usually 3000 bytes.

No modifications to the files in Figure 6.19 are required: ADABAS fully supports this logical model.

C. Refine the modified data model according to some obvious performance considerations.

Too many files in the inverted file logical model should be avoided. Data stored in many different files means that application programs must retrieve data from many files through calls to the DBMS. These calls must be queued, validated, interpreted, and executed. Physical I/Os must be done to the files. Too much of this activity leads to excessive overhead.

It is also desirable to reduce data duplication, if possible. For instance, in the SEMESTER + COURSE + STUDENT file, data values for a particular SEMESTER and NO-COURSE are being kept for each NO-STUDENT registering for that course in that semester. This leads to lowered storage efficiency.

While reducing the number of files will alleviate the problems described above, we do not want to pursue this course of action too far. In the extreme case there would remain a single file. The data independence, flexibility, and avoidance of anomalies gained by normalization in the conceptual model would be lost. The next two sections will examine how the choices are made in reducing the number of files and the duplication of data.

C.1. Don't overstructure.

As mentioned above, we would like to reduce the number of files in the logical model if this can be done in a way that preserves the desirable features of the model. To do this we look for files having small records (that is, few fields), containing nonvolatile data, or, in general, not contributing anything.

The COURSE file in Figure 6.19 is such a file. It contains no data which is not present in other files. It appears that there are no attributes which depend only on the attribute NO-COURSE. Since the COURSE file serves no useful purpose, we eliminate it.

The SEMESTER file in Figure 6.19 does contain fields which are present in no other file, DSTRTSEM and DENDSEM. However, there are only two such fields. Further, the values of these fields, once determined, are not likely to change. Therefore we would like to avoid devoting an entire file to holding only SEMESTER information. One widely used way to do this is to devote a single file, called a "table file," to contain all such small files (or tables) using the ADABAS feature of null suppression. Another, which we will use, is to incorporate the fields DSTRTSEM and DENDSEM into the SEMESTER + COURSE file, accepting the redundancy this creates.

After the COURSE and SEMESTER files are eliminated, as described above, we are left with three files in the logical model as shown in Figure 6.20. They are the STUDENT and SEMESTER + COURSE + STUDENT files, as before, and a modified SEMESTER + COURSE file.

C.2. Reduce the number of files and data duplication.

ADABAS provides several capabilities that allow the reduction of the number of files and data duplication. These are multiple value fields, periodic groups of fields, and multiple record types within a file.

Multiple Value Fields. A field defined to ADABAS is normally an elementary field. Such a field is permitted to have only one data value in each record occurrence. However, any field can be designated to ADABAS as a multiple value field. ADABAS will then allow this field to have several (in fact, up to 191) data values in a single record occurrence. ADABAS also has a feature called null suppression whereby contiguous fields having null values (zeros or blanks) can be represented using a single byte. Combining the two features of multiple value fields and null suppression permits 0 to 191 occurrences of a field in a record, but wastes little space if some occurrences are empty.

As an example of multiple value fields, consider a drug file in the surgical hospital environment where several side effects are required to be recorded for some drugs. The file could be defined as having two fields, Postoperative Drug and Side Effect of Drug.

STUDENT FILE

NO-STUDENT	NAME-STUDENT	STATUS	MAJOR	MINOR	FACULTY-ADVISOR
123456789	John F. Smith	Undergraduate	Computer Science	Gymnastics	Joseph A. Corrigan
"	"	"	"	"	"
					"

SEMESTER + COURSE FILE

SEMESTER	DSTRTSEM	DENDSEM	NO-COURSE	COURSE–TITLE	NAME–INSTR	CAMPUS	DAY–TIME	BLDG–NO–ROOM
Summer, 1987	May 12, 1987	Aug. 15, 1987	CS608	Compiler Switching & Digital Systems	A. B. Adams	Brooklyn	THU 8–10 PM	Main 601
Summer, 1987	May 12, 1987	Aug. 15, 1987	CS623	"	J. N. Dolm	White Plains	TU 6–8 PM	
"	"	"	"	"	"	"		
"	"	"	"	"	"	"	"	Acct 389
								"

Added Fields

Superdescriptor

SEMESTER + COURSE + STUDENT FILE

SEMESTER	NO–COURSE	NO–STUDENT	CREDITS
Summer, 1987	CS608	967831201	4
"	"	"	"
"	"	"	"

Descriptor

Figure 6.20. A logical model of three files after the elimination of the COURSE and SEMESTER files and the designation of descriptors (inverted fields).

If the latter is an elementary field, then three records are required to store the fact that Penicillin produces three side effects:

Penicillin	Rash
Penicillin	Fever
Penicillin	Dizziness

If the field Side Effect of Drug is defined to be multiple valued, then only one record is required and the data value "Penicillin" is stored only once:

| Penicillin | Rash | Fever | Dizziness |

Next we consider the case where data values for not just one but several related fields may be repeated.

Periodic Groups. ADABAS provides the capability for storing several data values, not just for a single field, but also for a group of contiguous fields that are related. A periodic group of fields defined to ADABAS is allowed to have up to 99 occurrences in a single record occurrence. Once again, this feature is usually combined with null suppression to save space otherwise occupied by null values.

For example, a surgery file in the surgical hospital environment could consist of four fields: Patient Number, Surgeon License Number, Date of Surgery, and Surgery. The Patient Number for a patient having several surgeries would be stored each time:

| 1111 | 145 | JAN. 1, 1985 | GALLSTONES REMOVAL |
| 1111 | 311 | JUNE 12, 1985 | KIDNEYSTONES REMOVAL |

If the last three fields were designated a periodic group, then one record would suffice:

| 311 | JUNE 12, 1985 | KIDNEYSTONES REMOVAL |
| 1111 | 145 | JAN. 1, 1985 | GALLSTONES REMOVAL |

Multiple Record Types within a File. Through the capability of null suppression, ADABAS effectively allows records of different types to be stored in a single file. This is done by defining a single record type containing all the fields of several different record types. Under program control, record occurrences stored in this file will contain data values for only one of the record types; the remaining fields will be null and reduce to an empty field count (EFC).

For example, data on Patient Number and Patient Details and on Patient Number and Surgery Details could be retained in two files:

| Patient Number | Patient Details | File 1 — Record Type 1
| Patient Number | Surgery Details | File 2 — Record Type 2

Alternatively, a single record type could be defined thus:

| Patient Number | Patient Details | Surgery Details |

↑
Composite Record Type

The record occurrences stored in the resulting single file would always be one of the following types:

| Patient Number | Patient Details | Record occurrence of Type 1

| Patient Number | EFC | Surgery Details | Record occurrence of Type 2

The EFC is stored in place of the null Patient Details fields; no EFC is needed in the first record occurrence since the empty fields in Surgery Details are at the end of the record.

When deciding the extent to which data duplication should be reduced, the high priority processing area should be considered first. The aim is to keep all the fields required by a processing area in one record. Duplication of fields that are frequently updated should be avoided. As a general rule, however, duplication of short fields that are frequently accessed but rarely updated need not be removed. In fact, it is sometimes useful to build in this type of data duplication to assist performance.

No change is made in the logical model of Figure 6.20. It is possible to include the fields SEMESTER, NO-COURSE, and CREDITS into the STUDENT file as a periodic group. However, this would restrict the number of courses for which an individual student could register. Similarly, incorporating the fields NO-STUDENT and CREDITS into the SEMESTER + COURSE file would eliminate a file, but would limit the students registering for a particular course.

D. Select the attributes to be inverted.

The attributes to be inverted (called descriptors in ADABAS) must be selected with care in an inverted file logical model. Designating a field as a descriptor implies that the DBMS will build and maintain an index file, perhaps to several levels, on the data values of that field. Storage efficiency will be reduced and processing time during updates increased.

On the other hand, fields must be inverted to allow quick access to and navigation of files. Descriptors are necessary to allow the easy and efficient implementation of the conceptual requirements, that is, to provide suitable external models.

In ADABAS, any field, or combination of (up to five) fields, or portion of a field may be declared a descriptor. An elementary descriptor may be designated as unique in which case ADABAS will not allow two records with the same descriptor value to be stored. In other words,

ADABAS will guarantee that a unique descriptor is what we called a primary key in the conceptual model.

Let us consider how a programmer would implement the conceptual requirement Student Schedule List/Semester (Figure 5.14) using the logical model of Figure 6.20. First, a program could read, in turn, each record in the STUDENT file since the report must be produced for each registered student; no descriptor is required to do this. Next, the program could easily retrieve those records in the SEMESTER + COURSE + STUDENT file for any individual student provided NO-STUDENT was declared a descriptor here. The program could then select those records for the current semester through program logic or, more easily, if the field SEMESTER was also inverted. Finally, the program could retrieve, from the SEMESTER + COURSE file, the course details (including DSTRTSEM and DENDSEM) for each course for which the student was currently registered—if SEMESTER and NO-COURSE were individually or collectively defined to be a descriptor. In the latter case, the two fields would be combined to form a superdescriptor (see Figure 6.20).

Viewed through the program just described, the files in the logical model of Figure 6.20 appear in the form of the hierarchical external model shown in Figure 6.14. Although this external model has no technical significance in ADABAS (it is never coded as such), the one-to-many hierarchical relationship between student and course is nevertheless achieved.

Finally, if desired, the field NO-STUDENT in the STUDENT file of Figure 6.20 could be defined as a unique descriptor. Then ADABAS would enforce the integrity of this field as arising from a primary key in the conceptual model.

E. Add relationships that exist between data but have not surfaced in the logical model so far.

It is not necessary to add any relationships to the logical model in Figure 6.20.

REFERENCES

1. Atre, S., "End-User Designed/Driven Data Bases," *Computerworld/Extra*, September 1, 1982.

2. Atre, S., "Integrating Tools Speeds and Simplifies Applications Building Process," *Product Spotlight/Applications Generation, Computerworld*, Vol. XX, No. 31, August 4, 1986.

3. Bachman, C. W., "Data Structure Diagrams," *Data Base*, Journal of ACM Special Interest Group British Data Processing, Vol. 1, No. 2 (Summer 1969).

4. *IMS/VS System/Application Design Guide*, IBM Corporation, 1133 Westchester Avenue, White Plains, New York.

5. Lyon, John K., *An Introduction to Data Base Design*, The Wiley Communigraph Series in Business Data Processing. New York: John Wiley & Sons, 1971.

6. Olle, T. William, *The CODASYL Approach to Data Base Management*. New York: John Wiley & Sons, 1978.

QUESTIONS

1. Describe the mapping from a conceptual model to a relational data model. Illustrate with an example.

2. List the general steps involved in mapping from a conceptual model to either a hierarchical or a network data model.

3. In mapping a conceptual model to a hierarchical logical model, it is best to derive a structure first without regard for a particular DBMS. What are the major objectives that a designer should consider in this phase? Discuss in particular the resolution procedure for parent selection and the possible decision points the designer may encounter in constructing the model.

4. Discuss possible steps that may be taken by the designer of a hierarchical logical model that may enhance the potential performance of a data base. Identify any inherent trade-offs that may exist in each optimization path.

5. In IMS what is the difference between a logical parent and a physical parent? What constraints are placed on logical children? How might key names of logical and physical children differ?

6. In the construction of a network logical model, the designer is often warned not to overstructure. What does this mean? In attempting to avoid this potential performance hazard, what issues of data redundancy and integrity must the designer evaluate?

7. List the general steps involved in mapping from a conceptual model to an inverted file data model.

8. How is it possible that some relationships that exist between data surface only after the conceptual model has been developed? Is this a weakness of the design, or is it to be expected that the awareness of new relationships is a desirable byproduct of the conceptual model? Discuss and give an example.

9. From the conceptual model of the hospital environment constructed for Chapter 5, question 11, construct a network, a hierarchical, and an inverted file logical model. Discuss resolution of transitivity, multiple parentage, and unique ownership, if needed. Show how alternative logical models may enhance or hinder performance.

Data Base Performance

CHAPTER 7

Data Storage and Access Methods

One of the major factors affecting the performance of programs interacting with the data base is the manner in which data is stored and accessed. A generalized data base management system uses some internal model access methods, in addition to the specialized access methods made available through the external model. The internal model is the physical model, and the external model is a user view. Some internal model access methods are identical to the access methods provided by the operating system. In most DBMS packages, the data base designer has the flexibility of choosing one or a combination of several access methods provided. To design a data base for efficient storage and access performance, the designer should be familiar with the internal model (physical model), as well as the external model (user view), access methods.

7.1 INTERFACES BETWEEN USER AND DATA BASE(S)

One can almost say that, as the number of physical inputs/outputs necessary for retrieving data to satisfy a user request increases, performance decreases.

To complete the loop beginning with the user request and ending with the satisfaction of that request, the system has to pass through a number of interfaces. (See Figure 7.1.)

Figure 7.1.   Fulfillment of a user request through the data base management system, external model access methods, internal model access methods, and operating system access methods.

Interface 1.   After a user request is passed on to the data base management system, the DBMS knows the description of the user view, of the application program, and of the security and privacy conditions. On the basis of the user view, it knows which physical data base(s) may be accessed. From the description of the physical data base(s), it also knows which internal model access method(s) may be used. This may differ from implementation to implementation, but most implementations support more than one user view of the data base.

Interface 2.   The data base management system in turn uses an internal model access method. This method (or methods) differs from one implementation to another. Some of these internal model access methods are specialized methods provided by the DBMS, and some are composed of the generalized access methods provided by the operating system. Two examples are ISAM (indexed sequential access method) and BDAM (basic direct access method).

Interface 3. The internal model access methods, together with the operating system access methods, access the physical data base record(s). Once access to the physical data base record(s) is gained, the requested data base record(s) may be found by using the access method(s) that describe the logical relationship between different parts of the data base record.

By using the operating system access methods and the internal and external model access methods, data from the physical data base(s) may be retrieved and presented to the DBMS. Then it is up to the DBMS to decide which part of the data may be presented to the user, in which format it will be presented, and so on. Descriptions of all these features must be provided to the DBMS by the data administrator prior to data base implementation.

Since the performance of a data base depends to a large extent on the internal as well as the external model access methods, we discuss them in this chapter. This discussion is intended to provide the reader with a conceptual knowledge of these access methods. The designer will need to study the implementation details of the different access methods of the specific data base management system purchased or leased.

7.2 INTERNAL MODEL (PHYSICAL MODEL) ACCESS METHODS

The internal model access methods discussed here are: physical sequential, indexed sequential, indexed random, inverted, direct, and hashing. (See Figures 7.2, 7.3, and 7.4.) For every internal model access method, we will consider two measures:

1. **Access Efficiency.** This measure is the inverse of the average number of physical accesses required per logical access. A logical access is a request for a specific data base record. Physical accesses take place to satisfy the request. For example, if the system needs to access two records to find the one desired, the access efficiency is 0.5.
2. **Storage Efficiency.** This measure is the inverse of the average number of bytes of secondary storage space required to store each byte of raw data. Space is required for the raw data, as well as for tables, control information, free space left for expansion, and space that is unusable because of fragmentation. A data base designer usually finds a trade-off between the access and storage efficiencies. As we move into the on-line environment, access efficiency becomes the primary issue. Some data base management systems are optimized for on-line updating. As we will see in Chapters 8, 9, and 10, access efficiency is indirectly dependent also on storage efficiency.

Physical Sequential	Indexed Sequential
• Key values of the physical records are in logical sequence.	• Key values of the physical records are in logical sequence.
• Main use is for "dump" and "restore."	• Access method may be used for storage as well as retrieval.
• Access method may be used for storage as well as retrieval.	• Index of key values is maintained with entries for the highest key values per block(s).
• Storage efficiency is near 100%.	• No duplicate key values are permitted.
	• Access efficiency depends on levels of index, storage allocated for index, number of data base records, and amount of overflow.
	• Storage efficiency depends on size of index and volatility of data base.

Figure 7.2. **Two of the internal model access methods: Physical Sequential and Indexed Sequential**

- **The access efficiency of the physical sequential leaves much to be desired. Every data base record has to be verified until the desired one can be retrieved.**
- **The access method in which only the key values are verified before the data base records are accessed is called the "indexed sequential access method."**

Figures 7.2, 7.3, and 7.4 provide an overview of the internal model access methods.

7.2.1 Physical Sequential

With the physical sequential access method, the physical records are stored in logical sequence. If the storage medium to be used is a tape, the

Indexed Random	Inverted
• Key values of the physical records are not necessarily in logical sequence.	• Key values of the physical records are not necessarily in logical sequence.
• Index may be stored and accessed with indexed sequential access method.	• Access method is better used for retrieval.
• Index has an entry for every data base record. These entries are in ascending order. The index keys are usually in logical sequence. If they are not in logical sequence, the index is accessed via a hashing algorithm. Data base records are not necessarily in ascending sequence.	• An index for every field to be inverted may be built.
	• Access efficiency depends on number of data base records, levels of index, and storage allocated for any index.
• Access method may be used for storage as well as retrieval.	

Figure 7.3. **Two of the internal model access methods: Indexed Random and Inverted.**

- **With the indexed random access method the records are stored at random. A separate file is created with entries of actual key values, together with the physical addresses of the records stored.**
- **The inverted access method is used, in general, for retrieval only. Some other access method is used for storage.**

Direct	Hashing
• Key values of the physical records are not necessarily in logical sequence.	• Key values of the physical records are not necessarily in logical sequence.
• There is one-to-one correspondence between a record key and the physical address of a record.	• Many key values may share the same physical address (block).
• Access method may be used for storage as well as retrieval.	• Access method may be used for storage as well as retrieval.
• Access efficiency is always 1.	• Access efficiency depends on distribution of keys, algorithm used for key transformation, and space allocated.
• Storage efficiency depends on density of keys.	
• No duplicate keys are permitted.	• Storage efficiency depends on distribution of keys and algorithm used for key transformation.

Figure 7.4.   **Two of the internal model access methods: Direct and Hashing.**
   • **With the direct access method the storage and retrieval of the physical record can be done at a unique storage location. For one record key there is a unique storage location.**
   • **There is a similarity between the direct access method and the hashing access method. With the hashing access method the address of the physical record is derived from the record key with the help of an algorithm.**

programmer has to present the physical records in logical sequence. If the storage medium is a direct access one, the system will interconnect the physical records so that they are in logical sequence, even if they were not presented in logical sequence.

Access Efficiency.   Let us assume that one physical record has been retrieved and another physical record with a higher key value is to be retrieved. In the worst case, the whole data base has to be accessed to retrieve the desired data base record, whereas in the best case only the next physical data base record must be retrieved to satisfy the requirement. On average, the number of data base records to be accessed for retrieval of the desired record is half the size of the data base.

Storage Efficiency.   If a tape is used as a storage medium, the programmer has to present the data base records in logical sequence. As a result there is no waste of storage on a tape. On the other hand, if a direct access device is to be used, the system assigns the next available physical storage to the next physical record presented. The data base records are then interconnected so that they can be retrieved in logical sequence.

The access efficiency of the physical sequential method leaves much to be desired. Every data base record has to be verified until the desired one can be retrieved. The fact that the physical records are stored in logical sequence can be used for faster access. It would be beneficial if only the key values could be verified before the data base records were accessed. The access method based on this concept is called "indexed sequential," and the repository of the key values is called an "index."

7.2.2   Indexed Sequential

There are a variety of indexed access methods. The basic principle for any such method is that a separate file or structure is created with entries of the actual key values. The entry of the actual key is called an "index entry," and the entire actual key file, as mentioned above, is termed an "index." The index file is much smaller than the data base itself and therefore can be searched much more rapidly because a number of entries may fit in memory.

In the indexed sequential access method, the index file is always sequential based on a key called the "primary key." The primary key is the major attribute of the physical record. On the basis of the value of the primary key, the physical records can be identified. As far as possible, records are stored in the same logical sequence as the index (hence the name indexed sequential access method). The index therefore needs a reference, not for every record in the data base, but only for the range of the records stored in one physical block. For example, if 10 records are stored in a block, only one entry in the index file is necessary, not 10 entries. In this case, the size of the index file will be reduced by a factor of 10.

Because the index file is sequentially ordered, it is possible to build an index on top of the index files. The index records can be grouped into blocks. In turn, these blocks can be indexed. For large files, this arrangement can be used effectively for better access performance.

Since the actual keys do not necessarily behave uniformly, it is not advisable to preassign the key values to the blocks in the data file. Instead, the data file is created by initially loading it with the physical records in the order of the primary key. The key value of the last record in the block, which is either the highest or the lowest (most vendor-supplied indexed sequential access methods load the data file in ascending sequence of the primary key value), is entered in the index file. (See Figure 7.5.)

In practice, how does the access method cope with the insertions of new records? Depending on the values of the added records, the index entries may have to be changed. What happens when a block does not have any more room for a new record?

There are two ways of handling this problem:

1. The record is stored in a separate area called an "overflow area," and the block is chained in the overflow area with the initial block where the record logically belongs. The access of the records in the overflow area may reduce the access efficiency considerably.

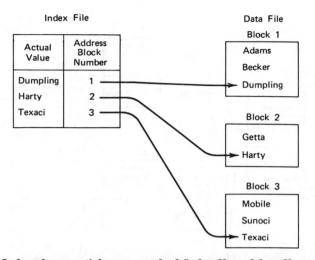

Figure 7.5.   **Indexed sequential access method. Index file and data file are in sequential order. Index file has only the highest value of the primary key in each block.**

2. When a block cannot accommodate any insertion, the block is divided
    in half. One new block contains half of the records of the initial block,
    and the other block contains the remaining half. (Sometimes the block
    is divided into two blocks such that one block contains two thirds,
    and the other block the remaining one third, of the records of the
    initial block.) A new entry is then made in the index file. In most
    cases, the access efficiency is better with this method as compared to
    chaining the records in the overflow area. But if the same blocks have
    to be split repeatedly, the file should be unloaded and reorganized
    and a new index file created. An example of this approach is IBM's
    VSAM (virtual storage access method).

    In the case of a very large file, it may be advisable to build a number
of index files. Another level of index file can be built pointing to these
index files. The building of this type of indexing may be done so that the
final index file is of reasonable size and can be kept in processor storage.
Figure 7.6 shows the building of higher level index files.

    The following major points must be considered in trying to achieve the
best performance with ISAM files.

Access Efficiency

1. **Size of the Data Base.**   As the size of the data base increases, more
    entries are made in the index. This probably results in a higher level
    of indexing. However, a large index file or a higher level of indexing

Figure 7.6. Indexed sequential access method. Index files with two levels. Because the index file is sequentially ordered, it is possible to build an index on top of the index files. The index records can be grouped into blocks. In turn these blocks can be indexed. This arrangement can be used effectively for large files for better access performance.

decreases access efficiency. In a large data base, the selection of primary and secondary keys is crucial.

2. **Record Size.** There is a trade-off between the size of the average record and the number of records in a data base. The bigger the size of the record, the smaller is the number of records in the data base, resulting in a smaller number of entries in the index. But the time

required for transferring the big data base records across the channels must be considered too. Determination of the optimum data base record size should be considered.

3. **Activity in the Data Base.** A higher level of insertion and deletion activity on the data base degrades access efficiency, that is, reorganization of the data base, together with the index files, should be planned from time to time. In some systems, this kind of activity does not significantly degrade access efficiency. However, the methods that make it possible to maintain access efficiency increase the size of the data base, that is, they decrease storage efficiency.

4. **Highest Level Index in the Processor Storage.** The allocation of enough processor storage for the highest level increases access efficiency.

Storage Efficiency

1. **Size of the Data Base.** As new records are added to the data base subsequent to the initial loading, the free space provided at the time of initial loading will be used. Storage efficiency depends on the percentage of free space provided. Since the records must preserve logical sequence, storage efficiency also depends on which part of the data base has the highest activity of addition and deletion of data base records. An analysis providing the value of free physical blocks and parts of blocks has to be carried out.

2. **Record Size.** The two factors affecting storage efficiency are record size and number of records. Larger records use less space for index entries. The number of records decreases as the size of the records increases. More levels of indexes are required as the number of records increases.

A final point that should be mentioned about the indexed sequential access method is that most vendors commonly restrict index keys to unique values.

For some applications, it is not necessary to process the data base records in logical sequence. In fact, it may be necessary to process the records in a random way. Nevertheless, the access method, called "indexed random," still relies on an index.

7.2.3 Indexed Random

For this access method, the records are stored at random, and a separate file is created with entries of the actual key values, together with the physical addresses of the records stored. The entry of the actual key, together with the address, is called an "index entry" and the entire file is termed an "index." In this access method there is an entry in the index for every data base record.

There are two major ways in which the index of the indexed random access method is created and accessed. In one way, the index is kept in collating sequence [e.g., IBM's Information Management System provides this facility, and it is called "secondary indexing" (see Figure 7.7)]. Access to the index is sequential, making it possible to process the records sequentially.

In the other way, the index itself is not kept in sequential order but a random access to the index is provided [e.g., Burrough's DMS-II provides random access to the index entries (see Figure 7.8)].

One aspect common to both ways of creating and accessing the index is that the records are not stored sequentially by the index key. That is the reason for calling this the indexed random access method.

The indexed random access method enables one to keep an index file on any field of the record, not necessarily on the primary key field. If duplicate key values exist, maintenance of the index file can be cumbersome.

Two major drawbacks of the indexed random access method are:

1. If the index is not kept in a sequential order, it is not possible to process the records sequentially with the help of the index only.

2. Because one entry exists for every record in the index file, the index file may become quite large.

Figure 7.7. Indexed random access method. The index file consists of an entry for every record, and the index entries are in ascending sequence. The target file is not necessarily in ascending sequence. Access to the index is sequential.

Figure 7.8. Indexed random access method. The actual key values go through the randomizing routine (RR), and the addresses for the records in the data file are calculated. There is a one-to-one correspondence between the address created and the physical record. Access to the index is through a randomizer.

To overcome these two major problems of the indexed random access method, the indexed sequential access method (ISAM) is widely used.

Access Efficiency

1. **Random Processing.** Because the index contains one entry for each record, the access efficiency is 1. This is true for only the primary key.
2. **Sequential Processing.** Because data base records are stored at random, and not necessarily in the logical sequence, the efficiency of sequential processing cannot be predicted. To mitigate the problem, the index may be kept in logical sequence.

Storage Efficiency

Size of the data base. The index will be quite large as a result of having one entry for every data base record. This may result in high levels of indexing.

If more than one attribute or a field of a record should be considered for retrieval by different applications, it may be necessary to build indices for the various attributes. The method based on this concept is called an "inverted" access method.

7.2.4 Inverted

The inverted access method is used, in general, for retrieval only, although some implementations do provide inverted updating capability too. In general, some other access method is used for storage. For example, a data base is loaded using any of the external model access methods discussed in this chapter. For each inverted field an entry is made in a table. The entry consists of the field name, the field value, and the record address. After the initial loading of the data base, sorting is performed on the field name and within the field name on the field value. For every field name, a separate index can be built. All the records with the same value for a field are grouped together, with the common value pointing to all the records with that value. As new records are added, entries are made to the appropriate index and to the appropriate value. And as records are deleted, the index entries from the appropriate index and for the appropriate values are removed. Figure 7.9 shows an example of the use of the inverted access method for the retrieval of records.

Access Efficiency. Before accessing the records from the data base, the index file(s) must be accessed. As a result, the access efficiency of

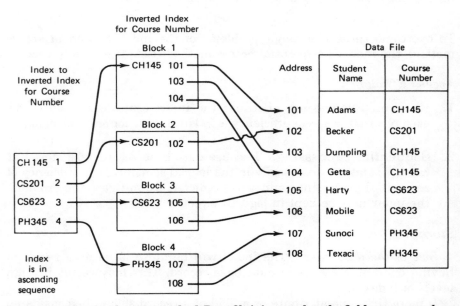

Figure 7.9. Inverted access method. Data file is inverted on the field course number. For each inverted field an entry is made in a table, also called an "index." The entry consists of the field name, the field value, and the record address. For every field a separate index can be built. This means that the data file is inverted on that field.

the inverted access method depends on the access method used for the index. In any event, at least one access is required to the index and at least one access to the data base record itself. The access efficiency is thus less than 0.5, at least two physical accesses being required for accessing one record. An analysis should be carried out to determine the access method for the index file(s). The access efficiency improves tremendously if the inverted index is kept in the storage during the data base processing.

Storage Efficiency.   The storage efficiency depends on the access method used for storing the data. If the only retrieval method to be used is the inverted one, the direct method (discussed in Section 7.2.5) using system-assigned keys can result in very efficient storage. The storage required for the index file will depend on the storage method used and the number of fields to be inverted.

7.2.5   Direct

The main characteristic of the direct access method is direct correspondence between the record key and the physical address of the record. The storage and retrieval of the physical record can be done at a unique storage location. The physical location of the record is derived from the key itself.

Access Efficiency.   The access efficiency is always 1 if the method is used in a direct way because of the one-to-one correspondence between the key value and the physical address of the record. If the physical records are not retrieved using this correspondence, the retrieval access efficiency will depend on the method of retrieval.

Storage Efficiency.   The storage efficiency depends on the density of the keys. If the keys are not dense, storage is wasted, because storage locations will be reserved for the missing keys. (See Figure 7.10.)

In the example of Figure 7.10, the algorithm used is: Strip off the X1 of all the source keys beginning with X1, and take the last two digits of the source key as the target key and the storage location. For the source keys that start with Y, strip off the Y and use the last three digits as in the target key and the storage location. Note that the physical record with the key Y102 is missing and that a storage location for that record will be reserved. Another drawback of this access method is that the keys have to be unique.

It is conceivable that, for some data bases, a one-to-one correspondence between the record key and the physical address of the record is not necessary. It may suffice to have a group of records point to the same physical address. This type of access method, called "hashing," is described in Section 7.2.6.

Student Numbers (source keys)	Keys Transformed (target keys)	Storage Locations (relative block numbers)	
X101	01	01	X101
X102	02	02	X102
X103	03	03	X103
•	•	•	•
•	•	•	•
•	•	•	•
X199	99	99	X199
Y100	100	100	Y100
Y101	101	101	Y101
(Missing)	(Missing)	Empty	
Y103	103	103	Y103

Figure 7.10. **Direct access method. Keys transformed (target keys) are based on the student numbers (source keys) giving the unique storage locations. The main characteristic of the direct access method is direct correspondence between the record key and the physical address of the record.**

7.2.6 Hashing

There is a similarity between the direct access method and the hashing access method in that the address of the physical record is derived from the record key with the help of an algorithm. The main difference between the two is the one-to-one mapping between the key and the address in the direct access method, and the potential many-to-one mapping between the keys and the address in the hashing access method (i.e., more than one key value may share the same address or the block).

The algorithm performing the key-to-address transformation is often called a "randomizing" or "hashing" routine. With this routine, the same key will always be transformed to the same address. The randomizing routine attempts to map a larger set of source key values to a smaller set of address places (usually relative block numbers). The keys mapped to the same physical address are called "synonyms." Since only one record can be stored in the randomized address, the synonyms have to be stored elsewhere. At the same time, some mechanism has to be provided to retrieve these synonyms. In most cases, the records with the synonym keys randomizing to the same physical address are chained, and the chain is called a "synonym chain." (See Figure 7.11.)

In Figure 7.11, the source key is Getta. The transformed key is 415, which is the address of the first record in the synonym chain. The Getta record points to the Mobile record at the address 423. The Mobile record points, in turn, to the Sunoci record with the address 852. And the Sunoci record points to the Texaci record at 900. This is the last record in the chain pointing to 0.

One major consideration when using a randomizing routine is the order of the transformed keys, that is, the order of the physically stored records does not match the order of the original keys. This may result in major difficulty in processing the physically stored records in sequential order by the original keys.

Access Efficiency.   The access efficiency of the random access method depends on three factors:

1. **Original Key Distribution.**   In many environments, the original key distribution is not totally random. The more the designer knows about the distribution, the better position he/she is in to select the number of blocks and the number of home addresses per block. The optimum selection of these factors will enable the designer to reduce the average length of the synonym chain. The access efficiency of the hashing access method depends greatly on the length of the synonym chain. In most data base management systems, the vendor-

Source Keys	Keys Trans- formed (target keys)	Address	Record Contents	Chain Pointer	Address	Record Contents	Chain Pointer
Adams	101	101	Adams	0	850		
Becker	213	213	Becker	0	852	Sunoci	900
Dumpling	311	311	Dumpling	0			
					900	Texaci	0
Getta	415	415	Getta	423			
Harty	420	420	Harty	0			
Mobile	415	423	Mobile	852			
Sunoci	415						
Texaci	415						
		Primary Storage Area			Overflow Storage Area		

Figure 7.11.   **Hashing access method. The algorithm performing the key-to-address transformation is often called a "randomizing" routine. It is also called a "hashing" routine. Note the synonym chain for the records with the keys Getta, Mobile, Sunoci, and Texaci.**

supplied hashing routines seem to do an excellent job and there is very little need for user-written routines.

2. **Space Allocated.** The key issue for access efficiency is even distribution of the actual keys over the number of blocks (i.e., the space allocated). If the output of the randomizing routine assigns many keys in one area, the result is a larger number of synonyms. Increasing the allocated space increases the number of addresses to which the randomizing routine can randomize.

3. **Randomizing or Hashing Routine** (also called algorithm or module). A good randomizing routine should distribute the actual keys evenly over the space allocated, thus reducing the average length of the synonym chain.

Storage Efficiency.   The storage efficiency depends on the space allocated and the randomizing routine. When using the hashing access method, it is advisable not to specify any free space within the blocks, as well as any free blocks. The reason is that the randomizing routine may randomize to the free blocks and to the free space within a block; this will result in putting the corresponding records into the overflow area. Determination of the page size also seems to be a major performance issue. Once the desired page is in the storage, searching the synonym chain is trivial compared to the physical input/outputs necessary if that is not the case.

Other, more complex access methods may be built with the help of the six internal model access methods described in Section 7.2.

7.3   EXTERNAL MODEL (USER VIEW) ACCESS METHODS

Access methods that describe the logical relationship may be called "external model access methods." Based on the data model used by the DBMS (e.g., relational, hierarchical, network, inverted file, or some combination), different user views may be provided for describing the logical relationship(s) between different parts of a physical record.

After gaining entry to the data base with the internal model access methods, the external model access methods are used for further retrieval of the data base records or of the parts of them. The external model access methods store or retrieve records on the basis of the relationships between the records. The relationships between the records depend on the data model used as an underlying data structure by the particular data base management system. It is possible that there are a number of external model access methods by which a record may be retrieved. But there is only one external model access method by which the record is stored.

7.3.1   Relationships between Two Records

To discuss the relationships between two records, let us examine the following case.

   Consider two records, X and Y. Record X is stored, and record Y is to be stored. Or record X is retrieved, and record Y is to be retrieved. If there is any relationship between the two records, X and Y, the possibilities are as follows for hierarchical and network data models:

1. **Sequence Field Relationship.**   Two records are related based on the key sequence field, that is, Y's key sequence field is next in sequence to X's key sequence field.

2. **Dependency Relationship.**   There is a dependency relationship between X and Y, that is, Y is a dependent of X.

   Hierarchical Data Model.   Y may be a child, and X may be a parent.

   Network Data Model.   Y may be a member record, and X may be an owner record.

3. **Parent Relationship.**   This is a dependency relationship with reversed roles of X and Y.

   Hierarchical Data Model.   The retrieved record X may be a child, and the record Y to be retrieved may be a parent.

   Network Data Model.   The retrieved record X may be a member, and the record Y to be retrieved may be the owner.

4. **"Near" Relationship.**   This relationship simply specifies that record Y should be stored near record X.

   Hierarchical Data Model.   There may or may not exist any specific relationship based on sequence field, dependency, or parentage between X and Y.

   Network Data Model.   There may or may not exist any specific relationship based on sequence field, dependency, or ownership between X and Y.

7.3.2   External Model Access Methods

Based on the four types of relationships between two records, there are four types of external model access methods. Two subcategories of these access methods are storage and retrieval. We will discuss the external model access methods for hierarchical and network data models.

1. **Sequence Field Access Method.**   Record Y to be stored is the one whose sequence field is next in sequence to record X.

   Hierarchical Data Model.   X and Y are of the same node type. If there is no node occurrence to establish the relationship, sequential next has no meaning.
   Network Data Model.   X and Y are of the same record type. If there is no record occurrence to establish the relationship, sequential next has no meaning.

The access methods for establishing the relationship based on the sequence field are as follows:

- *Prior*

   Hierarchical Data Model.   Either insert (store) or retrieve a node occurrence Y PRIOR to the node occurrence X.

   Network Data Model.   Either insert (store) or retrieve a record occurrence Y PRIOR to the record occurrence X.

- *Next*

   Hierarchical Data Model.   Either insert (store) or retrieve a node occurrence Y NEXT to the node occurrence X.

   Network Data Model.   Either insert (store) or retrieve a record occurrence Y NEXT to the record occurrence X.

2. **Dependency Access Method.**   Dependency access methods may be used for storage as well as retrieval of dependent nodes for hierarchical data model and of member records for the network data model.

The following options may be specified (see Figure 7.12):

- *First*

   Hierarchical Data Model.   Insert the most recent child as the first child Y of the parent X.

   Network Data Model.   Insert the most recent member as the first member Y of the owner X.

- *Last*

   Hierarchical Data Model.   Insert the most recent child as the last child Y of the parent X.

   Network Data Model.   Insert the most recent member as the last member Y of the owner X.

Figure 7.12. Dependency access methods: First, Last, Sorted (Next and Prior), and No Option. Dependency access methods may be used for storage as well as retrieval of dependent nodes for the hierarchical data model and of records for the network data model.

- *Sorted*

  Hierarchical Data Model. The dependent child should be inserted in the sorted sequence of the key. The child with the lowest sequence field is, therefore, logically the first one.

  Network Data Model. The dependent member should be inserted in the sorted sequence of the key. The member with the lowest sequence field is, therefore, logically the first one.

- *No Option*

  The data base management system will not maintain any dependency order.

The options for retrieval using the dependency access methods are as follows:

- *First*

  Hierarchical Data Model. Retrieve the first child. See Figure 7.12.
  Network Data Model. Retrieve the first member. See Figure 7.13.

- *Last*

  Hierarchical Data Model. Retrieve the last child.
  Network Data Model. Retrieve the last member.

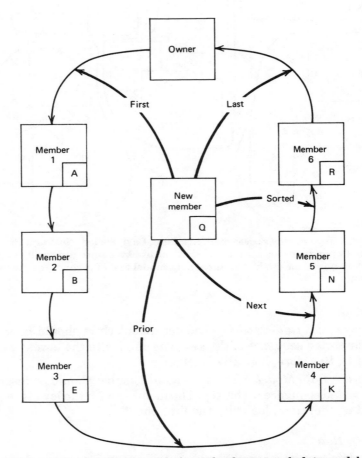

Figure 7.13. Set member relation rules for network data model.

- **First**
- **Last**
- **Prior**
- **Next**
- **Sorted (for insertion only)**

Parent or
owner

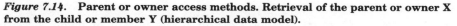

Figure 7.14. Parent or owner access methods. Retrieval of the parent or owner X from the child or member Y (hierarchical data model).

- *Prior*

   Hierarchical Data Model. Retrieve the prior child, with respect to the most recent retrieved.

   Network Data Model. Retrieve the prior member, with respect to the most recent retrieved. (The most recent member retrieved was Member 4 in Figure 7.13.)

- *Next*

   Hierarchical Data Model. Retrieve the next child with respect to the most recent one retrieved.

   Network Data Model. Retrieve the next member with respect to the most recent one retrieved. (The most recent member retrieved was Member 4 in Figure 7.13.)

- *Qualified*

   Hierarchical Data Model. Retrieve the child based on the qualification specified.

   Network Data Model. Retrieve the member based on the qualification specified.

When the dependency access method is used, the way in which node (or record) Y is inserted or retrieved depends on how the dependents are ordered, how the access is qualified, and which reference node (or record) was inserted or retrieved previously.

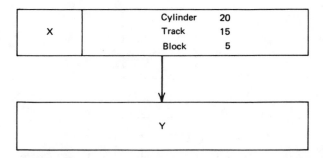

Figure 7.15. Direct pointer: the actual disk relative to the block address of record Y. For advantages and disadvantages, see Table 7.1.

3. **Parent or Owner Access Method.** The parent or owner access method is the reverse of the dependency access method.

    Hierarchical Data Model. A child cannot exist without its parent. This implies that the child cannot be stored before the parent. The parent access method thus cannot be used for the storage of the child and of the parent. This access method can be used, however, for retrieval of the parent from the child. (See Figure 7.14.)

    Network Data Model. In some implementations of the network data model, a member may exist without its owner. In such implementations the owner access method may be used for storage as well as for retrieval of the owner from the member. (See Figure 7.14.)

4. **Near Access Method.** The near access method is a storage-only data model access method.

Figure 7.16. Relative pointer: a relative pointer establishes itself in the context of something else. For advantages and disadvantages, see Table 7.2.

Figure 7.17. **Symbolic pointer: the key of record Y. The key makes possible access through one of the internal model access methods. For advantages and disadvantages, see Table 7.3.**

Hierarchical Data Model. A child is to be stored physically near its parent in a given hierarchical relationship.

Network Data Model. A member is to be stored physically near its owner in a given network relationship.

The external model access methods are often implemented with pointers. There are three types of pointers:

1. **Direct Pointer** (see Figure 7.15). The direct pointer is the actual disk relative block address of record Y pointed to and is stored in record X pointing to record Y.

Table 7.1. Advantages and Disadvantages of the Direct Pointer

Advantages

Access efficiency is the best. Once the direct address of a record is known, only one access is necessary for its retrieval. In most cases, a direct pointer is shorter than the corresponding symbolic address.

Disadvantages

A direct pointer is device dependent. If a record moves, all the direct pointers pointing to it must be updated.

Table 7.2. Advantages and Disadvantages of the Relative Pointer

Advantages

The advantage that the relative pointer has over the direct pointer is that, when files are moved to different devices (or just copied, for that matter), the only thing that the DBMS has to know is the location of the starting address. No other information has to be changed.

The advantage that the relative pointer has over the symbolic pointer is twofold: very little processing cost or time is involved in converting the key to a pointer, and the pointer is usually much smaller. The relative key is the concatenation of a data base page and a line number. The DBMS and the monitor then compute which page this is relative to the beginning of the file. After the page is accessed, the DBMS uses the line number as a negative offset on the bottom of the page. This offset contains a second offset, which is the exact location on the page.

Disadvantages

Although a relative pointer is not as device dependent as a direct pointer, it still relies on a preknowledge of the position. With a symbolic key, on the other hand, the records can be moved into a different arrangement, and all that needs to be changed is the algorithm that creates the address. Thus, in a system using symbolic pointers, no updating is necessary.

2. **Relative Pointer** (see Figure 7.16). The logical pointer is an identifier that can be mapped to an actual disk relative to the block address. For this type of pointer, the first part is the data base page, which can be transformed into a page offset from the beginning of an area. The second part of the pointer gives an offset from the bottom of this page that contains the real position on the page.

3. **Symbolic Pointer** (see Figure 7.17). The key of record Y pointed to is stored in record X pointing to it. The internal model access method has the responsibility of finding record Y.

The direct, relative, and symbolic pointers each have advantages and disadvantages, as listed in Tables 7.1, 7.2, and 7.3.

Table 7.3. Advantages and Disadvantages of the Symbolic Pointer

Advantages

A symbolic pointer is device independent. If a record moves, the symbolic pointers pointing to it do not have to be updated.

Disadvantages

Access efficiency may not be the best. The address of the record searched has to be resolved based on the symbolic pointer. A symbolic pointer is usually longer than a direct pointer.

REFERENCES

1. Atre, S., *Data Base Management Systems for the Eighties*. Wellesley, Massachusetts: QED Information Sciences.
2. Atre, S., "Technology, Intelligent Software Guide Market Growth," *Computerworld*, Special Report, June 24, 1985.
3. Curtice, Robert M. (Staff Member, Arthur D. Little, Inc.), *Data Base Management— Access Mechanisms and Data Structure Support in Data Base Management Systems*, Monograph Series. Wellesley, Massachusetts: QED Information Sciences.

QUESTIONS

1. What is meant by external model and internal model access methods? How do they differ? Relate? Why does the data base designer need to be familiar with both types of access methods?

2. After a user request is made, what information does the DBMS have available?

3. Access methods are measured by access efficiency and storage efficiency. Define each term and its major objectives. Which is the more important consideration in a) a batch environment and b) an on-line environment? Why?

4. Discuss the differences between physical sequential and indexed sequential organizations. Explain which method achieves superior access efficiency; which achieves superior storage efficiency. To what type of applications would each be suited?

5. How do the indexed sequential and physical sequential access methods cope with insertions of new records?

6. What are the advantages and disadvantages of the indexed random access method?

7. In what type of processing environment would an inverted file structure be most useful? How can the direct access method be incorporated with the inverted structure to overcome some of the inefficiencies of file inversion?

8. In which access method do synonyms occur? Describe this phenomenon and the techniques employed to handle its occurrence within a data base.

9. Discuss the similarities and differences of the direct and hashing internal model access methods. Compare their access and storage efficiencies. Name an application that would be suited to each.

10. Identify and define the four external model access methods. Explain how retrieval and storage of data is accomplished in each method for either the hierarchical or network data model.

11. External model access methods are often implemented using pointers. Describe the three types of pointers cited in the text. Under what circumstances would you prefer each type of pointer?

12. Assume a telephone book is a file whose entries are records containing the fields: name, address, and phone number. Describe the process to find the phone number of a person given that person's name and address using the:

   a) physical sequential access method
   b) indexed sequential access method.

Hierarchical Data Base Management Systems

Some of the oldest data base management systems are based on a hierarchical data model. One of them is IBM's Information Management System, IMS/VS. We shall see how the access methods are implemented in this system, and how the physical model is designed and evaluated.

8.1 IMPLEMENTATIONS OF THE ACCESS METHODS (IMS: INFORMATION MANAGEMENT SYSTEM)

A data base management system uses a combination of internal model access methods and external model access methods for storage and retrieval of the records in the data base. A data base designer is faced with a wide variety of options; and the selection of the appropriate ones is crucial, because these options affect the performance of the operations on the data base. To be able to appreciate the process of option selection, let us look at some of the implementations of the access methods available for IMS.

The main component of IMS is Data Language/I (DL/I). The data model and the access methods are contained in DL/I, which distinguishes between the physical data base(s) (called the internal model in Chapter 1), and the logical data bases (called the external model(s) in Chapter 1). The logical data bases are the views supplied to the application programmers. These views are always hierarchical. This is the main reason for putting IMS in the category of hierarchical data base management systems, although the logical relationships provide some network data model capabilities to IMS users.

The physical data base consists of a treelike structure. The node types referred to in Chapter 4, Section 4.4 on the hierarchical data model, are called "segment types." The root node type is called the "root segment type." The hierarchy of the segment types is defined as top to bottom and left to right. (See Figure 8.1.) The segment code assigned to the segment types is also in the same order. Every root occurrence starts a new physical record. (See Figures 8.2 and 8.3.) The child occurrences of the child segment type are called "twin occurrences." The segments in a physical data base are connected with physical relationships; the relationships in a physical hierarchy are physical parent, physical child, and physical twins.

Physical data bases may be split into several files, but a file may not contain segments from different physical data bases. In a physical data base with IMS:

1. The data base contains a single type of root segment.
2. The root may have dependent child segment types.
3. Each child of the root may also have any number of child segment types, up to a maximum of 15 segment types in any one path.
4. There can be up to 255 segment types in one physical data base.

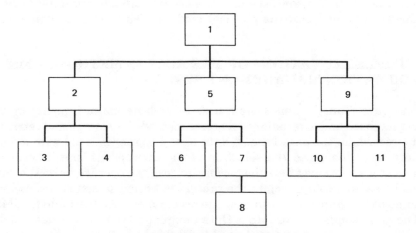

Segment Types Numbered in Hierarchical Sequence

Figure 8.1. Physical data base structure for IMS. The hierarchy of a physical record starts with the first occurrence of segment type 1. Depending on that occurrence, there is the first occurrence of segment type 2 and all the dependents of types 3 and 4. The hierarchy continues with the next occurrence of segment type 2 and all the dependents of types 3 and 4. When all the occurrences of type 2 are exhausted, the hierarchy continues to the right with segment type 5, and so on.

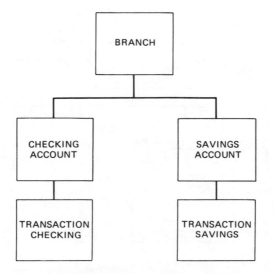

Figure 8.2. **Physical data base record starts with a root.**

5. For any occurrence of any given segment type, there may be any number of occurrences (possibly zero) of each of its children.

6. No child segment can exist without its parent.

Logical data bases are the views of the application programmers. These views are strictly hierarchical, but they can be constructed with the help of one or a number of physical data bases with the provision of logical relationships. Thus the capability of logical relationships in IMS provides some of the network data model properties. The logical relationships are explained later in this section.

Internal Model Access Methods for IMS. For a physical data base, there are four basic access methods, which use two methods for relating the segments:

Hierarchical Sequential (HS). The relationships among the segments of a hierarchy reflect the physical sequence in top-to-bottom, left-to-right order, that is, the segments of a data base record are related by physical adjacency. (See Figure 8.4.)

Hierarchical Direct (HD). The hierarchical relationships among the segments are represented by pointers, called "physical pointers." The pointers are physically stored in the prefixes of the segments. The dependency relationships are parent, child, and twins, and the relationships between parent and child are shown by first child, last

Figure 8.3. Every root occurrence starts a new physical record in IMS. One physical record starts with the occurrence of the root (Branch 123) and further consists of all its dependents (such as checking accounts, transactions on the checking accounts, savings accounts, and the dependent transactions).

Figure 8.4. In the hierarchical sequential access method, the segments are related by physical adjacency in the top-to-bottom, left-to-right, and front-to-back manners.

child, and physical parent. In IMS terminology, these pointers are physical child first (PCF), physical child last (PCL), and physical parent (PP). The dependency relationship next among twins is represented by physical twin forwards (PTF), and the relationship prior by physical twin backwards (PTB). (See Figure 8.5.) For a direct organization in IMS, the mandatory physical pointers are PCF and PTF, and the optional direct pointers are PCL, PTB, and PP.

Four internal model access methods that use the two methods, hierarchical sequential and hierarchical direct, for relating the segments, are:

HSAM: Hierarchical sequential access method.
HISAM: Hierarchical indexed sequential access method.

Figure 8.5. Direct pointers are used for relating the segments from the hierarchy in the hierarchical direct access method in IMS.

HIDAM: Hierarchical indexed direct access method.

HDAM: Hierarchical direct access method.

HSAM and HISAM use the hierarchical sequential method, and HIDAM and HDAM the hierarchical direct method, for relating the segments.

HSAM can be best described by saying that it is tapelike. The only basic access method used here is physical sequential.

HISAM uses a combination of the basic access methods indexed sequential and physical sequential. There is indexed access to the root and sequential access to the dependents. The index data set is stored and accessed by the indexed sequential access method (ISAM) or the virtual storage access method (VSAM). The index data set consists of root occurrences and as many dependent segments as will fit in a fixed length space in the primary data set (see Figure 8.6); that is, the index is nondense. Other segments are stored in the secondary data set. The segments do not get split, and there are no pointers between them. As a result, when new segments are to be inserted, the existing stored segments may have to move. At the time of loading, all the root occurrences are inserted in the primary data set. Subsequent additions of new root occurrences are inserted in the secondary data set, which is stored and accessed by the overflow sequential access method (OSAM) or by VSAM.

HIDAM uses indexed access to the root and direct access to the dependents; that is, once the basic access method indexed is used to gain access to the root, the data model access methods first, last, next, and prior are used for accessing the dependents. The index data set consists

Figure 8.6. **Hierarchical indexed sequential access method (HISAM) in IMS. HISAM provides indexed access to the root and sequential access to the dependents.**

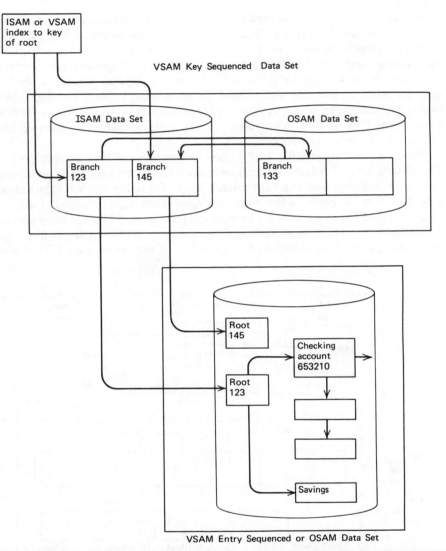

Figure 8.7. **Hierarchical indexed direct access method (HIDAM) in IMS. HIDAM provides indexed access to the root and direct access to the dependents.**

of only the root occurrences; that is, the index is dense. The storage and access to the roots are provided by ISAM or VSAM. The dependents of the root are stored in a secondary data set and accessed by OSAM or VSAM. (See Figure 8.7.) Among the root and the dependents, the pointers used are PCF and PTF, these two pointers being mandatory, and PCL, PTB, and PP, these three pointers being optional.

HDAM also uses the hierarchical direct access method for relating the segments of the hierarchy. The major difference between HDAM and HIDAM is that in the former the address where a root is stored is calculated using an algorithm called a "hashing algorithm" or a randomizing routine. The root and a specified number of bytes of the dependents are stored in the root addressable area (RAA), and the remaining bytes of the dependent segments are stored in the non-root-addressable area, which is an overflow area. (See Figure 8.8.) The basic access method used for storing and accessing the roots is random.

Every block in the RAA has a specified number of root anchor points. The HDAM randomizing algorithm takes the source key and produces the block number and the root anchor point from the block as the target key. If two roots hash to the same address, a synonym chain is built.

In HISAM the segments move, but in HIDAM and HDAM they do not. In HISAM, the space used by the deleted segments is not freed until the next reorganization, whereas the deletion of segments in HIDAM and

Figure 8.8. Hierarchical direct access method (HDAM) in IMS. HDAM provides random access to the root and direct access to the dependents.

Figure 8.9. Data base record occurrences of the CUSTOMER data base with inversion on account number.

HDAM frees the space. The HDAM organization also provides faster access to the dependent segments in the hierarchy. One drawback of HDAM is that the sequential processing of the root segments is awkward, as compared to HISAM and HIDAM.

HSAM, HISAM, HIDAM, and HDAM use a combination of the basic access methods and the data model access methods for storing and accessing the data base records using the hierarchical data model.

Secondary Indexing with IMS. The accessing of a data base record using HSAM, HISAM, HIDAM, or HDAM starts at the root level. To provide an entry at a lower level than the root, or to provide access on a secondary key to the root, IMS provides a capability called "secondary indexing." Secondary indexing is IMS's version of the inverted file structure.

In Figure 8.9, the root is CUSTOMER and the dependent segments are ACCOUNT and LOAN. If the data base is inverted on account number, a secondary indexing capability can be provided on account number. A secondary data set is maintained by IMS. The logical view provided to the application programmer is shown in Figure 8.10.

IMS also provides some network capability using its logical relationships.

Logical Relationships with IMS. The external models as explained in Chapter 1 are called "logical views" in IMS. The logical views are provided to application programmers for the coding of programs. In plain physical data bases, the segments are related to one another within a hierarchy. A facility provided by IMS called "logical relationships" enables one to span the relationships between segments across two or more physical data bases or between segments in different branches of the physical hierarchy. (See Figures 8.11, 8.12, and 8.13.) A logical view may be a subset of a physical data base or a view from a number of possible views provided by a physical data base(s) using logical relationships. A logical view may provide the user with an alternative view of data.

Two segments involved are said to have a logical relationship. The subordinate segment is called logical child; the other segment, logical parent. There are three possible ways of implementing logical relationships.

Unidirectional logical relationship. A logical parent pointer is used to point from logical child to logical parent. In Figure 8.14 (which is identical to Figure 4.14 in Chapter 4), there are two hierarchical structures with segment B a logical child of segment C, and D a logical child of segment A. Two logical relationships are involved. Pointers used are Physical Child First (PCF), Physical Twin Forwards (PTF), Physical Parent (PP), and Logical Parent (LP). Two of the possible logical views are shown

Figure 8.10. **Logical view based on inversion of account number as provided to application programmer.**

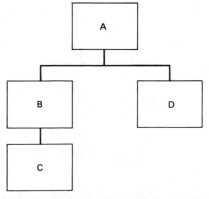

A physical data base without logical relationship

A logical view as a subset of the hierarchy above.

Figure 8.11.

in Figure 8.15. A logical view is the application programmer's view of the data base. There is total redundancy of data in segments B and D in the data bases of Figure 8.14. To have data integrity, the application programmer is responsible for updating any part of D if the identical part of B is to be updated and vice versa. IMS can remove this responsibility from the application programmer by providing a second type of logical relationship, called the "physically paired bidirectional logical relationship."

Physically paired bidirectional logical relationship. Segments B and D in Figure 8.16 are interconnected or "physically paired." Redundancy of data in B and D is still there. The main difference between two unidirectional logical relationships, as in Figure 8.14, and a physically paired bidirectional logical relationship, as in Figure 8.16, is that IMS automatically updates D if B is updated and vice versa. The pointers used are

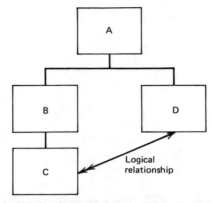

A physical data base with logical relationship between
segments in different branches of the physical hierarchy.

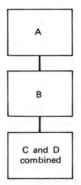

A logical view using the physical data base above with
the logical relationship.

Figure 8.12.

physical child first (PCF), physical twin forwards (PTF), physical parent
(PP), logical parent (LP), and pair (for pairing B and D). Two of the
possible logical views provided to the application programmer are the
same as in Figure 8.15. To avoid redundancy between B and D and to
avoid the overhead of updating D when B is updated and vice versa, there
is another way of providing the same logical views, called the "virtually
paired bidirectional logical relationship."

Virtually paired bidirectional logical relationship. To eliminate redundancy between B and D, one of the two may appear as a physical
segment. In Figure 8.17, B is physically present. The pointers used are

physical child first (PCF), physical twin forwards (PTF), physical parent (PP), logical parent (LP), logical child first (LCF), and logical twin forwards (LTF). The pair pointer has disappeared because D is not physically present; that is, D is virtually paired with B. Two of the possible logical views provided to the application programmer are the same as in Figure 8.15.

A logical data base (LDB) is composed of logical records based on a logical view. A logical record may be identical to a physical record or may be a combination of parts of different physical records from a single physical

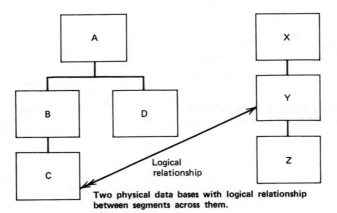

Two physical data bases with logical relationship between segments across them.

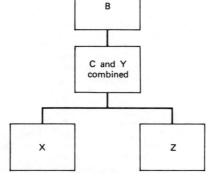

A logical view using the physical data bases above with the logical relationship.

Figure 8.13.

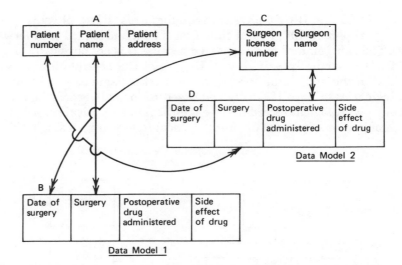

Data Model 2

Data Model 1

Figure 8.14. **Two physical data bases with two unidirectional logical relationships. B is a logical child of C, and D is a logical child of A.**

Application Programmer's View 1

Application Programmer's View 2

Figure 8.15. **Two of the possible logical views based on the physical data bases from Figure 8.14. The logical views are supplied to application programmers.**

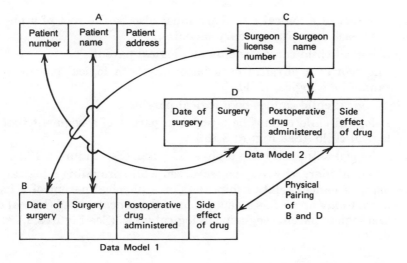

Figure 8.16. **Two physical data bases with physically paired bidirectional logical relationship. B and D are physically paired. If B is updated, IMS automatically updates D and vice versa.**

data base or from a number of them. There are some rules for supporting logical relationships.

Rules for Logical Relationships

1. Every logical view is a hierarchical view. But this hierarchical view may be different from the hierarchical structure represented by the underlying physical data bases.

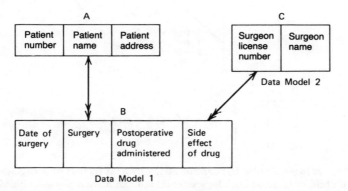

Figure 8.17. **Two physical data bases with virtually paired bidirectional logical relationship. B is physically present, and D is virtual.**

2. The root of a logical data base must also be the root of a physical data base (except secondary indexing).

3. A logical child can have only one logical parent.

4. The root of a physical data base may be a logical parent, but it cannot be a logical child.

5. A logical child cannot be a logical parent.

6. A logical child cannot be a physical parent of a segment that is a logical child. (See Figure 8.18.)

7. A logical child can have a physical child. (See Figure 8.18.)

8. Physical hierarchy may be traversed while providing a logical view using a logical relationship, that is, a physical parent of a logical parent may appear as a dependent of the concatenated (logical child and logical parent) segment in logical view. (See Figures 8.18a and 8.19.)

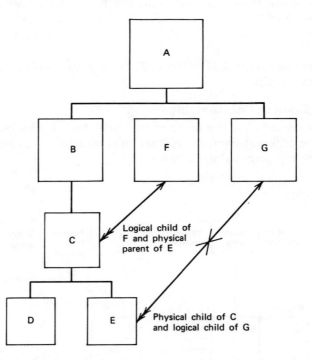

Figure 8.18. A logical child (C) cannot be a physical parent of a segment (E) that is a logical child of G (Rule 6). A logical child (C) can have a physical child (D) (Rule 7).

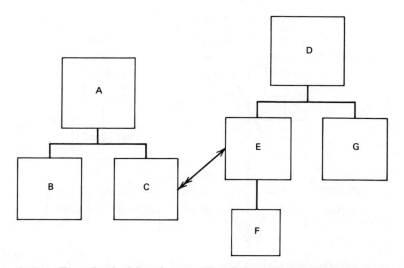

Figure 8.18a. Two physical data bases with a logical relationship. D is the physical parent of the logical parent E. F is a physical child of the logical parent E.

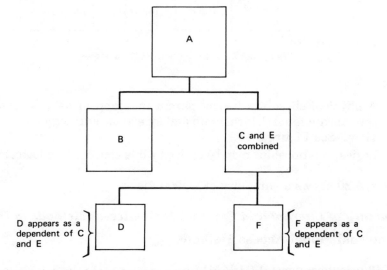

Figure 8.19. A logical view based on the two physical data bases with a logical relationship from Figure 8.18a.

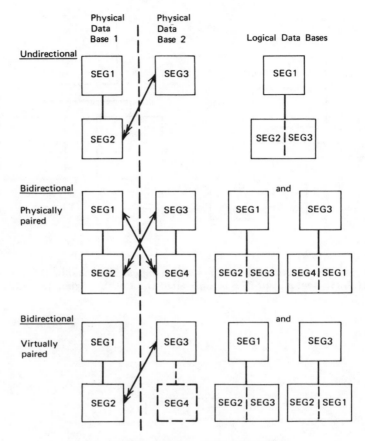

Figure 8.20. **Summary of logical views.**

9. A physical child of a logical parent may appear as a dependent of the concatenated (logical child and logical parent) segment in logical view. (See Figure 8.19.)
10. Logical relationships may be crossed while constructing logical views.

Figure 8.20 shows a summary of logical views.

Summary of Internal and External Model Access Methods in IMS/VS

Internal Model Access Methods

- Physical sequential (HSAM).
- Indexed sequential (HISAM, HIDAM).

- Random (HDAM).
- Inverted (secondary index).

External Model Access Methods

- Logical sequential (HSAM, HISAM, HIDAM).
- Physical hierarchy and modified hierarchy with logical relationships:

  Physical child (first, last).
  Physical twin (forwards, backwards).
  Physical parent.
  Logical child (first, last).
  Logical twin (forwards, backwards).
  Logical parent.
  Pair (physically paired bidirectional).

8.2 DESIGN A PHYSICAL MODEL OF A DATA BASE

In Part 2 we designed a conceptual and a logical model of a data base with obvious performance issues in mind. This and the following section discuss the next two data base design steps from Figure 1.8. The first of the two steps is designing a physical model of a data base for the chosen data base management system. The second of the two steps is evaluating the physical model for performance.

Two Steps of Data Base Design (Physical Model). The physical model is a framework of the data base to be stored on physical devices. Since a large percentage of data bases is used in an on-line environment, one has to be very concerned with visible performance. It is absolutely mandatory to evaluate the performance characteristics of the physical model before implementing the data base. Performance prediction is a multivariate analysis with the physical model as a major variable. One should carry out a quantitative analysis of the physical model with average frequencies of occurrences of the groupings of the data elements, with expected auxiliary space estimates, and with expected time estimates for retrieving and maintaining the data.

The applications using the data base can be categorized into groups based on their importance to the enterprise, as well as on the usage pattern. Time estimates for these applications may be predicted. A pencil and paper method will be used for the estimation process. Any major flaws in the design may be detected, and the physical design of the data base can be evaluated before it is put into production. Performance estimation in the design phase should have full support from management because, once a data base is installed, it is extremely difficult, if not impossible, to redesign it. It is like an arrow that has left the bow.

A data base designer generally tries to optimize the physical model for space and time considerations. Trade-offs between space and time are found in almost all DBMSs; that is, a number of physical input/outputs can be eliminated if some redundant data is carried; or not carrying redundant data may save space but cost more time. But one should not become absorbed by the space and time optimization and forget about the business requirements. It is possible that, from the business viewpoint, it is necessary to have multiple entry points into a data base, or to access a particular segment type with more than one key. To provide this type of access, it may be necessary to invert the segment on the keys, thereby posing some overhead on space and/or time. If so, that is the price that has to be paid for satisfying this particular business requirement.

Three major areas of expertise are needed by the designer of the physical model of a data base:

1. Knowledge of the DBMS functions.
2. Understanding of the characteristics of direct access devices.
3. Knowledge of the applications.

The first area where the physical model designer has to have expertise is knowledge of the DBMS, be it IMS, IDMS/R, ADABAS, IDS/II, DBMS-10/20, or TOTAL, to name just a few. The designer has to know how the DBMS performs its specific functions. Consider the example of DELETE. Delete means something to all of us. It means get rid of something. Some systems may get rid of a record physically; that is, the space is freed and compacted. Other systems may only mark the record as deleted without claiming the space on disk; that is, the record is deleted only logically. The second type of deletion may cause some problems in the long range as far as the disk space is concerned, as well as the time for fetching the desired records. Because of large unused space between the desired records, it may take longer to fetch the next record that is wanted. Knowledge of the DBMS to be used at the primitive function level is a necessity for the physical model designer.

The second area of expertise involves the characteristics of direct access devices. It is true that on many occasions we still think in terms of serial processing. When someone says get the next record, we expect the desired record to be physically close to the one we are working on. The thought that the next record may be three disk packs away may be disconcerting.

While designing the physical model of a data base, we need to worry about the physical aspects of the data base, that is, the record layout on disk, blocksizes, buffer sizes, and input/output characteristics, to name just a few examples. If these aspects are not considered in the physical model, the data base may collapse as a result of poor performance.

The third area is applications. The designer has to know the relationships of data elements and of entities referenced in the applications, that is, the external models. He or she must also know high-volume transactions, and response time requirements for an on-line environment. It is necessary to know the major batch programs and critical turnaround time requirements for a batch environment.

In the next section, a set of general rules for designing a physical model to avoid gross mistakes is discussed. These rules are sufficient only for first-pass analysis; they do not recognize specific circumstances.

Physical Model Design Guidelines. We will consider guidelines for a DBMS that uses a hierarchical data model as its underlying structure. Most of the guidelines given below can be used for any DBMS with a hierarchical data model; for example, SYSTEM 2000, marketed by SAS Institute, and Mark IV, marketed by Informatics, Inc. In particular, we will place some emphasis on IBM's Information Management System (IMS); especially, the terminology used is from IMS.

1. **Keep the Hierarchical Structure as Simple as Possible.** The hierarchy is defined in top-to-bottom and left-to-right order. The root is the dominant segment type. If secondary indexing capability is disregarded, access of any data base record takes place with the access of the root. The segments at the bottom and to the right of the hierarchy are the ones that are remote from the root. For this reason, the structure should be kept simple with fewer levels and less spread from left to right. The key issue here is not the number of segment types but the number of segment occurrences. A complex structure is usually an oversegmented structure. A result of over-segmentation is excessive DL/I calls and accesses of segments, as well as longer reorganization times. An analysis should be performed to find alternatives to secondary indexing and logical relationships. Secondary indexing provides multiple key retrievals at the cost of updating secondary data sets. Logical relationships give network capabilities at the cost of updating logical pointers and possibly of having to access a number of physical data bases. The key issue in designing a physical model is considering alternative solutions.

2. **Do Not Sacrifice Security and Data Independence Because of too Few Segments.** If the same amount of data is stored in fewer segments, the amount per segment is relatively large. As a result of the segment level access, an application programmer may be presented with data not required by the application. Fewer segments with the same amount of data affect security as well as data independence. The trade-off here is between too few and too many segments.

3. **Keep Frequently Accessed Segments Near the Top of the Hierarchy.** Since access to the data base records normally starts at

the root level, data in the root segment is accessed faster than that in any other segment in the hierarchy. Ideally, most frequently accessed data should be kept at the root level. If that is not possible for security, privacy, or redundancy reasons, the next desirable level is the second level, as far left in the hierarchy as possible. This minimizes the probability of physical I/O when the segment is accessed from the root. One of the factors that increases the probability of physical I/O for accessing a segment from the root is the distance between them.

4. **Split Segments in Accordance with the Key Ranges.** In a hierarchical data model, if the segments are split according to the key ranges, access to the desired segment will probably be more selective and faster.

The answers to the following questions should also be considered in developing guidelines:

5. **What about a Segment Type Whose Relative Frequency Under Its Parent Is 1?** One has to be suspicious about a segment of this type. The real question posed is why the segment is not included in the parent segment. Possible justifications for separation may be security, possibility of multiple occurrences of the segment, or no occurrences of the segment.

6. **What about a Segment Type Whose Prefix Length Is Greater Than Its Data Length?** The prefix for every segment consists of pointers, physical as well as logical. If the prefix length is greater than the data length for a segment, it is advisable to consider merging the segment with its parent. If, for security reasons, the segment cannot be included in the parent segment and if the segment is not keyed, it may be possible to reduce the multiple occurrences of the segment to one occurrence only. If the segment with a longer length of prefix than of data is a root segment, it may be possible to merge the root segment with some second level segments to form a new root segment.

7. **When to Use Variable-Length Segments and When Not to?** If a child segment is most likely to occur once or not at all, it is the best candidate to be moved to the parent segment. The parent can be made a variable-length segment.

If a segment is most likely to grow in size after the initial insertion, it will be split and inserted in the data base. This may require two I/O operations for its retrieval. A segment that may grow in size after the initial insertion is not the best candidate for a variable-length segment.

8. **How to Deal with Different Volatilities of the Segments? How to Separate Segments with Discrepancies in Sizes and Dis-**

crepancies in Usage? Problems of this nature may be resolved by using data set groups of a data base. A part of the data base may be stored as one data set group, whereas another part may be stored as another data set group. Different blocksizes and different free spaces may be specified for the data set groups. The segments that are accessed more frequently and together may be stored in one data set group. The segments to be accessed on-line may be separated from the segments to be accessed in batch. Data set groups may also be used to shorten the path to certain segments at the expense of others.

9. **When to Split One Physical Data Base into a Number of Physical Data Bases?** One physical data base of IMS is based on one hierarchical data model; that is, there is one root segment type per physical data base. If one physical data base is expected to become too big and there is a constraint (which most probably there will be in most data base environments on time availability for reorganization), or if because of high volatility there will be a need for frequent reorganizations, it may be advisable to split the physical data base.

But there is a trade-off between one physical data base and a number of physical data bases. The operational issues of backup and recovery become more complicated as the number of physical data bases increases. A costly process, as far as time is concerned, is opening and closing the data bases. As the number of physical data bases increases, the number of openings and closings increases too.

10. **How to Provide Alternative Access Paths besides the Strict Hierarchy?** Although IMS provides a hierarchical view to an application programmer, it offers a facility called "secondary indexing" that enables it to access a segment on its own without having to go through the strict hierarchy of a root and its dependents. IMS also provides a restricted network capability, called "logical relationships." Both these features, secondary indexing and logical relationships, have to be specified in the physical model of the data base.

   10.1. **Secondary Indexing.** With secondary indexing, IMS data base records can be accessed on data elements other than the primary key.

   The data element used as the entry point is called the "source segment." Secondary indexing enables the data base designer to invert the hierarchy. But secondary indexing should not be used for sequential processing. It is also not advisable to use secondary indexing on highly volatile source segments.

   Extensive use of inverting data base records is made by System 2000, marketed by SAS Institute.

   10.2 **Logical Relationships.** IMS provides many-to-many mapping with the help of logical relationships. This feature also helps to reduce the redundant data. The logical relationship must be specified in the physical data bases. The placement of the logical child in the physical data base may be critical from the viewpoint of performance; the logical child should be placed where the requests originate most frequently. Misplacement of the logical child may result in long logical twin chains, which may degrade the performance to a large extent because each access will probably result in an I/O.

Symbolic pointer and direct pointer have their benefits and drawbacks. An analysis should be performed to decide the types of pointers to be provided in the logical child segments. Unidirectional, physically paired bidirectional, and virtually paired bidirectional—each of the three methods has its benefits and drawbacks. Different trade-offs have to be made and decisions taken on an individual basis.

8.3 EVALUATE THE PHYSICAL MODEL OF A DATA BASE

Evaluating the physical model prior to implementing the data base and writing any application code seems to be a desirable method of comparing design alternatives. In Section 8.2, we studied some trade-offs in the process of migration from the logical model to a physical model. As a result of trade-offs, there may be a number of alternative physical models that have to be evaluated. Two estimates that play a major role in the evaluation process are space and time. The emphasis here is on desk checking.

The calculations made to answer the following questions often help in comparing the alternatives:

1. How many of each segment type are there?
2. What is the average data base record size, and how large is the data base?

Since one of the factors affecting time is the number of physical I/Os necessary to carry out a call, it is necessary to know the probability that two segments will be in different blocks or control intervals. With these probabilities and with the call patterns based on the applications, the designer is in a position to develop rough time estimates. We are not considering a data base that was loaded some time ago. Depending on its volatility, such a data base may consist of some fragmented space, some deleted parts of the data base records may still be occupying the physical space, and so on. The data base under consideration here is a newly loaded or a reorganized one. These basic facts about a data base also provide the usual side benefits of a programmed approach—consistent input, consistent output, and good documentation.

8.3.1 Space Estimates

A physical model can be evaluated only with detailed knowledge of a specific data base management system. Here we will consider IMS as the given DBMS.

At this point in design, one is not concerned with precise calculation of total direct access storage device space. It is usually sufficient to deal only with segment storage. As a result, we will not compute any index storage needed by the access methods.

The following assumptions are made for the data base design analysis, which uses a pencil and paper method described below.

1. All data bases are as they were at initial load, or just after reorganization.
2. Segment sizes are small relative to blocksizes.
3. The child segment occurrence frequencies relative to the parents within a data base are independent random variables.
4. The segments are assumed to be of fixed length.
5. If not specified otherwise, the frequency distribution of a child segment under its parent is uniform.
6. Data base records with distinctly different patterns of segment occurrences are not treated. They should be modeled as separate cases.
7. The I/O estimates help the designer translate segment accesses into I/O. However, the translation of DL/I CALLS into segment accesses has to be done with the help of the external models (called "logical" data bases in IMS) based on the internal model (called "physical" data bases in IMS).

The data base design analyzer will develop the space estimates and study the I/O characteristics. (See Figure 8.21.) Knowing the I/O characteristics, the call patterns, and the unit path length (i.e., the number of instructions necessary to carry out a CALL) it should provide quantitative estimates of DL/I (Data Language/I is the data base control part and the Data Manipulation Language of IMS) performance.

The basic facts necessary for estimating the space are the answers to these questions:

1. What is the hierarchy?
2. What is the length of every segment type? Here we consider not only the data length but the space taken by pointers too. The pointers used may be physical or logical ones, for example, Physical Child First, Physical Child Last, Physical Twin Forwards, Logical Child First, Logical Child Last, and Logical Parent.
3. What is the expected relative frequency of occurrence of every segment type relative to its parent? The length of a data base record depends

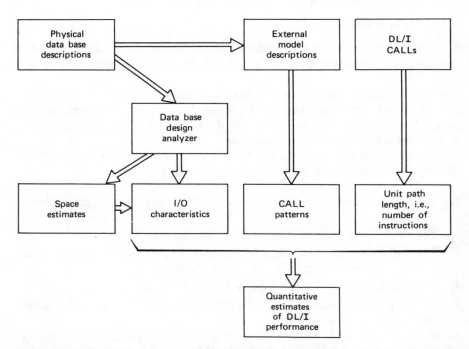

Figure 8.21.   **DL/I performance. DL/I is the data base control part and data manipulation language of IMS. The external model is called a "logical data base" in IMS.**

not only on the segment types in the data base but also (and mainly) on the segment occurrences. With the same reasoning, the distance between any two segment occurrences depends on the number of segment occurrences between them.

Using these factors, the designer can find:

1. The average physical data base record size in bytes.
2. The size of the data base.

IMS uses the hierarchical tree structure as its basic data model. A tree is composed of a number of subtrees. Since the hierarchical tree structure is an upside-down tree, we will take the bottom-up approach. The subtree of a segment A (S_A) is defined as one occurence of A and occurences of all its dependents. The subtree size of A (S_A) is then A's own length and the total of all the lengths of its dependents.

The space required on the direct access storage device is calculated in terms of SEGMENT BYTES, that is, the bytes occupied by the segments. SEGMENT BYTES is computed using the concept of a subtree.

In Figure 8.22, there are 2000 occurrences of segment A, and, for each occurrence of segment A, on an average 5 occurrences of segment B and 50 occurrences of segment C. With the bottom-up approach:

$$S_B \text{ (subtree of B)} = 30, \qquad S_C \text{ (subtree of C)} = 15, \qquad \text{and}$$

$$S_A \text{ (subtree of A)} = 1000$$

Figure 8.23 gives the subtree size of the isolated segment type X. The subtree size of any isolated segment type X is

$$S_x = L_x + (F_1 \times S_1) + (F_2 \times S_2) + \cdots + (F_N \times S_N)$$

The subtree size of the root is the same as the average physical data base record size. This leads the designer to the SEGMENT BYTES, that is, the number of bytes needed by the segments of the data base.

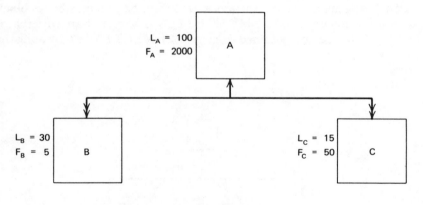

L = length of segment (including prefix)

F = relative frequency of occurrence of segment per occurrence of its parent

S = subtree size

Subtree size of a segment is one occurrence of the segment and all occurrences of all its dependents.

Calculate from the bottom up.

$$S_B = 30$$
$$S_C = 15$$
$$S_A = 100 + (5 \times S_B) + (50 \times S_C)$$
$$= 1000$$

Figure 8.22.   Estimation of the average physical data base record size.

SEGMENT BYTES = root subtree size

× frequency of occurrence of the root segment type

Estimate of the SEGMENT BYTES in Figure 8.22 = 1000 × 2000

= 2 million bytes.

The disk space to be used in bytes is dependent on the blocksize specified (BLK), the fraction of each block left free at load or reorganization time (FSW), the fraction of whole blocks left free at load time (FSB) or at reorganization time, and the end of block waste due to not splitting segments (W). (See Figure 8.24.)

As a result of FSW, FSB, and W, the effective blocksize is smaller than the specified blocksize.

Effective blocksize = [((1 − FSW) × BLK) − W] × (1 − FSB)

The bytes to be stored are SEGMENT BYTES. As a result of the effective blocksize being smaller than the blocksize assigned, the number of blocks necessary for storing the SEGMENT BYTES is bigger than anticipated. The BLOCK BYTES are obtained from the SEGMENT BYTES by adjusting

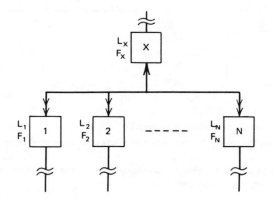

L = length of segment (including prefix)

F = relative frequency of occurrence of segment per occurrence of its parent

The subtree size of segment X is

$$S_X = L_X + (F_1 \times S_1) + (F_2 \times S_2) + \cdots + (F_N \times S_N)$$

Figure 8.23. **Determination of the subtree size of any isolated segment type X.**

DASD space to be used in bytes =
  f(BLK, FSW, FSB, W)

BLK = blocksize (CI: control interval size
  for VSAM)

FSW = free space within; fraction of each
  block left free at load

FSB = free space blocks; fraction of whole
  blocks left free at load

W = end of block waste due to not splitting segments .

Figure 8.24. **W is the end of block waste. The segment with the length of the shaded areas does not fit at the end of the block. The distance between the point Y and the end of the block is W.**

for free space and the unused space at the end of a block resulting from not splitting segments:

$$\text{BLOCK BYTES} = \text{SEGMENT BYTES} \times \frac{\text{blocksize}}{\text{effective blocksize}}$$

To find the distribution of W, two cases can be distinguished:

Case I. All the segments have the same length L in bytes.

Case II. The segments have different lengths L_X, where L_X is the length of segment X in bytes.

The essential information for space calculation is the physical hierarchical structure, that is, the parent-child relationships, the segment sizes, the data and the prefix, the segment frequencies relative to the parents, and any indexing relationships. The space computations are based on blocksize (control interval size for VSAM), free space, and data set grouping.

Case I. All the segments have the same length L in bytes.

BLK = blocksize
FSW = free space within block, the fraction of each block
  left free at load.
W = (1 − FSW) × BLK mod.* L

---

* mod. = "modulo." $X \text{ mod. } Y = \begin{cases} 0 \\ n \end{cases}$, where n is the remainder of the division $X \div Y$ and $n < Y$.

Example 1.

$$L = 100 \text{ bytes}$$
$$BLK = 4000 \text{ bytes}$$
$$FSW = 10\%, \text{ i.e., 400 bytes/block left free; at the initial load only 3600 bytes of each block will be used}$$
$$W = (1 - 0.1) \times 4000 \text{ mod. } 100$$
$$= 0$$

There is no end of block waste.

Case I.

Example 2.

$$L = 110 \text{ bytes}$$
$$BLK = 4000 \text{ bytes}$$
$$FSW = 10\%$$
$$W = (1 - 0.1) \times 4000 \text{ mod. } 110$$
$$= 80 \text{ bytes/block}$$

Because of not splitting segments, 80 bytes/block will be wasted.

Case II. The segments have different lengths L_x, where L_x is the length of segment X in bytes.

If simulation is carried out with the segments loaded in the blocks in a hierarchical sequence, the exact waste of bytes can be calculated. The simulation process would be extremely time consuming, however, and probably not worth the effort.

The pessimistic average estimate of W per block is the length of the longest segment in bytes $- 1$.

The optimistic average estimate of W per block is the length of the shortest segment in bytes $- 1$.

Case II.

Example.

$$FSW = 0.15$$
$$FSB = 0.10$$
$$BLK = 4096$$

Subtree size S_B = 30
Subtree size S_C = 15
Subtree size S_A = 100 + (5 × S_B) + (50 × S_C)
= 1000

$$\text{SEGMENT BYTES} = F_A \times S_A = 2{,}000{,}000$$
Estimated W = 99

$$\text{BLOCK BYTES} = \frac{2{,}000{,}000}{((1 - 0.15) \times 4096 - 99) \times 0.9} \times 4096$$
= 2,690,000

∴ DASD space is required for 2,690,000 bytes.

8.3.2 Time Estimates

In most data base management systems, one of the biggest time consumers in the execution of data base calls is physical I/O activity. In IMS every logical data base (external model in ANSI terminology) is composed of a physical data base or a number of physical data bases (internal model(s) in ANSI terminology). For a given application the access patterns can be estimated. Based on the access patterns, the sequence in which the segments are accessed is known. To access segment B from segment A, one needs to know all the segments that have to be touched on the way. One can estimate the number of I/Os necessary for accessing segment B from segment A if the probabilities of I/Os are known for all the intermediate segments that must be touched. If unit I/O time is known, it is possible to estimate the I/O time necessary for execution of the data base call when segment B has to be accessed from segment A.

The hierarchy of a physical data base, the length of every segment type, the expected frequency of occurrence of every segment type relative to its parent, and the sequence of segment accesses for a specific application can be used as input for finding the I/O activity necessary to access the required segments. The I/O activity needed to access the required segments also depends on the distance between the two desired segments, blocksize, buffer pool, and so on.

In DL/I (which is composed of the data base controlling component of IMS and of Data Manipulation Language), the pointers are embedded in the segments. The accessing of segment B from segment A is accomplished by using the pointers stored in the intermediate segments.

In HISAM data bases, the I/Os necessary for retrieving segment B from segment A can be calculated by summing the I/Os required for touching all the intermediate segments between A and B. There is no direct path between A and B, but the hierarchical order. For the direct access methods (HIDAM and HDAM), the possible pointers used may be physical child, physical twin, physical parent, logical child, logical twin, and logical parent. Since most of the segments related by logical relationships, which may be using logical child, logical twin, and logical parent pointers, are located in different physical records, the probability of I/O can be assumed to be 1 when using a logical relationship. An exception to this assumption may be made for any known physical relationships between the segments related logically.

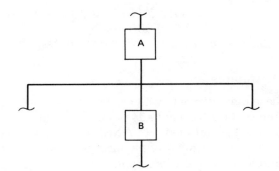

Segment Access Paths

- A to first B with PCF.
- B to next B with PTF.
- B to A with PP.

Segment distance from A to first B (i.e., from the end of A to the end of B):

$$PC_{A,B} = \text{length of B} + \text{all subtrees to left of B}$$

$$PCIO_{A,B} = \min. \left(1, \frac{PC_{A,B}}{[((1 - FSW) \times BLK) - W] \times (1 - FSB)} \right)$$

$PCIO_{A,B} = 1$ if A and B are in two different data set groups

where FSW = percentage of free space within block, W = end of block waste

      BLK = blocksize (control interval for VSAM),

      FSB = percentage of whole blocks left free at load time

Figure 8.25

The probability that the parent and the first occurrence of the child segment under the parent are not in the same block (called "control interval" for virtual storage access method: VSAM) is "PCIO" (physical child input/output). The assumption made here is that all occurrences of the child segment type are selected equally likely. The probability that a segment and its twin are not in the same block is "PTIO" (physical twin input/output). Finally, the probability that the segment and its parent are not in the same block is "PPIO" (physical parent input/output).

For an isolated parent-child relationship, as in Figure 8.25, the segment access paths between a segment of type A and a segment of type B are A to its first child B, B to its twin, and B to its parent A. The probability that segments A and B are in two different blocks depends on the distance between them, which is called the "SEGMENT DISTANCE." PCIO is dependent on the PC (physical child) bytes (SEGMENT DISTANCE) and the effective blocksize.

For HDAM overflow and for HIDAM:

$$PCIO_{A,B} = min.\left(1, \frac{PC_{A,B}}{[((1 - FSW) \times BLK) - W] \times (1 - FSB)}\right)$$

For HISAM:

$$Number\ of\ I/O_{A,B} = \left(\sum_{X=A}^{Y=B} probability\ IO_{X,Y}\right) \times 100$$

for every intermediate segment between A and B in the hierarchy, if probability $IO_{X,Y}$ is calculated to two decimal places.

In Figure 8.25, the segment distance between A and its immediate physical twin is the subtree size of segment A. The physical twin (PT) distance for segment A is the subtree size of A.

$$PTIO\ for\ segment\ type\ A = min.\left(1, \frac{S_A}{effective\ blocksize}\right)$$

$$PTIO_A = min.\left(1, \frac{subtree\ size\ of\ segment\ A}{[((1 - FSW) \times BLK) - W] \times (1 - FSB)}\right)$$

where FSW = percentage of free space within a block,
      W = end of block waste
   BLK = blocksize (control interval for VSAM)
   FSB = percentage of whole blocks left free at load time

For HDAM overflow and HIDAM:

$$PTIO_A = \min. \left(1, \frac{S_A}{[((1 - FSW) \times BLK) - W] \times (1 - FSB)}\right)$$

For HISAM:

$$\text{Number of I/O}_A = \left(\frac{S_A}{(1 - FSW) \times BLK}\right) \times 100$$

if

$$\frac{S_A}{[((1 - FSW) \times BLK) - W] \times (1 - FSB)}$$

is calculated to two decimal places.

$$PP_{B,A} = L_B + \left(\frac{f_B}{2} \times S_B\right) + \text{all the subtrees to the left of B}$$

where L_B = length of segment B

f_B = average frequency of occurrence of B under its parent A

S_B = average subtree size of B

Figure 8.26

The following assumptions are made in using the $PTIO_A$ to estimate the number of I/Os required for reaching the desired segment from the twin chain:

1. Every twin segment is equally likely to be selected.
2. The desired segment has an unknown position in the twin chain.
3. The expected number of segments to be touched before reaching the desired segment of the twin chain is equal to one-half the average number of segment occurrences in the twin chain.

In Figure 8.26, the segment distance between any B and its parent A is dependent on B's length, all the subtrees of the siblings before B (from the hierarchical order), and all the subtrees left to B (also from the hierarchical order). The PP (physical parent) distance is to be calculated for the segment Bi, that is, the distance between Bi and A.

$$PP_{Bi,A} = L_{Bi} \text{ (i.e., } B_i\text{'s own length in bytes)}$$

$$+ \text{ (subtree of the sibling } B_1)$$

$$+ \text{ (subtree of the sibling } B_2) + \cdots$$

$$+ \text{ (subtree of the sibling } B_{i-1})$$

$$+ \text{ all the subtrees to the left of B}$$

For the sake of simplicity we will assume that Bi is the middle segment of all the occurrences of B. For any occurrence of B:

$$PP_{B,A} = L_B + \left(\frac{f_B}{2} \times S_B\right) + \text{ all the subtrees to the left of B}$$

$$PPIO_{B,A} = \text{min.} \left(1, \frac{PP_{B,A}}{[((1 - FSW) \times BLK) - W] \times (1 - FSB)}\right)$$

PCIO, PTIO, and PPIO are valid for HDAM if both segments, that is, the from and to, are in overflow. The factors affecting the I/O activity for HDAM are byte limit, data base record size, blocksize (control interval size for VSAM), number of root anchor points per block, and number of roots that may be placed in a block, that is, the ratio of number of roots to number of blocks in the root addressable area. Because of the unique aspects of HDAM, it is necessary to calculate the average number of I/Os for retrieval of the root, average number of synonyms that must be read to retrieve an HDAM root, and probability of overflow of a given segment occurrence.

A DL/I CALL can be exploded into a number of segment calls. In Figure 8.27, a DL/I CALL is to retrieve a specific Z for a specific Y when positioned at a specific X:

$$\text{Number of I/Os} = \left[\text{PCIO}_{X,Y} + \left(\text{PTIO}_Y \times \left(\frac{f_Y}{2} - 1 \right) \right) \right]$$

$$+ \left[\text{PCIO}_{Y,Z} + \left(\text{PTIO}_Z \times \left(\frac{f_Z}{2} - 1 \right) \right) \right] \times 100 ,$$

if PCIO and PTIO are adjusted to two decimal places.

Figure 8.28 is an example of the calculations of PCIO and PTIO.

8.3.3 Data Base Applications

In estimating the time requirements for the data base applications, the major batch programs, the high volume transactions, and the transactions with critical response time specifications should be studied. The objective

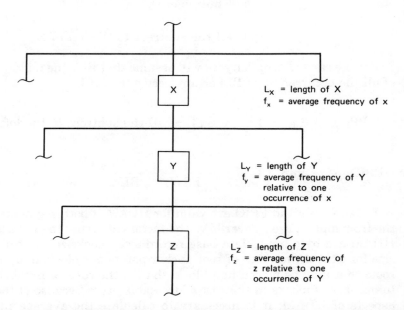

Figure 8.27. **A DL/I CALL is to retrieve a specific Z for a specific Y when positioned on X.**

$$\text{PCIO}_{A,B} = \frac{30}{740} = 0.040$$

that is, if B is accessed from A, out of 100 times most probably 4 times I/Os will be required.

$$\text{PCIO}_{A,C} = \frac{15 + 5 \times 30}{740} = 0.223$$

that is, if C is accessed from A, out of 100 times most probably 23 times I/Os will be required.

$$\text{PTIO}_A = \min.\left(1, \frac{1000}{740}\right) = 1$$

$$\text{PTIO}_B = \min.\left(1, \frac{30}{740}\right) = 0.040$$

$$\text{PTIO}_C = \min.\left(1, \frac{15}{740}\right) = 0.020$$

Figure 8.28

of the analysis is to estimate the average CPU time and the I/O time required for processing a transaction or for executing a specific CALL from the batch program. The primary objective of the analysis in the design phase is to locate the transactions that use the CPU and I/O time the most and to provide a comparison of the design alternatives for better performance. In our paper and pencil method, the CPU time and I/O time are estimated for a stand-alone, noncontention environment.

The analysis should be done for one CALL at a time; for example, for DL/I two of the CALLs are GU (Get Unique) and GN (Get Next). The CALL should be exploded to the segment or to the record level. In the case of DL/I, the segments, the logical records, and the I/O activities are used for calculating the estimates.

With the help of input such as the external models, the internal model, the access patterns for transactions, the I/O probabilities, the unit times for the possible data base calls (which have to be provided by the vendor of the DBMS used), and the unit times for the I/O, it is possible to estimate the CPU time and the I/O time required for the specific transactions.

REFERENCES

1. Atre, S., *Data Base Management Systems for the Eighties*. Wellesley, Massachusetts: Q.E.D. Information Sciences, 1983.

2. Atre, S., *Information Center: Strategies and Case Studies*. Rye, New York: Atre International Consultants, Inc., 1986.

3. Atre, S., "Mini and Mainframe DBMS, The Seven-Step Solution," Product Spotlight, *Computerworld* (March 31, 1986).

4. Brown, R. G., *Analysis of Data Base Design for Performance*, SHARE XLV, Vol. II.

5. Cardenas, Alfonso F., "Analysis and Performance of Inverted Data Base Structures," *Communications of the ACM*, Vol. 18, No. 5 (May 1975).

6. DBPROTOTYPE/II, Order No. G320-1535, SH20-1391, IBM Data Processing Division, 1133 Westchester Avenue, White Plains, New York.

7. Ghosh, Sakti P., "Pointers in Simple Hierarchical Structured Data," IBM Research Paper RJ 1775.

8. Dechow, Esther L., and Don C. Lundberg, *The IMS Data Base/Application Design Review*, Technical Bulletin, October 1977, Order No. G320-6009, IBM Palo Alto Systems Center, Palo Alto, California.

9. Gearhart, E. M., *The IMS Data Base/Application Design Review—Errata*, Technical Bulletin, January 1978, Order No. G320-6012, IBM Palo Alto Systems Center, Palo Alto, California.

10. *IMS/VS System/Application Design Guide*, IBM Corporation, 1133 Westchester Avenue, White Plains, New York.

11. Martin, James, *Computer Data Base Organization*. Englewood Cliffs, New Jersey: Prentice-Hall, 1977.

12. Wiederhold, Gio, *Database Design*, 2nd ed. New York: McGraw-Hill, 1983.

QUESTIONS

1. How are the entities of an enterprise, attributes of these entities, and relationships among them represented in IMS?

2. How is the hierarchical data model implemented in IMS?

3. What are the internal model access methods for IMS? How much physical data independence does each give?

4. What is a logical relationship in IMS? What is its use? Give an example of an external model or logical view made possible by a logical relationship.

5. Evaluate IMS with respect to logical data independence.

6. What is secondary indexing in IMS? When should it be used? Give an example of an external model or logical view made possible by a secondary index.

7. What are the three major areas of expertise needed by the designer of the physical model of a data base?

8. List and discuss guidelines for a hierarchical DBMS and for designing the physical model.

9. What are the key facts needed to estimate space for performance evaluation of the physical model of a hierarchical data base?

10. What factors need to be studied in estimating time requirements for data base applications? Once the relative importance of the CALLs are understood, what must then be considered to get a set of numbers for time predictions?

Network Data Base Management Systems

As stated in Chapter 4 (Section 4.5), much of today's awareness of the concepts of a data base can be credited to the work of CODASYL (Conference On Data Systems Languages) and its committees (DBTG being a major one). The underlying concepts of CODASYL specifications may be regarded as typical of a network-based system. There is a large number of data base management systems based on network data models, for example, Honeywell's IDS/II, Cullinet's IDMS/R, DEC's VAX DBMS, and UNIVAC's DMS 1100. Most of these conform to the CODASYL specifications. In this chapter we shall discuss some implementation details of the CODASYL-

DBTG data model in general, and of Cullinet's IDMS/R (Integrated Database* Management System/Relational) in particular. As the relational part of the name implies, IDMS/R supports the relational as well as the CODASYL data model; this is discussed further in Section 9.1.13.

9.1 IMPLEMENTATIONS OF THE ACCESS METHODS (IDMS/R: INTEGRATED DATABASE MANAGEMENT SYSTEM/RELATIONAL)

Entities, in the CODASYL data model, are represented by "record types." Each record type is a collection of data items or "fields" that are the attributes characterizing it. Record types are connected by one-to-many relationships called "set types." A set type is made up of an "owner" record type and one or many "member" record types. The rules for forming a set type are as follows:

1. A set type has only one owner record type.
2. A set type may have one or more member record types.
3. A record type cannot be an owner and a member of the same set type.
4. A record type can be an owner or a member in any number of different set types.

9.1.1 Areas and Pages

An IDMS/R data base consists of one or more (disjoint) portions called "areas." All occurrences of a particular record type are stored in a single area.

Each area is further subdivided into sequentially and uniquely numbered units called "pages." A page is the smallest unit that is read or written by IDMS/R. Its size is specified by the data base designer and can vary from area to area.

9.1.2 Database Keys

On each page can be stored one or more record occurrences, however many will fit. To each record occurrence on a page is assigned a unique number for the "line index," a position on the page containing the record's byte displacement. The concatenation of the page number and line number for a particular record occurrence is called the "database key." The database key has the following properties:

---

* We shall occasionally employ "database," Cullinet's single-word version of the term, in this chapter.

- It is assigned to the record occurrence upon entry to the data base
- It is associated with the record occurrence for as long as it remains in the data base
- It uniquely identifies and points to the record occurrence
- It is not stored with the record occurrence itself, but rather in set-related record occurrences (as we shall see later).

Record occurrences can be stored on the same page; that is, they can be physically contiguous but have no logical relationship. They can be of different types and can belong to different set occurrences as owners and members. How the page number is determined for a new record occurrence is examined next.

9.1.3   Internal Model Access Methods

When a new record occurrence is to be stored, IDMS/R has three methods of selecting its page within the assigned area. One of these methods, or "location modes," must be specified for each record type when the data base is designed. They are:

- CALC
- VIA SET
- DIRECT

The location modes are discussed in the following sections.

9.1.4   Location Mode CALC

When location mode CALC (short for calculation) is specified, then one field, or a combination of several fields, from the record type is also designated as the CALC key. IDMS/R then applies a hashing algorithm (see Section 7.2.6) to the value of the CALC key to give a page number. The record occurrence is stored on that page, if possible, otherwise on the next page in the area having sufficient space.

If location mode CALC is chosen, it is also necessary to specify to IDMS/R how to handle duplicate values of the CALC key. The designer must decide whether to allow or prohibit duplicate values of the key. For storing the records, we may want to allow duplicate occurrences of the same CALC key value, for example, if LAST-NAME is chosen as the CALC key. If SOCIAL-SECURITY-NUMBER is chosen as the CALC key, we would probably not want to allow duplicate values. Such a field would then correspond to what we called a primary key in the conceptual model and IDMS/R would assure its integrity.

Duplicates should not be confused with the problem of collisions, an aspect of the hashing algorithm. A collision occurs when two different CALC key values hash to the same target page number. Whether a record occurrence is stored on the page hashed to or on another page in the area, IDMS/R links the record occurrence into a chain associated with the target page. This assists the DBMS in subsequently retrieving by the value of the CALC key.

Location mode CALC can be specified for any record type in an IDMS/ R data base whether it is an owner or a member. We now consider a location mode which applies to members only.

9.1.5 Location Mode VIA SET

Any record type that is a member in some set type can have its location mode specified as VIA SET. The name of the set type is a part of this specification since the record type can be a member in several set types. IDMS/R then attempts to store a record occurrence in the same page with its owner and the other member occurrences for that set type. If owner and members are in different areas, then IDMS/R stores a member in a page whose location is proportional to the location of the owner in its area, that is, with its fellow members.

The idea behind location mode VIA SET is, of course, to improve access efficiency. If a set occurrence, called a "cluster" (owner and all members), can be contained in a single page, then many logical accesses to the cluster can be achieved with a single physical access.

In the two location modes just examined, the responsibility for placing a record occurrence rests with the DBMS. It is also possible to let the programmer decide.

9.1.6 Location Mode DIRECT

Any record type in an IDMS/R data base can have location mode DIRECT. In this event, the user or programmer specifies the page number for a record occurrence when it is stored. IDMS/R dutifully places the record occurrence on the given page, if possible, otherwise, on the next page in the area with sufficient space. The database key of the record occurrence is returned in either case.

Under location mode DIRECT the programmer assumes many of the functions of data management normally taken care of by the DBMS. Among these are location of record occurrences, distribution of record occurrences in the pages and the area, space availability management and, perhaps, eventual retrieval. For these reasons, DIRECT should normally be avoided.

Location mode determines where a new record occurrence is to be placed physically in the data base. A choice must be made by the data base designer for each record type. We next examine the various ways in which a new record occurrence may be logically positioned in an established set occurrence.

9.1.7   Set Order

A new member occurrence has been created and is to be placed into an existing set occurrence (Figure 9.1). Will it go first, before all member occurrences? Or last? Or perhaps next, or prior, to a specific member

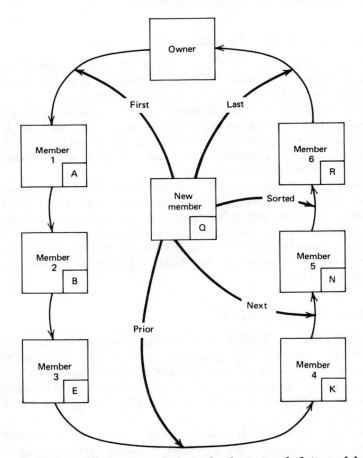

Figure 9.1. **Set member relation rules for network data model.**

- **First**
- **Last**
- **Prior**
- **Next**
- **Sorted (for insertion only)**

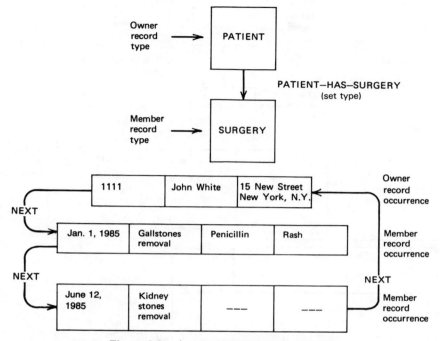

Figure 9.2.   **A set type with mode CHAIN.**

occurrence? Or sorted according to the data value of a particular field or "symbolic key" in the member?

All five of these CODASYL set ordering options are supported by IDMS/ R. The data base designer must select one of them for each set type in the data base.

CODASYL leaves the way of interrelating record types up to the individual implementors. We next examine the methods employed in IDMS/R.

9.1.8 Set Mode

IDMS/R supports two different methods of implementing sets: CHAIN and INDEX.

In set mode CHAIN (Figure 9.2), the owner occurrence points to (i.e., contains the database key of) the first member occurrence. Each member occurrence points to the next, and the last member occurrence points back to the owner occurrence, closing the chain, or "ring," as it is called.

If the PATIENT record was assigned location mode CALC, it is possible to access the "John White" record independently of the set, and then access the members consecutively with the pointers. If the SURGERY

Figure 9.3. **A set type with mode INDEX.**

record was stored with location mode CALC, each member record can also be accessed independently of the set and then processed with the other members of the set.

In set mode INDEX (Figure 9.3), one or more index occurrences are chained to the owner occurrence. The index occurrences contain pointers (once again, database keys) to the member record occurrences. The member occurrences, in turn, point back to the corresponding index occurrence.

Here, the member record occurrences do not have to be accessed through each other, by walking the chain. In fact, there is no direct link between members. The DBMS accesses any member from the index alone.

Both modes allow any of the five set order options of FIRST, LAST, NEXT, PRIOR, and SORTED (Section 9.1.7). Members can be sorted either ascending or descending either on the database key or on a symbolic key composed of one or more fields from the member record type.

Further, the owner of an indexed set can be either user defined or the DBMS (SYSTEM). An indexed set with a user defined owner implements the CODASYL concept of "pointer array": The owner points to all members and each member points back to the owner. The SYSTEM owner possibility is examined next.

9.1.9   File Inversion

An indexed set with owner SYSTEM that is sorted on a symbolic key implements the inverted access method (Section 7.2.4). Suppose, for example, that our data base contains a SURGERY record type with a field, named Date of Surgery. Suppose, further, that quick access to surgeries by date is desired. Then a set can be defined as in Figure 9.4, in addition to any

Figure 9.4.   **An indexed set with owner SYSTEM sorted (ascending) on Date of Surgery implements file inversion.**

others in which SURGERY participates as a member. The index occurrences are built and maintained to as many levels as appropriate by IDMS/R.

This has been an overview of the internal model access methods for IDMS/R. Let us now examine the external model access methods for the same DBMS.

9.1.10   External Model Access Methods

A programmer views data in an IDMS/R data base through an external model or "subschema." The subschemas, which must be explicitly coded, are subsets of the entire data base, which is described in a "schema." A subschema can contain some or all of the areas in the schema. Within an area, it can include some or all of the record and set types; and within a record type can be some or all of the fields appearing in the schema. The subschema can be created to provide the exact view of the data required by the programmer to satisfy the conceptual requirement.

We have seen how IDMS/R stores data at the internal model level. Let us look at how the programmer, using Data Manipulation language (DML), stores and retrieves data through access methods to the subschema.

9.1.11   Currency

To assist the programmer in navigating through the data base, IDMS/R maintains position or "currency" for each execution of the program, called a "run-unit." Currency is an elaborate concept with a simple basis. To put it simply, it is retaining the database key of a record occurrence that has just been accessed. The complication in this simple concept is that a great number of currencies can be active at one time. Unlike a sequential file where only one record is next, a programmer can and may want to move in many directions in a network. The following classes of currencies exist in IDMS/R:

- *Currency of Run-unit*
- Last record occurrence accessed by an execution of a program

- *Currency of Record*
- For each record type, last record occurrence accessed

- *Currency of Set*
- For each set type, last record occurrence (owner or member) accessed

- *Currency of Area*
- For each area, last record occurrence accessed

The action taken by a DML command depends upon the currencies in effect at the time of its execution. By the same token, the successful execution of a DML command will update related currencies. We now give an overview of some of the DML commands available.

9.1.12   DML Commands

A DML based upon the network data model must allow a programmer to access any member of a set from its owner, to move from one member to another, and to get from a member to its owner in any set. The usual operations of insertion, deletion, and modification must also be supported. How these capabilities are implemented can vary from one DBMS to another. Ignoring, for the moment, the details of the internal model, let us examine briefly some of the commands available to the IDMS/R programmer at the external model level.

STORE.   A new record occurrence is added to the data base. Where it is placed logically depends upon currencies previously established by the programmer. (Its physical location depends upon the location mode. See Sections 9.1.3–9.1.6.) A member record occurrence may be associated automatically with a particular owner or the programmer can establish this relationship using the next verb.

CONNECT.   An existing member record occurrence is incorporated into a particular set occurrence (that is, chained to a specific owner occurrence) determined by previously established currencies.

OBTAIN* CALC.   A record occurrence, whose location mode is CALC (see Section 9.1.4) is retrieved for a given value of the CALC key.

OBTAIN NEXT WITHIN SET.   Based on a previously established currency, the next member occurrence in a set occurrence is retrieved. The set type name must be specified. Variants include PRIOR, FIRST, and LAST instead of NEXT.

OBTAIN OWNER WITHIN SET.   The owner occurrence for a particular member occurrence is retrieved. Again, the action depends upon currency and the set type given.

OBTAIN NEXT WITHIN AREA.   The next record occurrence in a particular area is retrieved based on currency. The record type can be specified or not. Variants again include PRIOR, FIRST, and LAST. This access method, based only on physical location (and not logical relationships), is reminiscent of retrieval through physical sequential (Section 7.2.1).

---

* The OBTAIN command performs two distinct functions. One is to locate and establish currency on a specific record occurrence (FIND). The other is to transfer the data content of the record occurrence into the user work area (GET). Each of these commands can also be performed individually. Thus, OBTAIN = FIND + GET.

OBTAIN DB-KEY. A record occurrence whose database key is known is retrieved. This access method can be used in conjunction with location mode DIRECT (Section 9.1.6). Note that previously established currency has no effect on this command.

MODIFY. A record occurrence, or selected field values therein, which is in the user work area, replaces the record occurrence that is current of run-unit in the data base.

DISCONNECT. The record occurrence that is current of run-unit is removed from a specified set occurrence, but remains in the data base.

ERASE. The record occurrence that is current of run-unit is deleted from the data base. A variant, ERASE ALL, deletes an owner together with all its members (together with all their members, etc.).

The internal model access method of file inversion (Section 9.1.9) facilitates still other ways of retrieving data. Individual records containing a specific value for all or part of the symbolic key can be located randomly. Groups of records can be processed in ascending or descending sorted order by the symbolic key. Location mode VIA SET allows physical sequential processing of static data.

We see next how the relational, as well as the inverted file data model, makes an appearance in IDMS/R.

9.1.13 Relational External Models

IDMS/R also supports the relational data model (Section 4.3). Separate relations or tables can be defined, each representing an entity of the enterprise. External models composed of tables of stored or derived data values are presented to the end-users and programmers. The usual operations, including join, are permitted. The implementation is done under the facilities of IDMS/R described earlier using indexed sets. Generation of the necessary DBMS tables, schemas, and subschemas has been automated.

Summary of Internal and External Model Access Methods in IDMS/R

Internal Model Access Methods

- CALC
- VIA SET
- DIRECT
- CHAIN
- Pointer Array through INDEX
- File Inversion through INDEX

External Model Access Methods

- STORE and CONNECT
- OBTAIN CALC
- OBTAIN WITHIN SET
- OBTAIN WITHIN AREA
- OBTAIN DB-KEY
- MODIFY
- ERASE and DISCONNECT
- Relational

9.2   DESIGN A PHYSICAL MODEL OF A DATA BASE

The steps taken to map a conceptual model into a network or CODASYL logical model were discussed in Section 6.3. We now turn to the final steps in the data base design process, creating and evaluating an internal model for IDMS/R. The following must be finalized:

- Record types, their content and location mode
- Set types and options
- Subdivision of the data base into areas and physical files

First we consider the set options, and then we turn our attention to other choices to be made in structuring the data.

9.2.1   Set Options

Set Order.   The set order options of FIRST, LAST, NEXT, PRIOR, and SORTED determine where in a set occurrence a new member occurrence will be placed (Section 9.1.7). FIRST results in LIFO (last in/first out), LAST gives FIFO (first in/first out). These options are easy for the programmer to use, but lack flexibility. NEXT and PRIOR allow greater freedom in placement at the cost of imposing upon the programmer the burden of designating a specific member occurrence. SORTED sets are generally to be avoided because of the high maintenance overhead in the DBMS. NEXT is usually a good choice.

Set Linkage.   As discussed in Section 9.1.8, one way of implementing sets is to have each member occurrence contain a pointer to the next member occurrence, the owner point to the first member, and the last member back to the owner. These pointers, called NEXT, are required by IDMS/R when the mode of the set is CHAIN. Two other kinds of pointers, PRIOR and OWNER, are optional. (See Figures 9.5 and 9.6.)

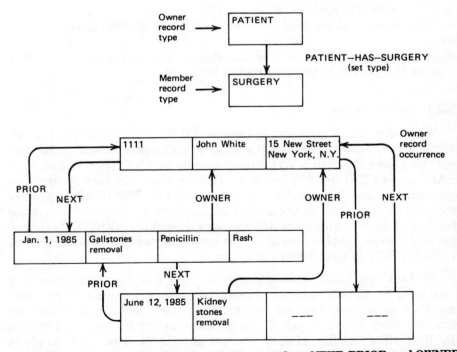

Figure 9.5. Chain for a set occurrence. Pointers used are NEXT and PRIOR.

Figure 9.6. Chain for a set occurrence. Pointers used are NEXT, PRIOR, and OWNER.

Members not clustered near owner.   If members are not clustered near owners, this situation provides a good rationale for OWNER pointer use. Even though, at the time of design, no user has any need for accessing the owner from the member, most probably three or six months after the implementation some of the users will want to access the owner directly from the member.

Many members in a set.   If the set is made up of several hundred members, the clustering may not store all the members on one page. If hundreds of members are scattered on five or six pages of storage, it may be advisable to have OWNER pointers. As alternatives, the designer can increase the page size so that all records fit on a page, or can give more buffer space to the application, so that all five or six pages are brought into memory simultaneously.

Processing considerations.   If there are different processing considerations, it may be advisable to have PRIOR pointers. In one situation we may be interested in the newest invoices stored, whereas in another situation we may be interested in paying off the oldest invoices to avoid higher interest. If the invoices are the members of the set, PRIOR pointers will be helpful.

Deletion of records.   PRIOR pointers are helpful also in the deletion process. If PRIOR pointers are not provided, the best way to get to the previous member record is most probably to go to the owner and use NEXT pointers. If PRIOR pointers are provided, the deletion process is often faster.

All three types of pointers should be specified unless an omission can be justified.

Insertion and Retention.   There are four combinations for insertion and retention of member record occurrences in a set:

Set Insertion or Storage Class	Set Retention or Removal Class
1. Automatic	Mandatory
2. Automatic	Optional
3. Manual	Mandatory
4. Manual	Optional

1. **Set Insertion: Automatic; Set Retention: Mandatory.**   The member record is linked into a set automatically when it is stored, and the record is retained in that set until it or the owner is deleted. (*Note*: This combination of the options is used quite frequently.)

2. **Set Insertion: Automatic; Set Retention: Optional.**   Insertion is the same as above. As far as retention is concerned, however, a member

may be disconnected from the set without necessarily deleting it from the data base or other sets. (*Note*: This combination of the options is not used quite so frequently.)

3. **Set Insertion: Manual; Set Retention: Mandatory.** The member record is not linked into the set automatically and must be connected by program logic. Once inserted, however, the member will be retained in the set until it or the owner is deleted. (*Note*: This combination of the options is used very seldom.)

4. **Set Insertion: Manual; Set Retention: Optional.** The member record is not linked into the set automatically and must be connected by program logic. As far as retention is concerned, however, a member may be disconnected from the set without necessarily deleting it from the data base or other sets. (*Note*: This combination of the options is used quite frequently.)

These combinations can be illustrated as follows:

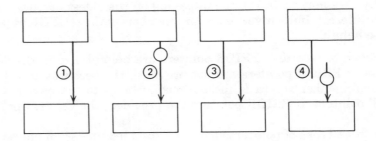

As mentioned in Chapter 4, the graphic notation was introduced by C. W. Bachman. A block represents an entity or a record type. The directed arrow, called the "Bachman arrow," connects two or more record types. The record type at the tail of the arrow is functioning as the owner record type, and the record type at the head of the arrow as the member record type.

Mandatory automatic gives the greatest control and validation while requiring the least programming effort. Under optional manual, the programmer must issue the CONNECT and DISCONNECT commands to insert and remove a member occurrence from a set occurrence. Unless greater flexibility is demanded, mandatory automatic is the option of choice.

9.2.2 Record Options

Location Mode. A location mode, normally either CALC or VIA SET (see Sections 9.1.3–9.1.6), must be assigned by the data base designer to each record type in an IDMS/R data base.

CALC generally allows retrieval of individual record occurrences with good access efficiency. It thus provides convenient direct entry into the data base. The random placement of the record occurrence frequently gives good distribution of the data. However, care must be taken when CALC is used on chained ring structures because of the physical I/Os required to walk the chain.

VIA SET, on the other hand, attempts to cluster the members of a set near the owner and near each other in the same physical block. It is most useful when the members of a set are inevitably processed whenever the owner is retrieved. Many logical accesses can then be done, and the chain walked, in a single physical I/O. Care must be taken that the page size is large compared to the cluster size so that the desired result is achieved. Of course, if a record type is a member in several set types, it can be stored VIA just one of them.

9.2.3 Areas and Files

Just as an IDMS/R data base is subdivided logically into one or more areas, it may be stored in one or many data sets or physical files. Many possibilities then exist for mapping the areas into files:

- All areas can be mapped into one file
- Several (not all) areas can be mapped into one file
- Each area can be mapped into a different file
- One area can be mapped into many files

Situations exist where the first (and obvious) choice would not be possible or advantageous. Since OS data sets cannot span packs, large areas must map into several files. Since page size can vary from area to area, large record types and clusters should go into areas with large page sizes. If areas used by different application processes are mapped to separate files, then those areas not required need not be on line. Seek time can frequently be reduced by mapping an area into files on different volumes.

We next turn to a list of DOs and DON'Ts of data structuring, which are helpful in finalizing the content of record types and the number of set types.

9.2.4 DOs and DON'Ts of Data Structuring

DO: Structure Variable Data.   In the logical model, study the owner-member relationships. For a given owner there may be many member occurrences within a set, and it may be valid to keep the set type. But if, for a given owner, there is only one member occurrence, be suspicious about the set type. The member may be included in the owner as well.

Figure 9.7. **Trade-off is between multiple retrieval capability and time to store.**

DO: *Recognize Trade-offs.* It is possible that the specific environment requires retrieval of some data in different contexts; for example, the EMPLOYEE record in Figure 9.7 may be retrieved based on PRIMARY SKILL or LOCATION or JOB CODE. Here the designer provides multiple retrieval capabilities at the cost of storing the employee data as a link, that is, establishing proper pointers between the three sets.

DO: *Avoid Lengthy Sets.* There is no definition of a lengthy set. The designer has to impose these limits. Is a set lengthy when it has 50 members, or is it lengthy when it has 500 members? The answer also depends on whether the members are physically clustered or distributed. A lengthy set may be divided into a number of groups. It is advisable to build ranges of the keys, as in Figure 9.8.

DO: *Consider Pointer Record Types.* Pointers do take up space. Suppose that in a particular situation there is an owner record and some

Figure 9.8

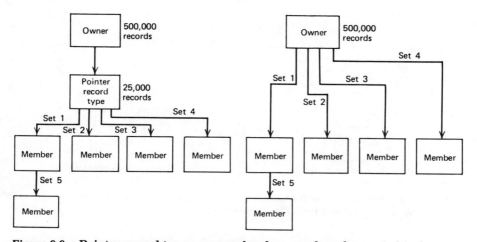

Figure 9.9.   **Pointer record type occurs only when members from sets 1 to 4 occur. More space is required without pointer record type because the 500,000 owner records have to provide pointer space.**

variables are associated with the owner. Let us assume that there are 500,000 owner records and four different sets. The volume of the sub-structure is very low; that is, out of 500,000 only 5 percent of the owner records need a substructure. In a case like this, consider using a pointer record type which is the member of a set. (See Figure 9.9.) As a result, the pointers are embedded in the pointer record type instead of in the owner record. The pointers will not be present in the 500,000 occurrences of the owner records. They will be present only in 25,000 records of the pointer record type.

DO: Weigh Record Clustering versus Distribution.   A trade-off that the data base designer has to consider involves distributing the data. In a network environment, the smoother the distribution, the better the performance of the data base. Consider an example where we have 5000 CUSTOMERS and 10,000 ACCOUNTS, and there are five TYPES OF ACCOUNTS. (See Figure 9.10.) If the 10,000 ACCOUNTS are clustered with the five TYPES OF ACCOUNTS, the result is a skewed distribution. If, on the other hand, the 10,000 ACCOUNTS are clustered with the 5000 CUSTOMERS, the result is a smoother distribution. It is advisable to consider record clustering versus distribution.

DON'T: Overstructure.   There may be a low ratio of owners to members; for example, for 100,000 INVOICES there are only 1000 BACK ORDERS. It may not be advisable to structure INVOICE and BACK ORDER as a set, as in Figure 9.11. It may be advisable to use the same invoice CALC key for accessing both the INVOICES and the BACK ORDERS.

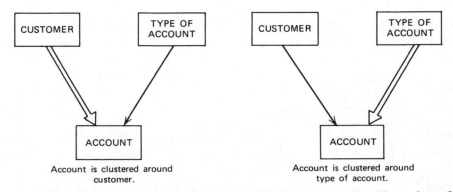

Account is clustered around customer.

Account is clustered around type of account.

Figure 9.10. **For better performance smooth distribution is preferable to skewed distribution. The arrow ◊ indicates clustering.**

DON'T: Sacrifice Selectivity. In Figure 9.12 the three paths provide selectivity at the cost of space. With the single path in the same figure, less space is used at the cost of time for acquiring some data.

DON'T: Neglect Pointer Placement Analysis. A data base usually consists of two types of records. One type is long duration; that is, the records stay in the data base for a relatively long time. The other type is short duration; that is, the records have a short life cycle. Data base records about CUSTOMERS, STUDENTS, and ACCOUNTS usually are of the long duration type, whereas records about INVOICES and ORDERS are of the short duration type. Short duration type records are usually the ones that have to be updated quite frequently. If pointers are placed

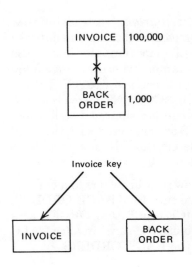

Figure 9.11. **For low ratio between owner and member, the same invoice CALC key is used for accessing the invoice as well as the back order.**

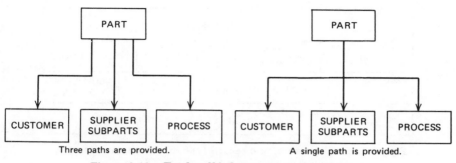

Figure 9.12. **Trade-off is between space and time.**

in short duration type records, the pointers "go away" when the record is deleted, unlike the pointers in long duration type records. See Figure 9.13.

DON'T: *Overlook Off-line Processing.* Off-line processing may be a preferable alternative to on-line processing if data is voluminous. Historical and inventory data may be good candidates for off-line processing. Sorting in batch may not necessarily be the worst solution for certain problems!

We next look at how the data structures in a CODASYL internal model can be graphically represented.

9.2.5 Bachman Diagram

It is apparent from the preceding sections that there are many choices to be made in the design of a CODASYL data base, many options to be exercised. Once a tentative design has been developed, it is advisable to have it reviewed for soundness by as many people as is feasible before it is coded for the DBMS. The processing for each conceptual requirement

Figure 9.13. **Pointers placed in the short duration records need more maintenance than pointers placed in the long duration records.**

Figure 9.14. **Representing a record type in a Bachman diagram.**

must be walked through to ensure that an effective and efficient external model can be provided. A diagram, drawn according to the method devised by C. W. Bachman, can be of material assistance in this review. Most of the decisions made earlier, together with the record and set types, can be displayed in a single picture.

A record type is represented by a rectangle subdivided into four rows (see Figure 9.14). The first row contains the name the designer has chosen for the entity or record type. The second contains the numeric identification (not greater than 9999), the length mode (fixed or variable), the length (actual or maximum), and the location mode (CALC, VIA SET, or DIRECT). For CALC, the field(s) serving as the CALC key, and for VIA SET, the set name, is recorded on line three. Finally, the area designated is placed on the last line.

As mentioned earlier, the set type is shown by a Bachman arrow pointing from the owner record type to the member record type as in Figure 9.15. Beside the arrow are listed the name of the set (one convention is to use owner and member names separated by a hyphen); the pointers to be used (required Next, optional Prior and Owner); the membership options

Figure 9.15. **Representing a set type in a Bach-man diagram.**

for insertion and retention (MA, OA, MM, OM); the set order (First, Last, Next, Prior, Sorted); and the mode (CHAIN or INDEX).

A complete Bachman diagram for the banking case study is given in Appendix A (Figure A.22).

9.3 EVALUATE THE PHYSICAL MODEL OF A DATA BASE

9.3.1 Space Estimates

In order to estimate the size of an IDMS/R data base, the following assumptions are made:

1. All data bases are as they were at initial load, or just after reorganization.
2. Record and cluster sizes are small relative to page sizes.
3. The member record occurrence frequencies relative to the owners are independent random variables.
4. The records are of fixed length.
5. The frequency distribution of a member under its owner is uniform.

The layout of a page in an IDMS/R area is shown in Figure 9.16. The record occurrences are stored contiguously immediately following the header. The line indexes, one for each record occurrence, are stored pro-

Figure 9.16. Page layout.

ceeding backward from the footer. The free space between is available for the addition of new record occurrences.

Record Size.   For each record type, find the sum of the following; this is the record size.

- Data Length (bytes)
- N,P Pointers as Owner (4 bytes each)
- N,P,O Pointers as Member (4 bytes each)
- CALC Record Type? (8 bytes for N,P Pointers in CALC Set Occurrence)
- Variable Length Record? (8 bytes for Pointers and Counters)
- Line Index (8 bytes)

Area Size.   For each area of the data base, proceed as follows:

- Multiply Record Size times number of record occurrences for each Record Type in Area and sum to get Data Size
- Divide Data Size by Page Size minus 32 (header and footer) to get (minimum) Number of Base Pages
- Divide by Space Utilization (70% for static file, 30% for volatile file) to get Total Number of Base Pages
- Divide Page Size minus 32 into twice Total Number of Base Pages to get Number of Space Management Pages
- Add Total Number of Base Pages to Number of Space Management Pages to get Number of Pages in Area
- Divide Number of Pages in Area by number of pages per disk volume track

The data base size is the sum of all Area Sizes.

DML Command		No. of I/Os
OBTAIN $\left\{ \begin{array}{l} \text{NEXT} \\ \text{PRIOR} \end{array} \right\}$ WITHIN SET (VIA)		1/N
OBTAIN $\left\{ \begin{array}{l} \text{NEXT} \\ \text{PRIOR} \end{array} \right\}$ WITHIN SET (NON-VIA)		1
OBTAIN OWNER WITHIN SET (WITH OWNER POINTERS)		1
OBTAIN CALC		1
MODIFY		1
DISCONNECT (NON-VIA WITH PRIOR POINTERS)		2
CONNECT (NON-VIA WITH PRIOR POINTERS)		2
ERASE = MODIFY + DISCONNECT (NO QUALIFIER)		3
STORE (CALC)		1
STORE (VIA)		2/N

Figure 9.17.   **Estimating Number of I/O's per Record Accessed assuming:**
- **N VIA records per page**
- **No pages found in Buffer Pool**

9.3.2 Time Estimates

In IDMS/R, as in most DBMSs, the biggest time consumer in the execution of calls to the DBMS is not the CPU, but physical I/O. If the call patterns are determined for the, say, four or five most critical processes, their performance can be estimated. The I/O requirement for each is the number of physical I/Os per record accessed times the number of records accessed by type. A table for estimating the number of I/Os for each of the common DML commands is given in Figure 9.17.

REFERENCES

1. Atre, S., *Data Base Management Systems for the Eighties*. Wellesley, Massachusetts: Q.E.D. Information Sciences, Inc., 1983.
2. Atre, S., *Information Center: Strategies and Case Studies*. Rye, New York: Atre International Consultants, Inc., 1986.
3. Atre, S., "Storing Data about Data," *Information Center*, July 1986.
4. Bachman, C. W., "Data Structure Diagrams," *Data Base*, Journal of ACM Special Interest Group British Data Processing, Vol. 1, No. 2 (Summer 1969).
5. Bachman, C. W., "Implementation Techniques for Data Structure Sets," from *Data Base Management Systems: Proceedings of the SHARE Working Conference on Data Base Management Systems, Montreal, Canada, July 23–27, 1973*, edited by D. A. Jardine, North-Holland, 1974.
6. "CODASYL," Data Description Language Committee, *Journal of Development*, January 1978. Box 1808, Washington, D.C. 20043.
7. Fadok, George T., *Effective Design of CODASYL Data Base*. New York: Macmillan, 1985.
8. Olle, William T., *The CODASYL Approach to Data Base Management*. New York: Wiley-Interscience, 1978.

QUESTIONS

1. How are the entities of an enterprise, attributes of these entities, and relationships among them represented in IDMS/R?
2. How is the CODASYL data model implemented in IDMS/R?
3. What are the internal model access methods for IDMS/R? How much physical data independence does each give?
4. Distinguish between automatic and manual set insertion and between mandatory and optional set retention in IDMS/R. When would each option be used?
5. Evaluate IDMS with respect to logical data independence.
6. Describe the Bachman diagram and the advantages of its use.
7. What types of questions must be addressed in designing the physical model if one is using the CODASYL data model?
8. When should a physical data base be split into a number of physical data bases?

CHAPTER 10

Inverted File Data Base Management Systems

Some data base management systems available today need not impose any specific formal structure on the records. The records do not have to be related by a hierarchy or by a network. There need be no parents, no owners, no children, no members, no twins. In short, the records can be just records. The data base using such a data base management system is composed of a number of files. The records in these files can be inverted on one or a number of fields. Relationships between files are present whenever two files contain a common field with common data values. Such a relationship can be implemented by inverting upon one or both of these common fields. As mentioned in Section 6.4, one of the major data base management systems using inversion of files is ADABAS

(Adaptable Data Base System) marketed in the U.S.A. by Software AG of North America, Inc.

10.1 IMPLEMENTATIONS OF THE ACCESS METHODS (ADABAS: ADAPTABLE DATA BASE SYSTEM)

An ADABAS data base consists of one or more files each representing an entity of the enterprise. A file contains records representing entity occurrences and a record contains the data values of the fields that are the attributes of the entity. Fields may be added to an ADABAS file at any time through the use of a utility; reorganizing or reloading the file is not required.

10.1.1 Descriptors

Any field, subfield, or combination of fields in an ADABAS file may be designated as a "descriptor" (or key). ADABAS constructs an index file or "inverted list" for the field in a separate area. Whenever a record is added to or deleted from the file or the value of a descriptor field is changed, ADABAS makes a corresponding update to the inverted list.

10.1.2 Internal Sequence Numbers

ADABAS assigns to each record entering a data base an identifying number called the "Internal Sequence Number" (ISN) which is unique to the file. The ISN is used by ADABAS to implement file inversion. The ISN is not the physical address of the record, but rather a logical identifier. ISNs are normally assigned by ADABAS, but may be user assigned.

10.1.3 Examples

Figure 10.1 shows two files. One file describes the Policy, and the other the Policyholder. The records in both files contain internal sequence numbers (ISNs). The field Last Name is defined as a descriptor in the Policy file allowing quick access by the values of that field. The descriptors in the Policyholder file are Policy-No and Policy-Type. As these files stand there is no relationship between them.

If, however, the field Policy-No is added to the Policyholder file as in Figure 10.2, a relationship between the files does exist. If, further, the Policy-No field is declared to be a descriptor in both files, as indicated, then this relationship is implemented.

This means that, given a record in the Policy file, it is easy to obtain the record(s) in the Policyholder file that contain the same Policy-No and vice versa.

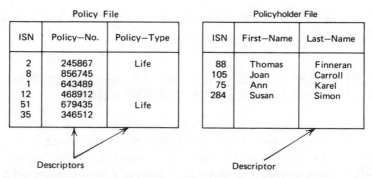

Figure 10.1. **Policy file with fields Policy-No and Policy-Type. Policy-No and Policy-Type are descriptors.**

Policyholder file with fields First-Name and Last-Name. Last-Name is a descriptor.

For unique identification of the policy holder, we may append the date of birth or address as fields to the Policyholder file.

With this basic capability ADABAS can support a network data model of many files with single or bidirectional, one-to-many or many-to-many relationships between records as in Figure 10.3. ADABAS also supports hierarchical and network views based on the common descriptors among the files. These external models (see Chapter 1) contain fields from related data base records. Figures 10.4*a*, 10.4*b*, and 10.4*c* display some of the views based on Figure 10.3.

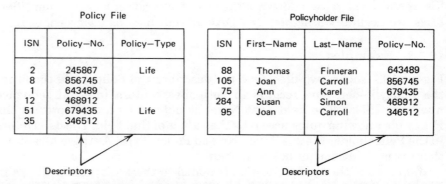

Figure 10.2. **Policyholder file is expanded with Policy-No as compared to Figure 10.1. Policy-No interconnects the two files, the Policy file and the Policyholder file.**

A policyholder may hold more than one policy; for example, Joan Carroll holds two policies.

Another way to express this one-to-many relationship is to make Policy-No a multiple value field, as described later, in the Policyholder file. This might be preferable to reduce or eliminate data redundancy.

Policy File

ISN	Policy—No.	Policy—Type	Policyholder Last—Name
2	245867	Life	Smith
8	856745		Carroll
1	643489	Life	Finneran
12	468912		Simon
51	679435		Karel
35	346512	...	Carroll
...	...		...

Policyholder File

ISN	First—Name	Last—Name	Policy—No	Rep—No.
88	Thomas	Finneran	643489	2345
105	Joan	Carroll	856745	6748
75	Ann	Karel	679435	1367
284	Susan	Simon	468912	4589
95	Joan	Carroll	346512	6748
...	...	...	...	...

Representative File

ISN	Rep—No.	Policy—No.
581	6748	856745
530	1367	679435
356	4589	468912
289	2345	643489
685	6748	346512
...	...	...

Claims File

ISN	Policy—No.	Claim—Date
855	643489	January 15, 1988
931	346512	March 30, 1988
863	856745	February 18, 1989
845	468912	April 11, 1990
698	643489	March 5, 1988
567	245867	February 8, 1988
...	...	

Figure 10.3. Policy, Policyholder, Claims, and Representative files are interrelated on certain descriptors.

(a)

(b)

Figure 10.4a. **A person may own many policies and may have put in many claims.**

Figure 10.4b. **On a certain policy many claims may be made.**

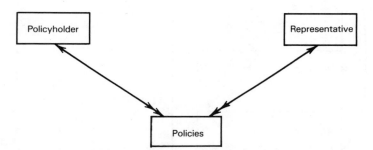

Figure 10.4c. **There may be a many-to-many relationship between policyholders and representatives through policies.**

10.1.4 Implementation of File Inversion in ADABAS

Figure 10.5 displays how the inverted file access method is implemented in ADABAS. The Policy file is placed in an area called "Data Storage." The Policy-Type field is defined as a descriptor. ADABAS places the inverted list for this field in another area called the "Associator." The inverted list is in order by the value of the descriptor. Each entry contains the number of records in which the value occurs and the ISNs, in ascending order, of those records. Figure 10.5 shows that there are 8010 records with Policy-Type "Life," those with ISNs 2 and 51 plus many others.

Since the ISN is a logical record identifier it does not specify where in Data Storage the record can be found. This is done through another structure in the Associator called the "Address Converter" (see Figure 10.5). An Address Converter exists for each file in the data base and contains one entry for each record in that file. The ISN is used as an index to the Address Converter entry for the record and this entry contains the number of the physical block, or RABN (relative ADABAS block

Associator   Data Storage

	Inverted List				Address Converter Block Number		Policy File			B l o c k
Value	Count	ISN	ISN	---	1	ISN	Policy—No.	Policy—Type	
					1				
Life	8010	2	51	---		2	245867	Life	
						8	856745		} 1
						1	643489		
						12	468912		
					1	51	679435	Life	} 2
						35	346512		
					2	⋮	⋮	⋮	
					⋮				

Figure 10.5.

- Inverted list for the descriptor Policy-Type in the Policy file. The value Life occurs 8010 times in this file, in records with ISN = 2 and 51, as shown, and some others.

  Address Converter shows that the records with ISN = 1, 2, and 8 are in block 1. The record with ISN = 12 is in block 2.

- Associator consists of the inverted list and the address converter. It contains the general description of the entire data base. It also contains the specific file directory for each file with the file description and field description table. The Associator also consists of the space management tables.

number), in which the record is stored. Thus, in Figure 10.5, the records with ISNs 1,2,8 are all in block number 1.

Suppose that the Policy-No in the Policy file of Figure 10.5 is also declared a descriptor and, further, that this descriptor is defined as unique. This means that ADABAS will insure the uniqueness of the data values of the Policy-No field. The inverted list in the associator will appear as in Figure 10.6. The values of the Policy-No field appear in order and the counts are all one.

Again, suppose that the record in Figure 10.5 for Policy-No=643489 is updated and the record no longer fits in block 1. ADABAS must move the record to another data storage block (this process is called "migration"). The block number of the new block is recorded in the first entry of the address converter to complete the migration. The ISN of the record did not change (it is still 1) and so the inverted lists are still accurate.

Inverted List for Policy-No

Value	Count	ISN
245867	1	2
346512	1	35
468912	1	12
643489	1	1
679435	1	51
856745	1	8
. . .		

Figure 10.6.   The inverted list in the associator of Figure 10.5 for the unique descriptor Policy-No.

10.1.5   ADABAS Components

ADABAS stores a data base in several distinct areas. Two of these components were described above. The data storage component contains the files of data of the enterprise as records with ISNs. The associator component contains the inverted lists for all descriptors and the address converters for all files in the data base. These two components, together with a third called "work," are now described in more detail.

The data storage component contains the variable length records for all ADABAS files. Each physical block of data storage can contain one or many records, as many as will fit. ADABAS does not use an operating system access method; all I/O is done by EXCP (execute channel program).

While ADABAS accepts data into the data base and presents it back to the user in expanded form, it compresses the data as kept in data storage to save space. Data compression is done on each field by default unless the user specifies otherwise when the field is defined:

- Trailing spaces on alphanumeric fields are removed
- Leading zeros on numeric data are removed
- Unpacked decimal numeric data is packed
- A series of consecutive null valued fields may be represented by a single byte empty field count

Figure 10.7 shows the results of data compression. ADABAS adds a length byte at the beginning of each compressed field to aid in decompression. Fields that are multiple valued and in periodic groups (see Section 6.4) are also compressed; ADABAS placed a byte before each such structure in the record giving the number of occurrences.

ADABAS reserves a percentage of free space in each physical block, called a padding area, for the growth of existing records in the block. Ranging from 3 percent to 97 percent, the padding factor is defined for each file when it is loaded and can be changed at any time by utilities. The padding area is not used to store new records, but only to avoid the

Data before compression

| 0 | 0 | 0 | 0 | 7 | 2 | 4 | 5 | 8 | 6 | 7 | L | I | F | E | | | | | | |

<---->
defined as 11 bytes
unpacked decimal

<---->
defined as 11 bytes
alphanumeric

Data after compression

| 0 5 | 7 2 | 4 5 | 8 6 | 7 5 | F | 5 | L | I | F | E |

↑   ↑
Inclusive length   Inclusive length

Figure 10.7. **Data compression:**

- **Removes trailing spaces on alphanumeric fields**
- **Packs unpacked numeric data and removes leading zeros on all numeric data**
- **Reduces one or many null valued field(s) to a single character**

migration to other blocks of old records that have expanded after an update.

The associator component contains internal control information for all files in the data base in addition to the inverted lists and address converters mentioned previously. The file definitions, the space allocations for the various components, security criteria, and the data storage space table giving space available block by block are all here. The associator also holds a Field Definition Table (FDT) for each file containing the names, lengths, formats, and all other characteristics for all the fields in the file. As shown in Figure 10.8, ADABAS keeps the data in one place and the logical relationships involving the data in another. This fact gives ADABAS a great deal of data independence. Fields can be added at any time (at the end of the record, of course) by changing the FDT in the associator. Fields can be added or removed as descriptors by adding or deleting

Figure 10.8. **ADABAS stores the data and the logical relationships between data in separate components of the data base.**

inverted lists in the associator; data storage remains untouched. However, when data is changed in data storage, which alters the logical relationships, then both components must be updated.

The work component contains temporary information associated with the data base. Data protection information required to restart ADABAS and back out uncompleted transactions is kept here. Lists of ISNs of records requested by users to satisfy complex search criteria while the users are retrieving the desired records are retained on the work. ADABAS also uses the work as a scratch area to hold intermediate ISN lists while satisfying searches.

10.1.6 Storage Methods (Internal Model)

ADABAS normally puts a record entering a file into a convenient physical block using linear storage mode. However, one of two other methods of record placement may be specified instead to increase access efficiency. Randomized storage mode can speed retrieval of records containing a unique descriptor. Physical ordering of records optimizes logical sequential access by any single descriptor.

Randomized storage mode, called ADAM (ADABAS direct access method), implements the hashing access method in ADABAS. A unique descriptor is selected as the ADAM key. When a record is stored in the ADAM file, the value of the ADAM key is passed through a hashing algorithm to determine the physical block number or RABN. Another block is used to hold the record if the block hashed to is full. ADABAS still builds and maintains the inverted list for the ADAM key. However, retrieval is always attempted using the hashing algorithm first before resorting to the inverted list. Specifying enough data storage blocks for the ADAM file and selecting the ADAM key to avoid collisions (any string of bits within the unique descriptor may be used) can lead, in many cases, to access efficiencies close to one for random retrievals. Since ADAM usage is completely transparent to the applications programmer, it is a true internal model access method in the sense of Chapter 7.

Linear storage mode is the default used by ADABAS. When the file is loaded, new records are placed in the next consecutive block of data storage until it fills to the padding area. Thereafter, when the file is in use, any memory resident block with adequate space is used.

Physical ordering of records causes the records in an ADABAS file to be stored in physical blocks in ascending sequence by the value of any one of its descriptors. A program retrieving records in logical sequence by that descriptor is thereby optimized. Physical ordering is achieved through a utility or by sorting the records before loading. Logical sequential access on physically ordered files that are static can be done by retrieving sequentially without the inverted list. However, in the latter case the access method is not (strictly speaking) internal since the programmer must know about the physical layout of the file.

10.1.7 Retrieval Methods (External Model)

ADABAS offers many ways for a user to retrieve data from an ADABAS file. Some of these employ the structures created by ADABAS in implementing file inversion: the address converter and the inverted lists. Or, the user can bypass these structures and go directly to the file. Since these retrieval methods are used by the programmer in interfacing with ADABAS, they are classified as external model access methods as described in Chapter 7. However, they impact upon the interface between the DBMS and the operating system at the internal model level as well. The retrieval methods to be considered are:

- Read physical
- Read ISN
- Read logical
- Find
- Histogram

"Read physical" returns the records from a file in the sequence in which they reside in data storage. Since it accesses only the data storage component, it is the most efficient of the retrieval methods. Read physical provides no selectivity; it is used only when the order in which the records are retrieved is irrelevant (see Figure 10.9a).

"Read ISN" returns the records from a file in sequence by ISN. Since it accesses the address converter in the associator as well as data storage blocks in possibly random order, it does not have such good access efficiency. Read ISN provides selectivity by ISN only; it is used when the ISN has some significance to the user as when the user has assigned the ISN (see Figure 10.9b).

"Read logical by descriptor" returns the records from a file in logical sequence by the values of the descriptor. Since it accesses both structures in the associator, the inverted list and the address converter, as well as data storage, it will have even poorer access efficiency. However, read logical provides perfect selectivity, delivering back only the records having the values, and in the order, desired (see Figure 10.9c).

"Find" accepts a search involving a single descriptor or many descriptors. Complex search criteria may be specified using the usual arithmetic relations and logical operators. ADABAS constructs a list of ISNs of all records together with the number of records, if any, satisfying these criteria and places it on the work component. The program may then retrieve any or all of these records from data storage; one read is issued for each record desired. Since it accesses all of the various components, it is the least efficient of the retrieval methods. However, it gives perfect selectivity on the values desired of the descriptors defined (see Figure 10.9d).

"Histogram" returns the range of values present in the file for any descriptor and the number of records containing each value. One read is

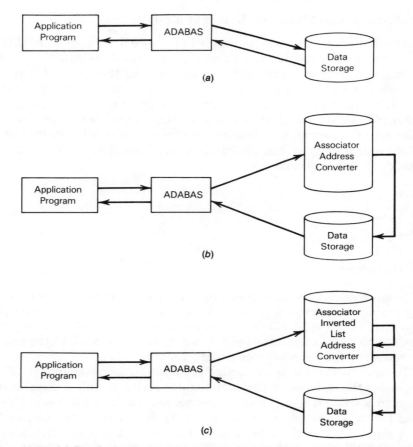

Figure 10.9. (*a*) **Read physical accesses data storage only. (*b*) Read ISN accesses the address converter as well as data storage. (*c*) Read logical accesses the inverted list, the address converter, and data storage.**

issued for each value. It is very efficient since only the inverted list, and not data storage, needs to be accessed. Histogram is used when only counts of records, and no further details, are required (see Figure 10.9*e*).

10.1.8 Accessing Related Records

Although the access methods just described are quite varied, and the search criteria can be quite complex, the data retrieved is from a single entity. The external model presented to the user contains all, or perhaps a portion of, the fields from one ADABAS file.

As mentioned earlier, a relationship exists between two files that contain a common field with common values. If either or both of these fields are defined as descriptors, then this relationship can be implemented by ADABAS in an external model. This facility is called "logical coupling."

Consider the Policy file and Claims file in Figure 10.3. Suppose that Policy-Type in the Policy file and the Policy-No (call it Claim-Policy-No) and Claim-Date fields in the Claims file are all defined to be descriptors. Then selecting data from both files can be done using the following two nested finds with implied reads:

FIND POLICY WITH POLICY-TYPE='LIFE'
FIND CLAIM WITH CLAIM-DATE
    BETWEEN January 1, 1988 and January 31, 1988
    AND CLAIM-POLICY-NO=POLICY-NO

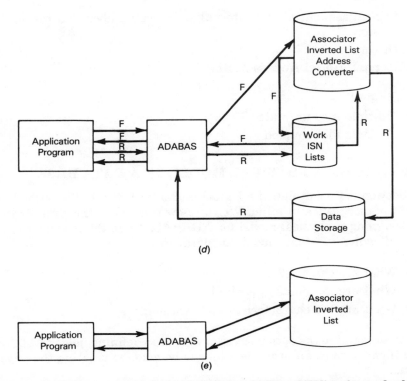

Figure 10.9. (*d*) Find accesses the inverted lists to build an ISN list of records placed on the work. These records may then be read from data storage using the address converter. (*e*) Histogram accesses the inverted list only; data storage is not required.

The record retrieved for this query is:

Policy-No=643489   Policy-Type=LIFE
Claim-Date=January 15, 1988

Such an operation is effective and meaningful only when the fields Policy-No and Claim-Policy-No contain the same data values and arise from the same attribute. The external model supported by ADABAS in this process is exactly the hierarchical view of Figure 10.4b.

Summary of Internal and External Model Access Methods in ADABAS

Internal Model Access Methods

- Physical sequential
- Inverted
- Logical sequential and internal sequence number as a result of inversion
- Direct

External Model Access Methods

- Single File
- Multiple files unrelated
- Multiple files coupled

10.2   DESIGN A PHYSICAL MODEL OF A DATA BASE

In Section 6.4 we designed a logical model for inverted file with obvious performance issues in mind. We can now proceed to the next step, that of designing a physical model for ADABAS. To do this we must answer the following questions about our data base:

- What are the files?
- What are the fields in each file?
- What are the characteristics of each field?

We first examine the options available to us in defining fields to ADABAS and then we consider other decisions to be made in creating the physical model.

10.2.1   Field Definition Options

Each field defined in an ADABAS file must be given a unique name together with a standard length and format. The formats permitted are alphanumeric, binary, fixed point, packed decimal, unpacked decimal, and floating point. The length and format are purely for external use by ADABAS in accepting input data and presenting output data to the user. The length and format of the data as actually stored may be different after compression. (See Figure 10.7.)

In addition, one or more of the following options can be associated with any field to declare it to be:

- A descriptor
- A unique descriptor
- Uncompressed
- Compressed
- Null suppressed
- Multiple valued
- A participant in a periodic group

These options are explained more fully in the following sections.

10.2.2 Compression

Three of the options defined in Section 10.2.1 concern ADABAS compression. The uncompressed option, or fixed length field, causes the data values to be placed in data storage using the standard length and format. No length byte is required. Normal compression, which is the default, instructs ADABAS to compress according to the rules in Figure 10.7. All field values then occupy a minimum of two bytes, one for data and one for the inclusive length. Null suppression allows the values of (up to 63) contiguous fields which are null (zeros if numeric, blanks if alphanumeric) to be stored in a single byte empty field count (EFC).

Null suppression is used for any field as a rule-of-thumb, especially for multiple value fields and those in periodic groups. Fields that are only one or two bytes long, that have a true fixed length (e.g., a telephone number), or that are seldom null, make good candidates for fixed-length fields. Normal compression is used for fields where fixed length is too restrictive and null suppression is not appropriate.

10.2.3 Multiple Value Fields and Periodic Groups

A field in an ADABAS file may have one or many values in a single record occurrence. An elementary field (the default) is allowed to have only one value. A field designated as multiple valued can have up to 191 values in a single record. Several contiguous fields in a record, defined as a periodic group, can have up to 99 occurrences. A field in a periodic group can be multiple valued, but nesting of periodic groups is not permitted.

We saw in Section 6.4, Step C.2, where these features can be used to reduce data redundancy and the number of files.

Occurrences of multiple value fields and periodic groups that are not used do not waste storage space. A one-byte count records the exact number of occurrences of an instance of either structure in a particular record occurrence.

Null suppression of all participating fields insures that empty fields will collapse to empty field counts.

Since the counts and occurrences of multiple value fields and periodic groups are stored with the main record, they can be retrieved and updated with the same ADABAS call and the same physical I/O as the record.

A multiple value field can be designated a descriptor. Searches are always unindexed. Example: Find Drug with (any) Side-Effect='Fever.' A field in a periodic group can also be a descriptor. Entries in the inverted list then include the occurrence number as well as the field value. Thus, indexed searches are also permitted and positionality maintained. Example: Find Drug with Side-Effect(1) [principal side effect]='Fever.'

Disadvantages of multiple value fields and periodic groups include increased program complexity and the overhead of one byte per record occurrence. Also, care must be taken to avoid exceeding the compressed record length limit (Section 6.4, Step B.6).

10.2.4 Descriptors

One of the most important questions in the creation of the physical model for ADABAS is: Which attributes should be inverted, that is, which fields should be defined as descriptors? We saw in Section 6.4, Step D, that descriptors provide quick access to the file and implement the relationships from the conceptual model. They are needed to support the external models. But, at the same time, each descriptor requires space for storage of inverted lists in the associator and processing time for updating these lists (see Section 10.1). Therefore, descriptors should be defined not just on the arbitrary whim of the designer, but only where fully justified by processing requirements. Additional descriptors can be created (and removed) at any time through the use of utilities.

As we have seen, any elementary field can be defined as a descriptor. Such a descriptor can further be defined as unique. In this case, ADABAS will automatically guarantee uniqueness of the values of the field. It should be noted that the feature of unique descriptor bundles together two unrelated capabilities: quick access and data integrity for the primary key from the conceptual model.

Any combination of up to five fields can be defined as a "superdescriptor." The individual fields may or may not be descriptors and need not be contiguous in the record. If desired, any byte string within a field, not necessarily the entire field, can participate in the superdescriptor. If two descriptors always participate in a search together, then they should be combined into a superdescriptor. Then only one inverted list will be built and maintained. Example: the fields SEMESTER and NO-COURSE in the university environment (see Section 6.4, Step D). A superdescriptor can also be defined as unique.

Any portion of a field can be declared a "subdescriptor." If queries on a particular field always involve a range of values rather than exact values, then define a subdescriptor. The resulting inverted list will contain far fewer values. Example: The SALARY field in an Employee file where retrievals are in ranges by thousands of dollars, and not to the penny.

An elementary alphabetic field can be designated a "phonetic descriptor." In this case, the inverted list contains phonetic equivalents of the field rather than the actual values. A search on the value SMITH would retrieve records containing SMYTHE and SMIT as well. The "hyperdescriptor" is a generalization that allows a user to implement his or her own phoneti- cization routine, or any other algorithm based on field values in a record.

Some fields do not make good descriptors. Fields that assume only a few values or take a particular value in many records will result in long and unwieldy ISN lists in the associator. As a rule-of-thumb, fields with a value selecting over one third of a file should be avoided as descriptors. Also, fields that further refine search criteria already narrowed by other descriptors should not be descriptors. Let the program do some of the work!

Several methods of avoiding descriptors exist:

- Read records in physical sequence. If an alphabetic directory of the students is required annually, do not define STUDENT-LAST-NAME as a descriptor to retrieve the records in logical order. Read the data storage directly (see Figure 10.9a) and sort the directory entries separately.
- Separate logical subsets into physical files. Do not define the STATUS field in the Student file as a descriptor so that programs can select currently registered students. Instead, have separate Student and Alumni files.
- Employ user-assigned internal sequence numbers (ISNs). Make the NO-STUDENT the ISN of the Student record. Then no inverted list is required and quick access to the Student file is provided through the address converter (see Figure 10.9b).

10.2.5 Field and Component Placement

In Section 10.1.6 we considered how the data base designer can place the records in an ADABAS file to improve access efficiency. In this section, we look at how placement of fields in a record and of components on auxiliary storage can also be done to advantage.

We recall from Section 10.2.2 that ADABAS normally stores data values as compressed fields in variable length records. Retrieving a value from a field in the middle of the record cannot be done positionally as with a fixed length record. ADABAS must decompress all fields, using the inclusive length bytes, up to and including the one desired.

Thus ordering the fields within a record carefully can reduce the CPU time needed for processing.

- Fields used most frequently should be placed at the beginning of the record.
- Fields seldom read, but used mainly in search criteria, should be placed at the end of the record.
- Fields read and updated together should be grouped as a single field.
- Fields frequently null should be placed together and null suppressed. This will allow them to be represented by single byte empty field count (see Section 10.2.1).

Three of the components of an ADABAS data base were discussed in Section 10.1.5: data storage, associator, and work. Two other temporary data sets are "sort" and "temp." For best performance, we should avoid placing any ADABAS component with sort-work data sets, compiler libraries, operating system packs, spool queues, or any other non-ADABAS data sets with high activity. ADABAS files which are used together should be placed on separate channels, if possible. The ADABAS components should be distributed according to the following rules insofar as is feasible:

- *Associator*
- Different physical volume from data storage and work
- Separate channel from data storage and work
- Never on same physical volume as sort

- *Data Storage*
- Different physical volume from associator
- Separate channel from associator
- Never on same physical volume as temp

- *Work*
- Different physical volume from associator
- Separate channel from associator
- Possibly on same physical volume as data storage

- *Sort*
- Never on same physical volume as associator
- Two equal parts on separate physical volumes

Given three volumes, a possible deployment of the ADABAS components conforming to the above rules would be:

10.2.6 Free Space

The data in ADABAS files is stored as compressed variable length records in data storage blocks. As noted in Section 10.1.4, an increase in size of an existing record can cause it to migrate to another block with space to accommodate it. To avoid the overhead of excessive movement of records, ADABAS permits the designer to specify a percentage of free space (or "padding factor") for each file.

A high padding factor implies lowered storage efficiency. Ranging between 3 percent and 97 percent, the padding factor is assigned at file load, but can be changed through a utility. Guidelines for the specification of the padding factor include:

- For static files or for files where records are unlikely to expand, assign a padding factor near the minimum.
- For files with high update activity, which causes records to grow in length, assign a high padding factor (say 50 percent where records double in size).
- For files with high update activity creating new values for descriptors, assign a high padding factor for the associator.

10.2.7 Buffer Pool

ADABAS, as with most modern data base management systems, reads physical blocks at session execution time from the data base into a buffer pool in memory. Algorithms insure that frequently used blocks remain in memory as long as possible. In general, then, the larger the buffer pool, the better will be the access efficiency. The buffer pool size for

ADABAS can range upward from 80,000 bytes, the minimum, and default. A rule-of-thumb is to begin with 250,000 bytes, or with 50,000 bytes per file concurrently active during the session. This can be increased by 50,000-byte increments until the access efficiency (called buffer efficiency and displayable by operator command) is optimal.

10.2.8 Number of Files

As indicated before in Section 6.4, Step C, it is not desirable either to have too many or too few ADABAS files in our physical model. There are no hard-and-fast rules that will determine the optimum number of files for a particular data base. A designer will proceed on a combination of past experience, hunches, knowledge of the applications to be supported, as well as the anticipated future requirements. There are, however, some issues to be considered while making these decisions.

Advantages of Many Small Files

- Simpler relational-like properties (each file is an entity)
- Simpler programs
- Increased flexibility
- Greater data independence
- Less prone to errors
- Improved security
- Shorter records giving more per block and per I/O
- Easier sequential processing
- Easier isolation of volatile data
- Reduced chance of exceeding record length restriction
- Fewer periodic groups and multiple value fields
- Reduced chance of file contention among programs

Advantages of Few Large Files

- Less data redundancy
- Less storage table overhead
- Fewer calls to ADABAS
- Less time required for backup and recovery
- Less synchronization of diverse files required
- Reduced chance of exceeding 255 file restriction

After designing one or more alternatives for an ADABAS physical model, and before implementing any of them, we turn to a comparative evaluation while they are still in the blueprint stage.

10.3   EVALUATE THE PHYSICAL MODEL OF A DATA BASE

10.3.1   Space Estimates

Estimating direct access storage requirements for the data storage component of an ADABAS data base entails estimating these requirements for each of the individual files. The basic units of a file are fields that combine to form (logical) records which, in turn, are stored in blocks, the physical subdivisions of data storage. (See Figure 10.10.)

Field size calculations differ according to the compression option specified (see Section 10.2.2). The number of bytes in an uncompressed, or fixed-length, field is the actual standard field length. For a compressed field, the average compressed field length is increased by one* to account for the inclusive length byte. Null suppressed fields with anticipated null values occupy only a fraction of a byte determined by the number of adjacent null suppressed fields whose values are also empty.

The space required by multiple value fields and periodic groups is easily calculated from the lengths of the constituent fields. A single count byte is required in both.

multiple value field:
$$(\text{field length}) \cdot (\text{average number of occurrences}) + 1$$
periodic group:
$$(\text{sum of field lengths}) \cdot (\text{average number of occurrences}) + 1$$

The byte length of a logical record is obtained by summing the lengths of all elementary fields, multiple value fields, and periodic groups that make it up. Six bytes are added for the inclusive length and ISN.

The number of bytes available in a physical block for the storage of logical records is:

$$\text{usable block length} = (\text{physical block length})$$
$$- (\text{padding factor} + 4)$$

The size of the ADABAS file is thus given by:

$$\text{logical records per block} = \frac{\text{usable block length}}{\text{logical record length}}$$

$$\text{number of blocks} = \frac{\text{no. of record occurrences}}{\text{logical records per block}}$$

---

* Two for alphanumeric fields whose value is longer than 126 bytes.

Figure 10.10. **In an ADABAS file, fields are combined into logical records together with the length and ISN. Logical records are placed in the portions of blocks not occupied by the header and the padding factor.**

For example, consider the Student file of Figure 6.20. Assume that there are 100,000 students, block size is 1510, padding factor is 10%, and field characteristics are:

Field	Compression Option	Length
NO-STUDENT	Fixed	9 bytes
NAME-STUDENT	Compressed	16 bytes average
STATUS	Fixed	2 bytes
MAJOR	Fixed	2 bytes
MINOR	Fixed	2 bytes
FACULTY-ADVISOR	Null suppressed	null (50%), 16 bytes average (50%)

The size of the Student file is estimated as follows:

$$\text{logical record length} = 6 + 9 + (1 + 16) + 2$$

$$+ \ 2 + 2 + \frac{1 + 16 + 1}{2}$$

$$= 47 \text{ bytes}$$

$$\text{logical records per block} = \frac{1510 - (151 + 4)}{47} = 28 \text{ records}$$

$$\text{number of blocks} = \frac{100,000}{28} = 3572 \text{ blocks}$$

The size of data storage is only a part of the story. When fields are inverted, additional direct access storage is required for the index files.

The inverted list for each descriptor defined for an ADABAS file occupies space in the associator component. To estimate this space we must be aware of the ADABAS index structure shown in Figure 10.11. ADABAS builds up to six levels of index for each inverted list; the number of levels is always great enough to insure that there is exactly one block at the highest level.

If the NO-STUDENT field is declared a unique descriptor in the Student file, then the size of the inverted list is calculated as follows:

The usable block length is 1510 less 151 (10% padding factor) less 3 (block indicator) or 1356 bytes.

NI entry contains:

EL		Value		Count		ISN	
1	+	9	+	1	+	3	= 14 bytes

$$\frac{1356}{14} = 96 \text{ entries per NI block}$$

$$\frac{100,000}{96} = 1042 \text{ NI blocks}$$

MI entry contains:

EL		Value		ISN		RABN	
1	+	9	+	3	+	3	= 16 bytes

$$\frac{1356}{16} = 84 \text{ entries per MI block}$$

$$\frac{1042}{84} = 12 \text{ MI blocks}$$

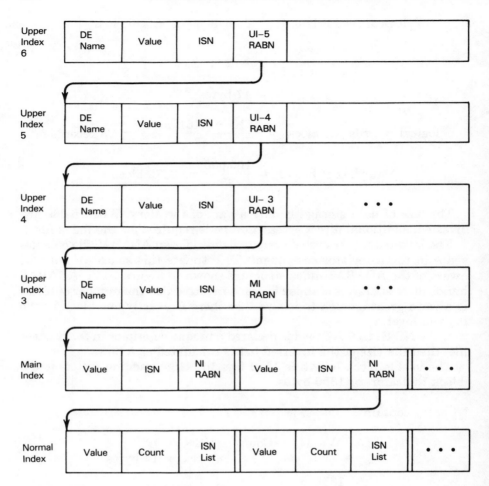

Figure 10.11. **ADABAS index structure. There is always one (1) block at the highest level.**

UI-3 entry contains:

$$\begin{array}{ccccccccccccc} \text{DE name} && \text{Flag} && \text{EL} && \text{Value} && \text{ISN} && \text{RABN} & \\ 2 &+& 1 &+& 1 &+& 9 &+& 3 &+& 3 &=& 9 \text{ bytes} \end{array}$$

$$\frac{1356}{19} = 71 \text{ entries per UI-3 block}$$

$$\frac{12}{71} = 1 \text{ UI-3 block}$$

Thus there are $1042 + 12 + 1 = 1055$ blocks in the associator containing the inverted list, and the inverted list consists of three levels of index. Knowing the number of levels allows us to calculate the number of physical I/Os, and thus the performance of operations, against the ADABAS file. We take a close look at these calculations in the next section.

10.3.2 Time Estimates

On-line transactions with critical response time are naturally among the first considerations when evaluating performance. Although CPU time, both in the program and in the data base management system, is a factor, it is usually minuscule in comparison to the I/O time required. This can be calculated if the number of physical I/Os performed in the execution of a transaction and the unit I/O time for the particular hardware and software configuration are known.

The number of physical I/Os required to retrieve randomly a record from an ADABAS file through an inverted list is a function of the number of levels of index. Since the highest level of index is a single block (see Section 10.3.1) we assume that it will be memory resident in the buffer pool. Thus one I/O is done for each level of index remaining, one I/O for the address converter which is positional (see Section 10.1.4), and one I/O to retrieve the physical block containing the record. The resulting number of I/Os is one greater than the number of index levels. For example, to retrieve a record from the Student file of Section 10.3.1, knowing the NO-STUDENT, would require four physical reads.

However, in any real execution of ADABAS, we would seldom see the worst case random retrieval situation just described. ADABAS keeps in its buffer pool (Section 10.2.7) frequently accessed blocks from data storage as well as from the inverted lists and the address converters. Access efficiency is improved by increasing the buffer pool size and also by adjusting the program call sequences with the exact characteristics of the internal model in mind.

It is also important to take a look at the major batch programs. It is always disconcerting to build a system and then find that the daily file update has run time of 37 hours! In Section 10.1.6 we examined several methods of physically ordering the records in an ADABAS file. If the batch input transactions are sorted in this same order, then the update program can process all records directly without resorting to any inverted list (see Section 10.1.7, Figure 10.9a). Similarily, batch reports can be produced by reading the ADABAS file in physical order and sorting the data extracted in a separate step. For example, the entire Student file of 100,000 records in Section 10.3.1 can be processed, in this way, with only 3572 I/Os.

REFERENCES

1. *ADABAS Design Guide*, Software AG of North America, Inc., Reston International Center, 11800 Sunrise Valley Drive, Reston, Virginia.
2. *ADABAS Introduction Manual*, Manual/Order Number: ADA-410-000, Software AG of North America, Inc., Reston International Center, 11800 Sunrise Valley Drive, Reston, Virginia.
3. Atre, S., *Data Base Management Systems for the Eighties*. Wellesley, Massachusetts: Q.E.D. Information Sciences, Inc., 1983.
4. Atre, S., "The Information Center Holds," *PC World*, August 1986.
5. Atre, S., *Information Center: Strategies and Case Studies*. Atre International Consultants, Inc., P.O. Box 727, Rye, New York, 1986.
6. Cardenas, Alfonso R., "Analysis and Performance of Inverted Data Base Structures," *Communications of the ACM*, Vol. 18, No. 5 (May 1975).

QUESTIONS

1. How are the entities of an enterprise, attributes of these entities, and relationships among them represented in ADABAS?
2. How is the inverted file data model implemented in ADABAS?
3. What are the internal model access methods for ADABAS? How much physical data independence does each give?
4. What are the external model access methods for ADABAS? How much physical data independence do they give?
5. Evaluate ADABAS with respect to logical data independence.
6. How and why is data compression done in ADABAS? When should it be used?
7. Discuss the considerations of data duplication in ADABAS: multiple value fields, periodic groups, multiple record types within a file, and multiple files.
8. What are the arguments favoring and opposing multiple ADABAS files to store data?

CHAPTER **11**

Performance Issues

Once the physical design is evaluated, it can be implemented. The structure of the physical design, the specifications of the access methods, and several details about retrieving, updating, adding, and deleting the data have to be supplied to the data base management system. Some of the existing data files will be converted and integrated into the physical data base. A number of performance issues need to be considered in the implementation phase.

The day-to-day chores will be performed on the implemented data base. Since software as well as hardware may fail, it is absolutely necessary to have established recovery and backup procedures in every data base environment. The best physical design in the world cannot provide consistently good performance for a volatile data base despite the self-reorganizing features of some data base management systems. Most DBMS packages provide reorganization routines, and the physical design of the data base must be evaluated with the possible reorganization in mind. There is also a need for continuous and long-term monitoring of service delivered by the data base environment. The data collected from these tools can be used for performance tuning. It is also mandatory to provide a certain measure of security and privacy, which will vary from environment to environment, even at the cost of some performance.

11.1 IMPLEMENTATION

11.1.1 Physical Creation

Usually it is not the best implementation strategy to store the data regarding the entire enterprise in one gigantic data base. Rather, it is advisable to describe the conceptually separate units of the enterprise in separate data bases. At the same time it may be advisable to provide linkages between these separate physical data bases. The actual storage of data in auxiliary storge with the physical design as the framework is called a physical data base in IMS terminology. As we saw in Chapter 10, however, ADABAS supports a number of files, and these files can be related to each other via a coupling feature. It is realistic to store the data regarding the entire enterprise in several physical data bases with a corresponding physical design underlying each physical data base. The existence of a number of physical data bases should not be the concern of the application programmers. The DBMS is the black box that supports the logical view or external model seen by the application programmer.

Two basic issues that need considerable attention are the options to be provided in the physical implementation and the physical placement of the data bases. One may go to the extreme of saying, "Show me a poorly performing data base, and you will find a poorly placed data base."

Almost every DBMS lets the data base implementor choose a number of combinations from a spectrum of possible options. The major issue here is which combination to pick to meet the desired performance level. The implementor faces almost the same dilemma as does a child in a candy store with limited money in his or her pocket.

We saw a number of alternatives for physical data structures in Chapters 8, 9, and 10. Other options are available in splitting a data base into a number of data bases or parts. Should the volatile part of the data base be separated from the nonvolatile part? Also, should any free space be provided at the time of initial loading or at the time of reorganization of a data base, and, if so, how much, and how should it be distributed? Free space provided may degrade performance today but be helpful for performance six months from now. How big should be the blocksize (control interval size for VSAM), and how big the logical record length? A large blocksize enhances the probability of finding two segments or two records in the same block. But what if the application does not require the two segments or two records to be in the same block? Then it will just take longer for a channel to transfer the big block of data without gaining any benefit from it.

How large should the buffers be and how many should exist? Buffers take away storage from real memory. One of the major issues in designing the physical structure of the data base is pointers, which use storage. As a result of using pointers, the distance between segments or records widens. But at the same time faster access from one record to another record is provided. If the implementor does not select the pointers, most DBMSs provide default pointers and sometimes, with the defaults, some surprises.

Most DBMSs provide a number of access methods to choose from. For some DBMSs one access method has to be selected for the entire data base, whereas for others different methods may be chosen for accessing different parts of the data base. Should the records of a data base be accessed sequentially or with the help of an index or directly, using some hashing algorithm? For some applications it may be advisable to access the records sequentially; for others, directly. The pointers to be chosen to reside in the data base records depend on the access method chosen. Although most DBMSs provide some kind of software with which the organization and access method can be changed, this change may be quite time consuming. In the data base environment, there is nothing better than getting things right the first time.

Another option that has to be considered is whether any compaction technique should be used. With some DBMSs and with some access methods, when a data base record is deleted, it is deleted logically and not physically. If the activity of deletion of data base records is heavy, a considerable part of the space on auxiliary storage may be unused. This unused space may widen the distance between the active data base records, resulting in longer time for retrieval. The question to be answered is whether compaction should be done on a daily basis during the third shift, on a weekly basis, or on a monthly basis or should be postponed until performance becomes unacceptable as a result of a disorganized data base.

Another basic issue that affects the performance of a data base is the placement. Most of the data is stored on auxiliary storage. Methods for giving fast response include combinations of the following:

1. Storing frequently referenced data on fast devices.
2. Positioning data so that lengthy seeks are avoided where possible.
3. Selection of address and search schemes that require few seeks, preferably only one per retrieval.
4. Use of multiple operations in parallel.

In space allocation and placement, it should be considered whether to separate index and data and put them on separate volumes. Before placing a data base on a device, an analysis of device and channel activity for other data processing should be made. It should be determined which applications or transactions refer to the data base and to part of the data base concurrently. It should also not be forgotten that a voluminous data base, if not required to be kept on-line, may be stored on magnetic tape(s).

11.1.2   Conversion and Integration

One of the biggest cost factors of the data base environment is the conversion of data from the existing data files to a data base. In most environments, the data to be converted will exist in different formats, scattered across a number of data files. There will be a considerable redundancy in the stored data. To move the scattered data to a central data base, a number of application programs will have to be written. It will not be easy to justify the considerable programmer time required to write these programs.

The programs to be written for the conversion are not trivial. They have to access a large number of data files, with redundant data. Only part of the data files are extracted in certain situations. Time is needed to understand the conversion "from" and "to," and writing the application code, testing and revising it, and coordinating a number of programs is not a trivial job. Management of an enterprise has to be aware of the fact that acquisition of a DBMS is not the end, but rather the beginning of a commitment.

Another major issue that should not be forgotten during the process of conversion and integration is that the data has to be validated and then the data base must be populated. Errors in the data conversion will have long lasting effects.

As a result, conversion to a data base is not a one-time shot. The conversion process is incremental. The enterprise and its various disciplines have to function during the process of conversion on the existing data files. The enterprise cannot shut its doors during the time period, which may extend over months, of conversion from data files to a data base. Application programs and the data manipulated by them will be transferred gradually to the data base as new application programs for the data base are written.

Most DBMSs do not provide a general purpose software to convert the existing data files to a data base, although some load utilities and aids are provided. The major obstacle in providing a tool for conversion is nonuniformity of data files in different environments. Most enterprises have developed data files tailored to their needs. Some research is being done in this area, however, and one of the results is EXPRESS: A Data EXtraction, Processing and REStructuring System. (See reference 13 in the list at the end of the chapter.) EXPRESS can access and restructure data from multiple files and produce multiple restructured files in a single run.

In most environments, it may be advisable to redesign the existing applications to be able to take advantage of the data base approach. In some environments, however, it may be advisable to let the existing applications alone and use the data base approach for new applications. But wherever conversion and integration is undertaken, it should work only on a small part of the functions of the enterprise. As with every project, there is a learning curve involved, and the most important and visible applications should not be the guinea pigs! To make any conversion project successful, standards should be adhered to strictly. But at the same time the standards should be easy to adhere to and adequate.

Any conversion and integration project is made up of two parts. One part is the data file conversion, and the other is the application program conversion. In the conversion phase, it may be necessary to maintain the same data in conventional data files for current operation of the business and in the data base for future use. This puts almost a double load on the maintenance staff. In most environments, it will be necessary to rewrite the application programs for the data base environment. Moreover, the application programs for a data base require different program writing habits than do the programs for a conventional environment. As a result there is a need for retraining on the part of application programmers.

11.2 OPERATIONS

11.2.1 Backup and Recovery

Once a data base is implemented, one of the major concerns of management is keeping it up and available to users. The major components of a data base environment are the operating system, data base management system, application programs, transactions for an on-line environment, hardware, and users. In a data base environment, damage to the data base has to be taken more seriously than in the conventional data file environment. In the latter environment, if one data file is damaged, there may be ways of reconstructing the damaged data because of its probable multiple appearance in various data files. In a data base environment, however, there may be a chain reaction in a number of places in the data base as a result of damage to data in one place. The following steps should be considered for backup and recovery.

STEP 1. Detecting the error that damaged the data base. At what time did the error take place? Which part of the data base was damaged? What or who triggered the error? The application program, the transaction, the logical and the physical terminal in an on-line environment, or the user?

STEP 2. Tracing all the activity against the data base that took place between the occurrence of the damage and the correction of the damage.

STEP 3. Restoring the data base to the most recent error-free stage and running all the activity detected in step 2.

In addition to these three steps, it may be wise on the part of management to establish a mechanism that will not let an error, as detected above, happen. "Prevention is better than cure" holds for the data base environment too.

To recover to the error-free stage, a backup copy of the healthy (i.e., undamaged) data base at a certain point in time has to be kept. In addition, a log of all the activities that took place against the data base after that point in time must be maintained. Merging the backup copy of the data base and all the activities against it should result in an accurate indication of the current state.

Most DBMSs provide a facility, called "logging," that records all the activities against the data base on a "log tape" or on an exchangeable disk. As the reader can imagine, a lot of information will be stored on the log tape, and the installation will need a number of log tapes.

The main components of the information stored on a log tape in a transaction-oriented environment may be:

1. **Transaction Record (Input and Output).** This component includes transaction identification, such as user identification, logical terminal identification, time of day, and date; input message, such as type of transaction to be processed and input message of the transaction; and output message, such as whether the transaction was completed successfully and list of blocks read.

2. **Before Images.** Whenever a change is made to the data base, the DBMS can write a copy of what the block, segment, page, or record looked like before the change. When a failure occurs, the DBMS can remove changes by writing these before copies (usually called "before images") back into the data base. This kind of restoration "rolls back" the data base from one point in time to an earlier point.

3. **After Images.** In a manner similar to writing before images, the DBMS can write copies that show the changes made. Thus, if a data base is damaged, these copies can be added to a backup copy of the data base. This kind of restoration "rolls forward" the data base from a point in time when it is known to be correct to a later time.

Before step 2, the access control mechanisms have to check whether the user is authorized to request the changes. If he or she is not authorized, the transaction should be interrupted without making any changes to the data base record. Log tapes may be used for auditing. They may also be used for checking the integrity of data in the data base by inspecting the before and after images for given transactions.

Checkpoints. If backing out is necessary for certain transactions or application programs because of the detection of an error, it may be quite time consuming to start the transaction or the application program from the beginning. To be able to start at certain points in the execution, "checkpoints" may be taken. In case of a possible backout, it may be possible to go back to the latest checkpoint instead of all the way to the beginning of the execution.

In on-line environments, checkpointing may be cumbersome because of concurrent processes. All the processes have to be made inactive before taking a checkpoint. In some environments where all the processes cannot be made inactive, checkpointing is done on individual processes separately. These checkpoints have to be synchronized at the time of recovery.

Checkpointing results in a degrading of performance. There is a trade-off between the number of checkpoints and the time interval between two checkpoints; the higher the number of checkpoints, the greater is the degradation of performance but the easier the recovery. If the time interval between two checkpoints is long, the degradation of performance is less at the cost of more difficult recovery.

The timing of checkpoints may depend on a number of factors:

1. An operator should issue a checkpoint command.
2. The system should automatically take a checkpoint after a certain time interval; the time interval may vary during the day. At the peak load the time span between two checkpoints may be smaller than for a sluggish load.
3. A checkpoint should be taken by the system after a certain number of changes to the data base.
4. A checkpoint should be taken by the system after a certain number of records are written out to the log tape or after a certain number of transactions have been processed.

In some environments, if these backup facilities are not sufficient, two identical copies of the data base should be maintained. The updating by the system has to be such that the two copies are identical.

The log tape or the journal is a way of backing up to an error-free stage of the data base if a recovery has to take place. The recovery process starts at the point where an error is discovered. The detection of the error (i.e., "What went wrong?") and the determination of the error source (i.e., "Who did it?") may be time consuming and may require considerable manual intervention.

If there is a system crash, the time period of incorrect operation is usually small. But if there is error detection on the basis of incorrect output, there may be a long time interval between occurrence and detection of error. In the latter case, considerable detective work may be necessary to restore the data base to an error-free stage.

Unfortunately, errors usually take place in groups. What happens if the log tape itself cannot be read properly? This means that a backup of a backup has to be provided. In most environments, however, multiple errors occur because proper attention is not paid to single errors. It is the data administrator's responsibility to provide adequate backup and recovery procedures and see to it that they are followed.

11.2.2 Reorganization

In most data base environments, it will be necessary from time to time to clean up the data base. After the initial loading or after the reloading of the data base, there will be unused space between the valid records as a result of a deletion of some records. There will also be some fragmention of space. Inserted records will not necessarily be stored in the logical sequence, and this may result in the creation of long chains. The fetch or sequential processing time may become excessive. Most DBMSs provide reorganization routines to rearrange the untidy data base in order to reclaim space occupied by deleted data and to move records from overflow areas to free space in prime data areas. The basic activities involved in the reorganization of a data base are copying the old data base onto another device, excluding records marked deleted; reblocking the valid records; and reloading them. One side effect of reorganization is that it provides a backup copy of the data base.

At the time of reorganization, it may also be possible to rearrange records so that, for most of them, their physical sequence is the same as their logical sequence. It may also be possible to rearrange the records so that the more frequently accessed ones are stored on a high speed medium, whereas the rarely accessed records are stored on a slower speed medium.

In the case of a sequentially organized data base, reorganization means taking the old data base and the transaction log file and combining the two into a new data base, omitting any data base records marked deleted on the transaction log file. In the case of an indexed sequentially organized data base, reorganization means taking the entire data base from the prime and overflow areas and reloading the data base without any records in the overflow areas. In the case of a directly organized data base, reorganization means moving the records from the overflow areas physically closer to the records from the prime area with the same synonyms. This will also recover space lost because of fragmentation. With most DBMSs, the access methods with direct organization reclaim space used by the deleted segments or records on an ongoing basis. As a result, reorganization is probably needed much less frequently for a data base using direct organization than for one with sequential or indexed sequential organization.

Ideally, reorganization should be under direct control of the DBMS on a continuous basis. As records are deleted, the space should be reclaimed automatically. The DBMS should be monitoring the changes to different sectors of the data base, and after a certain threshold of changes and insertions is reached, reorganization should take place for the corresponding sectors.

In most data base environments, although certain organization methods reclaim deleted space on a continuous basis, reorganization of the data base is a major effort. The frequency of reorganization varies from environment to environment. The major causes of frequent reorganizations may be heavy activity of insertions and deletions of data base records, failure to provide sufficient free space for later insertions at the time of initial loading or reloading of the data base, incorrect selection of the organization and access methods, and incorrect selection of storage media.

Reorganization should take place when the overflow area exceeds a certain percentage of utilization and the average daily increase in the overflow area reaches a certain percentage. These percentages vary from environment to environment. The DBMSs provide statistics about the utilization and increase of the overflow area.

The major impact of reorganization on users is the downtime or unavailability of the data base. Here the DA has two choices: either reorganize the data base on a continuous basis at the cost of some unavailability of the data base to the users, or reach the stage, without any reorganization, where more and more hardware has to be added to keep the same performance requirements. In some cases, more hardware is the only choice.

11.2.3 Restructuring

It is conceivable that in a dynamic environment, after a data base has been in operations phase for some time, the usage pattern of the data base has changed relative to the initial design and anticipation. The priorities of data base applications, transactions, and performance requirements have changed. The basic entities and relationships between them may not have deviated drastically, but the way in which the entities and their relationships are modeled may need restructuring. Besides the changes to the original structure, it is also possible that the data base needs expansion, not relative to the volume of data but relative to the addition of new record types, new data elements, and so on.

Implementing changes at the logical model and at the internal (physical) model levels is called "restructuring." Changing the access control and data base procedures may be categorized as restructuring too. The basic difference between reorganization and restructuring may be stated through the following analogy. Reorganization is something like spring cleaning a house, with the restoring of misplaced items like clothes, books, toys, and tools to their proper preassigned places and the throwing away of accumulated junk. Restructuring, on the other hand, is like expanding a house with an attic or a basement for a family that has grown bigger, providing new passages between some rooms, and so on. Reorganization basically does not affect the existing applications or procedures, whereas restructuring may affect them.

Let us distinguish between three types of restructuring changes: procedural changes, physical level (internal model) changes, and logical level changes.

1. Procedural Changes

Backup and Recovery. Any changes to the procedures will affect the operations staff only.

Access Control. If, for some business reason, any of the access control procedures relative to security, privacy, or integrity is changed, the users will be affected. If any of the access controls to be changed is anchored in applications, the applications must be changed.

2. Physical Level Changes

Hardware Configuration or Data Base Placement Changes. It may be possible that statistics from performance monitoring indicates that the hardware configuration relative to channels and direct access storage devices (DASDs) should be restructured to minimize contention. It may also be possible that, for better performance, a data base has to be split into two or more data bases. The placement of the data bases must be reconsidered. Changes of this nature do not affect the existing applications as far as modification is concerned.

Reconfiguration of Pointers. Before a data base can be implemented, specification of pointers used is presented to the DBMS with the internal model. (In IMS the physical and logical pointers are specified at the physical data base description level; for CODASYL systems NEXT, PRIOR, and other pointers to be used by the DBMS have to be specified at this level.) If a change in the pointer structure, adding or subtracting some pointers, is justified by performance statistics, the change should be conveyed to the DBMS. Most DBMSs provide utility routines for reconfiguring the pointers. The data base descriptions of the physical data base are changed, and the actual physical data base is unloaded and then reloaded with the new set of pointers. Existing applications do not need any modification if the pointers are not used explicitly.

Changing Blocksizes, Buffer Pool Sizes, Prime Areas, Overflow Areas. Most of these changes may be considered as reorganization changes.

Changing the Attributes for Inversion. Based on the latest requirements for searching data base records, it may be necessary to change the set of attributes for inversion. Ideally, this change should not affect the existing applications.

Changing the Randomizing (Also Called Hashing) Algorithm. The hashing algorithm may have been based on the key distribution of data base records at the time of implementation. The key distribution will probably change as time passes. A modified algorithm should not affect the existing applications.

3. **Logical Level Changes.**

All of the following changes at the logical level may affect the existing applications:

Adding or deleting data elements in existing segments or records.

Combining a number of records or segments into one, or splitting one record or segment into number of records or segments.

Changing the relationships between records, sets, or segments, for example, owner-member, parent-child.

Changing the roles of data elements as keys or nonkeys.

Restructuring may require modifying the internal model, logical model, and contents of the data base. It may also necessitate reassigning the contents of the data base to different devices and media. Considerable time may be consumed in rewriting and recompiling applications and in debugging the new applications. It is advisable to dedicate the whole data base for restructuring if the contents of the data base as far as pointers or data are to be changed.

In most installations, restructuring is a major effort similar to the initial loading. Most DBMSs today do not provide a utility for a major restructuring. Most of them provide a set of simple utilities for loading a data base from a dump, whereas the dump consists of data in blocks without any underlying structure. The application programs written for loading the initial data base may not be used for reloading the data base for the new structure.

Restructuring is a big project as far as machine time and involvement on the part of data base professionals are concerned. It should not be done on a production data base without a duplicate copy. The time to be spent on restructuring should be outweighed by the benefits resulting from data base change.

11.2.4 Performance Monitoring and Tuning

In a data base environment, continuous, long-term measurements are necessary to understand the service provided by a DBMS. The performance monitor should provide a detailed as well as a bottom line picture of the demand on the data base service, the service provided, the resource consumption in the delivery of that service, and any resource overcommitments. The monitor should be inexpensive to operate and should create concise reports on a few pages. Voluminous reports are not reviewed on a daily basis.

Performance tuning of a data base is done successfully only when detailed knowledge of the performance of the existing system is gained. A number of useful statistics can be collected on the data base activity. The major questions in performance evaluation are what data to collect, when and how much to collect, and how to analyze it.

Let us consider an on-line environment. In an environment where performance is seen chiefly in terms of response time in seconds to users at terminals, degradation of performance is highly visible.

Hundreds of factors determine the performance of transactions within an on-line system. Most data base and data communications packages are complex software packages, and the large number of performance-related factors present are due mostly to the high function nature of the products and the large number of user options that can be specified for the system.

Examples of these performance-related factors are data base structure, number of different segment types or record types, relationships between a number of physical data bases, pointer selection, size of buffer pools for data bases, and physical and logical data base descriptions. Performance-related factors for teleprocessing are transaction classes, transaction mixes and volumes, transaction format blocks, number of transaction processing regions, and size and execution time of transaction processing programs, to name a few. Most of these performance factors could be more accurately classified as performance tuning factors, that is, given adequate resources to perform the job required (even though we have not yet determined what resources we need), we need only to understand the real meaning and effect of these factors, apply knowledge of the application, and evaluate possible trade-offs.

This is not meant to minimize the importance of the performance tuning activity. It is very important that installations dependent on a data base and/or teleprocessing system have people who understand the factors and their effects, the relationships between these factors, and the trade-offs involved. This usually requires detailed knowledge of the DBMS and the teleprocessing interface, since many of the factors, relationships, and effects are undocumented, misdocumented, or ignored in the manuals provided. However, once the performance factors are understood, the system can, given adequate amounts of central processing unit (CPU) power, main storage space, direct access storge device (DASD) space, channels, teleprocessing lines, and terminals, be tuned to do the work required of it. However, the purpose of performance prediction is to determine system performance capabilities, not by building the whole system and tuning it to a suitable level, but rather by determining beforehand what the adequate resources are that will be required (how large a CPU, how many channels, how much DASD), and, given these adequate resources, what kind of performance results can reasonably be expected. We would like to restrict ourselves to the central system, ignoring the teleprocessing lines and line delays (which can be analyzed separately).

To determine what reasonable results are, it would be useful if we could reduce the hundreds of interacting factors to a few general, major determinants of transaction performance. The selection of the following factors can be partially justified by the fact that they tie into many of the detailed performance factors and affect the major performance factors strongly:

1. **Transaction Rates** (as seen by the DBMS). It is obvious that the transaction rate is a major determinant. Note that the DBMS transaction rate may be higher than the rate of transactions from the user to the system (as when one user transaction causes multiple DBMS transactions to be scheduled). Also, the relative transaction rates of different transactions (i.e., the transaction mix) can be important, particularly if the resource usages of different transactions are very different, for example, if one transaction type issues ten times more DBMS CALLs than all the others. Such a different nonhomogeneous transaction not only can result in poor performance for itself, but also can adversely affect other transactions in the system to a degree far out of proportion to its own high resource usage.

2. **Transaction Processing Program Loading and Scheduling.** Generally, the longest single time component of a transaction is the time taken to load the program. Also, the largest single piece of CPU time consumed, if all DBMS CALLs are counted as separate pieces, is the time used to schedule a transaction into a transaction processing region. In particular, the I/O time to locate the proper directory entry by scanning one or more partitioned data set directories and to read the program into storage often accounts for more than 50% of a transaction's total transit time through the system. Also, program loading by multiple transaction processing regions from a few common program libraries may cause channel contention problems.

   The DBMS transaction processing preload facilities are the most commonly used means of reducing or eliminating program load and overload. However, this is effective only for very highly active transaction processing programs, and depends on the availability of adequate real main storage (since page faulting one's way through a program may be more costly than program loading). Also, the operating systems page reuse algorithms (e.g., Multiprogramming with Virtual Storage: MVS) may defeat the desired effect of preloading.

3. **Data Base CALLs Issued per Transaction.** For all but the most trivial transaction, this is the major determinant of the CPU consumption of a transaction. Generally, the complexity of the data base CALLs and of the data base structures, and the type of CALLs (e.g., CALLs that scan the data base), are less important than the sheer volume of CALLs issued (except as they affect point 4 below). This is mostly due to the fixed overheads of data base CALLs, including interregion communication and CALL analysis. Generally, many of the trade-offs in the design and implementation of transactions and systems are made to minimize the number of data base CALLs and the number of I/O operations per CALL (point 4 below). Also, the number of data base CALLs estimated in the design phase of system implementation is usually low (often by a factor of two).

4. **Physical I/O Operations per Data Base CALL.** This affects both the transaction elapsed time and the CPU time, since the issuing and processing of I/Os by the DBMS and the operating system consume a significant amount of CPU time. Generally, reduction of physical I/O operations is the major factor in data base design for performance, affecting the choice of access methods, data base structure, data base CALL types used, and use of relationships between the data base structures. On the other hand, attempts to severely reduce this quantity may greatly increase the complexity of the application programming involved.

5. **System Interactions with Other Tasks.** The other tasks processed on a system [e.g., batch jobs, time sharing operations (TSOs)] may also seriously affect data base performance. This is probably the most difficult area to assess and estimate, particularly if data base transaction processing is not clearly identified as the most important work being done on the system. The most common way of handling this performance determinant is to ignore it, rationalizing that data base work is clearly the most important work in the system and as such will be given the highest system priority, and thus its performance will not be degraded by other applications. However, the assumption that the DBMS, having the highest priority, will get the resources it needs is not always correct. This is particularly important to consider when there is contention for a highly used system resource, such as the CPU, real storage pages, a system channel, or a DASD device. Generally, contention for common system resources must be closely considered whenever a common resource is heavily used. For example, a CPU more than 70% busy, a block multiplexor channel more than 35% busy, a selector channel more than 50% busy, or a device more than 50% busy would be considered to be heavily used. Even after a potential problem has been identified, it may not be clear how to evaluate its effects.

6. **Input Queue.** The number of transactions on the input queue is a good indicator of the DBMS's responsiveness. If there is no queue buildup, the response time probably cannot be made significantly better except by reducing the I/O activity. Response time worsens as the queue builds up. A benchmark transaction may be developed, entered, and clocked at various levels of queues to determine the relationship between the queue length and the response time.

In an on-line environment the components of response time and the servicing component are:

Transaction Activity	Servicing Component
Teleprocessing line time	Systems control program
Queuing	DBMS
Scheduling	DBMS and systems control program
Application processing code	DBMS and systems control program
Application terminal output	DBMS and systems control program
Termination	DBMS and systems control program

Thus the major response time components are the systems control program (SCP), DBMS, and application programs. The response time is affected by hardware configuration, terminal network, and data base design. The classical I/O approach to performance is based on the assumption that response time increases in an exponential fashion as the I/O rate increases in a linear fashion.

To understand the performance of the existing system and to be able to tune it to the desired level of responsiveness, statistics on the following factors may be collected:

1. **CPU, Channel, and Device Utilizations.** The information will indicate whether any of these major components affecting the performance of the data base are posing bottleneck problems. Statistics on these are normally provided by the operating system. A detailed analysis should be performed for the peak time utilizations.

2. **Memory Usage.** Paging rates and swapping rates (in a virtual system environment) are good indicators of whether enough real memory is available. The buffer pool can be expanded with more memory, resulting in fewer physical I/Os. Periodic snapshots should be taken to indicate the usage.

3. **Transaction Statistics.** The major source of information for the transaction statistics is the log tape. Analysis of the log tapes by vendor-supplied or user-written programs can provide information on:

Transaction rates and transaction rate distribution.

Transaction response times.

Transaction priorities and classes.

Number of data base calls per transaction.

CPU time used by transaction processing program per transaction.

4. **Distribution of Data Base Contents.** The absolute number of occurrences of owners and members or parents and children in the entire data base, as well as the relative frequency of occurrences, will be helpful in expanding or restructuring the data base. Statistics on space used by pointers, by data, by variable-length records, by prime data areas, and by overflows will be helpful for tuning the data base. Statistics on free space will be of assistance in reorganization.

5. **Statistics on Use of Data Base Contents.** This information will be useful in reorganizing and restructuring the data base on the basis of the frequently used data items and the rarely used data items.

6. **Use of Application Modules and DBMS Procedures.** Since the longest single time component of a transaction is the time taken to load the program, it will be better to keep the most frequently used programs, as well as the DBMS procedures, in memory.

7. **Use of the Data Base by People.** People are one of the major determinants of the effective use of the data base system. Statistics on the error rate in use may indicate whether any additional training is necessary for those using the data base system.

8. **Statistics Collected by the Monitor for Data Base and Teleprocessing.** This tool is by far the most important source of performance information for tuning a data base. It provides detailed information on the internal operations of the DBMS, but does impose some monitoring overhead on the measured system. Almost all the important performance information is contained somewhere in its reports (e.g., IMS/VS DB/DC Monitor), including:

Buffer pool statistics.

Region utilizations.

I/O times and I/O waits.

Program load time.

Data base CALLs by program.

Activity by data base.

Transaction counts and rates.

Schedulings per transaction.

I/Os per data base call.

Data base calls per transaction.

Data base calls by call type.

Deadlock and enqueue data.

11.2.5   Security in the Data Base Environment

The issue of data security is crucial in the era of the centralized data base. We use the term "data security" to mean protection of the data in the data base against unauthorized or accidental disclosure, alteration, or destruction.

Historically, the prime incentive for data security was the protection of critical business records. Recently, however, the importance gained by the social issue of privacy has forced organizations to protect their personal records from any unauthorized disclosure. Access to sensitive data must be controlled. This means that the security issue extends beyond the data stored in the data base and beyond the data processing department. It extends to all levels of management, and therefore they must be involved in establishing and maintaining data security.

Realizing that perfect security is unattainable, the objective of a data security program is to minimize the risk and probability of loss and disclosure to the lowest affordable level and also to be able to implement a full recovery program if a loss occurs.

With increasingly reliable hardware and software, it is people who may breach the security, either intentionally or unintentionally. Let us try to classify into three different groups the people who will have direct contact with the data base.

Users.   This group of people decides on an application requirement. As a result of the application requirement and its justification, the entities, the relationships between the entities, and so on are integrated into the data base design and the stored data base. The data administrator's staff, together with the users, determines the origin of each piece of data. The originator of data determines accessibility and types of access to the data. To provide integrity of data, there must be only one department responsible for the accuracy of a particular piece of data. Once the authorized use of the data is determined by the originator of the data, the data administrator's staff can control the data usage according to the originator's intention. Access to the data can be a combination of the following:

> *Partial Retrieval Only.*   The authorized user can see only a specific part of the data and cannot change it.
>
> *Retrieval of All Types of Records.*   The authorized user can see the entire data base but cannot change it.
>
> *Insertion of Certain Types of Records.*   The authorized user can insert only certain types of records to the data base and cannot change any existing ones.

Insertion of All Types of Records.   The authorized user can insert all types of records to the data base but cannot change the existing ones.

Deletion of Certain Types of Records.   The users can see only certain types of records, which they can delete too.

Deletion of All Types of Records.

Updating of Certain Types of Records.

Updating of All Types of Records.

This list is by no means an exhaustive one, but it gives an idea of the kind of checking required of a data base management system to determine whether a user who wants to access data from the data base is authorized to do so. For this purpose, the DA has to provide the users with some way of identifying themselves to the DBMS.

Identification, verification, and authorization.   Before accessing the data base, the user has to identify to the DBMS who he or she is. One method to accomplish this in an on-line environment is by using a sign-number coupled with a confidential password. The DBMS will check the user profile supplied by the DA and will let the user perform only the actions for which he or she is authorized. The user profile, which can consist of the user sign-on number with his or her authorization, confidential password, and so on, can be conveniently stored in a data dictionary. Security can be implemented on the physical locations of the terminals; that is, terminals located within an area can perform limited operations.

If the user cannot provide satisfactory identification and authentication, the DBMS should sign off the user with a message and keep a log of such instances, consisting of the terminal number, the day, the time of the day, the supplied sign-on number, and so on. There should be at least one person on the DA's staff who is responsible for keeping track of such potential threats to security.

For a detailed treatment of user identification, the reader is encouraged to read selected references from the bibliography at the end of the chapter.

Programmers.   A high percentage of disclosure, alteration, and destruction is done by programmers. Before we discuss embezzlement by programmers, let us distinguish between:

1. Application programmers.
2. Systems programmers.
3. Operators.

There should be a clear distinction in responsibilities among these three groups.

1. *An application programmer* writes only application programs, not systems programs. An application programmer has the same type of access to the data base as any other user using the application program; that is, the application programmer has to use the sign-on procedures and the passwords.
2. *The systems programmers* make changes only to the systems code. A systems programmer may not write or run any application programs.
3. *An operator* can run but not write application programs. An operator may not change the systems code.

A librarian on the DA's staff provides the following security protections:

*   Changes to application programs can be made only by the application programmers. These changes must go through and must be recorded by the librarian.
*   The librarian keeps only the latest version of the application program. This prevents the possibility of floating versions of an application program.
*   The librarian has to back up the latest version of all application programs and store them off-site to protect against a major disaster like fire or flood.
*   The librarian can request an operator to delete or load any programs.

Operations Staff.   Frequently the accidental destruction of data is the result of untrained operators, or it may be due to insufficient guidelines for running the applications or to procedures too complex for the operator to follow. It is a wise technique to remove as many responsibilities from an operator as possible and to put those responsibilities in the application programs. Usually a new employee is given the job of computer operator as a beginning assignment. As a result, there is frequent turnover. Therefore it is risky to ask an operator to take care of backup tapes, to decide what action should be taken in case of a job failure, and the like.

The following precautions should be taken by the operations staff in order to avoid any security problems due to operational errors:

A complete log should be kept of all the activities and of any errors. The error messages should be clearly stated. The system should also print on the log the run times of all the jobs. The log can be generated by the system off-line.

Important decisions should not be left to the operators.

An operator should not have any access to the source listings of the application programs.

Operator embezzlement.   An operator desiring to breach security may manipulate data or application programs. To prevent fraud of this type, the following precautions should be taken:

An operator should not write any application programs.

Console printouts should be checked every day by a DA staff member for all the activity on the data base.

The application source programs should be kept *only* in a library and run *only* when the librarian requests them.

There should be at least two people in the computer room.

Critical forms such as checks should be locked away.

Program errors. A vast majority of accidental destruction of data is caused by program errors. Program errors or "bugs" often do not surface until some combination of circumstances takes place for which the application program was not tested. Program bugs are often the result of flaws in design, errors in program logic, errors in coding, incomplete definitions, or inadequately tested programs.

Certain precautionary steps can be taken to provide reliable application programs. Principles of structured programming can enable an application programmer to write more reliable code, and code walk-throughs can help him or her to detect any errors in the logic of the program. Fictitious data for testing the program logic should be developed by some other person than the coder. The following checkpoints should be made before sending a program into production:

1. Does the program have validity checking of input data? Most data values in real life, such as account numbers, transaction amounts, and invoice amounts, have reasonable ranges. If the calculated invoice amount does not fall in the reasonable range, the program should take proper action.

2. Does the program run successfully in extreme situations, such as the processing of one transaction only? What happens if the first or the last transaction is in error? Remember an analogy: statistically, most airplane accidents occur while taking off or while landing.

3. Does the program provide a log of record counts, card counts, transaction counts, and so on? An unreasonably high or low number of records, cards, or transactions may indicate errors.

4. Has the program been tested by someone other than the programmer? Quite often the programmer who writes the programs is not the best person to detect the program bugs.

5. Are the programs simple to read and documented in an understandable manner? (*Note*: Usually the programmer and the maintainer are different people. A well documented program facilitates reconstruction of lost data.)

6. Do program error actions explain what the precise error is and the operator/user action necessary for correction?

To check all the items above, the DA's staff should be able to borrow competent people who have application programming background. To obtain the maximum benefits, the DA and other management should not participate in code walk-throughs or the like.

Physical Security. Not long ago computer facilities were considered showcases of prestige for the company. Recently the trend has been in the other direction, in that in many installations the computers receive less visibility. One of the major reasons for providing maximum physical security is to prevent loss due to a disaster like fire. Special precautions against fire are:

1. Most computer room fires start in areas adjacent to the computer room and then spread to the computer area. The site for the computers should be chosen with this fact in mind.
2. Smoking should not be allowed in the computer room. No exceptions should be granted.
3. Clearly marked fire extinguishers should be placed in conveniently located areas.
4. The emergency power-off switch should be clearly marked and easily accessible.
5. Safety exits for people should not be blocked.
6. Fire drills should be conducted from time to time.
7. Important records should be stored in fireproof vaults.
8. Fire alarm systems must notify the computer room and an attended remote location of every defect.
9. Updated source program copies should be stored off the computer room premises, preferably in a different building.
10. Data necessary to reconstruct the data base should be stored off-site.

For security measures against water, vandalism, and sabotage the reader is referred to the bibliography at the end of the chapter.

11.2.6 Privacy in the Data Base Environment

Privacy is the right of an individual to determine what type of information can be stored and when and how, about him or her and what type can be transferred for other purposes than the one for which the information was collected originally. The individual about whom the information will be collected is the sole owner of that information.

Privacy—or rather the lack of it—has become a matter of public concern. According to the Privacy Act of 1974, federal agencies, the state, and federally financed institutions must not use certain types of information about people illegally; for example, the social security number is not supposed to be used for identification purposes. Extension of the privacy act with further legislation may occur in the foreseeable future. This legislation will make major changes in the way we process information today. Legislation will also specify civil and criminal sanctions for violations of the individual's right to privacy.

Legislation will definitely provide for fines and imprisonment for executives and administrators who do not take reasonable precautions to safeguard the privacy of information. The word "reasonable" will be interpreted more precisely by the courts once the legislation has been passed. The following safeguards are recommended by the legislative committee:

There must be no personal data record-keeping systems whose very existence is secret.

There must be a way for an individual to find out what information about him or her is recorded and how it is used.

There must be a way for an individual to prevent information about him or her obtained for one purpose from being used or made available for other purposes without his or her consent.

There must be a way for an individual to correct or amend a record of identifiable information about him or her.

Any organization creating, maintaining, or disseminating records of identifiable personal data must assure the reliability of that data for its intended use and *must take precautions to prevent misuse of the data.*

Privacy is more an ethical and social issue than an information processing one. Information processing systems are normally established to process and protect the data, not the sources of the data. The privacy issue will have far reaching effects on the way future information processing systems will function.

Privacy versus Security.   The term "privacy" is often confused with the term "security," but the two words have different meanings. Information privacy includes the right of individuals to know that recorded personal information about them is accurate, pertinent, complete, up to date, and reasonably secure from unauthorized access, either accidental or intentional.

Moreover, according to the definition of privacy an individual has the right to control information that can readily be identified as applying to him or her.

As a result of the discussion above, it becomes clear that the data administrator and management have to make the protection of privacy an organizational objective. The best time for the DA and management to solve any privacy problems or to prevent problems of this type from happening is during data base design.

What Is Private?   Once information about people (e.g., their credit records, financial positions, criminal records, addresses, purchases with credit cards, tax information, medical information) is collected, the distinction between what information should be public and what information should remain confidential is not always clearly stated. This decision requires ethical, moral, and legal judgments that administrators may be ill prepared or reluctant to make. But the question remains, which an administrator and executive must answer, whether the organization provides maximum protection for the personal information within its systems.

Does the Organization Have Privacy Problems?   The data administrator should supply answers to the following questions:

What concern has there been for the individual and his or her personal privacy as the information systems were developed?
What were the priorities concerning privacy?
What are they now?
What other systems can access information within the data base system?
If the enterprise is storing any information regarding the individuals in the system, does a single individual have a chance to examine, update, refute, or generally know what the record contains about him or her?

If the answer to any of these questions is "I don't know," the organization probably has an information privacy problem. Moreover, the data administrator and the management are responsible for invasion of privacy by not taking proper care of the private information stored in the data base, as explained below.

The information privacy problem can involve one or a combination of the following:

- Erroneous or misleading information.
- Accidental disclosure or modification of information.
- Intentional infiltration of an information system.
- Loss of data.

This list makes it clear that security and privacy issues are interwoven. The last three items are security problems. This means that, if security measures are not in place, lack of privacy is probably not far off, and if a reasonable policy for protecting private information is not established, security is at stake.

Erroneous or misleading information.   Generally, people have a tendency to trust anything that is printed. But it must be understood that, when erroneous information is passed through the computer, it will still be erroneous. Inadequately tested programs, last minute conversions of data to computer-readable media, information collected from hearsay, and insufficiently controlled information systems can all contribute to misleading information about individuals. Inaccurate information about individuals can result in lawsuits!

Accidental disclosure.   Negligence is the biggest enemy of information systems. The best technological measures and most sophisticated systems are of no value if a careless administrator leaves a sensitive report on an unattended desk.

Intentional infiltration of an information system.   Certain types of data stored in a data base may offer financial incentives and as such become the targets of potential intruders. The data administrator must identify and categorize this type of information in the data base and establish measures to prevent any intrusion.

Loss of data.   The loss of data due to natural occurrences (e.g., floods, tornadoes, earthquakes), malfunctions of mechanical equipment (e.g., power failures, air-conditioning problems), or acts of violence (e.g., civil disturbances, malicious acts of disgruntled employees) can range in magnitude from minor, inconvenient disturbances or interruptions in operations to major disasters that may break down a total organization. As far as loss of data is concerned, the data administrator has to differentiate between the CONFIDENTIALITY of data and the CRITICALITY of data. Criticality of data is based on the length of time an organization can survive if it loses that information.

The answers to the following questions will assist the data administrator and management in establishing a specific plan to avoid the invasion of privacy:

What should be done?

Who should do it?

How will one know when—and if—it is done correctly?

STEP 1. Check the information processed.

In many installations, more information is collected than necessary. In a requirement analysis study made before designing a data base, it is advisable to answer the following questions with the help of the user organizations:

What data is being collected?

Who needs this data?

Why do they need it?

When do they need it?

Are all new items of data collection and all new uses of data being cleared through the proper level of management?

These questions show that managment must take an active interest in the privacy issue and support the data administrator in carrying out the duties involved. An efficient and important tool for storing this type of information is a data dictionary, discussed in Chapter 3. The questions above are crucial for any managment information system. The goals of information privacy must be consistent with the optimum management information system. When extraneous information is not introduced during the data base design, two main advantages result:

1.	Elimination of many unnecessary threats to information privacy.
2.	Potential cost avoidance as a result of having only an "optimum" information system.

STEP 2.   Identify personal, critical, and proprietary data.
Processed either manually or automatically by machines, the data used by an organization generally falls within three general categories:

Personal, for example, certain medical and criminal history information.

Proprietary, for example, research and development data or copyrighted or patented information.

Critical, for example, accounts receivable or airline reservation information.

Personal data and proprietary data are both confidential in nature. Critical data may be the basic necessity for the existence of the organization. If the data is not critical, proprietary, or personal, why collect it?

To be able to take an effective action, the following questions must be answered:

How complex should the information classification structure be (i.e., how many levels of security are required)?

What guidelines are available to assess the value of information?

What are the legal and social responsibilities regarding information privacy?

How much protection is required for each kind of information?

Senior management, including the organization's counsel, must be prepared to accept the responsibility for answering these questions.

STEP 3.   Investigate susceptibility to damage and risks.
Management should assess the risk of exposure of personal information in the data processing system. It should also study whether the risk can be reduced be increasing the security protection.

Making an assessment of this type is not an easy task. The best way to solve the problem is to make a list of all possible exposures and to try to estimate the value of the information, that is, how much it will cost to reconstruct any loss of information. In this process the DA will be aware of the effectiveness of the safeguards currently implemented. The information systems executive, together with the data administrator, should evaluate new technological security systems on comparable software systems, similar access control systems, and similar encryption techniques.

STEP 4. Determine the budget for information privacy.

To implement any security and privacy measures, a specific budget must be set aside. The cost of implementing and operating a security and privacy program must be estimated. The budget should reflect the value of information security and privacy to the organization. In general, the higher the value, the more one should be willing to adequately secure— thus budget properly. It should also be determined what percentage of the cost should be billed to the information systems users.

STEP 5. Organize for information privacy.

Depending on the size, the number of functions supported, and the criticality of the data base, one person, either half time or full time, should support the privacy and security program. The job description of such an individual could look like:

1. Research state-of-the-art security technology.
2. Classify information according to its use.
3. Authorize, after concurring with the data administrator and senior management, specific individuals to access confidential and critical resources; for example, only a pair of specific operators can run certain information-sensitive application programs, a specific operator has the responsibility for a critical resource such as a specific disk.
4. Insure that all new information systems are designed with information privacy controls in mind.
5. Administer a program of education to insure the proper collection, handling, processing, dissemination, storage, and disposal of information.
6. Execute periodic technical and financial audits.
7. Investigate security and privacy breaches, and enforce policy and procedures.
8. Test all procedures that are enacted to insure operability.

STEP 6. Establish individual accountability.

To establish the guidelines for data access, the data administrator has to be told:

Who has the need to know, the need to change, and the right to expunge information?

When do these persons need to know?

Have these individuals received security clearances?

In addition, the personnel department must inform the DA of all personnel transfers or terminations so that the authorization entries can be deleted.

STEP 7. Implement technological safeguards, and create a privacy-conscious environment.

The plans developed for the privacy area should be implemented. Since the implementation of a privacy and security plan will need systems and people resources, the data administrator should consider the following:

- What is the priority of information privacy objectives in relation to other organization objectives (e.g., production, efficiency, other projects)?
- How will the implementaion of an information system security and privacy program affect user information system development plans and vice versa?
- How much and what kind of vendor support will be required to implement new technology?
- What additional resources (e.g., people, computer time) will be required during the implementation?
- Who is responsible for periodically communicating project status and plans to the information system user community?
- Where is the implementation plan?
- How will the plan be monitored and tested on a continuous basis?

The best developed plan is of no value unless management through all levels makes full commitment to its implementation and control throughout time.

- The information privacy problem should be addressed in organization policies.
- The substantive procedures should be well documented, understood by all concerned parties, and enforced.
- The education program should be expanded to include courses in the privacy area.
- Individuals having information privacy responsibilities should be evaluated accordingly.

REFERENCES

1. Atre, S., *Data Base Management Systems for the Eighties.* Wellesley, Massachusetts: QED Information Sciences, Inc., 1984.
2. Atre, S., *Information Center: Strategies and Case Studies.* Rye, New York: Atre International Consultants, Inc., 1986.

3. *Data Security and Data Processing*, Vols. 1, 2, and 3, G320-1370, G320-1371, and G320-1372. IBM Corporation, Data Processing Division, 1133 Westchester Avenue, White Plains, New York.

4. Date, C. J., *An Introduction to Database Systems*, 4th ed., The Systems Programming Series. Reading, Massachusetts: Addison-Wesley Publishing Company, 1986.

5. *Guidelines for Automatic Data Processing Physical Security and Risk Management*, FIPS PUB 31, U.S. Department of Commerce, National Bureau of Standards, Washington, D.C.

6. Jardine, Donald A., *Data Base Management Systems*. Amsterdam and New York: North-Holland and American Elsevier, 1974.

7. Lyon, John K., *The Database Administrator*. New York: Wiley-Interscience, 1976.

8. Martin, James, *Security, Accuracy, and Privacy in Computer Systems*. Englewood Cliffs, New Jersey: Prentice-Hall, 1973.

9. Olle, T. William, *The Codasyl Approach to Data Base Management*. New York: Wiley-Interscience, 1978.

10. Palmer, Ian R., *Data Base Systems: A Practical Reference*. Wellesley, Massachusetts: Q.E.D. Information Sciences, Inc., 1978.

11. Ross, Ronald G., *Data Base Systems Design, Implementation, and Management*. AMACOM, American Management Association, 135 West 50th Street, New York.

12. Schramm, David A., *Managing IMS Performance via IMS Control Block and Buffer Pool Statistics*, Technical Bulletin, Order No. GG22-9013, IBM Washington Systems Center, January 1978.

13. Shu, N. C., B. C. Housel, R. W. Taylor, S. P. Ghosh, and V. Y. Lum, EXPRESS: A Data Extraction, Processing, and REStructuring System," *ACM Transactions on Database Systems*, Vol. 2, No. 2 (June 1977), 134–174.

14. Sockut, Gary H., and Robert P. Goldberg, "Database Reorganization—Principles and Practice," *ACM Computing Surveys*, Vol. 11, No. 4 (December 1979).

15. "Two Men Arrested on Bribery Attempt," Illinois State Register, Friday, November 11, 1972, p. 16.

16. Van Tassel, Dennis, *Computer Security Management*. Englewood Cliffs, New Jersey: Prentice-Hall, 1972.

17. Verhofstad, J. S. M., "Recovery Techniques for Database Systems," *ACM Computing Surveys*, Vol. 10, No. 2 (June 1978).

18. Wiederhold, Gio, *Database Design*. New York: McGraw-Hill, 1977.

QUESTIONS

1. When creating the physical data base, what are some of the decisions to be made regarding physical implementation and placement?

2. Why is conversion to and integration of a data base so costly?

3. Why is backup and recovery particularly important in a data base system? What precautions against errors can be taken?

4. Reorganization or restructuring may be applied to a data base. Distinguish between the two operations. What does each do?

5. The text lists six factors that can be evaluated to aid in performance prediction. List them and justify their use.

6. Although related, privacy and security are separate issues. Discuss.

Designing a Data Base
for a Banking Environment

"Popular Bank"—Case Study 1

The list of reports in pictorial format shown in Figure A.0 presents the information needs of a hypothetical "Popular Bank." The reports and transactions are shown in Figures A.1 to A.7. Design a data base for the Popular Bank as follows:

I. Design a conceptual model of a data base (refer to Chapters 1, 2, 3, 4, and 5).

 I.1. Study the environment, and document assumptions for it (Chapters 1 and 2).

 I.2. Determine the data elements referenced in every report individually (Chapter 3).

 I.3. Determine the relationships between the data elements, such as identifying the primary key data elements and the nonkey data elements (Chapters 4 and 5).

 I.4. Develop third normal form relations for each set of data elements. Where this is not possible for individual reports, merge data from reports to establish third normal form relations (Chapter 5).

 I.5. Draw a conceptual model on the basis of the third normal form relations (Chapter 5).

II. Design a logical model of a data base (refer to Chapters 4, 5, and 6).

 II.1. Draw a logical model based on the conceptual model above for a data base management system, using:

 1. A relational data model.
 2. A hierarchical data model.
 3. A network data model.
 4. An inverted file data model.

 II.2. Draw external models for the reports in Figures A.1 to A.5, INQUIRY Transaction, and DEPOSIT/WITHDRAWAL Transaction on the basis of the logical model above.

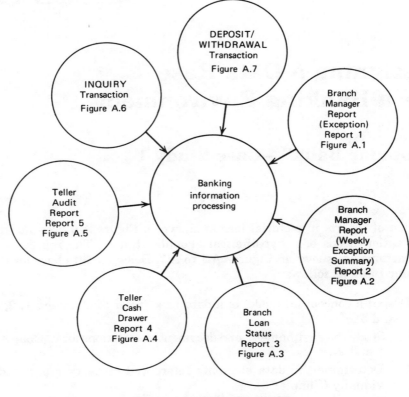

Figure A.0.   **"Popular Bank"**

III. Design a physical model of a data base (refer to Chapters 7, 8, 9, and 10).

    III.1. Draw an internal model (also called a physical model) on the basis of the logical model from step II.1.

IV. Evaluate the physical model of a data base (refer to Chapters 7, 8, 9, 10, and Appendix C on statistics).

    IV.1. Develop space estimates for the internal model above (as in step III.1). Develop input/output probabilities for the internal model above (as in step III.1).

    IV.2. Draw external models for the reports in Figures A.1 to A.5, INQUIRY Transaction, and DEPOSIT/WITHDRAWAL Transaction on the basis of the internal model above.

    IV.3. Develop time estimates for the external models as in step IV.2.

STEP I. DESIGN A CONCEPTUAL MODEL OF A DATA BASE (refer to Chapters 1, 2, 3, 4, and 5).

STEP I.1. Study the environment and document assumptions for it (refer to Chapters 1 and 2).

Popular Bank has a number of branches scattered throughout the city and the suburbs. A customer may walk into any branch and open an account. The customer is assigned a customer identification number (CID number) with the first account at the bank. The customer may open a number of accounts at that branch, but his or her CID number is not changed. The bank maintains checking accounts (accounts on which the customer may write personal checks), savings accounts (for which passbooks are required, and interest is given by the bank), loan accounts (customers must return the loans with interest), and mortgage accounts (customers must make regular payments with interest).

Branch Manager Report (Exception) (Figure A.1)

Every branch has a manager. At a certain point in time a branch has only one branch manager. A Branch Manager Report (Exception) is printed for the branch manager on a daily basis. The report consists of exceptional transactions only; for example, an automatic loan account called "Checking Plus" is overdrawn, or a savings account exceeds the balance of $100,000, which is the maximum amount insured by the Federal Deposit Insurance Corporation.

Branch Manager Report (Weekly Exception Summary) (Figure A.2)

Another type of report for the branch manager is the Weekly Exception Summary. This report is not based on individual accounts but is a summary. These two reports may be considered as batch reports.

Branch Loan Status (Figure A.3)

The branch manager also receives a Branch Loan Status. This report helps the branch manager to keep track of the loans given at the branch. It also serves as a source of new ideas for making loans at the branch attractive.

Teller Cash Drawer (Figure A.4)

The bank employs a number of tellers who cash checks and make deposits and withdrawals for the customers. The tellers are rotated among the branches, but it is assumed that once a teller is sent to a branch he or she will stay at that branch the whole day. A cash drawer is recorded every day for every teller. It keeps track of all the money flow for that

REPORT 1

DATE: January 11, 1988

Popular Bank
Branch Manager Report (Exception)

BRANCH–NO (Branch Number): 1234

BRANCH–NAME: Downtown Branch

BRANCH–ADDR (Branch Address): 1 First Street, New York, N.Y. 10001

MGR–NAME (Manager's Name) :J. J. Smith

Report for: January 10, 1988

CUST–NAME (Customer Name)	CID (Customer Identification Number)	ACCT–TYPE (Account Type)	ACCT–NO (Account Number)	AMOUNT (Involved)	X–DATE (Date of Transaction)	X–TIME (Time of Transaction)	X–TYPE (Trans. Code)	REASON–CODE	ACTION–CODE	REMARKS
Prof. Higgins	123456789	Checking	653210	268.50	1/10/88	10:15:20	Check withdraw	Checking overdrawn	Automatic loan	Notify customer Tel. 555-1234
Zalaf, Amir	345678901	Savings	12345–1	10,000.00	1/10/88	15:02:10	Check deposit	Savings exceed 100,000 limit	No deposit	Send back check and inform customer

Figure A.I. **Branch Manager Report (Exception)**

336

REPORT 2
_____

DATE: JANUARY 14, 1988

Popular Bank

Branch Manager Report (Weekly Exception Summary)

BRANCH—NO (Branch Number): 1234

BRANCH—NAME: Downtown Branch

BRANCH—ADDR (Branch Address): 1 First Street, New York, N.Y. 10001

MGR—NAME (Manager's Name): J. J. Smith

DSTRPT (Date Report Started): January 9, 1988

DENDRPT (Date Report Ended): January 13, 1988

REASON—CODE	NO—X—TOTAL (Total Number of Transactions Involved)	NO—ACCTS—TOTAL (Total Number of Accounts Involved)	AMT—TOTAL (Total Dollar Amount Involved)
Checking overdrawn	2072	1572	170,900.00
Checking overdrawn unavailable funds	650	560	100,000.00
Savings exceed 100,000 limit	24	20	2,150,000.00

Figure A.2. **Branch Manager Report (Weekly Exeception Summary)**

day, for that teller, and at that branch. Teller Cash Drawer may be considered as a batch application.

Teller Audit Report (Figure A.5)

The tellers are audited periodically, as well as for specific reasons. Every teller has a unique identification number called a teller number. Based on experience and on previous audit records, a teller may withdraw only up to a certain amount of money for a customer. If the customer wants to withdraw more money than the specific teller's maximum allowable upper limit, the teller has to request another teller who can withdraw the amount to do so. The Teller Audit Report, which could be considered a batch report, is sent to the central audit location for the bank.

REPORT 3
_____

DATE: January 11, 1988

Popular Bank

Branch Loan Status

BRANCH—NO (Branch Number): 1234

BRANCH—NAME: Downtown Branch

BRANCH—ADDR (Branch Address): 1 First Street, New York, N.Y. 10001

MGR—NAME (Manager's Name): J. J. Smith

LOAN—NO (Loan Number)	LOAN—TYPE	LOAN—ASSGND (Loan Assigned)	TOTAL—LOAN—COLLECTED (Total Loan Collected)	TOTAL—LOAN—TO—BE—COLLECTED (Including Interest)	INTEREST (Total Interest Received, i.e., profit)
1234	Car loan	4000	1000	3350	200
2389	Mortgage	45,500	5000	70,000	4550

Figure A.3. **Branch Loan Status**

Inquiry Transaction (Figure A.6)

It may happen occasionally that a customer walks into a branch and
wants to deposit or withdraw a certain amount of money or may want to
know the balance of a specific account. The customer may not be able to
provide the customer identification number (CID) or the account number(s).
In such a situation the teller should be able to provide the information
needed by the customer. This on-line transaction is only an INQUIRY
transaction; it does not deposit or withdraw any money from any of the
accounts but only provides information about the status of the accounts.

Report 4

Popular Bank

Teller Cash Drawer   DATE: January 11, 1988

TELLER—NO (Teller Number): 6789

DATE: January 11, 1988

TELLER—NAME: XYZ

BRANCH—NO (Branch Number): 1234

BRANCH—NAME: Downtown Branch

BRANCH—ADDR (Branch Address): 1 First Street, New York, N.Y. 10001

Total cash on hand start of day:	775.00
Plus total cash received during day:	5243.39
Less total cash dispensed during day:	4976.97
Final cash on hand end of day:	1041.42

Number of checks received drawn on us:	752
Number of checks received drawn on others	337

Total number of checks received: 1089

Dollar amount of checks received drawn on us:	$ 73,272.21	deposits made
Dollar amount of checks received drawn on others:	35,369.76	by customers

---

Total dollar amount of checks received: 108,641.97

Number of checks dispensed	972	withdrawals made
Dollar amount of checks dispensed	$ 76,197.60	by customers

Summary:

Final cash on hand:	1,041.42
Plus dollar amount of checks received:	108,641.97
Cash and checks for the day:	109,683.39
Less dollar amount of checks dispensed:	76,197.60
(certified checks, money orders)	33,485.79
Less initial cash on hand (start of day):	775.00
Net cash flow for day:	32,710.79

Figure A.4. **Teller Cash Drawer**

Popular Bank   DATE: January 11, 1988

Teller Audit Report

TELLER—NO (Teller Number): 6789
TELLER—NAME: XYZ
BRANCH—NO (Branch Number): 1234
BRANCH—NAME: Downtown Branch
BRANCH—ADDR (Branch Address): 1 First Street, New York, N.Y. 10001

Date audit started: January 2, 1988
Date audit ended: January 4, 1988
Reason code for audit: Regular audit

Total number of transactions by type processed:
  Type 1: 100 (Deposit)
  Type 2: 150 (Withdrawal)

Largest dollar amount involved for each transaction type:
  Type 1: 5000 (Deposit)
  Type 2: 2552 (Withdrawal)

Figure A.5. **Teller Audit Report**

Popular Bank

Inquiry Transaction   DATE: January 11, 1988

Input consists of:

(Customer name and birth date) or CID number
Transaction type (i.e., INQUIRY)

Output consists of:

CID number
Customer information (e.g., name, date of birth, address, telephone number)

Account number, account type (e.g., savings),
special type (e.g., time deposit), account balance

Loan number, loan balance (all loans given to the customer will be displayed)

(All accounts of a specific customer will be displayed.)

The assumption made here is that the customer name
and the customer date of birth uniquely identify the
customer, that is, the customer identification number
(CID number). If the teller does not know the customer,
the teller has to uniquely identify her/him by asking
the address, telephone number, and so on.

Figure A.6. **Inquiry Transaction**

Deposit/Withdrawal Transaction (Figure A.7)

These are two types of transactions. Type 1 is DEPOSIT, and Type 2 is WITHDRAWAL. Both are on-line transactions.

After studying the environment, the following assumptions may be made.

Assumptions about the Environment of "Popular Bank"

1. The customer identification number (CID number) is unique.
2. Account numbers are allotted bankwide; that is, the account numbers are unique. The account number uniquely identifies the account type, the branch in which the particular account was opened, and the customer's name; that is, the same account number will not be

---

Popular Bank

Deposit/Withdrawal   Transaction   DATE: January 11, 1988

BRANCH—NO (Branch Number): 1234

BRANCH—NAME: Downtown Branch

BRANCH—ADDR (Branch Address): 1 First Street, New York, N.Y. 10001

DEPOSIT   Transaction (type 1)   OR

WITHDRAWAL   Transaction (type 2)

Input consists of:

Branch number

Teller number

Transaction type

Account number

CID number (CID: customer identification number)

Amount

Output consists of:

Branch number   (Date of transaction and time of transaction

Teller number   are implied, that is, on a given day and at a

specific unit of time only one transaction can

Transaction type   take place.)

Account number

Type of account

Balance

Passbook line number (will be there only if the passbook is there)

Figure A.7. **Deposit/Withdrawal Transaction**

given to two or more accounts. The account number also uniquely identifies the customer.

3. Teller numbers are unique.

4. A teller can be assigned to different branches on different days, but, once assigned to a branch, works there the whole day.

5. The account number, with transaction date and transaction time, uniquely identifies the transaction.

6. The action to be taken and the remarks to be registered for an exception are dependent on the reason code and on the account number, that is, on the customer for whom an exceptional action has to be taken.

7. Branch number, together with reason code, the date of start of report, and the date of end of report, uniquely identify the total number of transactions for the weekly exception summary.

8. The loan number uniquely identifies the specific loan. The loan number is different from the account number. Account and loan are two separate entities.

9. A customer can have many account numbers at the same branch.

10. A passbook is provided only for savings accounts.

11. Transaction type and transaction code are synonymous.

12. An INQUIRY Transaction is only an information retrieval transaction.

13. If the teller worked in several branches during the audit period, a report for each branch will be printed. For each audit period for a given teller, there is only one reason code for the audit. Only the count of transactions and the largest dollar amount handled by teller being audited are taken into consideration.

14. The Exception Report and Weekly Exception Summary are for the branch where the account is kept. The reason is that the branch manager where the transaction was made is not too concerned if the account in another branch is overdrawn or if savings exceeds a certain limit. The branch manager is interested, however, if these things happen to his or her bank's accounts, even if the transaction triggering them takes place elsewhere.

15. Two types of transactions are recorded. Type 1 is the DEPOSIT Transaction, and Type 2 is the WITHDRAWAL Transaction. An INQUIRY Transaction is not recorded.

16. At a given point in time a branch has only one branch manager.

STEP I.2. Determine the data elements referenced in every report individually (refer to Chapter 3).

Examine every report individually, and build a cross-reference table showing the data elements and the reports where the information is referred to as in Table 1.

A list of all data elements referenced in the reports from Table 1 in alphabetical order is:

ACCT-NO
The account number uniquely identifies the particular account.

ACCT-TYPE
The account type can be checking, savings, etc.

ACTION-CODE
The action code specifies the action to be taken in exceptions. For example, if the checking plus account is overdrawn, it gives automatic loan not to exceed the total loan given by a particular amount.

AMOUNT
The amount involved in a particular transaction.

AMT-CHECKS-DISPENSED
Dollar amount of checks dispensed.

AMT-RECD-OTHER
Dollar amount of checks received drawn on others.

AMT-RECD-TOTAL
Total dollar amount of checks received.

AMT-RECD-US
Dollar amount of checks received drawn on us.

AMT-TOTAL
Dollar amount involved (total) in Weekly Exception Summary of the Branch Manager's Report.

AUDIT-REASON
Reason code for audit in the Teller Audit Report.

BALANCE
Balance of an account; either is asked for by a customer in an INQUIRY transaction or is the result of a DEPOSIT or a WITHDRAWAL transaction.

BRANCH-ADDR
The address of the branch.

BRANCH-NAME
The name of the branch.

BRANCH-NO
The number of the branch.

CASH-DISPENSED
Total cash dispensed during day; referred to in Teller Cash Drawer.

CASH-RECD	Total cash received during day; referred to in Teller Cash Drawer.
CHECKS-DISPENSED-TOTAL	Number of checks dispensed; referred to in Teller Cash Drawer.
CHECKS-RECD-OTHER	Number of checks received drawn on other banks; referred to in Teller Cash Drawer.
CHECKS-RECD-TOTAL	Total number of checks received.
CHECKS-RECD-US	Number of checks received drawn on us; referred to in Teller Cash Drawer.
CID	Customer identification number.
COH-EOD	Cash on hand at end of day.
COH-SOD	Cash on hand at start of day.
CUST-ADDR	Customer address.
CUST-DOB	Customer date of birth.
CUST-NAME	Customer name.
CUST-TEL-NO	Customer telephone number.
DATE	A business day. Every teller has a cash drawer report on a business day. A Teller Audit Report for a day or a group of days may be prepared. DATE is synonymous with X-DATE: transaction date.
DENDRPT	Date of end of report for the branch manager's Weekly Exception Summary.
DSTRPT	Date of start of report for the branch manager's Weekly Exception Summary.
INTEREST	Interest paid by the customer on a loan; referred to in Branch Loan Status Report.
LARGEST-AMT-TYPE 1	Largest amount of money for transaction type 1, which is depositing money.

LARGEST-AMT-TYPE2	Largest amount of money for transaction type 2, which is withdrawing money.
LOAN-ASSGND	Amount of money assigned as a loan.
LOAN-NO	Referred to in Branch Loan Status Report.
LOAN-TYPE	Mortgage loan, installment loan; referred to in Branch Loan Status Report.
MGR-NAME	Branch manager's name; the assumption is that there is only one branch manager per branch at a given point in time.
NET-FLOW	Net flow of money in Teller Cash Drawer.
NO-ACCTS-TOTAL	Exceptions took place on this number of accounts in a week.
NO-X-TOTAL	Total number of transactions that took place in a week; referred to in branch manager's Weekly Exception Summary.
NO-X-TYPE1	Number of transactions of type 1, i.e., depositing of money performed by a specific teller; referred to in Teller Audit Report.
NO-X-TYPE2	Number of transactions of type 2, i.e., withdrawals performed by a specific teller; referred to in Teller Audit Report.
PASSBOOK-LINE-NO	The passbook-line number is provided only for savings passbooks; referred to in DEPOSIT/ WITHDRAWAL Transaction. The passbook-line number is provided at the time when the transaction is processed.
REASON-CODE	Reason code for the exception at execution of a transaction; referred to in the Branch Manager Exception Report and the Weekly Exception Summary.

REMARKS	Any information provided to take care of an exception as a result of a transaction; referred to in the Branch Manager Exception Report.
TELLER-NAME	The teller name is uniquely identified by the teller number.
TELLER-NO	The teller number uniquely identifies the teller.
TOTAL-LOAN-COLLECTED	Total amount collected from an assigned loan.
TOTAL-LOAN-TO-BE-COLLECTED	Total amount to be collected from the loan; synonymous with loan balance.
X-DATE	The day on which the transaction took place.
X-TIME	The time at which a transaction took place.
X-TYPE	The type of transaction. There are two types of transactions: type 1 is depositing money, and type 2 is withdrawing money.

STEPS I.3 and I.4 (refer to Chapters 4 and 5).

STEP I.3. Determine the relationships between the data elements, such as identifying the primary key data elements and the nonkey data elements.

STEP I.4. Develop third normal form relations for each set of data elements. Where this is not possible for individual reports, merge data from reports to establish third normal form relations.

Branch Manager Report (Exception)

Data elements representing entities of this report are:

BRANCH-NO, BRANCH-NAME, BRANCH-ADDR, MGR-NAME, ACCT-NO, ACCT-TYPE, CID, CUST-NAME, X-DATE, X-TIME, X-TYPE, AMOUNT, REASON-CODE, ACTION-CODE, REMARKS

Table 1. Cross-Reference Table between Data Elements and Reports

Data Elements	Reports						
	Branch Manager Report (Exception)	Branch Manager Report (Weekly Exception Summary)	Branch Loan Status	Teller Cash Drawer	Teller Audit Report	Inquiry Transaction	Deposit/ Withdrawal Transaction
BRANCH-NO	X	X	X	X	X		X
BRANCH-NAME	X	X	X	X	X		X
BRANCH-ADDR	X	X	X	X	X		X
MGR-NAME	X	X	X				
ACCT-NO	X					X	X
ACCT-TYPE	X					X	X
CID	X					X	X
CUST-NAME	X					X	
CUST-ADDR						X	
CUST-TEL-NO						X	
X-DATE	X						X
X-TIME	X						X
X-TYPE	X						X

(Table continues on p. 348.)

Table 1. (*Continued*)

Data Elements	Branch Manager Report (Exception)	Branch Manager Report (Weekly Exception Summary)	Branch Loan Status	Teller Cash Drawer	Teller Audit Report	Inquiry Transaction	Deposit/ Withdrawal Transaction
AMOUNT	X						X
REASON-CODE	X	X					
ACTION-CODE	X						
REMARKS	X						
DSTRPT		X					
DENDRPT		X					
NO-X-TOTAL		X					
NO-ACCTS-TOTAL		X					
AMT-TOTAL		X					
LOAN-NO			X			X	
LOAN-TYPE			X				
LOAN-ASSGND			X				

Data Elements	Reports						
	Branch Manager Report (Exception)	Branch Manager Report (Weekly Exception Summary)	Branch Loan Status	Teller Cash Drawer	Teller Audit Report	Inquiry Transaction	Deposit/Withdrawal Transaction
TOTAL-LOAN-COLLECTED			X				
TOTAL-LOAN-TO-BE-COLLECTED			X			X	
INTEREST			X				
TELLER-NO				X	X		X
TELLER-NAME				X	X		
DATE				X	X		
COH-SOD				X			
COH-EOD				X			
CASH-RECD				X			
CASH-DISPENSED				X			

(Table continues on p. 350.)

Table 1. (*Continued*)

CHECKS-RECD-US	X			
CHECKS-RECD-OTHER	X			
CHECKS-RECD-TOTAL	X			
AMT-RECD-US	X			
AMT-RECD-OTHER	X			
AMT-RECD-TOTAL	X			
CHECKS-DISPENSED-TOTAL	X			
AMT-CHECKS-DISPENSED	X			
NET-FLOW	X			
AUDIT-REASON		X		
NO-X-TYPE 1		X		
NO-X-TYPE 2		X		
LARGEST-AMT-TYPE 1		X		
LARGEST-AMT-TYPE 2		X		
BALANCE			X	X
CUST-DOB			X	
PASSBOOK-LINE-NO				X

Relationships between data elements are:

1. **BRANCH-NO** ←→ **BRANCH-NAME, BRANCH-ADDR, MGR-NAME.** For a given BRANCH-NO there is only one BRANCH-NAME and BRANCH-ADDR (branch address), and also only one MGR-NAME (manager name). But several managers may have the same name. This is a one-to-many mapping, represented as ←→ or as $\underset{\text{many}}{\overset{\text{one}}{\rightleftarrows}}$.

2. **ACCT-NO** ←→ **ACCT-TYPE.** For a given ACCT-NO (account number) there is only one ACCT-TYPE (account type). But there may be many accounts of the same type. This is also a one-to-many mapping.

3. **CID** ←→ **CUST-NAME.** A given CID (customer identification number) uniquely identifies the CUST-NAME (customer name). But there may be many customers with the same name. This is also a one-to-many mapping.

4. **ACCT-NO*X-DATE*X-TIME** ←→ **X-TYPE, AMOUNT.** The ACCT-NO (account number) with X-DATE (transaction date) and X-TIME (transaction time) uniquely identify the transaction. The X-TYPE (transaction type) and the AMOUNT are uniquely determined.

5. **ACCT-NO*REASON-CODE** ←→ **ACTION-CODE, RE-MARKS.** The action to be taken (ACTION-CODE) and the RE-MARKS to be registered for an exception are dependent on the REA-SON-CODE and on the ACCT-NO (account number), that is, on the customer for whom an exceptional action has to be taken.

Third normal form relations for the Branch Manager Report (Exception) are represented in Figure A.8.

---

1   BRANCH-NO ←→ BRANCH-NAME, BRANCH-ADDR,
                    MGR-NAME
2   ACCT-NO ←→ ACCT-TYPE
3   CID ←→ CUST-NAME
4   ACCT-NO*X-DATE*X-TIME ←→ X-TYPE, AMOUNT
5   ACCT-NO*REASON-CODE ←→ ACTION-CODE, REMARKS

Figure A.8

Branch Manager Report (Weekly Exception Summary)

Data elements representing entities of this report are:

> BRANCH-NO, BRANCH-NAME, BRANCH-ADDR,
> MGR-NAME, REASON-CODE, DSTRPT,
> DENDRPT, NO-X-TOTAL, NO-ACCTS-TOTAL,
> AMT-TOTAL

Relationships between data elements are represented as third normal form relations in Figure A.9.

6   BRANCH-NO ◄◄───► BRANCH-NAME, BRANCH-ADDR,
                MGR-NAME
7   BRANCH-NO*REASON-CODE*DSTRPT*DENDRPT
    ◄◄───► NO-X-TOTAL, NO-ACCTS-TOTAL,
        AMT-TOTAL

Figure A.9

Branch Loan Status

Data elements representing entities of this report are:

> BRANCH-NO, BRANCH-NAME, BRANCH-ADDR,
> MGR-NAME, LOAN-NO, LOAN-TYPE, LOAN-
> ASSGND, TOTAL-LOAN-COLLECTED, TOTAL-LOAN-
> TO-BE-COLLECTED, INTEREST

Relationships between data elements are represented as third normal form relations in Figure A.10.

8   BRANCH-NO ◄◄───► BRANCH-NAME, BRANCH-
                ADDR, MGR-NAME
9   LOAN-NO ◄◄───► LOAN-TYPE, LOAN-ASSGND,
                TOTAL-LOAN-COLLECTED,
                TOTAL-LOAN-TO-BE-COLLECTED,
                INTEREST

Figure A.10

Teller Cash Drawer

Data elements representing entities of this report are:

> BRANCH-NO, BRANCH-NAME, BRANCH-ADDR, TELLER-NO,
> TELLER-NAME, DATE, COH-SOD, COH-EOD, CASH-RECD,
> CASH-DISPENSED, CHECKS-RECD-US, CHECKS-RECD-OTHER,
> CHECKS-RECD-TOTAL, AMT-RECD-US, AMT-RECD-OTHER,
> AMT-RECD-TOTAL, CHECKS-DISPENSED-TOTAL,
> AMT-CHECKS-DISPENSED, NET-FLOW

Relationships between data elements are represented as third normal form relations in Figure A.11.

> 10 <u>BRANCH-NO</u> ←←→ BRANCH-NAME, BRANCH-ADDR
> 11 <u>TELLER-NO</u> ←←→ TELLER-NAME
> 12 <u>TELLER-NO*DATE</u> ←←→ BRANCH-NO, COH-SOD,
> COH-EOD, CASH-RECD, CASH-DISPENSED,
> CHECKS-RECD-US, CHECKS-RECD-OTHER,
> CHECKS-RECD-TOTAL, AMT-RECD-US, AMT-RECD-OTHER,
> AMT-RECD-TOTAL, CHECKS-DISPENSED-TOTAL,
> AMT-CHECKS-DISPENSED, NET-FLOW

Figure A.11

Teller Audit Report

Data elements representing entities of this report are:

> BRANCH-NO, BRANCH-NAME, BRANCH-ADDR,
> TELLER-NO, TELLER-NAME, DATE, AUDIT-REASON,
> NO-X-TYPE1, NO-X-TYPE2, LARGEST-AMT-TYPE1,
> LARGEST-AMT-TYPE2

Relationships between data elements are represented as third normal form relations in Figure A.12.

> 13 <u>BRANCH-NO</u> ←←→ BRANCH-NAME, BRANCH-ADDR
> 14 <u>TELLER-NO</u>   TELLER-NAME
> 15 <u>BRANCH-NO*TELLER-NO*DATE</u> ←←→
> AUDIT-REASON, NO-X-TYPE1, NO-X-TYPE2,
> LARGEST-AMT-TYPE1, LARGEST-AMT-TYPE2

Figure A.12

INQUIRY Transaction

Data elements representing entities of this report are:

> ACCT-NO, ACCT-TYPE, BALANCE, CID, CUST-NAME,
> CUST-ADDR, CUST-TEL-NO, CUST-DOB, LOAN-NO,
> TOTAL-LOAN-TO-BE-COLLECTED

Relationships between data elements are represented as third normal form relations in Figure A.13.

> 16 ACCT-NO ←←——→ ACCT-TYPE, BALANCE
> 17 CID ←←——→ CUST-NAME, CUST-ADDR, CUST-TEL-NO
> 18 CUST-NAME*CUST-DOB ←——→ CID
> 19 LOAN-NO ←←——→ TOTAL-LOAN-TO-BE-COLLECTED

Figure A.13

DEPOSIT/WITHDRAWAL Transaction

Data elements representing entities of this report are:

> ACCT-NO, ACCT-TYPE, BALANCE,
> BRANCH-NO, BRANCH-NAME, BRANCH-ADDR,
> X-DATE, X-TIME, X-TYPE, CID,
> AMOUNT, TELLER-NO, PASSBOOK-LINE-NO

Relationships between data elements are represented as third normal form relations in Figure A.14.

> 20 ACCT-NO ←←——→ ACCT-TYPE, BALANCE, CID
> 21 BRANCH-NO ←←——→ BRANCH-NAME, BRANCH-ADDR
> 22 ACCT-NO*X-DATE*X-TIME ←←——→ X-TYPE,
>   AMOUNT, TELLER-NO, PASSBOOK-LINE-NO

Figure A.14

Merging third normal relations results in entities BRANCH, TELLER, CUSTOMER, LOAN, and ACCOUNT. Relationships between entities result in entities DRAWER, AUDIT, TRANSACTION, EXCEPTION, and EXCEPTION SUMMARY. Entities and relationships between them are represented in the total set as follows:

I.	BRANCH:	BRANCH-NO ←←——→ BRANCH-NAME, BRANCH-ADDR, MGR-NAME
II.	TELLER:	TELLER-NO ←←——→ TELLER-NAME
III.	CUSTOMER:	CID ←←——→ CUST-NAME, CUST-DOB, CUST-TEL-NO, CUST-ADDR, BRANCH-NO

CUST-NAME and CUST-DOB are underlined because they participate as part of a primary key in some other relations.
Included as a nonkey attribute is also BRANCH-NO for establishing the connection between the customer identification number (CID) and the branch where the customer banks.

IV.	LOAN	LOAN-NO ←←——→ LOAN-TYPE, LOAN-ASSGND, INTEREST, TOTAL-LOAN-COLLECTED, TOTAL-LOAN-TO-BE-COLLECTED, BRANCH-NO, CID

Included as two nonkey attributes also are BRANCH-NO and CID for establishing the connection between the loan and the branch where the loan was assigned and the customer (CID) to whom the loan was given.

V.	ACCOUNT:	ACCT-NO ←←——→ ACCT-TYPE, BALANCE, CID, BRANCH-NO

Included as two nonkey attributes also are CID and BRANCH-NO for establishing the connection between the account and the branch where the account is kept and the customer (CID) for whom the account was opened.

VI.	DRAWER:	TELLER-NO*DATE ←←——→ BRANCH-NO, COH-SOD, COH-EOD, CASH-RECD, CASH-DISPENSED, CHECKS-RECD-US, CHECKS-RECD-OTHER, CHECKS-RECD-TOTAL, AMT-RECD-US, AMT-RECD-OTHER, AMT-RECD-TOTAL, CHECKS-DISPENSED-TOTAL, NET-FLOW, AMT-CHECKS-DISPENSED

VII.	AUDIT:	BRANCH-NO*TELLER-NO*DATE ◄───► AUDIT-REASON, NO-X-TYPE1, NO-X-TYPE2, LARGEST-AMT-TYPE1, LARGEST-AMT-TYPE2
VIII.	TRANSACTION:	ACCT-NO*X-DATE*X-TIME ◄───► X-TYPE, AMOUNT, PASSBOOK-LINE-NO, TELLER-NO, CID, BRANCH-NO TELLER-NO is underlined as a nonkey attribute because it participates as part of a primary key in another relation. CID and BRANCH-NO are included as nonkey attributes for establishing the connection between the transaction performed, the customer for whom the transaction took place, and the branch where the transaction was executed.
IX.	EXCEPTION:	ACCT-NO*REASON-CODE ◄───► ACTION-CODE, REMARKS
X.	EXCEPTION SUMMARY:	BRANCH-NO*REASON-CODE* DSTRPT*DENDRPT ◄───► NO-X-TOTAL, NO-ACCTS-TOTAL, AMT-TOTAL

STEP I.5. Draw a conceptual model on the basis of the third normal form relations from step I.4 (refer to Chapter 5).

Figure A.15 represents the conceptual model based on the total set of third normal form relations I to X. The squares containing the roman numerals represent the numbered third formal form relations from the total set. DATE, TIME, and REASON-CODE participate in the third normal form relations as part of the primary keys but are not represented as entities anywhere. To show the participation of DATE, TIME, and REASON-CODE in the primary keys we have drawn squares for them at level 1. Relations VI, VII, VIII, IX, and X represent relationships between entities from level 1. Relation VIII in TRANSACTION represents the relationships between the entities TIME, DATE, ACCT, and TELLER.

The arrows drawn on the top of level 1 represent the relationships between ACCT and CUSTOMER, between LOAN and CUSTOMER, and between CUSTOMER and BRANCH, that is, a customer may have many accounts but a given account is assigned to a specific customer, a customer may have many loans but a given loan is assigned to a specific customer, and a branch has many customers, but a specific customer opens the first account at a branch [i.e., is assigned a customer identification number (CID) at the branch]. The arrows on the top of level 1 are introduced after the conceptual model for the total set of third normal form relations has

Figure A.15. Conceptual model.

been drawn. The relationships on the top of level 1 are fundamental to the enterprise and are not evident in the total set of third normal form relations based on the reports under consideration.

STEP II. DESIGN A LOGICAL MODEL OF A DATA BASE (refer to Chapters 4, 5, and 6).

STEP II.1. Draw a logical model based on the conceptual model from step I.5 above for a data base management system, using:

    1. **A relational data model.**
    2. **A hierarchical data model.**
    3. **A network data model.**
    4. **An inverted file data model.**

STEP II.1.1. Mapping to a relational data model

The tables represented will be relations I to X, for example, *Relation I:*

BRANCH—NO	BRANCH—NAME	BRANCH—ADDR	MGR—NAME
1234	Downtown Branch	1 First Street, New York, N.Y. 10001	J. J. Smith
2456	Midtown Branch	10 East 42nd Street, New York, N.Y. 10017	M. R. Berg
⋮	⋮	⋮	⋮

STEP II.1.2. Mapping to a hierarchical data model
            A. Derive a hierarchical data model without regard for a particular DBMS.
                      A.1. Eliminate superfluous relationships.

                      No superfluous relationships exist in the conceptual model of Figure A.15.

A.2. Derive parent-child relationships.

In the conceptual model of Figure A.15 the created entities TIME, DATE, and REASON-CODE do not have to exist in their own right. These entities may be integrated into the relations referring to them.

The conceptual model in Figure A.15 can be transferred into Figure A.16 (after removal of the boxes TIME, DATE, and REASON-CODE).

A.3. Resolve multiple parentage.

In performing step A.2, we resolved the problem of multiple parentage with the number of parents three or more. Figure A.16, redrawn in two hierarchical trees, is shown in Figure A.17. Some boxes, such as DRAWER, AUDIT, and TRANSACTION, have

Figure A.16. The modified conceptual model after removal of the boxes TIME, DATE, and REASON-CODE from Figure A.15.

Figure A.17. **The logical model from Figure A.16 redrawn in two hierarchical data models.**

two parents each. We will not resolve multiple parentage with two parents for consideration of logical relationships with IMS.

B. Modify the model to eliminate conflicts with the rules of the DBMS to be used.

In the logical model of Figure A.17, none of the conditions imposed by IMS is violated; hence no modifications are required.

C. Refine the modified model according to some obvious performance considerations.

D. Simplify key names.

In Figure A.17 the segment type EXCEPTION with REASON-CODE (relation IX) and the segment type EXCEPTION SUMMARY with REASON-CODE and DATE (relation X) take place as a result of TRANSACTION with TIME and DATE (relation VIII). Integrating the boxes with relations IX and X with the box with relation VIII results in the logical model shown in Figure A.18 for IMS.

Other versions of logical models are also possible.

E. Add intrinsic requirements.

In Figure A.18 there should be a possibility of accessing the customer information with CUST-NAME and CUST-DOB (date of birth). The primary key for CUSTOMER is CID (customer identification number). Accessing the segment with a secondary key, for example, CUST-NAME and CUST-DOB as in an INQUIRY transaction, is called a "secondary indexing" capability.

Figure A.18. **One version of the refined logical hierarchical model from Figure A.17.**

STEP II.1.3. Mapping to a network data model
A. Derive a network data model without regard for a particular DBMS.

A.1. Derive owner-member relationships.

After removing the boxes TIME and DATE, and after integrating REASON-CODE with the transaction, the conceptual model in Figure A.15 can be transferred to Figure A.19.

Figure A.19. **One version of the logical network model. TIME and DATE record types from Figure A.15 are integrated with the corresponding record types. DATE is integrated with DRAWER (VI), AUDIT (VII), and TRANSACTION (VIII). TIME is integrated with TRANSACTION (VIII). REASON-CODE, EXCEPTION SUMMARY (X), and EXCEPTION (IX) are integrated with TRANSACTION (VIII).**

     A.2. **Resolve any violations of unique ownership.**

There are no violations of unique ownership in the set types of Figure A.19.

B. **Modify the model to eliminate conflicts with the rules of the DBMS to be used.**

The CODASYL DBMS supports the set types of Figure A.19. No modifications are necessary.

C. **Refine the modified model according to some obvious performance considerations.**

D. **Simplify key names.**

Integrating the EXCEPTION and EXCEPTION SUMMARY in the TRANSACTION record type results in Figure A.19. The key names have been simplified too. Other versions of logical models are also possible.

E. **Add relationships that exist between data but have not surfaced in the logical model so far.**

We would like to access the customer information based not only on CID but also on CUST-NAME and CUST-DOB (date of birth). To obtain a facility of that nature, file inversion must be used.

STEP II.1.4. Mapping to an inverted file data model

A. **Derive an inverted file data model without regard for a particular DBMS.**

Each of the 13 third normal form relations of Figure A.15 becomes a file in the logical inverted file model.

B. **Modify the model to eliminate conflicts with the rules of the DBMS to be used.**

ADABAS supports the logical model; hence no modifications are required.

C. **Refine the modified model according to some obvious performance considerations.**

The files TIME, DATE, and REASON-CODE, which contain only a single field, may be dropped.

The EXCEPTION SUMMARY and AUDIT files are not retained inasmuch as the information they contain can be derived inexpensively.

Since an EXCEPTION occurs as a result of a TRANSACTION, its fields can be incorporated into the TRANSACTION file and null suppressed.

D. **Select the attributes to be inverted, that is, the fields to be defined as descriptors.**

The seven files in the resulting logical model are shown in Figure A.20. The fields are detailed together with the options selected for each: descriptor (DE), unique (UQ), superdescriptor (SP), null suppressed (NU), uncompressed (FI). Other versions of logical models are also possible.

E. **Add relationships that exist between data but have not surfaced in the logical model so far.**

It is not necessary to add any relationships to the logical model in Figure A.20.

STEP III. DESIGN A PHYSICAL MODEL OF A DATA BASE (refer to Chapters 7, 8, 9, and 10).

STEP III.1. Draw an internal model (also called a physical model) on the basis of the logical model from step II.1, using:

1. IMS
2. IDMS/R

STEP III.1.1. Internal model for IMS

Let us consider the following segment types: BRANCH, CUSTOMER, LOAN, ACCOUNT, TRANSACTION, TELLER, TELLER-CASH-DRAWER, and AUDIT. The EXCEPTION SUMMARY fields have been omitted from the AUDIT segment since they are easily derivable.

BRANCH FILE

BRANCH-NO   DE,UQ
BRANCH-NAME
BRANCH-ADDR
MGR-NAME

TELLER FILE

TELLER-NO   DE, UQ
TELLER-NAME

CUSTOMER FILE

CID   DE, UQ
CUST-NAME ⎫ SP
  CUST-DOB ⎰
CUST-TEL-NO
CUST-ADDR
BRANCH-NO

LOAN FILE

LOAN-NO   DE, UQ
LOAN-TYPE   FI
LOAN-ASSGND
INTEREST
TOTAL-LOAN-COLLECTED

TOTAL-LOAN-TO-BE-COLLECTED
BRANCH-NO   DE
CID   DE

ACCOUNT FILE

ACCT-NO   DE, UQ
ACCT-TYPE   FI
BALANCE
CID   DE

DRAWER FILE

TELLER-NO   DE
DATE   DE
BRANCH-NO
COH-SOD
COH-EOD
CASH-RECD
CASH-DISPENSED
CHECKS-RECD-US
CHECKS-RECD-OTHER
CHECKS-RECD-TOTAL
AMT-RECD-US
AMT-RECD-OTHER
AMT-RECD-TOTAL
CHECKS-DISPENSED-TOTAL
AMT-CHECKS-DISPENSED
NET-FLOW

TRANSACTION FILE

ACCT-NO
X-DATE   DE
X-TIME
X-TYPE   FI
AMOUNT
PASSBOOK-LINE-NO
TELLER-NO   DE
CID
BRANCH-NO   DE
REASON-CODE   DE, NU
ACTION-CODE   NU
REMARKS   NU

Figure A.20. One version of the logical inverted file model. The TIME, DATE, REASON-CODE, AUDIT, and EXCEPTION SUMMARY files have been eliminated. The EXCEPTION file has been combined with the TRANSACTION file. Field options, including descriptors (DE), have been selected.

Segment Sizes

An estimate of field size is made, and each field is assigned to a segment. The field and the segment sizes are entered into the data dictionary. It is assumed that, on average, three pointers are stored in every segment, that is, 12 bytes have to be added to each segment.

Segment	*Field*	*Length (bytes)*
BRANCH	BRANCH-NO	4
	BRANCH-NAME	25
	BRANCH-ADDR	55
	MGR-NAME	25
		109
CUSTOMER	CID	9
	CUST-NAME	25
	CUST-DOB	6
	CUST-ADDR	55
	CUST-TEL-NO	10
		105
LOAN	LOAN-NO	17
	LOAN-ASSGND	12
	LOAN-TYPE	2
	INTEREST	12
	TOTAL-LOAN-COLLECTED	12
	TOTAL-LOAN-TO-BE-COLLECTED	12
		67
ACCOUNT	ACCT-NO	17
	ACCT-TYPE	2
	BALANCE	12
		31
TRANSACTION	AMOUNT	12
	ACTION-CODE	2
	PASSBOOK-LINE-NO	15
	REASON-CODE	2
	X-DATE	6
	X-TIME	4
	X-TYPE	2
	REMARKS	60
	BRANCH-NO	4
	TELLER-NO	4
		111

Segment	Field	Length (bytes)
TELLER	TELLER-NO	4
	TELLER-NAME	25
		29
TELLER-CASH-DRAWER	AMT-CHECKS-DISPENSED	12
	AMT-RECD-OTHER	12
	AMT-RECD-US	12
	AMT-RECD-TOTAL	12
	CASH-DISPENSED	12
	CASH-RECD	12
	CHECKS-DISPENSED-TOTAL	5
	CHECKS-RECD-OTHER	5
	CHECKS-RECD-US	5
	CHECKS-RECD-TOTAL	6
	COH-EOD	12
	COH-SOD	12
	NET-FLOW	12
	BRANCH-NO	4
	DATE	6
		139
AUDIT	DATE	6
	AUDIT-REASON	2
	BRANCH-NO	4
	LARGEST-AMT-TYPE1	12
	LARGEST-AMT-TYPE2	12
	NO-X-TYPE1	7
	NO-X-TYPE2	7
		50

The following assumptions are made regarding segment frequencies:

1. There are 100 branch offices.
2. Each branch serves an average of 1000 customers.
3. Each branch employs an average of 10 tellers.
4. Each customer has an average of two accounts and one loan. Transactions for a loan are kept together with the loan information.
5. Detail information (i.e., transactions, Teller Cash Drawer, and Teller Audit Report) is retained for a current period of 2 months and then archived.
6. There is an average of 100 transactions for each account in the 2-month period.

Figure A.21. Two physical data bases TELLER and BRANCH for IBM's IMS. There are three logical relationships interconnecting the two physical data bases.

7. Each teller works an average of 50 days during each 2-month period.
8. Each teller is audited once every 4 months; that is, the average frequency of audits per teller for the 2-month period is 0.5.

These descriptions are an explanation of the frequencies that appear in Figure A.21.

The version of a logical model in Figure A.18 is reflected with the respective lengths (L) and average frequencies (F) relative to the parents in Figure A.21.

To calculate the space and time estimates, we will use a blocksize of 4096 bytes (4 × 1024, i.e., 4K) with FSB (free space blocks) and FSW (free space within a block) values of 10% each.

The version in Figure A.21 represents two physical data bases: TELLER and BRANCH. There are three logical relationships interconnecting the two physical data bases:

1. TELLER-CASH-DRAWER is a logical relationship between TELLER and BRANCH, TELLER being the physical parent and BRANCH the logical parent.
2. AUDIT is a logical relationship between TELLER and BRANCH, TELLER being the physical parent and BRANCH the logical parent.

3. TRANSACTION has ACCOUNT as its physical parent and TELLER as its logical parent.

To determine the effectiveness of the logical model of Figure A.21, we will take the approach of estimating data base size and times for the important transactions in STEP IV.

STEP III.1.2. Internal model for IDMS/R

The logical model of Figure A.19 has been redrawn in Figure A.22 as a Bachman diagram showing the options selected for the record and set types.

Figure A.22. **Bachman diagram representing one version of the internal model for IDMS/R.**

STEP IV. EVALUATE THE PHYSICAL MODEL OF A DATA BASE (refer to Chapters 7, 8, 9, and 10, and Appendix C on statistics).

STEP IV.1. Develop space estimates for the internal model above (as in step III.1). Develop input/output probabilities for the internal model above (as in step III.1). using:

    1.   **IMS**
    2.   **IDMS/R**

STEP IV.2. Draw external models for the reports in Figures A.1 to A.5, INQUIRY Transaction, and DEPOSIT/WITHDRAWAL Transaction on the basis of the internal model, as in step III.1. (*Exercise for the reader.*)

STEP IV.3. Develop time estimates for the external models, as in step IV.2. (*Exercise for the reader.*)

STEP IV.1.1. IMS Version from Figure A.21

Space Estimates: BLK = 4096, FSB = 0.1, FSW = 0.1

1.   TELLER data base

$S_{\text{TELLER-CASH-DRAWER}}$ (i.e., subtree size) = 151 bytes

S_{AUDIT} = 62 bytes

S_{TELLER} = 41 + 50 × 151 + 0.5 × 62 bytes

       = 7622 bytes

<u>SEGMENT BYTES</u> = 7622 × 1000

Wasted space (W)/block = the biggest segment size
151 (TELLER-CASH-DRAWER segment) − 1

       = 150 bytes

<u>Effective blocksize:</u>

Effective blocksize = [((1 − FSW) × BLK) − W] × (1 − FSB) (bytes)

       = [((1 − 0.1) × 4096) − 150] × 0.9

       = 3182 bytes

BLOCK BYTES:

$$\text{BLOCK BYTES} = \text{SEGMENT BYTES} \times \frac{\text{blocksize}}{\text{effective blocksize}}$$

$$= 7622000 \times \frac{4096}{3182}$$

$$= 9,811,349 \text{ bytes}$$

2. BRANCH data base

$S_{\text{TRANSACTION}} = 123$ bytes

$S_{\text{ACCOUNT}} = 43 + 100 \times 123 = 12343$ bytes

$S_{\text{LOAN}} = 79$ bytes

$S_{\text{CUSTOMER}} = 117 + (2 \times 12343) + 79$

$\qquad\qquad = 24882$ bytes

$S_{\text{BRANCH}} = 121 + 1000 \times 24882$

$\qquad\quad = 24,882,121$ bytes

SEGMENT BYTES $= 24,882,121 \times 100$ bytes

Wasted space (W)/block = the biggest segment size

$\qquad\qquad\qquad$ 123 (TRANSACTION segment) $- 1$

$\qquad\qquad\qquad = 122$ bytes

Effective blocksize $= (0.9 \times 4096 - 122) \times 0.9$

$\qquad\qquad\qquad\qquad = 3207.9$ bytes

BLOCK BYTES:

$$\text{BLOCK BYTES} = 2,488,212,100 \times \frac{4096}{3207.9}$$

$$= 3,177,068,100 \text{ bytes}$$

Input/Output Probabilities (Version from Figure A.21)

1. Teller data base

$PCIO_{\text{TELLER, TELLER-CASH-DRAWER}}$

$$= \text{min.} \left(1, \frac{\begin{array}{c}\text{Length of TELLER-CASH-DRAWER} \\ + \text{ all subtrees to left} \\ \text{of TELLER-CASH-DRAWER}\end{array}}{3182}\right)$$

$$= \text{min.} \left(1, \frac{151}{3182}\right) = 0.0474$$

$$\text{PCIO}_{\text{TELLER, AUDIT}} = \text{min.} \left(1, \frac{62 + 50 \times 151}{3182}\right)$$

$$= 1$$

$$\text{PTIO}_{\text{TELLER-CASH-DRAWER}} = \text{min.} \left(1, \frac{151}{3182}\right)$$

$$= 0.0474$$

$$\text{PTIO}_{\text{AUDIT}} = \text{min.} \left(1, \frac{62}{3182}\right)$$

$$= 0.0195$$

$$\text{PPIO}_{\text{TELLER-CASH-DRAWER, TELLER}} = \text{min.} \left(1, \frac{151 + 25 \times 151}{3182}\right)$$

$$= 1$$

$$\text{PPIO}_{\text{AUDIT, TELLER}} = \text{min.} \left(1, \frac{62 + 0.025 \times 62 + 50 \times 151}{3182}\right)$$

$$= 1$$

2. BRANCH data base

$$\text{PCIO}_{\text{BRANCH, CUSTOMER}} = \text{min.} \left(1, \frac{117}{3208}\right)$$

$$= 0.0365$$

$$\text{PTIO}_{\text{CUSTOMER}} = \text{min.} \left(1, \frac{24{,}882}{3208}\right)$$

$$= 1$$

$$\text{PPIO}_{\text{CUSTOMER, BRANCH}} = \text{min.} \left(1, \frac{117 + 500 \times 24{,}882}{3208}\right)$$

$$= 1$$

$$\text{PCIO}_{\text{CUSTOMER, ACCOUNT}} = \text{min.} \left(1, \frac{43}{3208}\right)$$
$$= 0.0134$$

$$\text{PTIO}_{\text{ACCOUNT}} = \text{min.} \left(1, \frac{12343}{3208}\right)$$
$$= 1$$

$$\text{PCIO}_{\text{CUSTOMER, LOAN}} = \text{min.} \left(1, \frac{79 + 2 \times 12343}{3208}\right)$$
$$= 1$$

$$\text{PTIO}_{\text{LOAN}} = \text{min.} \left(1, \frac{79}{3208}\right)$$
$$= 0.0246$$

$$\text{PCIO}_{\text{ACCOUNT, TRANSACTION}} = \text{min.} \left(1, \frac{123}{3208}\right)$$
$$= 0.0383$$

$$\text{PTIO}_{\text{TRANSACTION}} = \text{min.} \left(1, \frac{123}{3208}\right)$$
$$= 0.0383$$

$$\text{PPIO}_{\text{TRANSACTION, ACCOUNT}} = \text{min.} \left(1, \frac{123 + 50 \times 123}{3208}\right)$$
$$= 1$$

$$\text{PTIO}_{\text{BRANCH}} = \text{min.} \left(1, \frac{24{,}882{,}121}{3208}\right)$$
$$= 1$$

STEP IV.1.2. IDMS/R Version from Figure A.22
Space Estimates: Assume device type 3350 with 4628 bytes per page, 4 pages per track.

Record Sizes:

Teller record

Data length

29

N,P pointers as owner	24
CALC	8
Line index	8
	69 bytes

Drawer record
Data length	139
N,P,O pointers as member	20
Line index	8
	167 bytes

Audit record
Data length	50
N,P,O pointers as member	20
Line index	8
	78 bytes

Area Size: **Teller Region Area**
Teller $1,000 \times 69 = 69,000$
Cash Drawer $50,000 \times 167 = 8,350,000$
Audit $500 \times 78 = 39,000$
     TOTAL $8,458,000$ bytes

$$\frac{8,458,000}{4628\text{-}32} = 1841 \text{ base pages}$$

$$\frac{1841}{50\%} = 3682 \text{ total base pages}$$

$$\frac{7364}{4596} = 2 \text{ space management pages}$$

$$3682 + 2 = 3684 \text{ pages in area}$$

$$\frac{3684}{4} = 921 \text{ tracks}$$

Time Estimate: Deposit/Withdrawal Transaction (Figure A.7)

DML Command	No. of I/Os
OBTAIN BRANCH (CALC)	1
OBTAIN CUSTOMER (CALC)	1
OBTAIN ACCOUNT WITHIN SET (VIA)	0
OBTAIN TELLER (CALC)	1
STORE TRANSACTION (VIA AND NON-VIA)	0 + 2
MODIFY ACCOUNT	1
TOTAL	6 I/Os

Designing a Data Base for a University Environment

"The University"—Case Study 2

The list of reports in pictorial format shown in Figure B.0 presents the information needs of a hypothetical university. The reports are shown in Figures B.1 to B.8. Design a data base for "The University" as follows:

I. Design a conceptual model of a data base (refer to Chapters 1, 2, 3, 4, and 5).

　I.1. Study the environment and document assumptions for it (Chapters 1 and 2).

　I.2. Determine the data elements referenced in every report individually (Chapter 3).

　I.3. Determine the relationships between the data elements, such as identifying the primary key data elements and the nonkey data elements (Chapters 4 and 5).

　I.4. Develop third normal form relations for each set of data elements. Where this is not possible for individual reports, merge data from reports to establish third normal form relations (Chapter 5).

　I.5. Draw a conceptual model on the basis of the third normal form relations (Chapter 5).

II. Design a logical model of a data base (refer to Chapters 4, 5, and 6).

　II.1. Draw a logical model based on the conceptual model above for a data base management system, using:

　　1. A relational data model.
　　2. A hierarchical data model.
　　3. A network data model.
　　4. An inverted file data model.

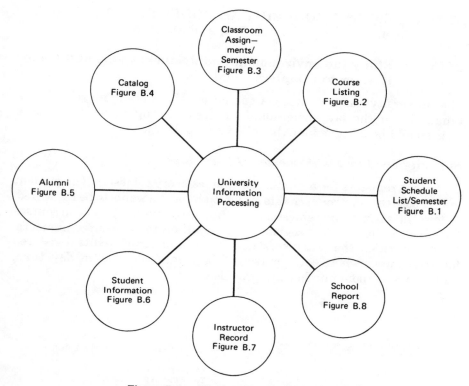

Figure B.0. **A university environment.**

II.2. Draw external models for the reports in Figures B.1 to B.8 on the basis of the logical model above.

III. Design a physical model of a data base (refer to Chapters 7, 8, 9, and 10). (Exercise for the reader.)

III.1. Draw an internal model (also called a physical model) on the basis of the logical model from step II.1.

IV. Evaluate the physical model of a data base (refer to Chapters 7, 8, 9, and 10 and Appendix C on statistics). (Exercise for the reader.)

IV.1. Develop space estimates for the internal model above (as in step III.1). Develop input/output probabilities for the internal model above (as in step III.1).

IV.2. Draw external models for the reports in Figures B.1 to B.8 on the basis of the internal model above.

IV.3. Develop time estimates for the external models as in step IV.2.

STEP I. DESIGN A CONCEPTUAL MODEL OF A DATA BASE (refer to Chapters 1, 2, 3, 4, and 5).

STEP I.1. Study the environment and document assumptions for it (refer to Chapters 1 and 2).

The university has a number of campuses. Undergraduate courses are taught during the day, and graduate courses are taught evenings. A data base should be designed for the following applications.

Student Schedule List/Semester (Figure B.1)

A student registers for a number of courses every semester. The student may choose the number of credits for which he or she wants to be registered. Before the start of the semester the student receives a list of the courses for which he or she has registered. In addition to the course numbers, the course titles, the instructors' names, the number of credits registered for, the campus where each course will be taught and also the day, time, building, and room number are provided.

Student Schedule List/Semester

DATE: SEPTEMBER 7, 1987

SEMESTER: FALL 1987:   SEPTEMBER 10, 1987
TO DECEMBER 22, 1987

SCHOOL: COLLEGE OF ENGINEERING
STUDENT: 123456789
NAME: JOHN F. SMITH
STATUS: UNDERGRADUATE
MAJOR: COMPUTER SCIENCE
MINOR: GYMNASTICS
FACULTY—
ADVISOR: JOSEPH A. CORRIGAN

NO—COURSE	COURSE—TITLE	NAME—INSTR	CREDITS	CAMPUS	DAY—TIME	BLDG—NO—ROOM
CS601	INTRO TO COMP SCIENCE	A.B. ADAMS	3	WHITE PLAINS	W6—8 P.M.	AL201
CS605	INFO STRUCT ALGORITHMS	J.S. FINK	3	BROOKLYN	TH8—10 A.M.	MAIN 605

Figure B.1.   **Every registered student at the school receives the report at the beginning of every semester. It is a confirmation of the courses for which the student has registered.**

Course Listing (Instructor's Copy)

DATE: SEPTEMBER 9, 1987

SEMESTER:	FALL 1987: SEPTEMBER 10, 1987 TO DECEMBER 22, 1987
SCHOOL:	COLLEGE OF ENGINEERING
DEPT:	COMPUTER SCIENCE
NO-COURSE:	CS601
COURSE-TITLE:	INTRO TO COMP SCIENCE
NAME-INSTR:	A. B. ADAMS
CAMPUS:	WHITE PLAINS
BLDG-NO-ROOM:	AL201
DAY-TIME:	W6-8 P.M.
PREREQ: (Prerequisite Courses)	NONE

NO-STUDENT	NAME-STUDENT	DEGREE-SOUGHT	GRADE
123456789	JOHN F. SMITH	B.S.	
897654321	FRANK H. FRAN	M.S.	
967831201	JANE F. BUNDY	M.S.	
⋮	⋮	⋮	

Figure B.2. **The Course Listing is printed for every course to be taught at the school. A copy is sent to the corresponding instructor.**

Course Listing (Instructor's Copy) (Figure B.2)

This is a list of all the students who have registered for a particular course. The instructor provides grades at the end of the semester.

Classroom Assignments/Semester (Figure B.3)

This report is for administrative purposes. The administrative people have a list of the classrooms and their corresponding capacities. This enables them to assign the classrooms with larger capacities to the courses with bigger enrollments.

Catalog (Figure B.4)

A catalog is printed before the start of every semester. It lists the name of the department offering the course, the course number and title, the

SEMESTER: FALL 1987: SEPTEMBER 10, 1987 TO DECEMBER 22, 1987

NO-COURSE	COURSE-TITLE	NAME-INSTR	CAMPUS	DAY-TIME	BLDG-NO-ROOM
CS601	INTRO TO COMP SCIENCE	A. B. ADAMS	WHITE PLAINS	W6-8 P.M.	AL201
CS605	INFO STRUCT & ALGORITHMS	J. S. FINK	BROOKLYN	THU8-10 A.M.	MAIN605
CS623	SWITCHING & DIGITAL SYSTEMS	A. M. JONES	LONG ISLAND	TU6-8 P.M.	MAIN238
PH500	FIELDS & WAVES	A. B. ADAMS	BROOKLYN	THU8-10 A.M.	ACCT389
⋮	⋮	⋮	⋮	⋮	⋮

Figure B.3.   **This report is for administrative purpose. Since introductory courses usually have larger enrollments than advanced courses, the bigger classrooms should be assigned to the introductory courses. The administrative people have a list of the classrooms and their corresponding capacities.**

Catalog

DATE: AUGUST 18, 1987

DEPT (Department):   COMPUTER SCIENCE

NO-COURSE: CS601

COURSE-TITLE: INTRO TO COMP SCIENCE

MAX-CREDITS (Maximum-Credits):   3

COURSE-DESC (Course Description):   THIS IS AN INTRODUCTORY
                                            COURSE IN COMPUTER
                                            SCIENCE

                                            TOPICS: – – –

                                            OBJECTIVES: – – –

PREREQ (Prerequisite Courses):   NONE

Figure B.4.   **A catalog is printed at the beginning of every semester.**

380

maximum credits a student can enroll for, the course description, and the prerequisite courses.

Alumni (Figure B.5)

Information about alumni will be kept up to date. The information will be mainly used for fund raising purposes.

Student Information (Figure B.6)

At the end of every semester the courses finished by the student and the corresponding credits will be added to the student's record.

Alumni

NO–STUDENT	NAME–STUDENT	ADDR–STUDENT–BUS (Student's Business Address)	
238912411	JAY R. KEIL	205 EAST 42 STREET, NEW YORK, N.Y. 10017	
364123889	MAUREEN F. SULLIVAN	19 WATER STREET, NEW YORK, N.Y. 10001	
⋮	⋮	⋮	

ADDR–STUDENT–RES (Student's Residential Address)	NO–TEL–BUS	NO–TEL–RES
15 MAIN STREET, LARCHMONT, N.Y.	(212) 411–2342	(914) 654–1489
241 HIGHLAND STREET, RYE, N.Y.	(212) 895–1245	(914) 894–3412
⋮	⋮	⋮

DEGREE–REC (Degrees Received)	DEGREE–DATE	NAME–EMPLOYER
B.S.	APRIL 15, 1950	AMC CORPORATION
M.S.	JANUARY 5, 1976	PQR INC.
⋮	⋮	⋮

ADDR–EMPLOYER	JOB–TITLE
205 EAST 42 STREET, NEW YORK, N.Y. 10017	SENIOR DESIGNER
19 WATER STREET, NEW YORK, N.Y. 10001	VICE PRESIDENT MARKETING
⋮	⋮

Figure B.5. **The information about alumni is kept up to date.**

Student Information (To Be Updated Every Semester)

NO-STUDENT:	967831201
NAME-STUDENT:	JANE F. BUNDY
ADDR-STUDENT-BUS: (Business)	44 EAST 86 STREET, NEW YORK, N.Y. 10028
ADDR-EMPLOYER:	44 EAST 86 STREET, NEW YORK, N.Y. 10028
ADDR-STUDENT-RES: (Residence)	5 BOSTON POST ROAD, RYE, N.Y. 10580
NO-TEL-BUS:	212-345-4412
NO-TEL-RES: (Residence)	914-684-1242
NEXT-OF-KIN:	JOHN J. BUNDY
FACULTY-ADVISOR:	ABRAHAM S. GOLDSTEIN
CREDITS-EARNED-HERE:	24
CREDITS-TRANSFERRED:	9
TOTAL-CREDITS:	33
NO-COURSE-FINISHED-SEMESTER:	NERVOUS SYSTEM IN MAMMALS, SPRING 1986
GRADE:	A
NO-COURSE-FINISHED-SEMESTER:	ORGANIC CHEMISTRY I, FALL 1985
GRADE:	B
⋮	⋮

Figure B.6. **At the end of every semester the courses completed by the student are added to the corresponding record.**

Instructor Record (Figure B.7)

Information will be kept for every instructor. In case an instructor becomes unable to teach a course, the Instructor Records can be checked for candidates who can take over the course with minimum preparation and schedule conflicts.

School Report (Figure B.8)

This report gives information about all the departments of the school, such as Electrical Engineering, Computer Science, Physics, and Business Administration.

Assumptions about the Environment of the University

The purpose of stating the assumptions is not to solve the environment's problems regarding these assumptions but rather to reflect the assumptions in our conceptual model.

NAME—INSTR: A.B. ADAMS

SEMESTER: FALL 1987

COURSE(S)—TAUGHT	STUDENTS'—COMMENTS
CS601	INFORMATIVE, COMPETENT INSTRUCTOR
PH500	EXCELLENT
$\vdots$	$\vdots$
CS601	COURSE—CAN—TEACH
CS622	COURSE—CAN—TEACH
CS625	COURSE—CAN—TEACH
PH500	COURSE—CAN—TEACH
CS777	COURSE—CAN—BACKUP
CS897	COURSE—CAN—BACKUP
$\vdots$	$\vdots$

Figure B.7. The information will be kept for every instructor. In case an instructor becomes unable to teach a course, the Instructor Records can be checked for candidates who can teach the course with minimum preparation and conflicts.

School   Report

DATE: SEPTEMBER 19, 1987

DIRECTOR:	A.B. BRIGHT
NO—TEL—DIRECTOR: (Director's Telephone Number):	212—845—1243
DEPT:	COMPUTER SCIENCE
TOTAL—STUDENTS—DEPT (Number of Students Registered in the Department):	150
DEPT:	PHYSICS
TOTAL—STUDENTS—DEPT:	120
$\vdots$	$\vdots$
TOTAL—STUDENTS—SCHOOL:	11,523

Figure B.8.   School report for all the departments of the school.

383

1. Every semester starts on a specific day and ends on a specific day.
2. The student number uniquely identifies the student, that is, the name of the student, the address of the student, the status (whether undergraduate or graduate), the major discipline, the minor discipline, and so on.
3. Every student is assigned to a faculty advisor.
4. A student can register for a number of courses in a semester.
5. The same course (e.g., CS601) can be taught in different semesters with different course titles. It can also be taught by different instructors. In two different semesters it can be taught on different campuses. The course schedules can be different, and the courses can be taught in different buildings.
6. If multiple offerings of a course are given, the course number will be made unique by means of a section number; for example, CS601.1 and CS601.2 are two offerings of the same course, CS601.
7. A student has the freedom to register for fewer credits for a given course in a given semester (e.g., auditors are permitted).
8. An offered course is taken by a number of students.
9. The Course Listing (instructor's copy) has a blank column for GRADE at the beginning of the course. The instructor enters the grade achieved by the student at the end of the semester and submits the listing to the administration office.
10. The Catalog lists the courses offered in a specific semester.
11. A student enrolling for a course in a specific semester can register for the maximum number of credits.
12. A course offered in the catalog may have more than one prerequisite course, which students have to finish successfully before registering for the desired course.
13. Alumni information is kept up to date for mailing purposes, such as informing the alumni about special program courses offered and fund raising.
14. The Student Information will be updated at the end of every semester. A student can receive credits for a limited number of courses taken at a different school.
15. At the end of every semester the students' comments about the course will be entered on the Instructor Record.
16. An instructor may not be listed as CAN-TEACH or CAN-BACKUP unless he or she has taught the course in question at least once.

STEP I.2 Determine the data elements referenced in every report individually (refer to Chapter 3).

Examine every report individually and build a cross-reference table showing the data elements and the reports where the information is referred to as in Table 1.

A list of all the data elements referenced in the reports from Table 1 in alphabetical order is:

ADDR-EMPLOYER	Address of the employer of the student, either a current student or an alumnus.
ADDR-STUDENT-BUS	Address of the student's business; it could be the same as ADDR-EMPLOYER or different.
ADDR-STUDENT-RES	Address of the student's residence.
BLDG-NO-ROOM	Building number and room number where the course will be taught.
CAMPUS	Campus where the course will be taught.
COURSE-CAN-BACKUP	The instructor can back up the course.
COURSE-CAN-TEACH	The instructor can teach the course.
COURSE-DESCR	Course description.
COURSE-TITLE	Course title.
CREDITS	Credits for which the student has registered.
CREDITS-EARNED-HERE	Credits earned at this school by the student.
CREDITS-TRANSFERRED	Credits transferred from another school.
DAY-TIME	Which day and what time the course will be taught.
DEGREE-DATE	Date on which the student received a degree.
DEGREE-REC	Degree received by the student.
DEGREE-SOUGHT	Degree toward which the student is earning credits.
DENDSEM	Date of end of semester.
DEPT	Department of the university.
DIRECTOR	Director's name.
DSTRTSEM	Date of start of semester.
FACULTY-ADVISOR	Faculty advisor.
GRADE	Grade received by the student for a course.
JOB-TITLE	Job title of alumnus.
MAJOR	Major discipline.
MAX-CREDITS	Maximum credits for which a student can register.

Table 1. Cross-Reference Table between Data Elements and Reports

Data Elements	Student Schedule List/Semester	Course Listing	Classroom Assignment/Semester	Catalog	Alumni	Student Infor-mation	Instructor Record	School Report
SEMESTER	X	X	X	X		X	X	
DSTRTSEM	X	X	X					
DENDSEM	X	X	X					
NO-STUDENT	X	X			X	X		
NAME-STUDENT	X	X			X	X		
STATUS	X							
MAJOR	X							
MINOR	X							
FACULTY-ADVISOR	X					X		
NO-COURSE	X	X	X	X		X	X	
COURSE-TITLE	X	X	X	X				
NAME-INSTR	X	X	X				X	
CREDITS	X							

Data Elements	Reports							
	Student Schedule List/ Semester	Course Listing	Classroom Assignment/ Semester	Catalog	Alumni	Student Infor- mation	Instructor Record	School Report
CAMPUS	X	X	X					
DAY-TIME	X	X	X					
BLDG-NO-ROOM	X	X	X					
DEPT		X		X				X
PREREQ		X		X				
DEGREE-SOUGHT		X						
GRADE		X				X		
TOTAL-STUDENTS-COURSE		X						
MAX-CREDITS				X				
COURSE-DESCR				X				
ADDR-STUDENT-BUS					X	X		
ADDR-STUDENT-RES					X	X		
DEGREE-REC					X			
DEGREE-DATE					X			

(Table continues on p. 388.)

Table 1. (*Continued*)

Data Elements	Student Schedule List/ Semester	Course Listing	Classroom Assignment/ Semester	Catalog	Reports Alumni	Student Infor- mation	Instructor Record	School Report
NAME-EMPLOYER					X			
ADDR-EMPLOYER					X	X		
JOB-TITLE					X			
NO-TEL-BUS					X	X		
NO-TEL-RES					X	X		
NEXT-OF-KIN						X		
CREDITS-EARNED-HERE						X		

388

CREDITS-TRANSFERRED		X		
TOTAL-CREDITS		X		
STUDENTS'-COMMENTS			X	
COURSE-CAN-TEACH			X	
COURSE-CAN-BACKUP			X	
DIRECTOR				X
NO-TEL-DIRECTOR				X
TOTAL-STUDENTS-DEPT				X
TOTAL-STUDENTS-SCHOOL				X
SCHOOL	X			X

MINOR	Minor discipline.
NAME-EMPLOYER	Name of employer.
NAME-INSTR	Name of instructor.
NAME-STUDENT	Name of student.
NEXT-OF-KIN	Name and address of the next of kin of the student for emergency purposes.
NO-COURSE	Number of course.
NO-STUDENT	Number of student.
NO-TEL-BUS	Telephone number at business of the student, if any.
NO-TEL-DIRECTOR	Telephone number of the director.
NO-TEL-RES	Telephone number at residence of the student.
PREREQ	Prerequisite courses that must be successfully finished before taking a specific course.
SCHOOL	Name of a school within the university.
SEMESTER	Every semester starts on a specific day and ends on a specific day.
STATUS	Status of student.
STUDENTS'-COMMENTS	Students' comments about a course.
TOTAL-CREDITS	Total credits earned by the student.
TOTAL-STUDENTS-COURSE	Total number of students enrolled in a course.
TOTAL-STUDENTS-DEPT	Total number of students in a department.
TOTAL-STUDENTS-SCHOOL	Total number of students in a school.

Suggestion to the Reader: Use some names with fewer qualifiers (e.g., phone number, address, name) in the reports, and use this combined list to detect and resolve synonyms and homonyms. This is an important part of the real life design process.

STEPS I.3 and I.4 (refer to Chapters 4 and 5).

STEP I.3. Determine the relationships between the data elements, such as identifying the primary key data elements and the nonkey data elements.

STEP I.4. Develop third normal form relations for each set of data elements. Where this is not possible for individual reports, merge data from reports to establish third normal form relations.

Student Schedule List/Semester

Data elements representing entities of this report are shown in Figure B.8a.

SEMESTER, DSTRTSEM, DENDSEM, NO-STUDENT,
NAME-STUDENT, STATUS, MAJOR, MINOR,
FACULTY-ADVISOR, NO-COURSE, COURSE-TITLE,
NAME-INSTR, CREDITS, CAMPUS, DAY-TIME,
BLDG-NO-ROOM, SCHOOL

Figure B.8a

Relationships between data elements from Figure B.8a are:

1. SEMESTER ←——→ DSTRTSEM, DENDSEM. For a given SE-
MESTER there is only one DSTRTSEM (date of start of semester)
and also only one DENDSEM (date of end of semester) and vice versa.

This is one-to-one mapping, represented as ←——→ or as $\overset{one}{\underset{one}{\rightleftarrows}}$. The
primary key picked is SEMESTER from the candidate keys SEMES-
TER, DSTRTSEM, and DENDSEM.

2. NO-STUDENT ←←——→ NAME-STUDENT, STATUS, MAJOR, MI-
NOR, FACULTY-ADVISOR, SCHOOL. For a given NO-STUDENT
(number of student) there is only one NAME-STUDENT, STATUS
(of the student), MAJOR (major discipline of the student), MINOR
(minor discipline of the student), and FACULTY-ADVISOR. But for
a given status there can be many students. There can be many students
with the same major and minor disciplines. And a faculty advisor
may be advising more than one student. This is a one-to-many mapping,

represented as ←←——→ or $\overset{one}{\underset{many}{\rightleftarrows}}$.

3. SEMESTER*NO-COURSE ←←——→ COURSE-TITLE, NAME-INSTR,
CAMPUS, DAY-TIME, BLDG-NO-ROOM. In a given SEMESTER
and for a given NO-COURSE (number of course) there is only one
COURSE-TITLE, one NAME-INSTR (instructor teaching the course;
if more than one instructor is teaching the course, we consider it one
team of instructors), one CAMPUS, one DAY-TIME and one BLDG-
NO-ROOM where the course will be taught.

But there may be a number of courses with the same course title
(e.g., Introduction to Computer Science, taught in different sections
with course numbers CS601.1, CS601.2, etc.). The same instructor
may be teaching a number of courses in a semester, and a number of

courses may be taught on a specific campus in a specific semester at the same time on the same day and in the same room in the same building.

This is a one-to-many mapping with SEMESTER and NO-COURSE being the compound key, represented as ←←→ or $\underset{\text{many}}{\overset{\text{one}}{\rightleftarrows}}$.

3a. NO-STUDENT*SEMESTER ←←→→ NO-COURSE, CREDITS. A given student (NO-STUDENT) may be taking in a given SEMESTER many courses (NO-COURSE) and also a set of CREDITS. A given course may also be taken by many students in a specific semester, and a given number of credits may be taken by many students as well. This is a many-to-many mapping, represented as ←←→→ or $\underset{\text{many}}{\overset{\text{many}}{\rightleftarrows}}$.

Relations 1, 2, and 3 are in third normal form, because nonkey data elements from these relations require the full keys for their identification. There is no transitive dependency between nonkey data elements as well. But relation 3a is not even in first normal form, because the mapping is many-to-many. First normal form requires the mapping between the primary key and nonkey data elements to be one-to-many (←←→) or one-to-one (←→). Second normal form requires that nonkey data elements have the full primary key for their unique identification. And third normal form requires that there be no transitive dependency between nonkey data elements.

Relation 3a can be transferred into a third normal form relation if the primary key is further qualified; that is, if the primary key is further compounded with NO-COURSE.

3b. NO-STUDENT*SEMESTER*NO-COURSE ←←→ CREDITS. Relation 3b is now in third normal form. A given student (NO-STUDENT), in a given SEMESTER, and for a given course (NO-COURSE) takes a specific number of CREDITS.

Figure B.8*b* shows four third normal form relations for the end-user's view from Figure B.1 regarding Student Schedule List/Semester.

---

4 SEMESTER ←→ DSTRTSEM, DENDSEM
5 NO-STUDENT ←←→ NAME-STUDENT, STATUS, MAJOR, MINOR, FACULTY-ADVISOR, SCHOOL
6 SEMESTER*NO-COURSE ←←→ COURSE-TITLE, NAME-INSTR, CAMPUS, DAY-TIME, BLDG-NO-ROOM
7 SEMESTER*NO-COURSE*NO-STUDENT ←←→ CREDITS

Figure B.8b. **Third normal form relations for the end-user's view from Figure B.1.**

Course Listing (Instructor's Copy)

Data elements representing entities of this report are:

> SEMESTER, DSTRTSEM, DENDSEM, DEPT, NO-COURSE,
> COURSE-TITLE, NAME-INSTR, CAMPUS, BLDG-NO-
> ROOM, DAY-TIME, PREREQ, NO-STUDENT, NAME-
> STUDENT, DEGREE-SOUGHT, GRADE, TOTAL-
> STUDENTS-COURSE, SCHOOL

Relationships between data elements are:

> 8 SEMESTER ◄───► DSTRTSEM, DENDSEM
> 9 SEMESTER*NO-COURSE ◄◄──► COURSE-TITLE,
>   NAME-INSTR, CAMPUS
>   BLDG-NO-ROOM, DAY-TIME,
>   TOTAL-STUDENTS-COURSE,
>   DEPT, SCHOOL
> 10 SEMESTER*NO-COURSE*NO-STUDENT ◄◄──►
>   NAME-STUDENT,
>   DEGREE-SOUGHT
>   GRADE
> 11 SEMESTER*NO-COURSE*PREREQ

Relations 8 and 9 are in third normal form; relation 10 is in first normal form. Relation 11 is in third normal form. The data elements NAME-STUDENT and DEGREE-SOUGHT depend only on part (NO-STUDENT) of the full key. The resulting third normal form relations are:

> 12 SEMESTER ◄───► DSTRTSEM, DENDSEM
> 13 SEMESTER*NO-COURSE ◄◄──► COURSE-TITLE,
>   NAME-INSTR, CAMPUS,
>   BLDG-NO-ROOM, DAY-TIME,
>   TOTAL-STUDENTS-COURSE,
>   DEPT, SCHOOL
> 14 NO-STUDENT ◄◄──► NAME-STUDENT,
>   DEGREE-SOUGHT
> 15 SEMESTER*NO-COURSE*NO-STUDENT ◄◄──► GRADE
> 16 SEMESTER*NO-COURSE*PREREQ

The five relations 12, 13, 14, 15, and 16 are in third normal form with data element(s) underlined as primary keys.

Classroom Assignments/Semester

Data elements representing entities of this report are:

> SEMESTER, DSTRTSEM, DENDSEM,
> NO-COURSE, COURSE-TITLE, NAME-INSTR,
> CAMPUS, DAY-TIME, BLDG-NO-ROOM

Relationships between data elements are:

> 17 SEMESTER ⟷ DSTRTSEM, DENDSEM
> 18 SEMESTER*NO-COURSE ⟷ COURSE-TITLE,
> NAME-INSTR, CAMPUS,
> DAY-TIME, BLDG-NO-ROOM

The two relations are third normal form relations with data element(s) underlined as primary keys.

Catalog

Data elements representing entities of this report are:

> DEPT, NO-COURSE, COURSE-TITLE,
> MAX-CREDITS, COURSE-DESCR,
> PREREQ

SEMESTER is a hidden data element not printed in this report. Relationships between data elements are:

> 19 SEMESTER*NO-COURSE ⟷ COURSE-TITLE,
> MAX-CREDITS,
> COURSE-DESCR, DEPT
> 20 SEMESTER*NO-COURSE*PREREQ

Relations 19 and 20 are third normal form relations with data element(s) underlined as primary keys.

Alumni

Data elements representing entities of this report are:

> NO-STUDENT, NAME-STUDENT,
> ADDR-STUDENT-BUS,
> ADDR-STUDENT-RES,
> NO-TEL-BUS, NO-TEL-RES,
> DEGREE-REC, DEGREE-DATE,
> NAME-EMPLOYER, ADDR-EMPLOYER,
> JOB-TITLE

Relationships between data elements are:

> 21 NO-STUDENT ◄───► NAME-STUDENT, ADDR-STUDENT-
> BUS, ADDR-STUDENT-RES, NO-TEL-
> BUS, NO-TEL-RES, DEGREE-REC,
> DEGREE-DATE, NAME-EMPLOYER,
> ADDR-EMPLOYER, JOB-TITLE

The relation is a third normal form relation with data element(s) underlined as a primary key.

Student Information (to Be Updated Every Semester)

Data elements representing entities of this report are:

> NO-STUDENT, NAME-STUDENT, ADDR-EMPLOYER,
> ADDR-STUDENT-BUS, ADDR-STUDENT-RES,
> NO-TEL-BUS, NO-TEL-RES, NEXT-OF-KIN,
> FACULTY-ADVISOR, CREDITS-EARNED-HERE,
> CREDITS-TRANSFERRED, TOTAL-CREDITS,
> NO-COURSE, SEMESTER, GRADE

Relationships between data elements are:

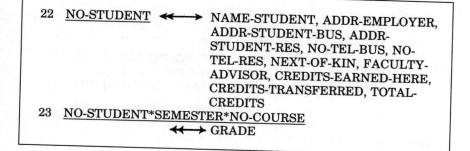

> 22 NO-STUDENT ◄───► NAME-STUDENT, ADDR-EMPLOYER,
> ADDR-STUDENT-BUS, ADDR-
> STUDENT-RES, NO-TEL-BUS, NO-
> TEL-RES, NEXT-OF-KIN, FACULTY-
> ADVISOR, CREDITS-EARNED-HERE,
> CREDITS-TRANSFERRED, TOTAL-
> CREDITS
> 23 NO-STUDENT*SEMESTER*NO-COURSE
> ◄───► GRADE

Relations 22 and 23 are in third normal form.

Instructor Record

Data elements representing entities of this report are:

> NAME-INSTR, NO-COURSE,
> STUDENTS'-COMMENTS, SEMESTER,
> COURSE-CAN-TEACH,
> COURSE-CAN-BACKUP

Relationships between data elements are:

> 24   SEMESTER*NO-COURSE ←←——→ STUDENTS'-COMMENTS,
>   NAME-INSTR
> 25   NAME-INSTR*NO-COURSE ←←——→ COURSE-CAN-TEACH,
>   COURSE-CAN-BACKUP

Relations 24 and 25 are in third normal form.

School Report

Data elements representing entities of this report are:

> DIRECTOR, NO-TEL-DIRECTOR,
> DEPT, TOTAL-STUDENTS-DEPT,
> TOTAL-STUDENTS-SCHOOL, SCHOOL

Relationships between data elements are:

> 26   SCHOOL ←←——→ DIRECTOR, NO-TEL-DIRECTOR,
>   TOTAL-STUDENTS-SCHOOL
> 27   SCHOOL*DEPT ←←——→ TOTAL-STUDENTS-DEPT

The resulting third normal form relations are:

I. Relations 4, 12, and 17 are identical:
  <u>SEMESTER</u> ←——→ DSTRTSEM, DENDSEM

II. Combining relations 5, 14, 21, and 22 results in:

  <u>NO-STUDENT</u> ←——→ NAME-STUDENT, STATUS, MAJOR, MINOR, FACULTY-ADVISOR, DEGREE-SOUGHT, ADDR-STUDENT-BUS, ADDR-STUDENT-RES, NO-TEL-BUS, NO-TEL-RES, DEGREE-REC, DEGREE-DATE, NAME-EMPLOYER, JOB-TITLE, ADDR-EMPLOYER, NEXT-OF-KIN, CREDITS-EARNED-HERE, CREDITS-TRANSFERRED, TOTAL-CREDITS, SCHOOL

III. The composite keys of relations 6, 13, 18, 19, and 24 are identical. The resulting relation is:

  <u>SEMESTER*NO-COURSE</u> ←——→ COURSE-TITLE, NAME-INSTR, CAMPUS, DAY-TIME, BLDG-NO-ROOM, TOTAL-STUDENTS-COURSE, MAX-CREDITS, COURSE-DESCR, DEPT, SCHOOL, STUDENTS'-COMMENTS

IV. Relations 7, 15, and 23 have identical composite keys. The combination of these two relations results in:

  <u>NO-STUDENT*SEMESTER*NO-COURSE</u> ←——→ CREDITS, GRADE

V. Relation 25 can be carried over:

  <u>NAME-INSTR*NO-COURSE</u> ←——→ COURSE-CAN-TEACH, COURSE-CAN-BACKUP

VI. Relation 26 can be carried over:

  <u>SCHOOL</u> ←——→ DIRECTOR, NO-TEL-DIRECTOR, TOTAL-STUDENTS-SCHOOL

VII. Relation 27 can be carried over:

SCHOOL*DEPT ◄───► TOTAL-STUDENTS-DEPT

VIII. Relations 11, 16, and 20 are identical:

SEMESTER*NO-COURSE*PREREQ

I. SEMESTER ◄───► DSTRTSEM, DENDSEM
II. NO-STUDENT ◄───► NAME-STUDENT, STATUS, MAJOR, MINOR, FACULTY-ADVISOR, DEGREE-SOUGHT, ADDR-STUDENT-BUS, ADDR-STUDENT-RES, NO-TEL-BUS, NO-TEL-RES, DEGREE-REC, DEGREE-DATE, NAME-EMPLOYER, JOB-TITLE, ADDR-EMPLOYER, NEXT-OF-KIN, CREDITS-EARNED-HERE, CREDITS-TRANSFERRED, TOTAL-CREDITS, SCHOOL
III. SEMESTER*NO-COURSE ◄───► COURSE-TITLE, NAME-INSTR, CAMPUS, DAY-TIME, BLDG-NO-ROOM, TOTAL-STUDENTS-COURSE, MAX-CREDITS, COURSE-DESCR, DEPT, SCHOOL, STUDENTS'-COMMENTS
IV. NO-STUDENT*SEMESTER*NO-COURSE ◄───► CREDITS, GRADE
V. NAME-INSTR*NO-COURSE ◄───► COURSE-CAN-TEACH, COURSE-CAN-BACKUP
VI. SCHOOL ◄───► DIRECTOR, NO-TEL-DIRECTOR, TOTAL-STUDENTS-SCHOOL
VII. SCHOOL*DEPT ◄───► TOTAL-STUDENTS-DEPT
VIII. SEMESTER*NO-COURSE*PREREQ

Figure B.9. The set of third normal form relations. (PREREQ are the courses that must be taken as prerequisites.)

STEP I.5. Draw a conceptual model on the basis of the third normal form relations from step I.4 (refer to Chapter 5).

Relations I to VIII can be represented in a pictorial format as follows:

1. A relation for which the primary key consists of only one data element represents an entity. Relations I, II, and VI represent the entities SEMESTER, STUDENT, and SCHOOL, respectively. All entities of this type are placed on level 1. In Figure B.10 the boxes SEMESTER, STUDENT, and SCHOOL on level 1 represent the entities in relations I, II, and VI. The data elements are written inside the boxes. The primary keys of the entities are underlined. If a box cannot hold all the data elements representing an entity, they are shown by three dashes, - - -.

2. Relations with primary keys of two data elements are placed on the second level. In relations III, V, and VII, the primary keys consist of two data elements each. The boxes for relations III, V, and VII are drawn on level 2. The primary keys in boxes III, V, and VII are compound keys and are underlined. The compound key of relation III is SEMESTER*NO-COURSE. This key represents the relationships between the two entities SEMESTER and COURSE. There is a box for the entity SEMESTER on level 1, but no box for the entity COURSE on level 1. To establish the relationship between the entities SEMESTER and COURSE on level 2, a new entity relation for COURSE will be created on level 1, because no unique relationship in Figure B.9 is defined only by number of course (NO-COURSE). The box with relation III on level 2 interconnects the relation SEMESTER and the newly created relation COURSE on level 1. Relation V on level 2 interconnects the entity COURSE and the newly created entity INSTRUCTOR on level 1. Relation VII shows the relationship between the entity SCHOOL and the newly created entity DEPARTMENT on level 1.

   The single-headed and double-headed arrows between relations I and III from Figure B.10 mean that in a given semester many courses can be taught, and a given course may be taught in many semesters.

3. The procedure for level 2 is repeated for level 3 and so on.

The resulting diagram for relations I to VIII is shown in Figure B.10. The resulting third normal form relations are based on the assumptions made regarding the specific environment. Since the assumptions are subjective, there is a good chance that someone will challenge them. It is possible that some of the following questions have entered the reader's mind:

Figure B.10. Conceptual model for the university environment. (Created relations are shown in dashed boxes.)

400

Q.1. If there is no student with a specific MAJOR or MINOR subject, how can any information on the MAJOR or MINOR exist?

A.1. The assumption we are making here is that MAJOR and/or MINOR subjects are the same as DEPARTMENTS. A student may take computer science as a major or a minor but may not take the subject "artificial intelligence," taught in the department, as a major or a minor. In other words, even if no student takes a specific major or minor, the information about the DEPARTMENTS, that is, about all possible MAJORS and MINORS is there.

Q.2. Why are COURSE-DESCR (course description) and COURSE-TITLE (course title) nonkey attributes of relation III with SEMESTER and NO-COURSE as the primary key? Why aren't COURSE-DESCR and COURSE-TITLE nonkey attributes of the relation COURSE with NO-COURSE as the primary key?

A.2. It is possible that the same course (i.e., the same NO-COURSE) is taught in two different semesters with different course descriptions and different course titles. Given a SEMESTER and given a NO-COURSE, however, the COURSE-DESCR and the COURSE-TITLE are uniquely determined.

Q.3. Why is NAME-INSTR a part of relation III with SEMESTER and NO-COURSE as the primary key?

A.3. It is possible that the same course (NO-COURSE) is taught by two different instructors in two different semesters. But in a specific semester the course is taught by a particular instructor. As a result of this assumption, given a specific SEMESTER and a specific NO-COURSE, the NAME-INSTR is uniquely identified. Note that the assumption was made that a course is taught by only one instructor. If more than one instructor teaches a course, the team is considered as one instructor.

Q.4. Aren't COURSE-CAN-TEACH and COURSE-CAN-BACKUP the same as the course?

A.4. COURSE-CAN-TEACH and COURSE-CAN-BACKUP reflect the association between an instructor and a course. If an instructor can teach a course, the implication is that relatively little time will be required for preparation before actually teaching the course. If an instructor can back up a course, the implication is that relatively more time will be required for preparation before actually teaching the course.

Q.5. Is a faculty advisor the same as an instructor?

A.5. In some instances a faculty advisor is not necessarily an instructor. A program director or someone from the departmental staff may be a faculty advisor but not necessarily an instructor.

If these or the other assumptions are changed, the third normal form relations change. The moral is, then, that the data base design staff has to be competent with an excellent understanding of the way the environment runs.

STEP II. DESIGN A LOGICAL MODEL OF A DATA BASE (refer to Chapters 4, 5, and 6).

STEP II.1. Draw a logical model based on the conceptual model from step I.5 above for a data base management system, using:

    1. **A relational data model.**
    2. **A hierarchical data model.**
    3. **A network data model.**
    4. **An inverted file data model.**

STEP II.1.1. Mapping to a relational data model

In Chapter 4 we saw that a relational data model is made up of a number of relations (tables). A table is a user's interface.

A logical model for a data base management system using a relational data model consists of the following relations and the corresponding attributes. All of the following tables from Figures B.11 to B.22 are related to one another, as shown in the conceptual model of Figure B.10.

STEP II.1.2. Mapping to a hierarchical data model

    A. Derive a hierarchical data model without regard for a particular DBMS.

        A.1. Eliminate superfluous relationships.

        No superfluous relationships exist in the conceptual model of Figure B.10.

        A.2. Derive parent-child relationships.

        In the conceptual model of Figure B.10, the boxes represent segments, and the arrows, ◄———►► , represent parent-child relationships between these segments.

        A.3. Resolve multiple parentage.

        When the rules for resolving multiple parentage are applied to the conceptual model of Figure B.10, the intermediate result in Figure B.23 is obtained. This is the hierarchical model.

Relations from Level 1

SCHOOL:

SCHOOL	DIRECTOR	NO—TEL—DIRECTOR	TOTAL—STUDENTS—SCHOOL
COLLEGE OF ENGI-NEERING	A.B. BRIGHT	212—845—1243	11,523
⋮	⋮	⋮	⋮

Figure B.11

DEPARTMENT:

DEPT
BUSINESS ADMINISTRA-TION
CHEMISTRY
COMPUTER SCIENCE
MATHEMATICS
PSYCHOLOGY
⋮

Figure B.12

INSTRUCTOR:

NAME—INSTR
A.B. ADAMS
J.S. FINK
⋮ Etc.

Figure B.13

COURSE:

NO—COURSE
CS601
CS605
CS623
PH500
⋮

Figure B.14

STUDENT:

NO–STUDENT	NAME–STUDENT	STATUS	MAJOR	MINOR	FACULTY–ADVISOR	DEGREE–SOUGHT	ADDR–STUDENT BUS	ADDR–STUDENT RES
123456789	JOHN F. SMITH	UNDER–GRADUATE	COMPUTER SCIENCE	GYMNASTICS	JOSEPH A. CORRIGAN	B.S.	81 Blind Bank Stamford, Conn. 34562	52 Birch Boulevard Old Greenwich, Conn. 36581
897645123	FRANK H. FRAN	GRADUATE	ELECTRICAL ENGINEER–ING	PHYSICS	JOHN F. SLATTER	M.S.	55 Main Street New Rochelle, N.Y. 16481	83 School Street, Rye, N.Y. 10580
967831201	JANE F. BUNDY	GRADUATE	BIO–CHEMISTRY	RADIOLOGY	ABRAHAM S. GOLDSTEIN	M.S.	44 East 86 Street New York, N.Y. 10028	5 Boston Post Road, Rye, N.Y. 10580
⋮	⋮	⋮	⋮	⋮	⋮	⋮	⋮	⋮

Figure B.15

SEMESTER:

SEMESTER	DSTRTSEM	DENDSEM
FALL 1987	SEPTEMBER 10, 1987	DECEMBER 22, 1987
⋮	⋮	⋮

Figure B.16

PREREQUISITE:

PREREQ
CS601
CS602
⋮

Figure B.17

NO-TEL-BUS	NO-TEL-RES	DEGREE-REC	DEGREE-DATE	NAME-EMPLOYER	ADDR-EMPLOYER	NEXT-OF-KIN	CREDITS-EARNED-HERE	CREDITS-TRANS-FERRED	TOTAL CREDITS	SCHOOL
203–423–1489	203–513–6774	----	----	PROGRAM-MING CORP.	81 Blind Bank, Stamford, Conn. 34562	LAURA M. CORRIGAN	15	----	15	COLLEGE OF ENGI-NEERING
914–462–1248	914–456–1489	B.S.	AUGUST 15, 1972	CHIP COMPANY	55 Main Street, New Rochelle, N.Y. 16481	BRIGITTE H. SLATTER	21	9	30	GRADU-ATE SCHOOL
212–345–4412	914–684–1242	B.S.	MAY 30, 1973	ABM Inc.	44 East 86th Street, New York, N.Y. 10028	JOHN J. BUNDY	24	9	33	GRADU-ATE SCHOOL
⋮	⋮	⋮	⋮	⋮	⋮	⋮	⋮	⋮	⋮	

Figure B.15 (*continued*)

Relations from Level 2

SCHOOL and DEPARTMENT:

SCHOOL	DEPT	TOTAL-STUDENT-DEPT
COLLEGE OF BUSINESS	BUSINESS ADMINISTRA-TION	180
COLLEGE OF ENGINEERING	CHEMISTRY	35
COLLEGE OF ENGINEERING	COMPUTER SCIENCE	150
COLLEGE OF ENGINEERING	MATHEMATICS	53
COLLEGE OF ENGINEERING	PHYSICS	120

Figure B.18

INSTRUCTOR and COURSE:

NAME-INSTR	NO-COURSE	COURSE-CAN-TEACH	COURSE-CAN-BACKUP
A.B. ADAMS	CS601	YES	YES
A.B. ADAMS	CS622	YES	YES
A.B. ADAMS	CS625	YES	YES
A.B. ADAMS	PH500	YES	YES
A.B. ADAMS	CS777	NO	YES
A.B. ADAMS	CS897	NO	YES
J.S. FINK	CS605	YES	YES
⋮	⋮	⋮	⋮

Figure B.19 If an instructor can teach a course, he or she can also back up the same course. But an instructor who can back up a course may need preparatory time before teaching it.

SEMESTER and COURSE:

SEMESTER	NO–COURSE	COURSE–TITLE	NAME–INSTR	CAMPUS	DAY–TIME	BLDG–NO–ROOM	TOTAL–STUDENTS–COURSE	MAX–CREDITS	COURSE–DESCR
FALL 1987	CS601	INTRO TO COMP SCIENCE	A.B. ADAMS	WHITE PLAINS	W 6–8 P.M.	AL201	35	4	———
FALL 1987	CS605	INFO STRUCT & ALGORITHMS	J.S. FINK	BROOKLYN	THU 8–10 P.M.	MAIN 605	22	4	———
FALL 1987	CS623	SWITCHING & DIGITAL SYSTEMS	A.M. JONES	LONG ISLAND	TU 6–8 P.M.	Main 238	15	3	———
FALL 1987	PH500	FIELDS & WAVES	A.B. ADAMS	BROOKLYN	THU 8–10 A.M.	ACCT 389	18	3	———
SPRING 1988	...	...	...	...	...	...	...	...	...

Figure B.20

406

DEPT	SCHOOL	STUDENTS'-COMMENTS
COMPUTER SCIENCE	COLLEGE OF ENGINEERING	EXCELLENT
COMPUTER SCIENCE	COLLEGE OF ENGINEERING	VERY GOOD
COMPUTER SCIENCE	COLLEGE OF ENGINEERING	FAIR
PHYSICS	COLLGE OF ENGINEERING	VERY GOOD
. . .	. . .	. . .

Figure B.20 (continued)

Relations from Level 3
SEMESTER, COURSE, AND PREREQUISITE:

SEMESTER	NO-COURSE	PREREQ
FALL 1987	CS605	CS601
FALL 1987	CS605	CS602
⋮	⋮	⋮

Figure B.21

STUDENT, COURSE, and SEMESTER:

NO— STUDENT	NO— COURSE	SEMESTER	GRADE	CREDITS
123456789	CS601	FALL 1987	A	3
123456789	CS605	FALL 1987	B	3
897654321	CS601	FALL 1987	A	3
⋮	⋮	⋮	⋮	⋮

Figure B.22

We are now ready to apply the rules of the data base management system to be used.

B. Modify the hierarchical data model to eliminate conflicts with the rules of the DBMS to be used.

If we decide to use IMS (Information Management System of IBM) as the DBMS, none of the conditions of IMS is violated in Figure B.23; hence no modifications are required.

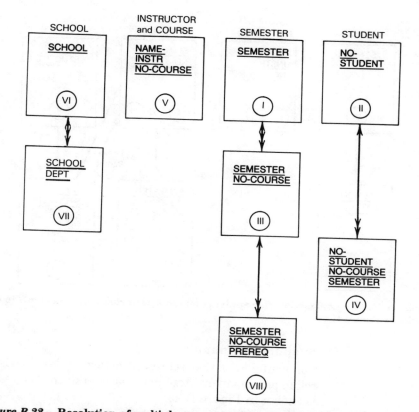

Figure B.23.   Resolution of multiple parentage from Figure B.10 for the university environment.

C. Refine the modified data model according to obvious performance considerations.

Parents having only one child segment type are candidates for combination with their children. In Figure B.23, SEMESTER has only one child, SEMESTER*NO-COURSE. The trade-off is between redundancy and performance. The SEMESTER has only two data elements, DSTRTSEM and DENDSEM. This suggests that very little redundancy is created; and since these data elements are permanent, no updating of redundant data is necessary. Thus combining SEMESTER with its child seems intuitively to be a good move.

This is the only obvious performance refinement until quantitative information becomes available. Our second intermediate result is shown in Figure B.24.

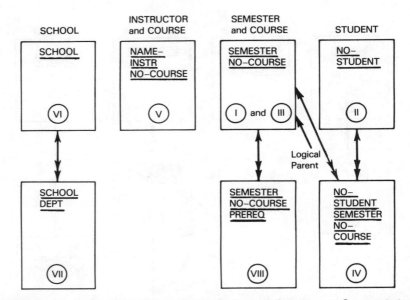

Figure B.24. Logical model after applying obvious performance refinements to the model in Figure B.23.

    D. Simplify key names.

        Compound keys that represent logical children, which relate parents in different paths, are retained. The result is shown in Figure B.25.

    E. Add relationships that exist between the data (i.e., add intrinsic requirements).

        It is not necessary to add any relationships to the logical model in Figure B.25.

STEP II.2. Draw external models for the reports in Figures B.1 to B.8 on the basis of the logical model from Figure B.25 (a hierarchical data model).

    The external models for Student Schedule List/Semester and for Course Listing are shown in Figure B.26 and B.27, respectively.

STEP II.1.3. Mapping to a network data model

    A. Derive a network data model without regard for a particular DBMS.

        A.1. Derive owner-member relationships.

            The record types that can be identified from Figure B.10 (conceptual model) are SCHOOL (relation

Figure B.25. Mapping of the conceptual model from Figure B.10 to a hierarchical data model, using IBM's Information Management System (IMS)—University Environment.

Figure B.26. External model for Student Schedule List/Semester, based on the logical model from Figure B.25 for IMS.

411

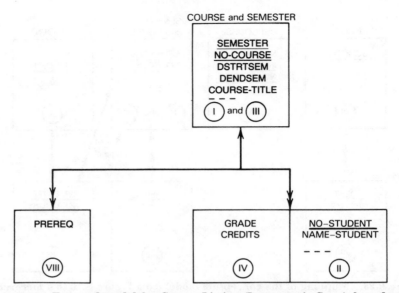

Figure B.27. **External model for Course Listing (Instructor's Copy), based on the logical model from Figure B.25 for IMS.**

VI), DEPARTMENT (created relation), LINK between SCHOOL and DEPARTMENT (relation VII), INSTRUCTOR (created relation), COURSE (created relation), PREREQ (relation VIII), GRADE (relation IV), SEMESTER (relation I), STUDENT (relation II), LINK between SEMESTER and COURSE (relation III), PREREQUISITE (created relation), and QUALIFICATION (relation V).

A.2. Resolve any violations of unique ownership.

There are no violations of unique ownership in the 10 set types arising from Figure B.10.

B. Modify the model to eliminate conflicts with the rules of the DBMS to be used.

IDMS/R (Integrated Database Management System/Relational), the CODASYL data base management system of Cullinet Corporation, fully supports the logical model; hence, no modifications are required.

C. Refine the modified model according to some obvious performance considerations.

C.1. Don't Overstructure.

The owners DEPARTMENT, COURSE and PREREQUISITE do not provide any data in their own right; hence, they are removed. The INSTRUCTOR record type is retained to provide an entry into the data base by NAME-INSTR, to avoid the storage anomalies created by its elimination, and to allow the university to store additional data on its instructors in the future.

The record type SEMESTER contains only a small amount of static data and is an owner in only one set type. Hence, it is combined with the member record type SEMESTER + COURSE. The refined logical model is shown in Figure B.28.

D. Simplify key names.

The key names have been simplified in Figure B.28.

E. Add relationships that exist between data but have not surfaced in the logical model so far.

Figure B.28. Mapping of the conceptual model from Figure B.10 to a CODASYL model, using Cullinet's IDMS/R—University Environment.

Figure B.29. **A Bachman diagram representing one version of the model for IDMS/R.**

There is an unsurfaced relationship between IN-STRUCTOR and COURSE. The NAME-INSTRUCTOR of the instructor teaching the course is a field in the COURSE record type. This relationship is implemented by adding the set type INSTR-COURSE as in Figure B.28. The STUDENTS'-COMMENTS for any IN-STRUCTOR are then easily obtained.

A version of the Bachman diagram for the university environment logical model of Figure B.28 is shown in Figure B.29.

STEP II.2. Draw external models for the reports in Figures B.1 to B.8 on the basis of the logical model from Figure B.29 (a CODASYL data model).

The external models for Student Schedule List/Semester, for School Report, and for Instructor Record are shown in Figures B.30, B.31, and B.32, respectively.

STEP II.1.4. Mapping to an inverted file data model

A. Derive an inverted file data model without regard for a particular DBMS.

Each of the 12 third normal form relations of Figure B.10 becomes a file in the logical inverted file model.

Figure B.30. **External model for Student Schedule List/Semester, based on the logical model from Figure B.29 for IDMS/R.**

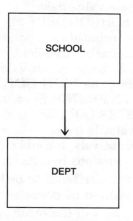

Figure B.31. **External model for School Report, based on the logical model from Figure B.29 for IDMS/R.**

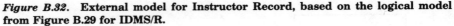

Figure B.32. **External model for Instructor Record, based on the logical model from Figure B.29 for IDMS/R.**

B. Modify the model to eliminate conflicts with the rules of the DBMS to be used.

ADABAS supports the logical model; hence no modifications are required.

C. Refine the modified model according to some obvious performance considerations.

The files DEPARTMENT, COURSE, and PREREQUISITE, which contain only a single field, may be dropped.

The PREREQ file, arising from relation VIII, may be incorporated into the SEMESTER-COURSE file as a multiple value field.

The SCHOOL-DEPT file, arising from relation VII, may be included as a periodic group in the SCHOOL file. Similarly, the fields from the INSTRUCTOR-COURSE file (relation V) may be placed as a periodic group into the INSTRUCTOR file.

The SEMESTER file could be pulled down into the SEMESTER-COURSE file at the cost of some redundancy of nonvolatile data.

Alternatively, it could participate with future codes and descriptions in a "table file."

D. Select the attributes to be inverted, that is, the fields to be defined as descriptors.

The five files in the resulting logical model are shown in Figure B.33. The fields are detailed together with the options selected for each: descriptor (DE), unique

(UQ), superdescriptor (SP), multiple value field (MU), periodic group (PE), null suppressed (NU).

Other versions of logical models are also possible.

E. Add relationships that exist between data but have not surfaced in the logical model so far.

It is not necessary to add any relationships to the logical model in Figure B.33.

STUDENT FILE
NO-STUDENT DE,UQ
NAME-STUDENT
STATUS
MAJOR
MINOR
FACULTY-ADVISOR
DEGREE-SOUGHT
ADDR-STUDENT-BUS
ADDR-STUDENT-RES
NO-TEL-BUS
NO-TEL-RES
DEGREE-REC
DEGREE-DATE
NAME-EMPLOYER
JOB-TITLE
ADDR-EMPLOYER
NEXT-OF-KIN
CREDITS-EARNED-HERE
CREDITS-TRANSFERRED
TOTAL-CREDITS
SCHOOL

GRADE FILE
NO-STUDENT DE
SEMESTER ⎱ SP
NO-COURSE ⎰

CREDITS
GRADE

SEMESTER-COURSE FILE
SEMESTER ⎱ SP
NO-COURSE ⎰
COURSE-TITLE
NAME-INSTR DE
CAMPUS
DAY-TIME
BLDG-NO-ROOM
TOTAL-STUDENTS-COURSE
MAX-CREDITS
COURSE-DESCR
DEPT
SCHOOL
STUDENTS'-COMMENTS
PREREQ MU,NU

INSTRUCTOR FILE
NAME-INSTR

NO-COURSE ⎫
COURSE-CAN-TEACH ⎬ PE,NU
COURSE-CAN-BACKUP ⎭

SCHOOL FILE
SCHOOL

DIRECTOR
NO-TEL-DIRECTOR
TOTAL-STUDENTS-SCHOOL
DEPT ⎱ PE,NU
TOTAL-STUDENTS-DEPT ⎰

Figure B.33. One version of the logical inverted file model. The DEPARTMENT, COURSE, and PREREQUISITE files have been eliminated. The PREREQ, SCHOOL-DEPT, and INSTRUCTOR-COURSE files have been included in other files. SEMESTER is part of a table file. Field options, including descriptors (DE), have been selected.

STEP III. DESIGN A PHYSICAL MODEL OF A DATA BASE (refer to Chapters 7, 8, 9, and 10). (Exercise for reader.)

STEP III.1. Draw an internal model (also called a physical model) on the basis of the logical model from step II.1.

STEP IV. EVALUATE THE PHYSICAL MODEL OF A DATA BASE (refer to Chapters 7, 8, 9, and 10, and Appendix C on statistics). (Exercise for the reader.)

STEP IV.1. Develop space estimates for the internal model above (as in step III.1). Develop input/output probabilities for the internal model above (as in step III.1).

STEP IV.2. Draw external models for the reports in Figures B.1 to B.8 on the basis of the internal model as in step III.1.

STEP IV.3. Develop time estimates for the external models as in step IV.2.

Basic Concepts: Probability Theory and Mathematical Statistics

PROBABILITY

Suppose that an event E can happen in N ways out of M possible and equally likely ways. Then the probability of occurrence of the event is denoted by

$$p = \text{probability (E)} = \frac{N}{M}$$

The probability of nonoccurrence of the event is denoted by

$$q = \text{probability (not E)} = 1 - \frac{N}{M} = 1 - p$$

Thus $p + q$ is 1 or

$$\text{Probability (E)} + \text{probability (not E)} = 1$$

that is, the probability of an event is a number between 0 and 1. Since the words "equally likely" basically mean "equally probable," the definition of probability is made up of probability itself. To avoid this pitfall, the estimated probability or empirical probability of an event is the relative frequency of occurrence of the event when the number of observations is very large. The probability itself is the limit of relative frequency with the number of observations approaching infinity.

A variable quantity, such as the length of a segment, is called a variate (or a variable), and the frequency distribution specifies how frequently the variate takes each of its possible values. If the variable does not take any intermediate value within its range of variation, it is called a discrete valued random variable.

Example. (refer to Chapter 8). Suppose that the length of a segment type has the following distribution:

Length in Bytes	Probability of Occurrence
1	p_1
2	p_2
3	p_3
4	p_4
$\vdots$	$\vdots$
N	p_N

$$L = \begin{cases} \end{cases}$$

The variable L does not take any values between 1 and 2, 2 and 3, 3 and 4, and so on. Therefore, L is a discrete valued random variable, and

$$\text{Probability } (L = i) = p_i \quad \text{for } i = 1, 2, 3, 4, \ldots, N$$

MATHEMATICAL EXPECTATION

If X denotes a discrete random variable that can assume the values x_1, x_2, x_3, x_4, $\ldots$, x_N with respective probabilities p_1, p_2, p_3, p_4, $\ldots$, p_N, where $p_1 + p_2 + p_3 + p_4 + \ldots + p_N = 1$, the mathematical expectation of X or simply the expectation of X, denoted by E(X), is defined as

$$E(X) = x_1 \times p_1 + x_2 \times p_2 + x_3 \times p_3 + x_4 \times p_4 + \cdots + x_N \times p_N$$

$$= \sum_{i=1}^{N} x_i \times p_i$$

If the probabilities p_i in this expectation are replaced by the relative frequencies f_i/M, where $M = \sum_{i=1}^{N} f_i$, the expectation reduces to

$$\frac{\sum_{i=1}^{N} x_i \times f_i}{M}.$$

This is the arithmetic mean $\overline{X}$ of a sample of size M in which x_1, x_2, x_3, x_4, $\ldots$, x_N appear with the relative frequencies

$$\frac{f_1}{M}, \frac{f_2}{M}, \frac{f_3}{M}, \frac{f_4}{M}, \ldots, \frac{f_N}{M}.$$

Example. For the distribution of the length of a segment type,

$$E(L) = 1 \times p_1 + 2 \times p_2 + 3 \times p_3 + 4 \times p_4 + \cdots + N \times p_N$$

is the average segment length.

Index

Access efficiency, 193
Access method, 7. *See also* External
    model access methods; Internal
    model access methods;
    external model, 191–193, 206–213
        dependency, 208–211
        near, 212–213
        owner, 212
        parent, 212
        sequence field, 208
    generalized, 7–8
        internal model, 191–206
        direct, 203
        hashing, 204–206
            in ADABAS, 288
            in IDMS/R, 258–259
            in IMS/VS, 224
        indexed random, 199–201
        indexed sequential, 196–199
        inverted, 202–203
            in ADABAS, 284–286
            in IDMS/R, 263–264
            in IMS/VS, 225–226
        physical sequential, 194–196
    operating system, 191–193
ADABAS direct access method, 288
ADAM (ADABAS), 288
Address converter (ADABAS), 284
After image, 310
Alias, 73
American National Standards
    Institute, 18
ANSI/X3/Sparc, 18
Archiving, 123
Area:
    CODASYL, 104
    IDMS/R, 257, 271

Associator component (ADABAS),
    284, 286
    placement of, 296–297
Attribute, 3. *See also* Data element
    in hierarchical data model, 91
    key, 4–5, 86, 126–127
    in network data model, 103
    nonkey, 127
    in relational data model, 85
Auditor, 49, 55
Automatic set insertion (IDMS/R),
    269–270

Bachman, C. W., 103, 270, 276
Bachman arrow, 172–173, 270, 276
Bachman diagram, 275–277
    examples of, 369, 414
Backup, 309–312
Banking environment, 3–12, 333–
    342
BDAM, 192
Before image, 310
Block, 196
Buffer, 306–307
Buffer pool (ADABAS), 297–298

CALC location mode (IDMS/R), 258–
    259
Candidate key, 5, 86, 126
Chain (IDMS/R), 261
CHAIN set mode (IDMS/R), 261
Checkpoint, 310–311
Child node, 91
Child segment type (IMS/VS), 218
Cluster (IDMS/R), 259
COBOL, 103
COBOL Journal of Development, 103